P9-AEU-690

TH
0705
.R78

THE COMPLETE SECURITY HANDBOOK
— for home, office, car, boat, RV, anything

BY C. A. ROPER

TAB TAB BOOKS Inc.

BLUE RIDGE SUMMIT, PA. 17214

FIRST EDITION

FIRST PRINTING

Copyright © 1981 by TAB BOOKS Inc.

Printed in the United States of America

Reproduction or publication of the content in any manner, without express permission of the publisher, is prohibited. No liability is assumed with respect to the use of the information herein. Library of Congress Cataloging in Publication Data

Roper, C.A. (Carl A.)
    The complete security handbook.

    Includes index.
    1. Burglary protection. 2. Security systems. I. Title.

TH9705.R66   643'.16   81-9214
ISBN 0-8306-0037-X   AACR2
ISBN 0-8306-1320-X (pbk.)

Cover photo courtesy of Medeco Security Locks, Inc.

Contents

Acknowledgments

There are many individuals and firms that I am indebted to for their time and assistance in furnishing much material, with no questions asked, for review and possible consideration in this book. While I cannot give a personal thank you to every one of them, I take this opportunity to acknowledge their advice and assistance.

A special thanks to Nancy Matuska, of Matuska Enterprises, for her insight in providing information on the crime problems faced by many people; to Peter Field, Billy Edwards, Bill O'Connor and Bill Kemp, Medeco Security Locks, for their invaluable advice and consultation on locking devices and applications; Marian Finney, of the NuTone Division of Scovill, for her constant effort and deliberations in tracking down much needed material in order to ensure the comprehensiveness of the sections on alarms; and to Henry Luks, of Controllor Systems Corp., for his advice and assistance in discussing the great advantages of various alarm systems that allowed me to better understand the problems and needs of the homeowner in this area.

Of course, a very special thank you goes to my wife, Lynda, for keeping me going and pushing to get the book done and also for reviewing sections of the book. And finally, to Roy and Virginia, for staying out of my way during the critical weeks of finishing the book by not constantly interrupting me with a problem or situation that only a daddy can solve.

Introduction

I recognize, without limitation, the necessity for the dissemination of current information in the design, use and installation of various products related to residential security. Accordingly, this book contains a wealth of information which is presented to facilitate the creation or upgrading of effective security systems.

Depending upon which book or government report is read, you will find that *statistically* there will be a home robbed or burglarized every 8, 10, 15 or 20 seconds. When you eliminate certain high-risk areas that have "beefed-up" police or private security patrols, you are indeed a target for burglary.

Consider also that some homes are burglarized several weeks after the original burglary. Why? It takes about two to three weeks for the insurance company to make a settlement and another week or two for the homeowner to "restock" his home or apartment with new furniture and appliances. If the person hasn't increased his security by installing various protective devices for warning that another burglary is about to happen, he becomes a very prime target—again.

From the outset it must be understood that no home, apartment or other type building is totally immune from burglar attack. Success for the burglar depends wholly upon what security measures have been installed, to what extent they can be circumvented or defeated, and the extent to which the owner is willing to go to make burglary as difficult and dangerous for the burglar as possible.

People, time, lights and noise are the enemies of the average burglar. Sure, there are the daring ones who will try anything and the desperate ones like drug addicts (the most dangerous) needing money to meet their "needs." But these people are not the average burglars. They will attempt to burglarize just about any home, no matter what preventative security measures have been taken by the owner. Reasonable care, caution and preventative security measures can ensure to a great extent that you will not be the target of an attempted or successful burglary.

Want to minimize your risk of becoming a victim of a robbery, burglary or home disaster? Well, step one has been accomplished; you decided to purchase this book. This home security handbook is just that: a comprehensive, all-inclusive handbook covering the many facets of home security, from attic to basement, from your front gate to the garage to the cabin cruiser at the lake. Now you can compare, select systems or do-it-yourself, or whatever, in a variety of modes and techniques.

With some 5,000 burglaries every 24 hours, you have an overriding concern and awareness for the safety of home and property. Add to this your car, motorcycle, mobile home, trailer or bicycle, and you can see a myriad of opportunities for burglary or theft.

We also have the potential disasters of rain, fire, flash flooding and lightning, which every home dweller should be concerned about. This book isn't just for the homeowner; it's for anyone who desires a guide to the selection, installation and use of many different devices that increase personal security in a home, apartment or even a trailer.

Whether you value something in dollars or in memories, such as a high school scrapbook, you want to protect it to the best of your ability. Remember that the cost of security is in direct proportion to and commensurate with the value you place upon one or more objects that you may possess.

The products in this book are the ones that have performed well, are readily available and represent a high degree of service and dependability to the user. You will find various products that can perform the basic functions of security, some more fancy than others. This is not to say that these products are the only ones available; they are the ones I have carefully studied, actually used and, for the most part, are the items that would best be suited to a wide cross section of people who want above-average home security—not just a barely adequate system that would not really deter even an amateur burglar.

The various products included herein will make your home more secure and more safe from fire, the threat of lightning, burglary or an attempted forced entry into the home. The selection is based on the premise that everyone wants to be safe and have peace of mind. Installation procedures have also been included so that you can see from various systems what is involved and what the installation, when completed, represents to your safety and security.

You will read and consider basic battery-operated door and window alarms, exterior lighting, alarm horns, various installation procedures, tools, window locks (all types), door locks, how to change a door lock, security grills and screens, burglar and fire alarm systems (and various component parts), latches, padlocks, auto horns and high-security ignition locks. What you won't find in this book are ideas and products that don't work; every item has been included as if I would select it. Having many years of experience in the security field, I am careful about what products to use. With this in mind, I am careful about what I tell (or write for) others about security. Good luck with this book. Use it carefully, and you and your home will be much more secure.

Home Security Planning

The home security planning concept means that in order to determine your needs, you must look at your home with a very critical view. You just can't say that you need to put in a home security system and then jump in the car, purchase a system at the local home improvement store and install it. If you did this, you would probably still have some very serious security deficiencies. Even with an off-the-shelf system, you might have a very poor system. The one that was purchased probably doesn't really meet your needs, or requirements, and can be easily defeated by a burglar in less than five minutes. You may have attached sensors to both doors, wired them to the alarm unit master control, put in a couple of window locks on the first floor, and that was it. You haven't really checked your locks, your upper and basement windows or the basement door. You haven't checked your auto security, nor that of your detached garage. You don't have your valuables marked with an identification number. Your bushes have not been trimmed in over three years, and you have a very nice tree, growing right next to the home where a burglar can climb up it and into the house through the second floor window.

I really don't feel too sorry for you if you get burglarized. You didn't really consider your home and its particularities when you went out and purchased a security system. In fact, you didn't consider anything at all.

That's what this chapter is all about and what the book is about: getting you to consider all elements of your home so that you can do something about the security, upgrading it to a proper and very acceptable level. It's getting you to think and then to act in your self-interest.

CIRCUMSTANCES WHICH DICTATE SECURITY REQUIREMENTS

Individual circumstances, such as location, type of building, crime statistics in the area (city, town, and suburban locations), value of your property, value of contents, and the type of security measures now in effect will dictate your security requirements and how much you really want to do to improve the security. As an example, consider five homes on one block in a town; all are of the same general construction characteristics, since they were all built at the same time. They can, very possibly, run into different levels of security. The corner house has a street light, and so does house number three. Numbers two, four and five have no street lights. Number three, right in the middle, has exterior lighting covering all sides of the house, and the bushes have been cut away so no one can hide near the door or windows. Number five has bushes that are overgrown and several trees that are just a mite too close to the house, extending up to the second story windows that are never closed and locked.

House number two has a privacy fence on both sides and the back is by the alley, but there are no lights at all. The garage is never closed and locked when the owner is away.

House number four has a small fence in front, and a hedge that goes across the front (setting just behind the fence) and down both sides. The back side has a high privacy fence.

Now here's the question. Which house would you rather live in and why?

Well, the relevant amount of security integrity given to these five homes is very different. It is based upon the time and money, plus the amount of security consciousness that the homeowner has, and what he wants to do in order to improve his home security.

USING THE HOME SECURITY CHECKLIST

What I'm driving at is that only you can determine how effective you want your security to be. Appendix A is a home security checklist. This is your first step in developing a security plan that will upgrade your present security to one of optimum value, which will give you a reasonable amount of protection and warning against the various types of home disasters and emergencies that can occur.

Home security is not just deterring burglars; it includes much more—fire prevention and fire/smoke warning devices, lightning protection for the home, water protection, protection against gas leaks in the home, electrical wiring faults and other potential disastrous conditions. Also, home security includes your auto, RV van, truck or home business office that you may have just started this year, along with the protection of the home valuables and the family members when a disaster strikes. All these facets are part of home security planning.

Let's get started. The home security checklist is essential for the proper planning and preparation in developing, designing, purchasing and installing a basic home security system, and all the various devices and considerations that go along with the system, not to mention the responsibilities. Whether the security system that you finally decide upon is one specially built for your particular home or apartment, a do-it-yourself type, or one that has been installed by a professional installer company that specializes in home security, the security survey should still be done. The survey gives you a very good idea of where your weaknesses are, so you know which areas to concentrate on in improving the security of your home.

It is highly recommended that you perform the home security survey by using the checklist in Appendix A before really going into detail on the various options available to you in this book. If nothing else, at least read through the survey and make mental notes. When you are studying the rest of the book, you can relate the various security measures to your areas of weakness.

Once you have read the checklist through and studied the book thoroughly, it's time to do your homework. First of all, compare your home to the one in Fig. 1-1. Using this as a sample home, you can see what has been considered for the basic security system by its owner. You should rough out a plan of your home and yard area, and do basically the same.

Using the checklist, and noting the various weaknesses, indicate on your drawing all the areas that need improvement of some form. Don't forget to include those frequently forgotten areas such as water and gas in the home, much less your exterior lighting and the garage.

In performing this little ritual, remember that one definition of home protection is "the anticipation and recognition of a risk, and then the initiation of certain actions that will remove or reduce the risk." This definition is quite broad, but it can be changed to read the recognition of a burglary, fire or whatever.

Now start looking at the various systems and individual devices, units and techniques that are available to you in order to improve, upgrade, or start from scratch the development of a home security system.

Tentatively, select the most important items that you would really like to have in your home. In your mind, or on separate pieces of paper, work out the wiring of a system (if it is hard-wired), the location of various component parts of a comprehensive system, or the individual self-contained units.

Determine whether or not you will have a telephone dialer with the system. The possible location of an outdoor alarm device should be noted.

Check the trees, shrubs, exterior doors and locks. Are they adequate or will they need replacement? Can they just be improved without a new device being installed?

After this homework, you can readily discuss, in realistic terms, exactly where your major and minor security problems are and where future problems may arise. The next phase is up to you. Corrective measures are now in order, and only you can direct the purchase of various items, call in specialists to work on the locks, replace the doors, etc. Only you can make the final determination of whether or not your home will have adequate security to alert you to the presence of a would-be burglar, and if you will have a proper fire alerting system and family escape plan. And only you will concern yourself as to whether or not your car deserves any security against attempted theft.

The area of corrective measures becomes a stickler for many, but it is one of the primary purposes for which the book you are holding was written: to help you to increase and improve your home so it is the most safe and secure that is feasibly possible.

COSTS

The cost of improving the home is dependent upon how much you really want to spend to protect the home against the various types of problems that you learned about from the home security survey. Realistically speaking, how much cash outlay are you willing to invest?

What you have to spend, what you desire in the end, and what you end up with are three different things. You can purchase the individualized, and somewhat limited, security system devices for $20 and up. You can go over $1000 for a complex, all-purpose system specifically tailored to your every whim and desire.

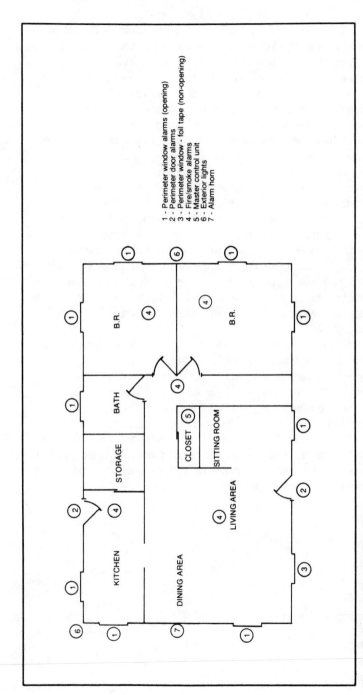

1 - Perimeter window alarms (opening)
2 - Perimeter door alarms
3 - Perimeter window - foil tape (non-opening)
4 - Fire/smoke alarms
5 - Master control unit
6 - Exterior lights
7 - Alarm horn

Fig. 1-1. Basic security system for a home.

15

You can build it yourself. A serviceable system that is developed by the homeowner, based on the general and specific information in this book, might cost anywhere from $10 to $100 and be just as effective, or more so, than an off-the-shelf system that costs $300. Overall, what you get in a system is dependent upon what level of security you want, what you are trying to protect, and what you are willing to spend, in cash and in time.

Finally, implementing the security plan that you have developed based on the security survey may mean giving up some degree of yourself. If it is privacy you want, and total security for everyone and everything, I would suggest, although it is unrealistic, that you purchase several acres of land in a remote area and build yourself a small stone and steel castle. Make sure the windows are no more than 6" x 6" and, just in case, better put some bars over them. Have a sealed exterior and be sure that every door is constantly bolted, double-bolted and locked 24 hours a day. Ideally, the entrance should have an armed guard for maximum exterior protection. You had better include a self-contained electrical system, your own air supply, and food and water to last indefinitely.

Now, that's real security. It's also totally unrealistic, self-defeating and psychologically immature.

The following chapters of this book have been designed to provide the most up-to-date and advanced technological products to meet the needs of homeowners. Each product described has been selected because it meets certain criteria and needs within the home. Assuredly, many other products are available on the market, but the items included are those that can be considered the best suited to meet the needs of improved security and overall safety for you, the reader.

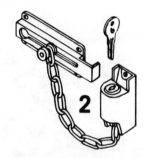

Tools and Equipment

Tools are the instruments by which the homeowner installs, builds, repairs and/or modifies the home. Tools are used in installing home security systems and individual devices. Every person has some knowledge of tools, and this knowledge is furthered still by the use of the proper tool for each task that is undertaken in the improvement of the home and its security. Remember that any project can be accomplished better, easier and more correctly when the proper tools are at hand and are used only for their intended purpose. As an example, you don't use a screwdriver when a pry bar is really what is necessary to pry two pieces of wood apart at a nail joint. It is true that the first step towards your own safety in working with tools is to use the right one—not just a tool that can, and is, an unacceptable alternate.

While the tools presented here are not discussed in great detail, each tool or piece of hardware has a specific function. They are all important for the homeowner in the installation of various home security systems that are presented in this book. Virtually all the tools and hardware can be used for the upgrading of both the interior and exterior portions of home security improvement. The most commonly known nomenclature is used in this book, although alternate names have worked their way into our daily vocabulary. The more basic tools are probably found in the home workshop. If not, prepare a short list, based on the following pages, of the specific items that you require and obtain them at your local hardware store.

Fig. 2-1. These tools belong in your tool cabinet (courtesy of Stanley Tools).

As a note here, don't just buy the hammer or screwdriver or whatever because the price is low, as in many foreign-made tools (especially those from the Far East). They are not made to high standards of workmanship and tend to break, bend, splinter or wear down quickly, making them ineffective.

Without the special interest and assistance of members of the Stanley Tool and Stanley Hardware Divisions of The Stanley Works, the many specific items pictured on the following pages would not be available. The extraordinary effort in meeting the needs of this book, by making available these products, means that

Fig. 2-2. Screwdrivers and holding devices (courtesy of Stanley Tools).

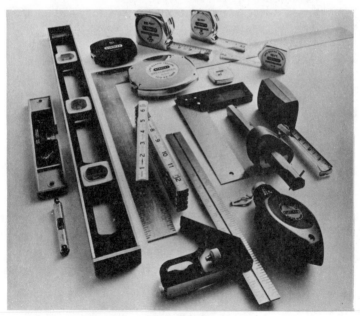

Fig. 2-3. Measuring tools (courtesy of Stanley Tools).

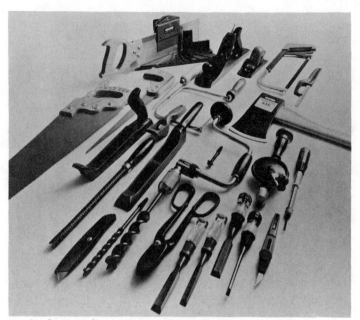

Fig. 2-4. Saws, planes and other tools (courtesy of Stanley Tools).

you will not be left in the dark as to the precise tools that are necessary to set up, upgrade and otherwise improve your home security. As you review the products herein, remember that Stanley Tools will provide you with very dependable service.

TOOLS

First, let's take a general look at some of the tools that you should have, remembering that depending upon your current tool chest items, you may only need some of these tools.

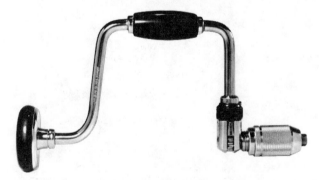

Fig. 2-5. Open ratchet bit brace (courtesy of Stanley Tools).

Fig. 2-6. Expansive bit (courtesy of Stanley Tools).

Fig. 2-7. Use this item to bore into concrete (courtesy of Stanley Tools).

Fig. 2-8. Screw-Sink combination Countersink-Counterbore set (courtesy of Stanley Tools).

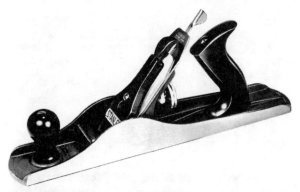

Fig. 2-9. Jack plane (courtesy of Stanley Tools).

—Hammers, hand drills and various bits (Fig. 2-1).

—Screwdrivers of all types, "C" clamps and other holding devices (Fig. 2-2).

—All types of measuring tools (Fig. 2-3).

Fig. 2-10. All-purpose snips (courtesy of Stanley Tools).

—Saws, planes, the Surform tools, metal-cutting shears, wood chisels and various drill bits (Fig. 2-4).

Now, getting down to specifics, let's look at and learn just a bit about the various tools you will need.

Fig. 2-11. Compass saw (courtesy of Stanley Tools).

Fig. 2-12. Hacksaw (courtesy of Stanley Tools).

Fig. 2-13. Pennsylvania saw (courtesy of Stanley Tools).

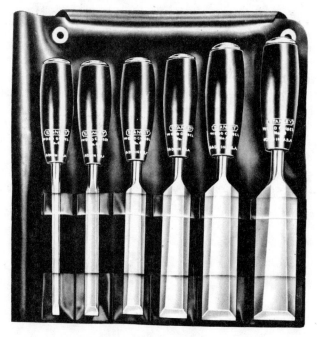

Fig. 2-14. Wood chisel set (courtesy of Stanley Tools).

Fig. 2-15. Tape rule (courtesy of Stanley Tools).

—Steel clad with ball bearing head open ratchet bit brace (Fig. 2-5).

—Expansive bit (Fig. 2-6) for a positive adjustment of hole diameters. A full turn of the adjusting screw enlarges the hole ⅛".

—Heavy duty carbide tipped masonry drill (Fig. 2-7) for fast boring into concrete, slate, brick, etc. The wide spiral flute provides for fast, easy drilling and quick dust removal.

—Power drill extension fits ¼" and larger power drill chucks and is used with ¼" shank power bits.

—Circle cutters for cutting circles in sheet metal, mild steel, laminated materials, hardboard, wood, plywood, etc. Adjustable bit of high speed steel is held firmly in the arm with a setscrew.

—The *Screw-Sink* combination Countersink Counterbore prepares wood for screws (flush or deep-seated) without damaging

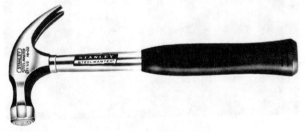

Fig. 2-16. Steelmaster hammer (courtesy of Stanley Tools).

24

Fig. 2-17. Tack hammer (courtesy of Stanley Tools).

or splintering the wood surface. It fits ¼″ and larger drill chucks. The Screw-Sink can drill an accurate pilot hole and clearance hole. The scored area permits countersinking. More pressure allows for a counterbore. With a Stanley plug cutter, you can form a perfectly mated plug. The Countersink-Counterbore-Drill set is pictured in Fig. 2-8.

    —*Jack plane* (Fig. 2-9) for trimming long boards to size.

    —All purpose snips (duckbill pattern shown) (Fig. 2-10).

    —Compass saw (Fig. 2-11) for cutouts of curved shapes in wood or plywood. The 12″ blade gives efficient cutting action, with the teeth precision set and filed for fast and smooth cutting.

Fig. 2-18. Magnetic stud finder (courtesy of Stanley Tools).

Fig. 2-19. Hexagonal blade screwdriver (courtesy of Stanley Tools).

—Professional rigid steel frame hacksaw (Fig. 2-12) adjustable for 8″ & 12″ blade lengths.

—Pennsylvania saw (Fig. 2-13) with precision set bevel filed teeth and tempered for long life.

Fig. 2-20. Home screwdriver set (courtesy of Stanley Tools).

—Wood chisel set (Fig. 2-14) containing ¼″, ½″, ¾″, 1″, 1¼″ and 1½″ chisels for all your home security installations.

—Leverlock tape rule (Fig. 2-15) with ¾″ wide power return and automatic bottom lock.

—Professional *Steelmaster* high carbon steel hammer (Fig. 2-16).

Fig. 2-21. Yankee offset ratchet screwdriver (courtesy of Stanley Tools).

Fig. 2-22. Yankee spiral ratchet screwdriver (courtesy of Stanley Tools).

—Tack hammer (Fig. 2-17) with magnetic tip is extremely useful.

Fig. 2-23. Angle wrench (courtesy of Stanley Tools).

—Magnetic stud finder (Fig. 2-18) for locating wall studs easily. It quickly and accurately locates the steel nails in the studs.

Fig. 2-24. Woodworker's vise (courtesy of Stanley Tools).

27

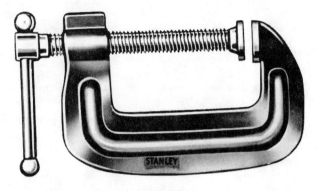

Fig. 2-25. C-clamp (courtesy of Stanley Tools).

The base of the stud finder is grooved for marking once studs are located.

—Hexagonal blade screwdriver with quick opening steel jaws to hold firmly screws for quick starting (Fig. 2-19).

—Handyman home screwdriver set (Fig. 2-20). The set contains seven pieces.

—Offset screwdriver for slotted and Phillips head screws.

—Yankee offset ratchet screwdriver (Fig. 2-21) for slotted head screws.

—Yankee spiral ratchet screwdriver (Fig. 2-22) is a time and labor saver during installations. It has right and left hand drive as well as a rigid setting.

—Angle wrench (Fig. 2-23) for smooth, easy adjustment.
—Woodworker's vise (Fig. 2-24).
—C-clamp (Fig. 2-25).
—Jobmaster plier (Fig. 2-26).

Fig. 2-26. Jobmaster plier (courtesy of Stanley Tools).

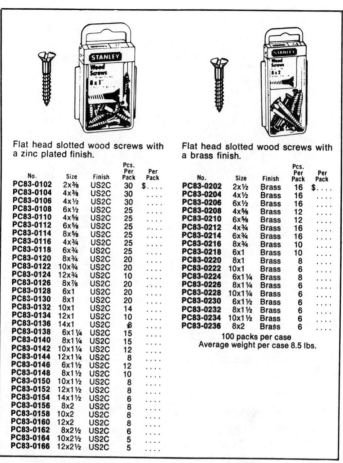

Flat head slotted wood screws with a zinc plated finish.

No.	Size	Finish	Pcs. Per Pack	Per Pack
PC83-0102	2x3/8	US2C	30	$....
PC83-0104	4x3/8	US2C	30	....
PC83-0106	4x1/2	US2C	30	....
PC83-0108	6x1/2	US2C	25	....
PC83-0110	4x5/8	US2C	25	....
PC83-0112	6x5/8	US2C	25	....
PC83-0114	8x5/8	US2C	25	....
PC83-0116	4x3/4	US2C	25	....
PC83-0118	6x3/4	US2C	25	....
PC83-0120	8x3/4	US2C	20	....
PC83-0122	10x3/4	US2C	20	....
PC83-0124	12x3/4	US2C	10	....
PC83-0126	8x7/8	US2C	20	....
PC83-0128	6x1	US2C	20	....
PC83-0130	8x1	US2C	20	....
PC83-0132	10x1	US2C	14	....
PC83-0134	12x1	US2C	10	....
PC83-0136	14x1	US2C	8	....
PC83-0138	6x1¼	US2C	15	....
PC83-0140	8x1¼	US2C	15	....
PC83-0142	10x1¼	US2C	12	....
PC83-0144	12x1¼	US2C	8	....
PC83-0146	6x1½	US2C	12	....
PC83-0148	8x1½	US2C	10	....
PC83-0150	10x1½	US2C	8	....
PC83-0152	12x1½	US2C	8	....
PC83-0154	14x1½	US2C	6	....
PC83-0156	8x2	US2C	8	....
PC83-0158	10x2	US2C	8	....
PC83-0160	12x2	US2C	8	....
PC83-0162	8x2½	US2C	6	....
PC83-0164	10x2½	US2C	5	....
PC83-0166	12x2½	US2C	5	....

Flat head slotted wood screws with a brass finish.

No.	Size	Finish	Pcs. Per Pack	Per Pack
PC83-0202	2x½	Brass	16	$....
PC83-0204	4x½	Brass	16	....
PC83-0206	6x½	Brass	16	....
PC83-0208	4x5/8	Brass	12	....
PC83-0210	6x5/8	Brass	12	....
PC83-0212	4x3/4	Brass	16	....
PC83-0214	6x3/4	Brass	16	....
PC83-0216	8x3/4	Brass	10	....
PC83-0218	6x1	Brass	10	....
PC83-0220	8x1	Brass	8	....
PC83-0222	10x1	Brass	6	....
PC83-0224	6x1¼	Brass	8	....
PC83-0226	8x1¼	Brass	6	....
PC83-0228	10x1¼	Brass	6	....
PC83-0230	6x1½	Brass	6	....
PC83-0232	8x1½	Brass	6	....
PC83-0234	10x1½	Brass	6	....
PC83-0236	8x2	Brass	6	....

100 packs per case
Average weight per case 8.5 lbs.

Fig. 2-27. Flat head wood screws (courtesy of Stanley Hardware).

HARDWARE

Having the various tools is the most basic step toward being prepared to work on the many projects involved in home security. But tools are useless without the proper and varied hardware items that seem so inconsequential until they are needed. When substitutes are used in their place, the job just doesn't have the "professional looking" touch when finished. Following is a breakdown of the various hardware items of that should be in your tool chest or hardware organizer.

—Flat head wood screws (zinc or brass finish) (Fig. 2-27) with sizes ranging from 3/8" to 2½".

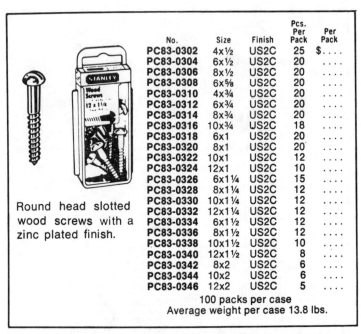

No.	Size	Finish	Pcs. Per Pack	Per Pack
PC83-0302	4x½	US2C	25	$ . . . .
PC83-0304	6x½	US2C	20	. . . .
PC83-0306	8x½	US2C	20	. . . .
PC83-0308	6x⅝	US2C	20	. . . .
PC83-0310	4x¾	US2C	20	. . . .
PC83-0312	6x¾	US2C	20	. . . .
PC83-0314	8x¾	US2C	20	. . . .
PC83-0316	10x¾	US2C	18	. . . .
PC83-0318	6x1	US2C	20	. . . .
PC83-0320	8x1	US2C	20	. . . .
PC83-0322	10x1	US2C	12	. . . .
PC83-0324	12x1	US2C	10	. . . .
PC83-0326	6x1¼	US2C	15	. . . .
PC83-0328	8x1¼	US2C	12	. . . .
PC83-0330	10x1¼	US2C	12	. . . .
PC83-0332	12x1¼	US2C	12	. . . .
PC83-0334	6x1½	US2C	12	. . . .
PC83-0336	8x1½	US2C	12	. . . .
PC83-0338	10x1½	US2C	10	. . . .
PC83-0340	12x1½	US2C	8	. . . .
PC83-0342	8x2	US2C	6	. . . .
PC83-0344	10x2	US2C	6	. . . .
PC83-0346	12x2	US2C	5	. . . .

100 packs per case
Average weight per case 13.8 lbs.

Round head slotted wood screws with a zinc plated finish.

Fig. 2-28. Round head wood screws (courtesy of Stanley Hardware).

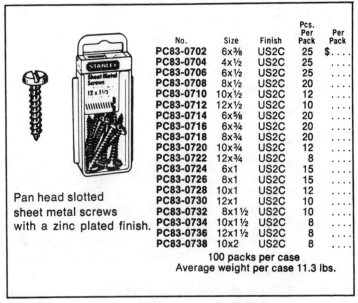

No.	Size	Finish	Pcs. Per Pack	Per Pack
PC83-0702	6x⅜	US2C	25	$ . . . .
PC83-0704	4x½	US2C	25	. . . .
PC83-0706	6x½	US2C	25	. . . .
PC83-0708	8x½	US2C	20	. . . .
PC83-0710	10x½	US2C	12	. . . .
PC83-0712	12x½	US2C	10	. . . .
PC83-0714	6x⅝	US2C	20	. . . .
PC83-0716	6x¾	US2C	20	. . . .
PC83-0718	8x¾	US2C	20	. . . .
PC83-0720	10x¾	US2C	12	. . . .
PC83-0722	12x¾	US2C	8	. . . .
PC83-0724	6x1	US2C	15	. . . .
PC83-0726	8x1	US2C	15	. . . .
PC83-0728	10x1	US2C	12	. . . .
PC83-0730	12x1	US2C	10	. . . .
PC83-0732	8x1½	US2C	10	. . . .
PC83-0734	10x1½	US2C	8	. . . .
PC83-0736	12x1½	US2C	8	. . . .
PC83-0738	10x2	US2C	8	. . . .

100 packs per case
Average weight per case 11.3 lbs.

Pan head slotted sheet metal screws with a zinc plated finish.

Fig. 2-29. Pan head sheet metal screws (courtesy of Stanley Hardware).

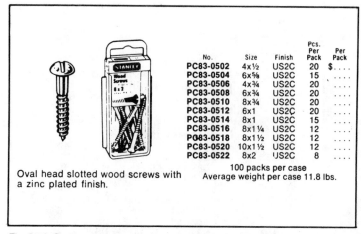

No.	Size	Finish	Pcs. Per Pack	Per Pack
PC83-0502	4x½	US2C	20	$ . . . .
PC83-0504	6x⅝	US2C	15	. . . .
PC83-0506	4x¾	US2C	20	. . . .
PC83-0508	6x¾	US2C	20	. . . .
PC83-0510	8x¾	US2C	20	. . . .
PC83-0512	6x1	US2C	20	. . . .
PC83-0514	8x1	US2C	15	. . . .
PC83-0516	8x1¼	US2C	12	. . . .
PC83-0518	8x1½	US2C	12	. . . .
PC83-0520	10x1½	US2C	12	. . . .
PC83-0522	8x2	US2C	8	. . . .

100 packs per case
Average weight per case 11.8 lbs.

Oval head slotted wood screws with a zinc plated finish.

Fig. 2-30. Oval head wood screws (courtesy of Stanley Hardware).

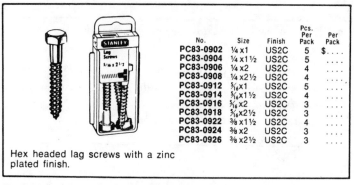

No.	Size	Finish	Pcs. Per Pack	Per Pack
PC83-0902	¼ x1	US2C	5	$ . . . .
PC83-0904	¼ x1½	US2C	5	. . . .
PC83-0906	¼ x2	US2C	4	. . . .
PC83-0908	¼ x2½	US2C	4	. . . .
PC83-0912	5⁄16x1	US2C	5	. . . .
PC83-0914	5⁄16x1½	US2C	4	. . . .
PC83-0916	5⁄16x2	US2C	3	. . . .
PC83-0918	5⁄16x2½	US2C	3	. . . .
PC83-0922	⅜ x1½	US2C	4	. . . .
PC83-0924	⅜ x2	US2C	3	. . . .
PC83-0926	⅜ x2½	US2C	3	. . . .

Hex headed lag screws with a zinc plated finish.

Fig. 2-31. Lag screws (courtesy of Stanley Hardware).

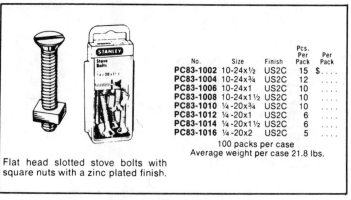

No.	Size	Finish	Pcs. Per Pack	Per Pack
PC83-1002	10-24x½	US2C	15	$ . . . .
PC83-1004	10-24x¾	US2C	12	. . . .
PC83-1006	10-24x1	US2C	10	. . . .
PC83-1008	10-24x1½	US2C	10	. . . .
PC83-1010	¼ -20x¾	US2C	10	. . . .
PC83-1012	¼ -20x1	US2C	6	. . . .
PC83-1014	¼ -20x1½	US2C	6	. . . .
PC83-1016	¼ -20x2	US2C	5	. . . .

100 packs per case
Average weight per case 21.8 lbs.

Flat head slotted stove bolts with square nuts with a zinc plated finish.

Fig. 2-32. Flat head stove bolts (courtesy of Stanley Hardware).

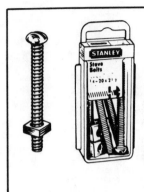

Round head slotted stove bolts with square nuts with a zinc plated finish.

No.	Size	Finish	Pcs. Per Pack	Per Pack
PC83-1102	10-24x½	US2C	15	$....
PC83-1104	10-24x¾	US2C	12	....
PC83-1106	10-24x1	US2C	10	....
PC83-1108	10-24x1½	US2C	10	....
PC83-1110	10-24x2	US2C	10	....
PC83-1112	¼-20x½	US2C	10	....
PC83-1114	¼-20x¾	US2C	10	....
PC83-1116	¼-20x1	US2C	6	....
PC83-1118	¼-20x1½	US2C	6	....
PC83-1120	¼-20x2	US2C	5	....
PC83-1122	¼-20x2½	US2C	4	....

100 packs per case
Average weight per case 19.8 lbs.

Fig. 2-33. Round head stove bolts (courtesy of Stanley Hardware).

—Round head wood screws (Fig. 2-28) ½" to 2".
—Pan head sheet metal screws (Fig. 2-29) ⅜" to 2".
—Oval head wood screws (Fig. 2-30) ½" to 2".
—Lag screws (Fig. 2-31) 1" to 2½".
—Flat head stove bolts (Fig. 2-32) ½" to 2".

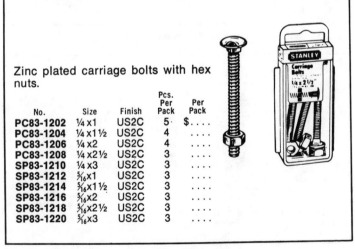

Zinc plated carriage bolts with hex nuts.

No.	Size	Finish	Pcs. Per Pack	Per Pack
PC83-1202	¼ x1	US2C	5	$....
PC83-1204	¼ x1½	US2C	4	....
PC83-1206	¼ x2	US2C	4	....
PC83-1208	¼ x2½	US2C	3	....
SP83-1210	¼ x3	US2C	3	....
SP83-1212	5⁄16x1	US2C	3	....
SP83-1214	5⁄16x1½	US2C	3	....
SP83-1216	5⁄16x2	US2C	3	....
SP83-1218	5⁄16x2½	US2C	3	....
SP83-1220	5⁄16x3	US2C	3	....

Fig. 2-34. Carriage bolts (courtesy of Stanley Hardware).

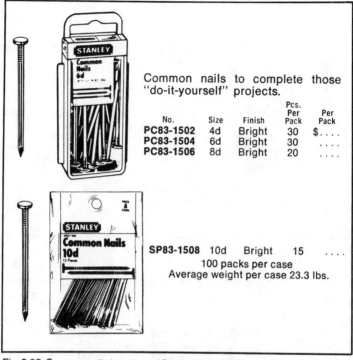

Common nails to complete those "do-it-yourself" projects.

No.	Size	Finish	Pcs. Per Pack	Per Pack
PC83-1502	4d	Bright	30	$ . . . .
PC83-1504	6d	Bright	30	. . . .
PC83-1506	8d	Bright	20	. . . .

SP83-1508	10d	Bright	15	. . . .

100 packs per case
Average weight per case 23.3 lbs.

Fig. 2-35. Common nails (courtesy of Stanley Hardware).

—Round head stove bolts (Fig. 2-33) ½″ to 2½″.
—Carriage bolts (Fig. 2-34) 1″ to 3″.
—Common Nails (Fig. 2-35) 4d to 10d.
—Finishing nails (Fig. 2-36) 4d to 8d.

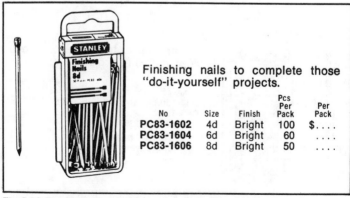

Finishing nails to complete those "do-it-yourself" projects.

No	Size	Finish	Pcs Per Pack	Per Pack
PC83-1602	4d	Bright	100	$ . . . .
PC83-1604	6d	Bright	60	. . . .
PC83-1606	8d	Bright	50	. . . .

Fig. 2-36. Finishing nails (courtesy of Stanley Hardware).

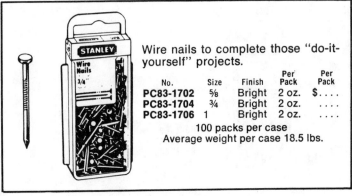

Wire nails to complete those "do-it-yourself" projects.

No.	Size	Finish	Per Pack	Per Pack
PC83-1702	⅝	Bright	2 oz.	$ . . . .
PC83-1704	¾	Bright	2 oz.	. . . .
PC83-1706	1	Bright	2 oz.	. . . .

100 packs per case
Average weight per case 18.5 lbs.

Fig. 2-37. Wire nails (courtesy of Stanley Hardware).

Zinc plated flat washers to complete those "do-it-yourself" projects.

No.	Size	Finish	Pcs. Per Pack	Per Pack
PC83-2202	³⁄₁₆″	US2C	25	$ . . . .
PC83-2204	¼″	US2C	20	. . . .
PC83-2206	⁵⁄₁₆″	US2C	15	. . . .
PC83-2208	⅜″	US2C	10	. . . .

Fig. 2-38. Flat washers (courtesy of Stanley Hardware).

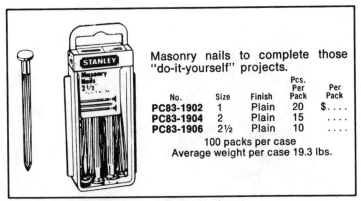

Masonry nails to complete those "do-it-yourself" projects.

No.	Size	Finish	Pcs. Per Pack	Per Pack
PC83-1902	1	Plain	20	$ . . . .
PC83-1904	2	Plain	15	. . . .
PC83-1906	2½	Plain	10	. . . .

100 packs per case
Average weight per case 19.3 lbs.

Fig. 2-39. Masonry nails (courtesy of Stanley Hardware).

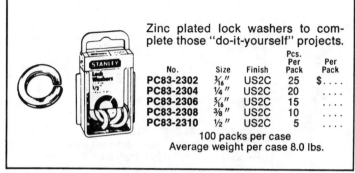

Zinc plated lock washers to complete those "do-it-yourself" projects.

No.	Size	Finish	Pcs. Per Pack	Per Pack
PC83-2302	³⁄₁₆ "	US2C	25	$ . . . .
PC83-2304	¼ "	US2C	20	. . . .
PC83-2306	⁵⁄₁₆ "	US2C	15	. . . .
PC83-2308	³⁄₈ "	US2C	10	. . . .
PC83-2310	½ "	US2C	5	. . . .

100 packs per case
Average weight per case 8.0 lbs.

Fig. 2-40. Lock washers (courtesy of Stanley Hardware).

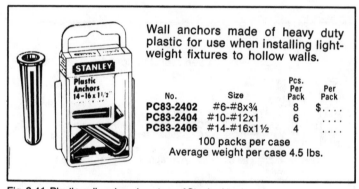

Wall anchors made of heavy duty plastic for use when installing lightweight fixtures to hollow walls.

No.	Size	Pcs. Per Pack	Per Pack
PC83-2402	#6-#8x¾	8	$ . . . .
PC83-2404	#10-#12x1	6	. . . .
PC83-2406	#14-#16x1½	4	. . . .

100 packs per case
Average weight per case 4.5 lbs.

Fig. 2-41. Plastic wall anchors (courtesy of Stanley Hardware).

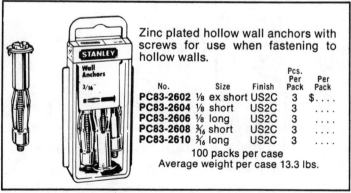

Zinc plated hollow wall anchors with screws for use when fastening to hollow walls.

No.	Size	Finish	Pcs. Per Pack	Per Pack
PC83-2602	⅛ ex short	US2C	3	$ . . . .
PC83-2604	⅛ short	US2C	3	. . . .
PC83-2606	⅛ long	US2C	3	. . . .
PC83-2608	³⁄₁₆ short	US2C	3	. . . .
PC83-2610	³⁄₁₆ long	US2C	3	. . . .

100 packs per case
Average weight per case 13.3 lbs.

Fig. 2-42. Hollow wall anchors (courtesy of Stanley Hardware).

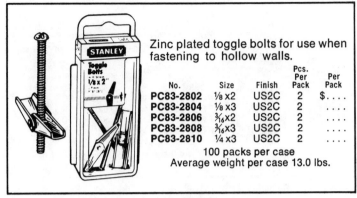

Zinc plated toggle bolts for use when fastening to hollow walls.

No.	Size	Finish	Pcs. Per Pack	Per Pack
PC83-2802	1/8 x2	US2C	2	$....
PC83-2804	1/8 x3	US2C	2	....
PC83-2806	3/16 x2	US2C	2	....
PC83-2808	3/16 x3	US2C	2	....
PC83-2810	1/4 x3	US2C	2	....

100 packs per case
Average weight per case 13.0 lbs.

Fig. 2-43. Toggle bolts (courtesy of Stanley Hardware).

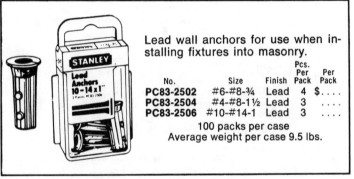

Lead wall anchors for use when installing fixtures into masonry.

No.	Size	Finish	Pcs. Per Pack	Per Pack
PC83-2502	#6-#8-3/4	Lead	4	$....
PC83-2504	#4-#8-1½	Lead	3	....
PC83-2506	#10-#14-1	Lead	3	....

100 packs per case
Average weight per case 9.5 lbs.

Fig. 2-44. Lead wall anchors (courtesy of Stanley Hardware).

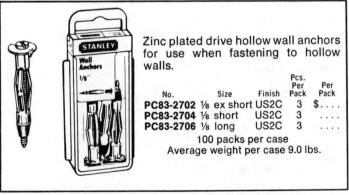

Zinc plated drive hollow wall anchors for use when fastening to hollow walls.

No.	Size	Finish	Pcs. Per Pack	Per Pack
PC83-2702	1/8 ex short	US2C	3	$....
PC83-2704	1/8 short	US2C	3	....
PC83-2706	1/8 long	US2C	3	....

100 packs per case
Average weight per case 9.0 lbs.

Fig. 2-45. Drive hollow wall anchors (courtesy of Stanley Hardware).

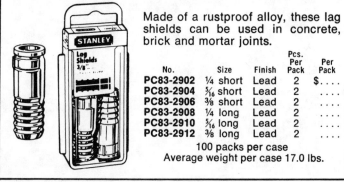

Made of a rustproof alloy, these lag shields can be used in concrete, brick and mortar joints.

No.	Size	Finish	Pcs. Per Pack	Per Pack
PC83-2902	¼ short	Lead	2	$ . . . .
PC83-2904	⁵⁄₁₆ short	Lead	2	. . . .
PC83-2906	⅜ short	Lead	2	. . . .
PC83-2908	¼ long	Lead	2	. . . .
PC83-2910	⁵⁄₁₆ long	Lead	2	. . . .
PC83-2912	⅜ long	Lead	2	. . . .

100 packs per case
Average weight per case 17.0 lbs.

Fig. 2-46. Lag shields (courtesy of Stanley Hardware).

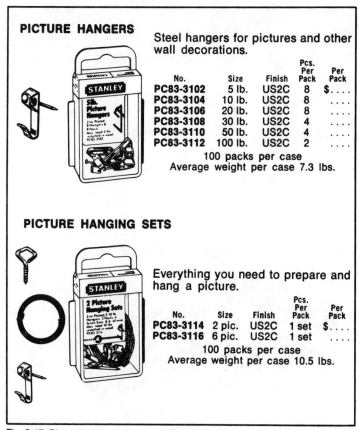

PICTURE HANGERS

Steel hangers for pictures and other wall decorations.

No.	Size	Finish	Pcs. Per Pack	Per Pack
PC83-3102	5 lb.	US2C	8	$ . . . .
PC83-3104	10 lb.	US2C	8	. . . .
PC83-3106	20 lb.	US2C	8	. . . .
PC83-3108	30 lb.	US2C	4	. . . .
PC83-3110	50 lb.	US2C	4	. . . .
PC83-3112	100 lb.	US2C	2	. . . .

100 packs per case
Average weight per case 7.3 lbs.

PICTURE HANGING SETS

Everything you need to prepare and hang a picture.

No.	Size	Finish	Pcs. Per Pack	Per Pack
PC83-3114	2 pic.	US2C	1 set	$ . . . .
PC83-3116	6 pic.	US2C	1 set	. . . .

100 packs per case
Average weight per case 10.5 lbs.

Fig. 2-47. Picture hangers (courtesy of Stanley Hardware).

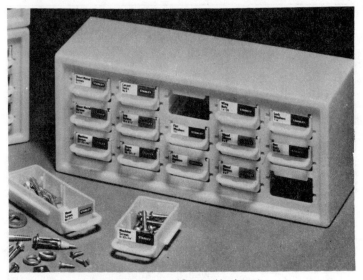

Fig. 2-48. Stanley organizer (courtesy of Stanley Hardware).

—Wire nails (Fig. 2-37) ⅝" to 1".
—Flat washers (Fig. 2-38) 3/16" to ⅜".
—Masonry nails (Fig. 2-39) 1" to 2½".
—Lock washers (Fig. 2-40) 3/16 to ½".

Fig. 2-49. Arrow wiring tacker (courtesy of Arrow Fastener Co., Inc.).

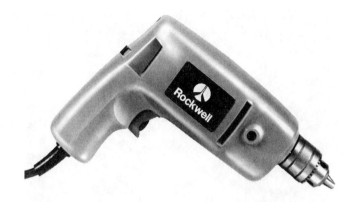

Fig. 2-50. The ⅜″ adjustable variable speed reversing drill (courtesy of Rockwell International).

- —Plastic wall anchors (Fig. 2-41).
- —Hollow wall anchors (Fig. 2-42).
- —Toggle bolts (Fig. 2-43).
- —Lead wall anchors (Fig. 2-44).
- —Drive hollow wall anchors (Fig. 2-45).
- —Lag shields (Fig. 2-46).
- —Picture hangers (Fig. 2-47).

Fig. 2-51. Jigsaw (courtesy of Rockwell International).

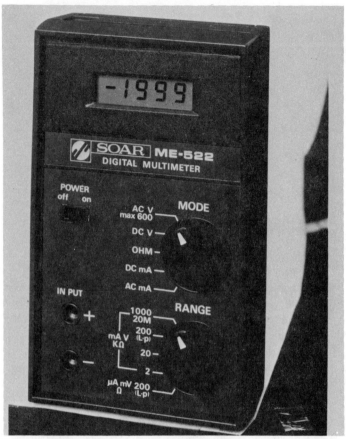

Fig. 2-52. ME-522 multimeter (courtesy of Soar Electronics (U.S.A.) Corporation).

OTHER AIDS

Now that you have all these items, what are you going to do with them? A suggestion might be to consider using the Stanley *organizer* (Fig. 2-48). This is a reusable, impact-resistant case with 15 convenient storage drawers. Depending upon how many different pieces of fastening hardware you have, several units can be safely stacked on top of each other. Note the easy to read identification markers on each drawer; this will cut down your time finding which particular fastener is in which storage drawer of the organizer.

You may have to permanently attach wires to the wall, but you want to be able to remove the wire, if necessary. Also, you may be worried about damaging the wire, which would ruin the circuit and possibly damage the electrical or electronic components of a security alarm unit or lighting fixture. Well, worry no more; you can use the Arrow *wiring tacker* (Fig. 2-49). Safety, speed and efficiency are part of the built-in performance for fastening all sizes of wires. The T-75, is ideally suited for the homeowner in the installation of various wiring systems. It loads staples with a ½" crown and divergent points. The built-in groove guide positions wire and cable for proper staple envelopment. The grooved ejector blade in the stapler halts staple drive at a safe height to prevent wire damage and short circuits.

Installing a security system will probably involve a certain amount of drilling and sawing. You may want to consider power tools in some uses. The ⅜" adjustable variable speed reversing drill (Fig. 2-50) is probably the most versatile drill for the home handyman. Depending upon the material you are working with, the variable speed control permits drilling in it. It has a powerful 2.7 amp motor with a developed .25 horsepower.

Fig. 2-53. Electrical pliers (courtesy of Milbar Corporation).

Also from Rockwell International is the two-speed jigsaw (Fig. 2-51) that is lightweight, easy to use and versatile. It cuts wood composition, light and heavy metals, Plexiglass, plastic and laminates. A fingertip speed selector allows you to control the speed of the blade, a great advantage when working with different hardnesses, strengths and flexible materials. The anti-splinter insert prevents the splintering of paneling.

Multimeters to check the ac voltage, dc voltage, ohms, etc. with precision should be used with the various systems that are included in the book. Two such multimeters are excellent for this use. The ME-221 is a portable unit with the standard easy reading mirrored scale on the front. The ME-522 is the newly developed and popular digital model (Fig. 2-52).

The Milbar electrical pliers feature a wire stripper AWG, metric wire cutter and bolt cutter. They can be used to cut the various wires in your hard-wired home security systems (Fig. 2-53).

Exterior Security

Exterior security is more than a fence, padlocks and *hasps* on outbuildings and lights. It is also the psychology of visual deterrence. Coupled with this is the unknown element for the home itself. How so? If you have a well defined perimeter line that might use a brick, metal or wood fence, and several lights covering the yard, the thief knows that his advantage of being seen is greatly increased. Further, based on the use of psychology, he can assume (but will never know for sure) that you have other forms of security. Perhaps you have a ground sensor to detect him walking across your yard or up the driveway late at night. Maybe you have infrared or other types of electronic sensing devices to "see" and detect his movement, and also the possibility of hidden "traps" awaiting him. As a professional in the security field, I, too, would be most hesitant to walk into somebody else's home in such a situation. The fear of the unknown and what the possible consequences can be are a major part of the psychology of deterrence that the homeowner must consider when selecting items for exterior security.

PERIMETER LINE

The very basic perimeter line outside the home can take a variety of forms. Specific types are dependent upon the size, location and vulnerability to the safety and security of the residence. Perimeter security, in this case, can take in the areas of fences, hedges, electronic circuits, lighting, etc.

In actuality, none of these by themselves can totally ensure top security of a ground perimeter line. When used properly, the deterrence factor is pushed to the utmost.

Fences and *hedges* are only two of the various forms of barriers that can reduce property penetration. In essence, they keep the honest person honest, provide for visual security and also define the property line limits.

In considering the fence, what type do you want? Figure 3-1 illustrates some basic types that are very popular and in use today. Do you want a privacy fence or something that is aesthetically appealing and matches the design of the home and property theme?

The *privacy* fence does not allow individuals to see what is on the opposite side of the fence due to the closeness of the boards and their height. The *basketweave* fence, while essentially a perimeter defining fence, can be heightened to provide some of the attributes of the privacy fence, but the spaces between the boards where they bend rule out complete privacy.

The *chain link* fence and other metal fencing types are only property line defining fences. They offer no real protection and are only a deterrence factor.

Masonry walls, brick walls and the like provide for a greater sense of security. If built to the 6-8' level, they are indeed privacy fences and very strong deterrents.

In some areas, by local ordinances, it is illegal to have walls with spikes, broken glass, or barbed wire or electrified fencing. But the question here would be, "How innocent is the person who is slightly hurt or injured in the process of climbing over your fence at 2 a.m. in the morning?" Regretably, legal liability of the homeowner may far outweigh the security aspects.

The height of the wall, fencing or hedge may be restricted in some communities. Thus, you may have to consider variations, such as putting up a 6' chain link fence and then growing a hedge around it.

SECURITY ASPECTS OF WALLS AND FENCES

Low walls are used to define the perimeter, channeling movement and limiting access. As a definite barrier, they only define and separate the private from the public areas.

High walls are usually constructed at the 6' level and form a relatively impenetrable barrier. They can eliminate (to a great extent) uncontrolled and unauthorized entrance into certain areas. They offer visual privacy and can be of poured concrete, concrete blocks, brick or wood.

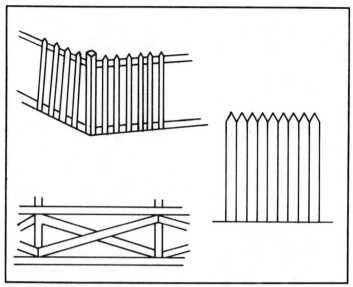

Fig. 3-1. Basic types of fences.

Low fences form a symbolic barrier, but contribute toward the minimizing of site penetrability. Metal picket or chain link fences do not hinder visual surveillance. They can be of wrought iron, tubular steel or chain link.

High fences form a reasonably impenetrable barrier when they are 6' high. They can also be used to secure and screen certain areas for privacy. They include wrought iron, tubular steel and chain link fences.

Exterior security planning starts with these types of fences and walls. Remember that fences control and direct traffic. How access to a residential property is structured and controlled is a major element in exterior planning for security purposes. If people can cross the yard at will, then the perimeter security is nil. If crossing the property line means going over a 3' fence, the perimeter security is good. If it means climbing a 6' brick or chain link fence, then the residence moves into the excellent category.

These physical and psychological barriers are created with any form of perimeter defense walls. Whether the wall be 2 or 6' high, a psychological barrier is formed for the would-be burglar. Symbolic barriers are subtle approaches to perimeter security, but offer no real security. The barrier is an implied stop point. Such barriers include low ground shrubs, low retaining walls, mid-sized shrubs and trees along the property line border.

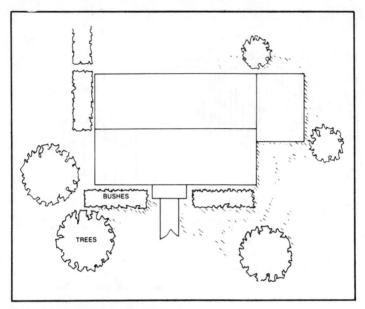

Fig. 3-2. A typical home without lighting.

I didn't discuss shrubs and trees earlier for the simple reason that they tend to provide assistance to the burglar rather than a deterrence. Whenever possible, there should be no trees near the property line; the same applies to bushes.

To limit access, define the perimeter and provide above average security, medium to high fences or walls should be installed, with gates that have a latch (not necessarily a locking one). With these, penetrability is minimized. They control access, but yet allow life to remain normal.

Minimal, symbolic and psychological security is a very important element by reducing site penetrability and designating perimeter lines, which delineate the public from the private access routes. A screen or buffer zone is formed, as with medium-sized shrubbery. While shrubbery is aesthetically appealing, it provides for concealment and only slows down a person crossing the property line *through* the shrubbery—rather than *over* as with a fence or wall.

EXTERIOR LIGHTING

The burglar prefers the cover of darkness to perform his dastardly deeds. Concealment from detection is a major factor and the use of light becomes the burglar's enemy. Even the light

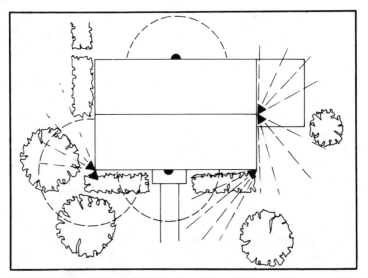

Fig. 3-3. A home with exterior lighting.

reflected off the home can become a deterrent to the burglar if it is bright enough on a clear night. Home lighting, when set up properly, greatly reduces the chances of burglary. It must be noted, though, that a lot of housebreakings and burglaries occur during the daylight hours. This is where the home alarms and locking devices come into play. These are discussed later in this book.

Effective and safe levels of light greatly increase a sense of security for the homeowner. When used in the proper setting, they also increase the home's resistance to attempts of burglary.

The levels of illumination do not, however, have to be the same across the entire property area or even cover all points. They should be concentrated in the areas wherein the potential is greater for concealment and also near the home. For the average home, lights are usually found about the garage, by the sidewalk/front steps, back door and possibly at the edge of the property line at the foot of the sidewalk. By adding, in strategically designed locations, extra lighting, this is all that may be required to cut the potential threat to almost nothing.

Figure 3-2 illustrates a typical home without lighting. The shaded areas represent potential hiding areas for the burglar. Figure 3-3 is the same home that has included exterior lighting as a deterrence. The differences readily demonstrate what light can do to cut down the chances of a burglar hiding on your property.

Remcraft Lighting Fixtures

Remcraft lighting fixtures have provided general and specific home lighting for many years. A variety of their units are available for use in your home protection.

The *security light* (Fig. 3-4) provides an excellent protection for pennies a day. An automatic unit once installed, it contains a photoelectrically controlled device which will automatically turn on a light, giving dusk to dawn protection. A single unit (Fig. 3-5) can also be used, depending upon unit location. Figure 3-6 illustrates several points where either type of unit could be installed and used effectively.

Floodlighting trees and shrubbery also are very important to the overall security of the home. Today's society is concerned with aesthetics. Thus, home decor includes numerous bushes, foliage plants and a variety of trees surrounding the home. Unfortunately, as mentioned earlier, these provide a base point for the would-be burglar to hide, preventing detection by casual observation at night. Light installation can "spotlight" a specific shrubbery area or "flood" an entire portion of the yard to deter the burglar.

Exactly what features and specifications are in these units? Let's look:

☐ A heavy gauge aluminum reflector that blends with your home style decor.

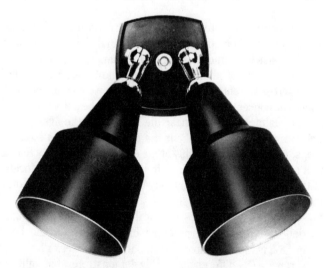

Fig. 3-4. Security light (courtesy of Robboy Electric Mfg. Co.).

Fig. 3-5. Single reflector exterior lighting unit (courtesy of Robboy Electric Mfg. Co.).

☐ All-around reflectors to protect the lamp from accidental or intentional damage.

☐ Complete adjustability, so the light goes where it is needed—not in unwanted areas (including the neighbor's windows).

☐ Heavy duty electric unit that mounts directly into a standard outlet box (minimal installation cost and time).

☐ Fast and simple wiring.

☐ Built-in photoelectric control sensor.

The decor provides that extra amount of increased security that is needed today, while also highlighting specific exterior portions of the home to enhance the nighttime beauty. Figure 3-7 illustrates such a unit.

Light Square and Decorator Units

Home security lighting is sometimes called emergency exterior lighting. The lighting has far too often received little of the attention it deserves in security deterrence for the homeowner.

Like various types of home security alarm devices, the homeowner doesn't bother until after a burglary or another home disaster.

The *National Electric Code* states that emergency lighting systems should be installed in any place where artificial lighting is required. This includes the exterior points of the home, especially at night.

Don Gilbert Industries specializes in emergency lighting systems for both business and home applications. I will discuss two typical units that can fit very nicely into the home without lowering the aesthetic decor considerations.

The *model 4-C1* (popularly known as the *light square*) is an excellent choice for the home because of the decorative value it provides. Although it was initially designed for use in hallways, bedrooms, and the basement of the home, the unit is excellent for a front or rear porch light, or an enclosed side porch, where the light will also cover portions of the lawn area next to the home (Fig. 3-8).

It uses a specially designed miniature *halogen* lamp which produces a high lumen output. Combined with the reflector and a prismatic acrylic lens, the unit produces a light pattern free of the fragmentation and hot spots that are closely associated with other units. The uniformity of light distribution ensures clear vision.

If your garage has a number of windows at the sides, or in the doors, then the light square can also be used here. Placement

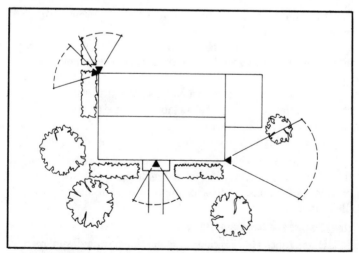

Fig. 3-6. Locations where automatic and single lighting units can be installed and used effectively.

Fig. 3-7. An exterior lighting unit (courtesy of Robboy Electric Mfg. Co.).

Fig. 3-8. Model 4-C1 light square (courtesy of Don Gilbert Industries, Inc.).

51

inside allows the light to penetrate and cover portions of the exterior ground area.

The SLC-2 model (the *Decorator*) can be applied also to either the interior or exterior, if need be (Fig. 3-9). Using simplified wall mounting, it can be obtained with an exterior power cord for use in standard ac circuits. Small in size, the two small 6-watt halogen lamps provide approximately 500 beam candlepower output each. This unit can also have a battery put in for an emergency measure should the home's power fail. Because of the unit's size and design, it can be applied anywhere outside the home for external lighting coverage without detracting from the beauty of the home.

Low Voltage Electrical System

Exterior effect lighting that highlights your bushes and the sides of the home can provide a dramatic effect. Such lighting can also be used, albeit subtly, to spot a hidden intruder up close to the home. A Malibu lighting system can make the home safer, more secure and also more beautiful.

A safe, low voltage (12 volt) electrical system that will illuminate the home and landscaping for pennies a night is shown in Fig. 3-10. These six easily placed weather and shockproof lights can be inserted anywhere in the ground and quickly wired up to a 24-hour automatic timer that will save you having to activate the lighting every evening and also turning it off in the morning. An automatic timer is built into the basic unit.

SECURITY LIGHT CONTROL (SLC-1)

Let's discuss in detail one particular home lighting object. The *Security Light Control* (SLC-1) from *Colorado Electro-Optics* (CEO)

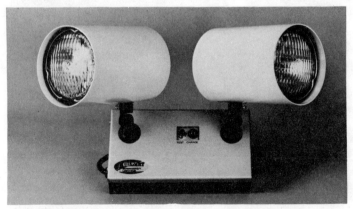

Fig. 3-9. Decorator SLC-2 model (courtesy of Don Gilbert Industries, Inc.).

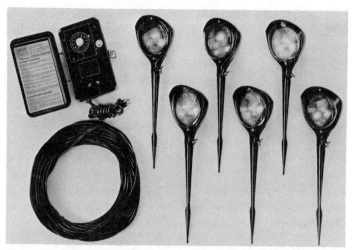

Fig. 3-10. A low voltage electrical system (courtesy of Intermatic Inc.).

is a unique home security unit designed to automatically turn on outdoor lights as somebody approaches your home (Fig. 3-11). Automatically, the unit turns the lights off when they are gone. The SLC-1 applies remarkable space-age technology to make your home a better and safer place. Depending upon how your home, driveway or front parking is situated, the unit will detect the approach of persons or vehicles. Several minutes after their departure, the lights go off. But the unit continues to let you know, and them, that their approach has been signaled by the light going on. For the burglar, the light becomes an effective deterrent. The surprise of a light activating automatically as the burglar approaches your home definitely lets him know you are security conscious, and that your home is one that he should avoid.

The benefits of the SLC-1 include:

☐ A relay output that is normally open for the activation of auxiliary devices.

☐ An area coverage of up to 2' x 25'.

☐ A sensing device that is fully adjustable by the homeowner.

☐ Direction and sensitivity can be adjusted to fit the specific needs of the home.

☐ A light switching capability of up to 500 watts.

☐ A timing circuit to automatically turn off the lights four minutes after interruption.

☐ A phototransistor to deactivate the unit during daylight hours.

☐ UL standards applied to all circuitry in the unit.

☐ All-weather housing (matches any decor).

☐ An override switch for manual operation.

The SLC-1 uses a passive infrared sensing device which detects the relative change in temperature as an object, such as an automobile or a person, moves through the detection pattern. It senses targets moving into and through the pattern which are relatively warmer or colder than the background. Once motion is sensed, the unit activates the connected lights for a period of approximately four minutes. It has a built-in phototransistor which will deactivate the system during the hours of daylight to give a longer unit life.

The unit operates from the standard ac home power. Lighting provided through the unit cannot exceed 500 watts, but this does not mean it has to be just one lamp that is attached to the unit.

Fig. 3-11. The SLC-1 (courtesy of Colorado Electro-Optics, Inc.).

Several lamps can be successively applied in different locations for maximum lighting coverage.

The ideal mounting location for the SLC-1 is on the side of the home viewing the controlled area with a downward looking tilt. This type of location often provides an overhang or semi-protected mounting location which is more desirable but not always necessary for proper operation. The unit should be mounted in such a fashion to allow the optical assembly (a mirror surfaced lens) to view areas with the heaviest traffic patterns such as a driveway or walkway. It is most important to mount the unit in the upright position to achieve the optimum 25' x 25' coverage area (Figs. 3-12 and 3-13).

Within the sensing pattern, there are six zones. A person is detected as he passes through the zones. The device is most sensitive to motion across the pattern and least sensitive to motion toward or away from the sensor. This fact should be a consideration when choosing the mounting location.

Mounting the SLC-1 Unit

Tools required include large and small regular screwdrivers a small Phillips screwdriver, and a wire cutter and stripper tool. Note that when working with the ac wiring, be sure the electricity is turned off.

The SLC-1 is simple and straightforward. The connection involves power to the unit and power out to the desired light(s). After mounting the SLC-1 to the wall, proceed as follows:

☐ Remove the outdoor light fixture which you desire to control.

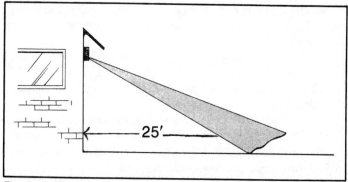

Fig. 3-12. Mount the SLC-1 in an upright position (courtesy of Colorado Electro-Optics, Inc.).

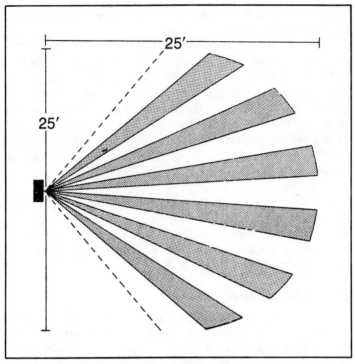

Fig. 3-13. Mount the SLC-1 to achieve the optimum coverage area (courtesy of Colorado Electro-Optics, Inc.).

☐ Route the ac power input that originally went to the light fixture to the SLC-1. Use either the bottom or back of the SLC-1 for cable routing.

☐ Connect the power input to the black and white SLC-1 wires. The white wire is common to both the power in and power out so that either white wire can be used. Use wire connectors for connection.

☐ Route the new wire to the light fixture. Use outdoor rated wire such as AWG 14 two-conductor (with ground if required).

☐ Connect the wires together in the unit to the light fixture wires by use of wire connectors.

☐ If the power input and lower outlet cables include a ground wire, twist the two copper ground wires together that contains the ground circuit through the SLC-1 without connection to the sensor. Fold all wires and connections into the center wiring compartment of the SLC-1.

☐ Turn on the ac.

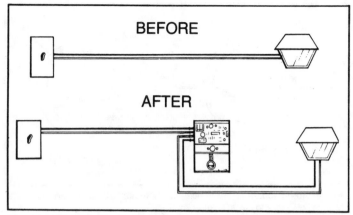

Fig. 3-14. The before and after wiring system of a SLC-1 installation (courtesy of Colorado Electro-Optics, Inc.).

Figure 3-14 illustrates the before and after wiring system of a SLC-1 installation.

Adjustment of the Optical Assembly

In looking at the mechanism of the unit, there are two loops. These loops were added to the unit to make the aiming of the optical assembly safer, easier and quicker. Figure 3-15 shows the optical assembly on the mounting bracket. By loosening the nut

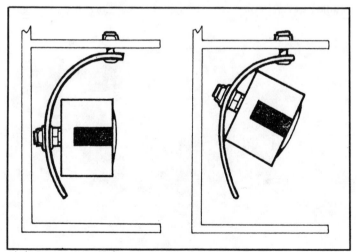

Fig. 3-15. The optical assembly on the mounting bracket (courtesy of Colorado Electro-Optics, Inc.).

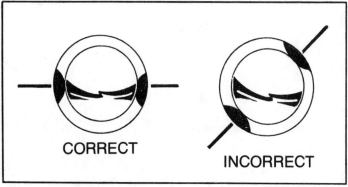

CORRECT

INCORRECT

Fig. 3-16. It is important that the optical assembly aiming lines be kept horizontal (courtesy of Colorado Electro-Optics, Inc.).

behind the assembly, aiming the optical assembly (up and down sliding) on the mounting post is achieved. The entire optical assembly can be swiveled around the pivot points. In order to achieve the 25′ x 25′ coverage, it is very important that the optical assembly aiming lines be kept horizontal, as shown in Fig. 3-16.

DRIVE-ALERT DRIVEWAY ALARM

There are numerous homes in every city that have a long driveway; some are so long and curved that the owner cannot see an approaching vehicle until it almost reaches the house. What would happen, in such a situation, if a burglar drove in at night only

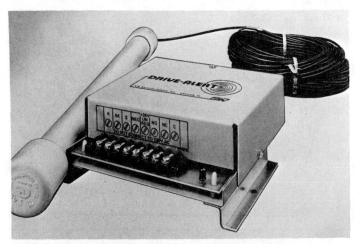

Fig. 3-17. The Drive-Alert system (courtesy of B-W Manufacturers, Inc.).

Fig. 3-18. Garage door opener (courtesy of NuTone Division, Scovill Inc.).

partway and parked? The homeowner would have no idea of the impending danger.

Such a situation can now be alleviated. The Drive-Alert driveway alarm has been developed by B-W Manufacturers to counteract such a situation. The DA-500 *Drive-Alert* system is a multi-purpose electronic system designed to detect any vehicular traffic in the driveway or any area where knowledge of vehicular movement is desired (Fig. 3-17). For rural homes and in farm communities, it is also available and highly recommended.

The installation allows the homeowner to know when someone enters the driveway. This is accomplished by an out-of-sight sensor which detects moving metal objects—cars, trucks, motorcycles, etc., within a 15′ radius. This sensor sends a signal to the master control unit and sounds an electronic whistle. When placed along side a stationary metal object, the device will also detect any movement and sound the alarm, aiding in the prevention of theft or vandalism to the object.

B-W Manufacturers also provide the DA-505 timer control which is used in conjunction with the Drive-Alert system. This greatly expands the versatility of the system. The timer control can turn on lights and sound sirens or bells.

With the timer added to the basic unit, the Drive-Alert owner can feel more secure as he turns into the driveway at night. The time control automatically turns on the outside lights. Installation procedures for the Drive-Alert system are provided in the chapter on various installation procedures for home security devices.

GARAGE DOOR OPENER

You have the exterior lighting, the home security alarm and other devices, but what about your garage? Imagine coming home late at night and the exterior light over the garage is out. Is someone hiding in the shadows waiting for you to exit the car? Hopefully not. But, as the old adage goes, better safe than sorry. With this in mind, you should look at a garage door opening device that can be radio-operated from the safety of your car. NuTone has such a system (Fig. 3-18). The unit also turns on the interior garage light so you can see before you enter. Detailed installation instructions and information on how the NuTone radio controlled unit works are provided in the installation chapter.

Home Perimeter Security

The first lines of defense in any home are the doors and windows. The outer structure and component parts such as the structural framing, the locks, latches and chains are included, along with sliding doors and windows, grills and accessory devices that can be attached thereto.

Basically, when considering home security, much emphasis is given to the door, as it should be. Regrettably, not enough thought is given to the door components, which include the door framing, the surrounding wall and the locks. In this chapter, we will discuss and detail the ways to ensure a good home perimeter.

In the majority of residential crimes, as can be noted in the annual FBI reports, the door is the major point of entry for burglars and daytime thieves. It is usually the easiest point of access. Why? The average homeowner tends to consider the door as a secure instrument for his home security. No thought is given to the construction of the doors, the various vulnerable points, the possible weaknesses in the frame, and also the possibility that a cheaply manufactured or poorly installed lock may be the weakest point of the door. You can reduce the threat by ensuring that the construction of your door and associated structural parts are "up to snuff" and by investing in a top quality residential door locking device.

The average burglar wants to enter the home as rapidly as possible. He wants no obstacles that will give him trouble or take time to defeat. He really doesn't have a lot of time to get in without being seen. If the door is really solid, carries an excellent security lock, and if the framing is such that great difficulty will arise, entry via the door will be nil.

DOOR TYPES

Basically, there are three door types: the *solid, hollow core* and the panel door. Within these types, you can have *one panel, two panel, flush, ledged* or *braced* doors.

Doors are graded in a descending order. This descending order represents the resistance to attack as determined by the strength of each, the types of materials that make up their construction and also the framing of the door. Steel, hardwood, hardwood with solid panels, softwood with panels, glazed (glass) panels, and framed and braced doors are found in many homes.

An entire book could be written just about door types, their weaknesses and advantages, and how each can best be used to the homeowner's advantage. To suffice, it is enough to say that no matter what type of door you currently have, or plan to install in the place of a current door, it may not adequately protect you from burglary unless it is the strongest possible.

Door panels cannot, in many instances, be reinforced without the loss of some aesthetic qualities which, in most cases, the owner will not do. Doors with panels that are not reinforced but remain as a thin panel offer virtually no protection. This notion, plus the fact that any door with an opening including glass is not effective, means that you should seriously consider replacing the door or else improving its strengthening qualities.

Besides the door itself, the frame must be carefully examined. Is it old, slightly deteriorated, rotting, or coming out of proper alignment because the home is slowly settling? Then the frame must be looked at in terms of its overall security, which at the present is not really very much, if any.

Let's just talk in some general terms about doors and the frames. The doors, as I have said, are of wood or metal and so are the frames. Along with these, you have the metal jambs that are normally of a one-piece construction, whereas the wood jambs will have a minimum of three pieces.

The doors are fastened to the frame by three hinges, although older homes may have two hinges, as will many metal doors and frames. Opposite the hinge side is the locking device. It can consist of a single unit, and in many instances for older homes a warded (skeleton key) or a key-in-the-knob lock. It may have separate units, one containing the lock itself, and then the door knob. Also, there could be an older door with a newer, more recent and better lock, plus an auxiliary lock or inside latch affixed to the door.

Weaknesses of the door are most prevalent since it may be less secure than the solid construction and framing into which it is set, much less the associated wall structure. Doors can be constructed of thin wooden panels or glass panels set in between wooden rails and stiles of the door. The panels may be excessively thin and easily removed or kicked in. Also, when not properly installed, the frame itself becomes a weak point, whether or not the door itself is also weak.

If the door is of wood, installation usually consists of nailing it against the wall studs after which the doorstop would be nailed to the jamb. If done improperly, this type of installation allows for shims or levers to be inserted so that the locking bolt is disengaged, allowing the door to be opened. Fortunately, the all-metal one-piece door frame precludes such relatively easy entrances into the home. It is of sufficient strength and will not give and allow the door to be pried out of the frame or the locking bolt to become disengaged.

If not correctly installed, the door itself tilts slightly and the locking bolt does not properly line up, so the owner may enlarge the strike plate hole to save the time of rehanging the door. This, in effect, decreases the security integrity of the entire door unit.

HINGES

Hinges are another matter. When incorrectly positioned, they can also contribute to the weakness and possibility of the door being a secure security deterrent. If the hinges are surface mounted so that the hinge pins are on the outside (for doors opening out), or the hinges are mounted flat against the door and frame, either the pins or screws can quickly be removed. Thus, the hinges must be positioned so that the hinge pin is on the inside and the hinge screws are concealed.

Outside mounted hinges require bolts, not screws, to give any type of security at all to the door. Also, the use of hinges that do not allow for the pin to be removed, or by welding or brazing the pin to the hinge, can also stop pin removal.

DOOR WEAKNESSES

Weaknesses of the door include seven possible areas that can be vulnerable to the burglar. They are:

☐ Poor or rotting door or frame, or portions thereof.

☐ Thin wood panels in the door.

☐ Having a window in the door that may be within 25-35″ of the inside door handle.

☐ Having a cheap lock on the door.

☐ Having a space between the door and frame.

☐ Having the hinge pins located on the exterior of the door.

☐ Having a hollow core door.

Figure 4-1 illustrates these faults in the average door.

Figure 4-2 shows the potential of an unacceptable windowed door. If a windowed door is necessary to see who is outside, then it should be replaced with a solid door and a peephole door viewer

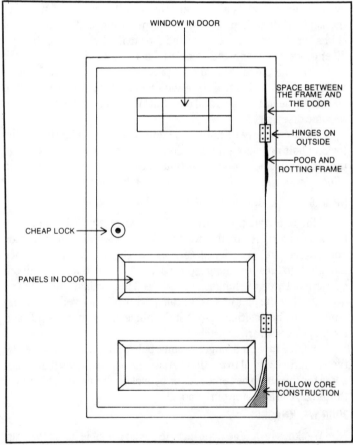

Fig. 4-1. Door faults.

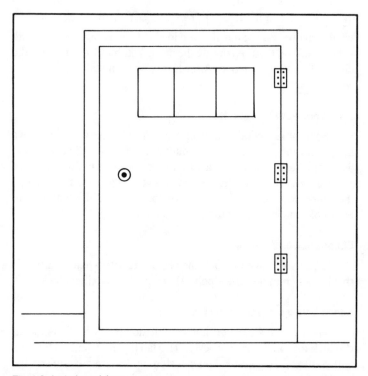

Fig. 4-2. A windowed door.

(Fig. 4-3). Taking each item one at a time, let's look at these faults and see what can be done to remedy them.

Poor or Rotting Frame or Door Edge

Realize that such a condition is an open invitation to burglary and the ultimate theft of possessions. Such a door indicates that the owner cares not for good effective home security and is willing to let nature take its course with his home. The cure for this is to replace the frame and/or the door with a new one.

Window in the Door

If the window is within 25-35″ of the inside door handle, it can be broken through and the handle reached and turned. Replace the glass with wire glass or one of the acrylic plastics. Also, when considering replacement, remember that the replacement may not be broken but would, more than likely, be forced all the way out of the door by use of heavy blows with a blunt instrument, such as a heavy hammer with the aid of a screwdriver. The best method would involve taking out the window and resealing the area with solid wood and then repainting the door. You could also replace the door with a solid core one. After this is done, install a peephole to see who is outside.

Thin Wood Panels in the Door

Several remedies are available to the homeowner. Remove the panels and put in a piece of solid wood. Remove the panels and put in thicker panels. Take another piece of wood (solid hardwood preferably) and cover over the panels so the edges are smooth with the other door edges. Remove the door and install another one, either of solid wood or with a metal cladding.

Cheap Lock on the Door

Totally remove the lock and replace it with a heavy-duty lock that has a 1″ minimum deadbolt. Also, install an auxiliary lock.

Space Between the Door and Frame

Over the years, older homes will slowly settle. This means the lock may not work properly. The latch plate is cut so the lock will continue to operate. You can shim up the frame; remove the door and frame and reinstall it, realigning it as you do so. Replace the door and frame.

Hinge Pins on the Outside of the Door

I have no idea why anyone would want a home with a door that opens outward. Safe and sensible security deems it necessary that the door swing inward. By swinging outward, the hinge pins are exposed to the tools of the burglar. His job is thus made over 300% easier. The proper remedy is to remove the door and hinges and replace them on the inside. Temporary stop-gap measures might mean welding or brazing the pin to one of the hinge halves. This would prevent someone from lifting the pins out and removing the door to gain entry. Also, a metal plate bolted over the latching area between the door handle and the door frame would stop a person from easily forcing back the locking back.

Hollow Core Doors

About the only really effective remedy for this is the replacement of the door with a solid-core one. A hollow core door

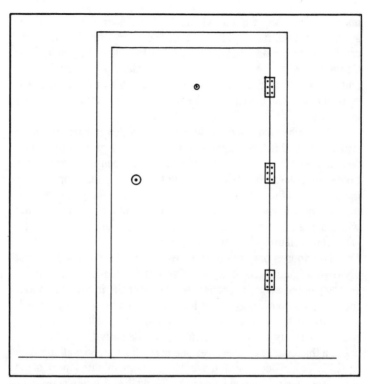

Fig. 4-3. Note the peephole viewer.

of wood is easily detected by the simple method of rapping on the door in a couple of places. Once a burglar determines that the door is hollow, a real good kick with the foot or a couple of hammer blows will cause the wood to give way. A burglar's hand can reach through and open the door from the inside.

DOOR CONSTRUCTION

As the optimum and most often used point in the home for entry, the door must provide for the maximum flexibility in design, but also have the security commensurate with the valuables stored within the home. The optimum choice in doors which provides the flexibility and security desired is the *steel door*. Its weight and cost are somewhat higher than what the average homeowner is usually willing to pay, but such an investment is well worth it in the long run.

Without paying as much for a steel door, a homeowner can still build up the home security quite a bit by considering not only the door, but also the framing about it. Remember that within the average residential dwelling, the doors are most commonly constructed of wood—but not always hardwood, as they should be. Combined with the basic wood can be aluminum, some steel and glass. Often, the construction is a combination of all these materials and can also include hardboard, fiberboard and, in some instances, plastic.

Remember from the earlier discussion that most of the door types may well include a panel or a flush type construction. Panel design doors have vertical and horizontal members framing a rectangular area that may have glass, other panels or *louvers* included. The flush door, on the other hand, is a flat panel with no inserts being framed. The all-wood door of solid core construction will provide excellent security, but not the optimum security that a steel door will provide against a burglar.

The door is only the first of several considerations you must improve to guarantee that your front door is above average in its security deterrence. You must also consider the framework about the door, the materials of that framework and the associated wall structure. After all, it does no good to have an excellent door if the frame is slightly out of alignment, or a little rotted, and the walls are of a thin coat of plaster over one layer of lath, and wallboard on the interior has been painted over. For several minutes more of his time, the burglar can go through the wall and open your door through the wall.

DOOR FRAMING

The improvements that can be made include strengthening the entire area around the frame with additional structural members, the inclusion of a hardwood barrier that cannot easily be punched through from the outside, and the insertion of a thin strip of steel at the prime point that entry would be attempted through a home wall. This solidification or hardening of the wall ensures that it will not become the focal point for a person breaking into the home when the door is too hard to break through, and there are no other alternatives.

The framing about the door, if of wood, can be covered over with sheet metal before the exterior framing is put on. This provides another hardening about the door. Metal covered wood frames are a good cost-security investment, especially when used in combination with a metal clad wood door.

When hollow steel door framing is used, an air gap is behind the framing. This must be taken care of for proper security. The gap can be filled in with mortar or steel bars. This prevents the use of a spreader device which is basically an auto jack being used to spread the steel frame far enough back so the door can be forced open.

The standard door frame construction is shown in Fig. 4-4. Improvements to these type frames in order to upgrade the physical security integrity include cross bracing, a metal sleeve insert, plywood covering (both sides to be covered), shims and use of the steel insert. For units that have a metal door frame, the cross

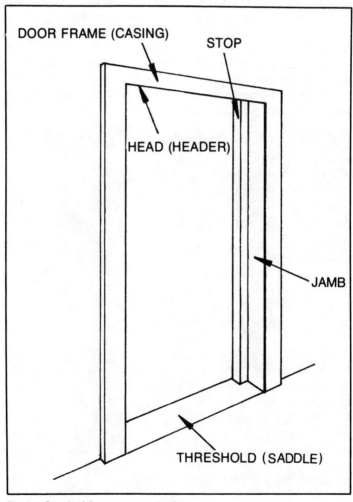

Fig. 4-4. Standard door frame construction.

bracing should be considered; setting the metal frame into a standard wood construction usually means the use of shims to adjust the frame.

PERMA/DOOR

Steelcraft, major manufacturer of steel doors for industry and home, has developed entranceway units that offer a maximum design flexibility coupled with a maximum door security. Because of the construction of the Steelcraft doors, the *Perma-Door* (Fig. 4-5) is an excellent replacement for the older home and also for the newer home that does not yet have that extra edge on proper security.

Replacing the poorly fitted wooden door with a Perma-Door replacement package is relatively easy. These doors are prehung into a steel frame which fits into the older door frame area. The replacement door units are available in various sizes for either single or double door replacements.

Fig. 4-5. The Perma-Door (courtesy of Steelcraft Manufacturing Co.).

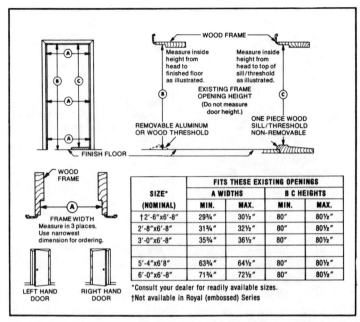

Fig. 4-6. Determining replacement door size (courtesy of Steelcraft Manufacturing Co.).

The table within the figure:

| SIZE* (NOMINAL) | FITS THESE EXISTING OPENINGS | | | |
| | A WIDTHS | | B C HEIGHTS | |
	MIN.	MAX.	MIN.	MAX.
†2'-6"x6'-8"	29¾"	30½"	80"	80½"
2'-8"x6'-8"	31¾"	32½"	80"	80½"
3'-0"x6'-8"	35¾"	36½"	80"	80½"
5'-4"x6'8"	63¾"	64½"	80"	80½"
6'-0"x6'-8"	71¾"	72½"	80"	80½"

*Consult your dealer for readily available sizes.
†Not available in Royal (embossed) Series

In determining the replacement door size, you will need to do the following (See Fig. 4-6). Measure the frame width in three places. Use the narrowest dimension for the size of the replacement door unit. Measure the inside existing frame opening height from the head to the finished floor. If there is a wooden or aluminum threshold, remove it when measuring. Measure the inside existing frame opening height from the top of the sill/threshold for one-piece sill/thresholds that are non-removable. With these dimensions, go out and obtain the Perma-Door replacement unit for your home.

The steel entrance frame is quite uniquely constructed. You may already have a steel door, but if it was hung on a wooden frame (this has been done), it would be wise to change the frame to a steel one. Steelcraft offers the frame because of a simple reason. It offers that extra security and also the durability that a wooden frame cannot provide.

Like installing a complete Perma-Door and frame, installation time and effort by the homeowner is relatively easy and takes less than a couple of hours. Installation is in three easy steps (Figs. 4-7 through 4-9).

Fig. 4-7. Remove the old door, hardware, threshold and inside trim (courtesy of Steelcraft Manufacturing Co.).

□ Set the prehung unit into the rough door opening.

□ Nail it in place through the predrilled nailing holes in the security flange.

□ Install the siding as with a wooden door frame.

Note that when selecting these doors for self installing, it is only the single doors that are prehung. Doors in pairs are not.

Once you have taken the doors, the door frames, and the adjoining walls into consideration and upgraded them, you still don't really have a secure door. This is because you still have to secure that door, or doors, with a proper retaining device that will hold it securely closed—the lock.

Fig. 4-8. Nail the replacement unit into place. Attach anchor screws. Cut bands and open door (courtesy of Steelcraft Manufacturing Co.).

Fig. 4-9. Apply pre-weatherstripped wood stops. Fasten and caulk the sill. Reinstall inside trim (courtesy of Steelcraft Manufacturing Co.).

QUICK 'N EASY

LOCK TECHNOLOGY

Depending upon the age of the home, plus the considerations of the builder and previous owners, you may or may not have truly effective and secure primary and secondary locks on your front, side and back doors. From the time that the basic cylinder lock was developed, constant work has been performed to improve and upgrade the security integrity of all locks. Is your lock the most technically developed and secure lock possible for the protection and safety of your home and its contents? Before getting into the most popularly available locks that you should consider for the home, a mini-review of some lock technology is in order.

The basic *cylinder* lock (Fig. 4-10) is designed to provide a measure of adequate security for the home. The average cylinder lock is constructed of brass with five pin sets and springs (Fig. 4-11), although some of the later models currently available use six pin sets. These pins and the springs hold the cylinder from turning. As the proper key is inserted, the pins "line up" at the top of the

Fig. 4-10. Basic cylinder lock (courtesy of Scovill Security Products).

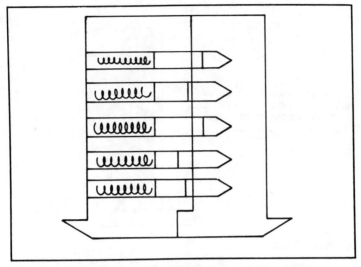

Fig. 4-11. The average cylinder lock is constructed of brass with five pin sets and springs.

cylinder edge (the shear line) allowing the key to turn, and either locking or unlocking the lock (Fig. 4-12).

The most commonly available locks can be defeated (Fig. 4-13). The time required to defeat such locks can vary from a few seconds to an hour or more for the non-professional burglar who is not adept at picking locks. It should also be noted that a burglar, when looking over your home with the intent of burglary is, most naturally, concerned primarily with your external security

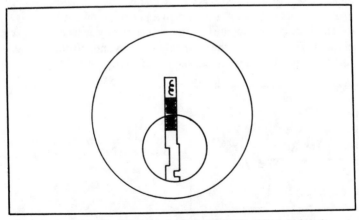

Fig. 4-12. As the key is inserted, the pins line up at the top of the cylinder edge.

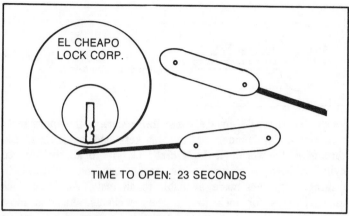

TIME TO OPEN: 23 SECONDS

Fig. 4-13. Common locks can be defeated.

features—specifically the locking devices. The burglar realizes the more secure and technologically designed the lock is, the less chance he will have of gaining entry through the door.

Within the standard cylinder (Fig. 4-14), notice the pins are cylindrically shaped. The matching key has the standard types of cuts that are found on most keys, and the cuts in the key will match up to the cylinder pin (Fig. 4-15).

MEDECO CYLINDER LOCK

Manufacturers have consistently sought methods to improve the security of various facets of the lock to greatly increase the

Fig. 4-14. Standard cylinder.

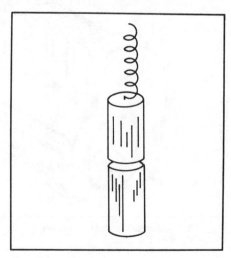

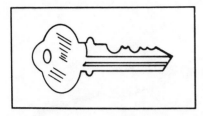

Fig. 4-15. The cuts in the key will match up to the cylinder pin.

lock's security. To ensure *maximum* security, the most pick-resistant lock cylinder on the market—and made available throughout the world—is the *Medeco* lock. First of all, the Medeco cylinder, because of its superior technology and resistance to picking, has been made available to all major American lock manufacturers for inclusion in their locksets. As this most sophisticated lock is discussed, consider its varied and unique design features that are shown in the accompanying illustrations.

Viewing the basic cylinder (in a cutaway view), it uses a double-locking feature unlike any other cylinder on the market. The modification to the basic cylinder design is the addition of the longitudinal slot running the length of the pin chambers (Fig. 4-16). A side bar locking device has been added, strengthening the lock's integrity (Fig. 4-17).

From the exterior front view, it is seen that the cylinder possesses two locking points—the side bar and the cylinder pins

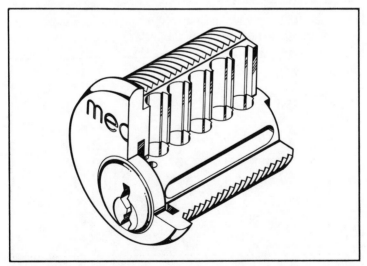

Fig. 4-16. The longitudinal slot runs the length of the pin chambers (courtesy of Medeco Security Locks, Inc.).

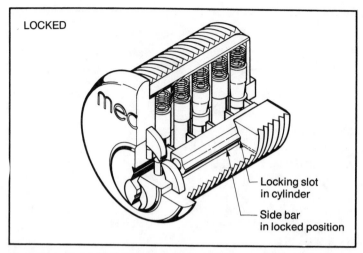

LOCKED

Locking slot
in cylinder

Side bar
in locked position

Fig. 4-17. A side bar locking device strengthens the lock's integrity (courtesy of Medeco Security Locks, Inc.).

(Fig. 4-18). When the proper key is inserted into the cylinder keyway, the tumblers will align properly at the shear point, allowing for the side bar to move inward (Fig. 4-19).

Because of the unique cutting of the key (Fig. 4-20), it is plain that no average key will operate the lock, much less a lock pick.

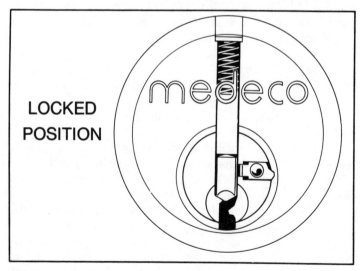

LOCKED
POSITION

medeco

Fig. 4-18. The cylinder possesses two locking points (courtesy of Medeco Security Locks, Inc.).

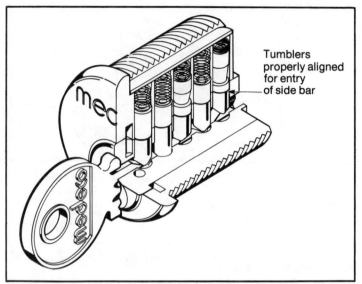

Tumblers
properly aligned
for entry
of side bar

Fig. 4-19. When the key is inserted into the cylinder keyway, the tumblers will align properly at the shear point (courtesy of Medeco Security Locks, Inc.).

Each cylinder, in this case, must be moved to the proper height. The key cuts, because of their angle, also rotate the tumbler pins to a specific angle for the side bar to engage the slots cut within each tumbler pin (Fig. 4-21). The key cut angles and the pins are prepared at very critical angles to ensure that only the properly authorized key will operate the lock.

Figure 4-22 shows in more detail the alignment factors of the tumbler and the side bar. Once proper alignment is achieved, the cylinder tumblers and side bar have shifted to allow the cylinder to turn (Fig. 4-23).

The next area to consider for the Medeco lock is that six hardened anti-drilling inserts have been included to prevent an individual from taking a drill and drilling away the basic cylinder portions to further manipulate the lock and gain entry (Fig. 4-24). These portions can also be noted in detail, along with the other features of the lock in the exploded lock view (Fig. 4-25).

The exploded view clearly shows the many features of the lock. Specifically, note items 15 (hardened steel inserts), 16 (hardened steel ball to prevent drilling of the side bar locking feature), 18 and 19 (security pins), 21 (the mushroom shaped pins) and 11 (uniquely configured tumbler pin designed to accept and operate only with a specially cut Medeco key).

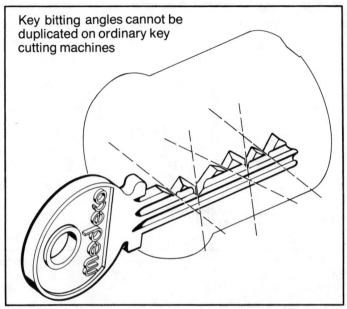

Fig. 4-20. Note the unique cutting of the key (courtesy of Medeco Security Locks, Inc.).

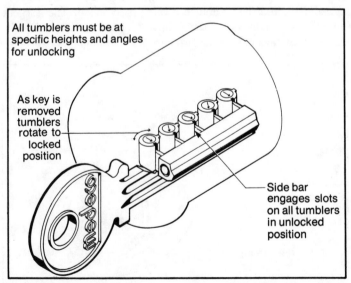

Fig. 4-21. The key cuts rotate the tumbler pins to a specific angle for the side bar to engage the slots cut within each tumbler pin (courtesy of Medeco Security Locks, Inc.).

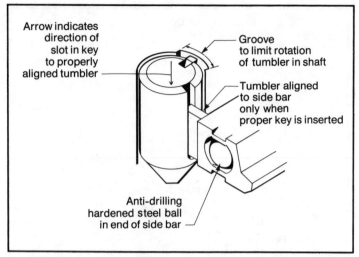

Fig. 4-22. Alignment factors of the tumbler and side bar (courtesy of Medeco Security Locks, Inc.).

SARGENT KESO LOCK

Second in line for the home security-conscious homeowner is probably the *Sargent Keso* lock (Fig. 4-26). Like the Medeco cylinder, it, too, has a unique locking mechanism. The Sargent Keso has two sets of tumblers (Fig. 4-27) built into the lock and a key that, instead of the standard key cuts that might be expected,

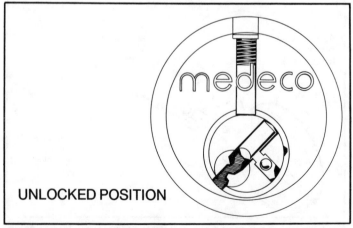

Fig. 4-23. The cylinder tumblers and side bar have shifted to allow the cylinder to turn (courtesy of Medeco Security Locks, Inc.).

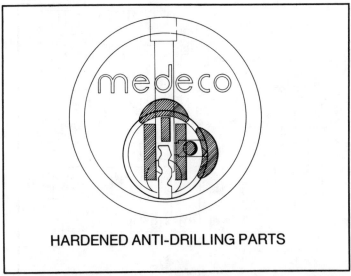

HARDENED ANTI-DRILLING PARTS

Fig. 4-24. The lock has six hardened anti-drilling inserts (courtesy of Medeco Security Locks, Inc.).

has what looks like partially drilled holes (Fig. 4-28). Again, like the Medeco, the key cannot be duplicated because of the unique configuration of the key cuts or holes in it.

ULTRA 700 SECURITY DEADBOLT LOCK

The *Ultra 700 security deadbolt* lock by Medeco is designed to complement the appearance of any door and, at the same time, prevent entry via the locking device (Fig. 4-29). Built to provide a maximum deterrence to the unlawful removal of the lock or any portion thereof to gain entry, its uniqueness is that there are no attaching screws on either side of the lock. The design will prevent prying or twisting of the cylinder off the door. This is due to the type of lock construction and attachment to the door. If the homeowner selects a steel door instead of a solid wood door for increased security, the Ultra 700 can be mounted on it, also. Any door with a thickness from 1⅝″ to 1 13/16″ is acceptable.

Figure 4-30 shows an exploded view of the Ultra 700 lock with the following features:

(1) The escutcheon covers are replaceable.

(2) Each cylinder has two individual screws to secure it.

(3) The protective lock cover is of steel.

(4) The escutcheon castings are of a special metal alloy.

ASSEMBLY NUMBER 10-200— MORTISE CYLINDER

ITEM	DESCRIPTION	REQ'D	PART NO
1	Key 6 Pin	1	10-011
2	Plug Mortise 6 Pin	1	10-012
3	Shell Mortise 6 Pin	1	10-017
4	Fence 6 Pin	1	10-022
5	Washer	1	10-025
6	Cam	1	as required
7	Set Screws	6	40-005
8	Screw #2-56 Slotted F H	2	10-032
9	Spring 'Tumbler'	6	10-034
10	Driver (Hardened on application)	6	10-035—10-040
11	Tumbler	6	Listed below
12	Spring Fence	2	10-047
13	Master Pin Disc	As required	10-048—10-052

ASSEMBLY NUMBER 10-400 RIM CYLINDER

ITEM	DESCRIPTION	REQ'D	PART NO
1	Key 6 Pin	1	10-011
2	Plug Rim 6 Pin	1	10-020
3	Shell Rim 6 Pin	1	10-024
4	Fence 6 Pin	1	10-022
5	Retainer	1	10-026
6	Connecting Bar	1	as required
7	Set Screws	1	40-005
9	Spring 'Tumbler'	6	10-034
10	Driver (Hardened on application)	6	10-035—10-040
11	Tumbler	6	Listed below
12	Spring Fence	2	10-047
13	Master Pin Disc	As required	10-048—10-052
14	Mounting Screws	2	10-055
*15	Steel Insert (Hardened)	2	10-057
*16	Steel Ball (Hardened)	1	10-058
*17	Escutcheon Ring	1	10-059
*18	Security Pin	2	10-062
*19	Security Pin	1	10-063
20	Plate (Back)	1	10-064
*21	Mushroom Drivers	As required	10-065—10-071

*These parts included on 10-200 MORTISE CYLINDER
Patent No. 3499502

TUMBLERS

1	Right	10-041
2	Right	10-042
3	Right	40-133
4	Right	40-134
5	Right	40-135
6	Right	40-136
1	Center	40-141
2	Center	40-142
3	Center	40-233
4	Center	40-234
5	Center	40-235
6	Center	40-236
1	Left	40-241
2	Left	40-242
3	Left	40-333
4	Left	40-334
5	Left	40-335
6	Left	40-336

Fig. 4-25. Exploded view of the Medeco lock (courtesy of Medeco Security Locks, Inc.).

Fig. 4-26. Sargent Keso lock (courtesy of Sargent, Division of Walter Kidde & Company, Inc.).

(5) The locking bolt is of solid steel and provides for a full 1⅛" throw. A hardened roller insert is within the bolt. When in the locked position, a full 1" of the bolt will always remain within the lock body.

(6) Hardened steel cylinder guards are free turning. Also, the cylinder guards are recessed into the escutcheons for maximum protection of the cylinders.

(7) The cylinders thread directly into the escutcheon with more than a ¼" engagement.

(8) The lock is clamped securely to the door by a unique means that is accessible only from the edge of the door. This means there

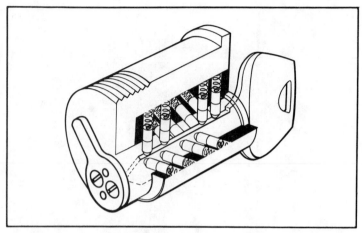

Fig. 4-27. Note the tumblers (courtesy of Sargent, Division of Walter Kidde & Company, Inc.).

Fig. 4-28. The Sargent Keso key (courtesy of Sargent, Division of Walter Kidde & Company, Inc.).

Fig. 4-29. Ultra 700 security deadbolt lock (courtesy of Medeco Security Locks, Inc.).

are no screws on either side of the door, which ensures maximum security integrity.

(9) The moving lock mechanism parts are of stainless steel for long lasting wear and tear, which would normally weaken other locking mechanisms.

(10) The free-turning hardened pin.

(11) The strike plate uses 2″ screws of *hardened* metal.

Installation of the Ultra 700, because of its design, is relatively simple. Notch out the door edge according to the factory supplied template. Insert the lock body into the cutout and tighten the two screws from the door edge for firm clamping action.

Add the lock faceplate. The cutout dimensions are 2¾″ high × 3¾″ long with a ½″ radii at the two inside corners.

The Ultra 700 comes in three variations: a double-locking cylinder (locks on both sides), the cylinder on the outside and a thumbturn on the inside, and a cylinder on the outside and a cylinder blank on the inside.

Cylinder deadlocks come in several styles. Some are units that are separate from the door knob mechanism and others are built into the mechanism. Whichever is selected by the homeowner, only one real thing must be kept in mind. The lock selected must provide an optimum amount of security.

KWIKSET'S 800 SERIES LOCKS

In recent years, the importance of redesigned engineering and construction improvements for greater strength have allowed a greater quality line of security cylinder deadlocks to become available to the homeowner. Kwikset's *880 series* (Fig. 4-31) provides an ideal companion to the basic home door lock. The improved lock features a full 1″ solid steel deadbolt with a revolving hardened steel insert to deter the sawing of the bolt, two heavy duty steel reinforcing rings to resist prying or pulling of the cylinder from the door, and a tapered steel cylinder guard that is free turning to resist any attempt to twist or pry the cylinder away from the door and the lock. Kwikset has also added specially heat-treated, special alloy steel bolts (¼″ diameter) which install *directly* to the cylinder to protect against prying.

Functions of the 880 series locks are:

☐ **880.** It has a 1″ deadbolt exterior keyed cylinder and a thumb key turn on the inside.

☐ **881.** It has a 1″ deadbolt exterior keyed cylinder and no interior thumb key turn.

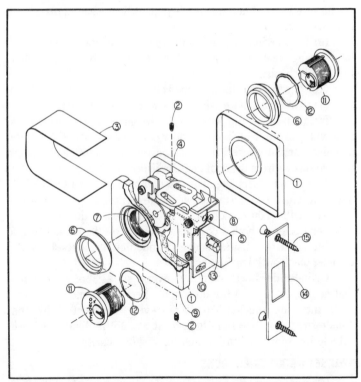

Fig. 4-30. Exploded view of the Ultra 700 security deadbolt lock (courtesy of Medeco Security Locks, Inc.).

New Kwikset 880 Series
Cylinder Deadlocks

No. 880
Cylinder deadlock with 1" deadbolt.

No. 881
One-way deadlock with 1" deadbolt.

No. 885
Double cylinder deadlock with 1" deadbolt.

No. 886
Keyless deadlock with 1" deadbolt.

Fig. 4-31. The 800 series (courtesy of Kwikset, Division of Emhart Industries, Inc.).

☐ **885.** This is a double cylinder deadlock. The key operates a 1″ bolt from either the interior or the exterior.

☐ **886.** A one-sided deadlock, the thumb key turn piece operates the 1″ bolt from the interior side only. There is no exterior locking. This lock is considered an auxiliary (secondary) locking device, but it may be mounted in the same door as the primary lock, according to the purchaser's wishes. As such, this is probably the best nighttime latch available on today's home security market.

All Kwikset deadlocks with 1″ deadbolts are adjustable for 1⅜″ up to 1¾″ doors. For thicker doors, up to 2¼″, contact should be made directly with the local Kwikset distributor or locksmith for specific information on obtaining one to fit a specific thickness door.

Note that these locks have a backset (the distance from the door edge) of 2⅜″, 2¾″ and 5″, so they are configured for any popular door currently available for home use.

PROTECTO-LOK

The Kwikset double security *Protecto-Lok* (Fig. 4-32) is designed specifically as an extra deterrent to illegal entry.

87

Protecto-Lok can be opened from the inside by turning just the interior knob. It provides two-way security; it has anti-panic and anti-burglar features built into the lock.

The lock combines an extra security cylinder deadlock together with a key-in-knob lockset. Unlike other ordinary deadlock and lockset combinations, the new Protecto-Lok can be opened from the inside by simply turning the knob.

There is no need to turn both the thumb key and knob before the door will open. Just one action retracts both the deadbolt and the deadlocking latch. The deadlock and lockset are keyed alike (same key opens both locks) for easy locking and unlocking.

The Protecto-Lok features instant reversibility for both right hand and left hand doors (doors that open from different sides). This feature allows you to simply pull and rotate the lock spindle 180 degrees and install the lock so that the "hand" of the lock matches the "hand" of the door. If the lock was purchased for a right hand door opening and it should have been for a left hand one, you won't be stuck with an extra lock. Kwikset has saved you the time and money by having the instant reversibility feature.

Additional protection is provided against burglary through the use of a 1″ steel deadbolt with a hacksaw-resistant steel rod, plus a solid steel housing assembly that is protected by a very heavy duty steel cylinder guard and solid steel reinforcing rings and plates.

Depending on the function, the companion lockset is also equipped with an extra security latchbolt that deadlatches when the door is closed.

Since some people like the decorative finish or knob designs that go with the lock and may match the house in some way, Kwikset also provides for these aesthetic qualities, with no lessening of the security integrity of the lock.

MEDECO D-11 SERIES DEADBOLT LOCK

The *Medeco D-11 series deadbolt lock* comes with the standard locking features discussed earlier. The deadbolt is designed for all doors with a thickness from 1¼″ to 2⅝″ and includes a wrench-resistant cylinder guard collar to prevent forced removal. Unlike some other deadbolt locks on today's market, the ¼″ diameter mounting bolts are of high tensile strength steel and are totally concealed when the lock installation is complete.

The strike is of 14-gauge brass and uses 2″ screws. There is an additional measure for wood frame installation that can also be

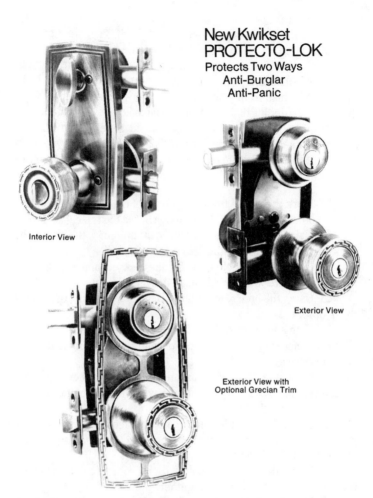

New Kwikset
PROTECTO-LOK
Protects Two Ways
Anti-Burglar
Anti-Panic

Interior View

Exterior View

Exterior View with
Optional Grecian Trim

Fig. 4-32. Double security Protecto-Lok (courtesy of Kwikset, Division of Emhart Industries, Inc.).

used—a steel reinforcement plate with 3″ screws for additional strength and security.

This is only a sampling of the types of locks that can be considered for installation to upgrade the security of the door and the home. Each homeowner must decide for himself the particular lock that he wishes to install.

INSTALLING A DOOR LOCK

Installing your door lock is not as difficult as you may imagine. You may think that the exact location of the hole for the lock, once cut, will be a slight fraction of an inch off. Well, your worries have been alleviated. Howard Hardware has come up with a variety of lock installation kits, such as the one in Fig. 4-33. In addition to the basic tools (less the power drill and screwdrivers for the lock, which you furnish from your own home workshop), a template for the exact positioning of the lockset and latch holes is provided.

Besides the electric drill, you should have a screwdriver, chisel, hammer, ⅛" twist drill and a 3/32" twist drill from your own toolbox. Simple procedures provide for the easy installation of your lockset.

☐ Mark the height from the bottom of the door. Use existing locks in other doors as a guide, although 38" is the typical height.

☐ Using the template, mark the center point of the knobs (the backset) and the center of the door edge.

☐ Drill the pilot holes, ⅛" for the lockset, and a 3/32" hole for the latch plate where it is indicated in the template.

☐ Using the hole saw, drill the large hole through the side of the door for the lockset.

☐ Using the wood drill, drill the latch hole into the door edge. This hole should meet the lockset hole and continue for another ¾" past the large hole.

☐ Insert the latch. Mark around the edge and then chisel out the area to make the latch plate fit flush with the edge of the door.

☐ Screw in the latch.

☐ Insert the outside knob (with the accompanying rosette plate), putting the spindles through the latch (or engaging the lock "tongue" in the latch grooves).

☐ Insert the opposite knob (with its rosette plate), aligning the screw stems. Screw them together.

☐ Measure the height from the floor to the center of the latch that you have just installed. Measure the distance from the door edge to the center of the latch and mark this on the door jamb.

☐ Place the strike plate over this, with the mark in the center of the strike plate. Using the wood drill, drill a hole at least ⅝" deep. Clean the wood out of the hole and put the strike plate in place. Mark around the edge and chisel out an area so the strike plate will be flush with the door jamb. Drill 3/32" pilot holes for the strike plate installation screws and affix the strike plate to the jamb.

This completes the installation. For less than a $5 investment in a lock installation kit, you have saved a minimum of $25 for a

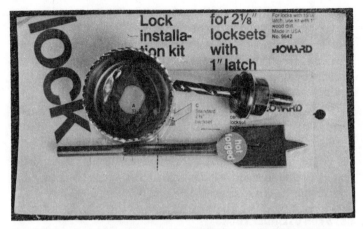

Fig. 4-33. Lock installation kit (courtesy of Howard Hardware Products, Inc.).

professional installation. You also have the installation kit to use when installing another lock in the home.

IDEAL SECURITY HARDWARE SUPER GUARD LOCK II

When installing or replacing a lock with one that is more secure, it becomes imperative that the new lock provide greater security to the door and the home. The *Ideal Security Hardware Super Guard Lock II* is probably America's only jimmy proof *prime* door lock that is up to eight times stronger than the current door lock you may have. It replaces any of the millions of key-in-knob locksets of low or questionable and dubious security integrity that now grace many homes. It will replace virtually any lockset you may have.

The Ideal Super Guard Lock II has such qualities as:

—Automatic locking. Just close the door and it's locked.

—Lockout button. By throwing the lockout button into the locked position, entry from the outside *even with a key* is prevented.

—Protective sliding bolt so the door cannot shut on you, accidentially locking you out.

—An adjustable ball catch feature allows the door to remain in the closed position when the lock is not engaged.

—Aesthetic design. A modern lever on the inside handle will also turn both ways for left and right handed locking doors. (Modern style door companion handles are also available for outside the door.)

—A through bolting system. All screws are concealed.

—Jimmy-proof construction.

The Super Guard II lock is easy to install. Remove the present lock unit. Insert the Super Guard II ball catch strike. Install the outside handle and key cylinder *into the existing hole.* (Note that no new holes must be drilled to install this lock.)

Screw the lock together from the inside. Attach the strike plate to the door framing. Your new lock is now ready to use; time required for installation is less than 30 minutes.

Note that the lock also comes with a double cylinder for doors that have side lights or windows. Your key would be required to operate the door from either side.

KEYS FOR CYLINDER LOCKS

Before moving on with secondary and auxiliary locks for the home, here is a quick look at keys for cylinder locks. Standard lockpicking equipment will defeat the majority of these in short order. The Medeco key (Fig. 4-20) and the Sargent key (Fig. 4-28) are different in the key cuts; they are not as those on the regular keys. If you live in a very high crime area, consider the type of key when considering the type of lock to install. Beware of the person who will sell you just any lock, indicating that it will stop the average burglar. A lock is only as good as the type of key that goes into it; if the key is easy to duplicate or has key cuts that can be picked even by the amateur, the lock is not for you.

FOX POLICE BRACE LOCK

For many homes, especially those in which elderly people and those in community housing projects live, the doors do not have an auxiliary lock. The management may not permit one to be installed. So, what can the resident do to create a greater sense of security for the door? The best bet, and a very popular one, is to install a Fox jimmy-proof *police brace lock* (Fig. 4-34).

The lock can be installed with a cylinder or without (if the management so deems). It should be pointed out, though, that it is to the management's advantage to have the secondary lock cylinder installed. In 99% of all cases, management will agree to having the entire unit installed. Many times they will undertake the expense of having a man come in and perform the work. In other instances, the apartment dweller will have to hire out or perform the work himself.

Fig. 4-34. Police brace lock (courtesy of The Fox Police Lock Co.).

This is not to say that the lock should not be used in the single family dwelling. On the contrary, it is another line of defense against the would-be intruder or burglar.

The Fox police lock can be used when you are home or when you are out. It is always in place and takes only a moment to remove the brace bar for entry or exiting. Further, it is endorsed and recommended by many police departments and approved by various burglary insurance underwriter firms.

Note that it applies only to those residences where the door opens inward. It is the only lock using this positive steel bar to prevent forced entry. The lock is designed to fit all size doors.

Installation procedure is as follows. Determine the hand of the door. Close the door from the inside. If the door knob is on the right side, then you will be using the right lock; if the knob is to the left, then the left lock will be used.

With the door in the closed position, measure 48″ up from the floor (Fig. 4-35). This is the approximate height at which the lock will be installed. If there is a lock or other obstruction at this location, it will have to be removed.

When there is another location or obstruction at the 48″ level on the door that cannot be removed, a special longer steel bar may be obtained and used in place of the regular bar. The standard bar is 56″ long; the special bar will be 60-62″ long. This will allow for the lock to be installed at 54″ instead of 48″. If there is an auxiliary lock at the 48″ height, remove the lock from the door.

With the door fully closed, measure 30″ out from the bottom edge of the door (Fig. 4-36). From this point, measure 2″ in toward the hinge side of the door; this will give the most effective bracing. This is the point at which the floor socket will be installed.

In the event the Fox police lock must be installed where there is a cement floor, use the following procedure (Fig. 4-37). Drill a hole in the center of the floor socket and countersink it so a flat head screw may be used. Chisel the cement to countersink the floor socket so it is level with the floor surface. Then remove the floor socket and continue the hole deep enough to insert a wood plug or lead shield under the socket. Set the wood plug or shield in place and reset the socket in the floor. Secure it with the flat head screw. If too much cement has been chiseled away after the floor socket

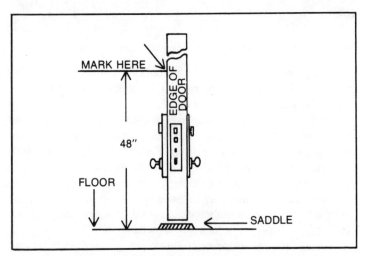

Fig. 4-35. The height at which the lock will be installed.

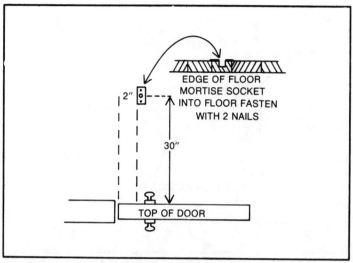

Fig. 4-36. Measure 30″ out from the bottom edge of the door.

has been secured, fill the excess with patching cement. Do not use the lock until the cement has sufficiently hardened.

Remove the cover from the lock and remove the movable parts. Note the position of the parts before removing them.

Hold the base of the lock on the door (48″ from the floor) and about ¼″ from the edge of the door. Insert the steel brace bar into

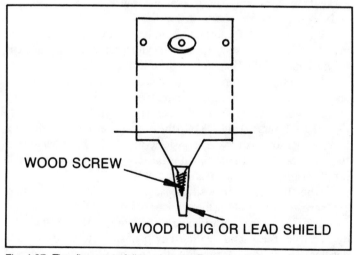

Fig. 4-37. The diagram to follow when the Fox police lock must be installed where there is a cement floor.

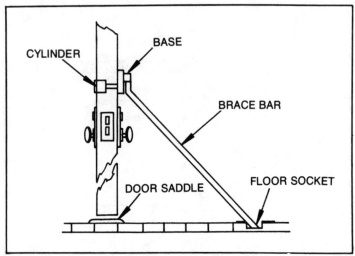

Fig. 4-38. Insert the steel brace bar into the floor socket and bring it into the locked position on the base of the lock.

the floor socket and bring it into the locked position on the base of the lock (Fig. 4-38).

With the lock held in this position, scribe a circle on the disk socket hole (Fig. 4-39). Remove the lock, exposing the scribed circle.

Draw a vertical line through the center of the circle of the disk socket hole. Now draw a horizontal line where the top of the circle and vertical lines intersect (Fig. 4-40).

Bore a 1¼″ hole for the cylinder where the vertical and horizontal lines intersect. Insert the cylinder into the hole and cut off the tailpiece 1/16″ longer than the thickness of the door.

Cut off the cylinder screws (if necessary) to the proper length and mount the base and cylinder on the door with these screws. Don't tighten down the screws too securely at this time!

Place the brace bar back into the floor socket and set it into the locking position on the base of the lock (Fig. 4-41). If the bar seems too short, tap the base down; if it is too long, tap the base up until it is tight against the bar with the door closed.

When the base is in position, fasten to the door with the four 1½″ screws. Also, tighten the cylinder screws.

The Fox police lock will operate as either a latch (that can be opened from the outside with a key or inside by hand), or as a deadlock (when locked outside with the key, it cannot be opened from the inside), by a simple change of the eccentric cam. With the

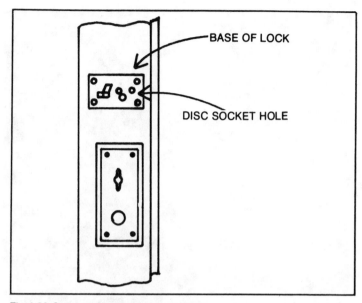

Fig. 4-39. Scribe a circle on the disc socket hole.

cam pin in the top position, the lock will work as a latch; with the cam pin left or right, the lock becomes a deadlock. After the eccentric cam is in place, insert the slide bolt into position. Place the cover over the lock and secure it with two 10/24″ machine screws.

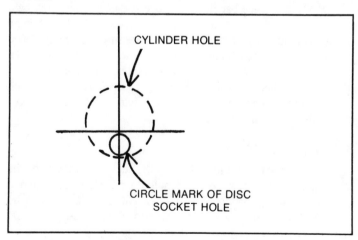

Fig. 4-40. Draw a horizontal line where the top of the circle and vertical lines intersect.

Fig. 4-41. Place the brace bar back into the floor socket and set it into the locking position on the base of the lock (courtesy of The Fox Police Lock Co.).

Place the brace bar into the floor socket and into the lock. Open the door and see that the bar slides freely into the retaining guide. Try locking from the outside to make sure the door is closed securely. If the lock binds and the key will not close the lock smoothly, file a very small amount of metal off the top of the bar. If the Fox police lock is installed properly, this is the best protection you can buy with your money for an auxiliary device for the door, and it has been well worth it.

FOX DOUBLE BOLT LOCK

The *Fox double bolt lock* (Fig. 4-42) is designed to provide the maximum security required for single doors. Although designed primarily for use on doors that open outward, it can also be installed on other types of doors through the use of special hardware.

Properly installed, the lock works smoothly from the outside of the door as the key is inserted and cylinder turned. Turning the

Fig. 4-42. Fox double bolt lock (courtesy of The Fox Police Lock).

cylinder rotates the spindle and bolt activating gear. As the bolt gear turns, the teeth of the gear engage the bolt teeth to extend the bolts and lock the door. The bolts enter the door frame through the two strike plates and go 2½″ into the jamb (Fig. 4-43).

The double bolt lock uses a standard five-pin tumbler cylinder in a brass case that is covered over (except for the keyway) with a steel safety plate that is bolted into place so that the cylinder cannot be wrenched out. The tailpiece mechanism, however, differs from the usual lock tailpiece. The Fox tailpiece is rigid and connects to the cylinder by a backplate held by two screws. Figure 4-44 details the various parts of the lock in an exploded view.

Installation is as follows. Drill a 1½″ hole in the exact center of the door, approximately 50″ above the floor.

From the outside of the door, insert the lock cylinder (and cylinder ring) through the hole. Position the outside steel safety plate over the cylinder face so that only the keyway is accessible through the opening in the plate.

Mark the position of the four corner holes and remove the plate. Drill four holes ¼″ in diameter and fasten the plate to the

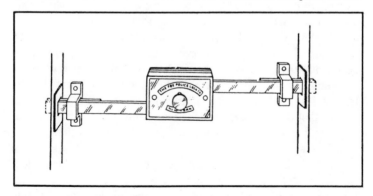

Fig. 4-43. The bolts enter the door frame through the two strike plates (courtesy of The Fox Police Lock Co.).

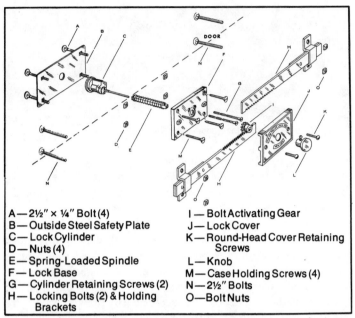

A — 2½″ × ¼″ Bolt (4)
B — Outside Steel Safety Plate
C — Lock Cylinder
D — Nuts (4)
E — Spring-Loaded Spindle
F — Lock Base
G — Cylinder Retaining Screws (2)
H — Locking Bolts (2) & Holding
     Brackets

I — Bolt Activating Gear
J — Lock Cover
K — Round-Head Cover Retaining
     Screws
L — Knob
M — Case Holding Screws (4)
N — 2½″ Bolts
O — Bolt Nuts

Fig. 4-44. Exploded view of the double bolt lock (courtesy of The Fox Police Lock Co.).

door with the four 2½″ quarter-inch bolts and nuts. When completed, it should look like Fig. 4-45.

Working on the inside of the door, fasten the lock base to the lock cylinder with the two cylinder retaining screws. Depending upon the thickness of the door, the screws might have to be shortened. In the case of a panel door, a block of wood will have to be used to increase the effective thickness in the area where the base is to be fastened. Ensure that the lock base is level and fasten it to the door with four 1½″ sheet metal screws.

Align the locking bolts on the base, extending each bolt outward to the jamb. Place the brackets over the bars as close to the jambs as possible. The Fox Police Lock Company highly recommends ¼″ between the bracket and the jamb. This will ensure that the bars cannot be sprung. Mark the position of the brackets. Laying the bolts aside, install the brackets with four 3″ × 5/16″ bolts and nuts.

Slip the bolt activating gear over the end of the spring loaded spindle, with the gear edge facing the center of the spindle. Take the inside lock cover and, from the inside of the cover, fit the spindle and gear into the opening.

Fasten the knob to the portion of the spindle protruding through the opening. Then, align the bolts on the base plate and through the brackets.

Holding the bolts in position, slip the cover and spindle unit into place. (During this operation, make sure that the cylinder tailpiece slides into the square bore of the spindle.) Fasten the cover to the base plate with two round head screws.

To install the strike plates, extend the bars against the door jambs and, with a pencil, mark the position of the strike hole. Drill the strike hole deep enough to allow the bolts to protrude a minimum of 2½" into the jamb. Finish the job by installing the strike plates over the two holes.

The Fox police double bolt lock comes in three different configurations, depending upon your particular desires and needs. All three are shown in Fig. 4-46.

AUXILIARY DOOR LOCKS

Auxiliary locks are secondary locks used in conjunction with the primary lock for any door. They are in addition to the basic locking mechanism and should always be considered as such. They do not take the place of the primary lock, and they do not offer the full value of security protection as the primary locking device. Various auxiliary locks are shown in Fig. 4-47.

In many instances, the auxiliary lock is the same one that was located on the door when a person moved into the residence. This can mean the device is 10, 15, or 20 years old or more. The auxiliary lock is sometimes, though, a very good quality lock, such

Fig. 4-45. The plate is fastened to the door (courtesy of The Fox Police Lock Co.).

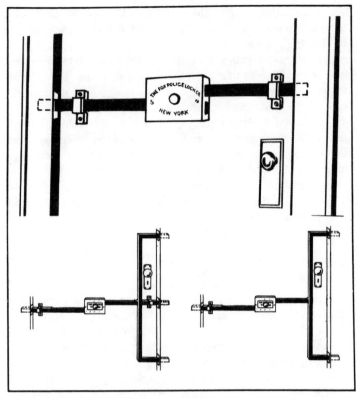

Fig. 4-46. Three different police double bolt lock configurations (courtesy of The Fox Police Lock Co.).

as the jimmy proof lock (Fig. 4-48). Again, the auxiliary lock can be almost any device such as a rim latch, deadbolt latch, surface mounted cylinder, chain guard, etc. (Fig. 4-49).

Since many locks are surface-mounted, you should be aware that there are a number of disadvantages associated with them. The locks are held *against* the door with screws. Forcing of the door can weaken the screw holding power with the wood. Repeated forcing attempts over even a short period of time can weaken the screws enough to allow entry.

The strike box for the latchbolt is held with two screws, neither of them very long. Again, several repeated blows against the door can loosen these screws, also.

The internally mounted lock has relatively few disadvantages. A person looking at the door will know that there is an auxiliary locking device, whereas he often wouldn't with the surface-

102

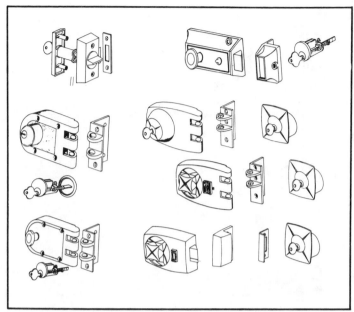

Fig. 4-47. Auxiliary locks (courtesy of Ideal Security Hardware).

mounted lock. The surface-mounted lock doesn't require that a cylinder be installed along with it.

From a burglar's point of view, having a secondary lock that is merely a surface-mounted one may be to his advantage. He picks open your primary lock and prepares to enter—only to discover that he cannot because there is something else holding the door closed. He can assume that a person is on the inside, or that the

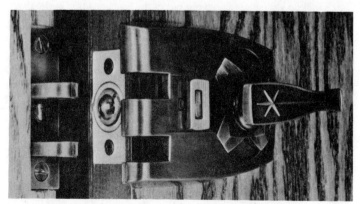

Fig. 4-48. Jimmy-proof lock (courtesy of Ideal Security Hardware).

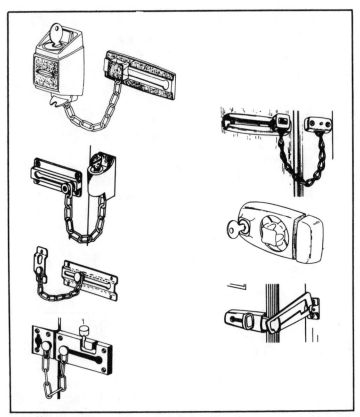

Fig. 4-49. Various door security locks and devices (courtesy of Ideal Security Hardware).

latch locked also when you went out of the house. If this is the case, then he might as well go ahead and force the door. It will only take an extra 30 seconds or so. Also, he is usually safe in the knowledge that if you are cheap enough to install such a lock, you probably are cheap about all your home security devices, so he should have no further trouble. He won't thank you for it in writing, but he thanks you just the same.

This example is just one prime reason for considering an auxiliary locking device that is enclosed within the door, whenever possible. If you must use a surface-mounted lock, use longer screws (2″ length), and only use them in areas where the security factor is low, such as a side door to the garage or the side porch of the home (where the main entry door off the house is covered with an in-door lock).

Several latch and bolt locks are available which will suffice for the average homeowner or apartment dweller. Figure 4-50 illustrates several of them. Easily installed with screws, they are rapidly attached to the door and serve the basic use of a night latch. If the door happens to be of metal, use only metal screws, never wood screws.

If the door is solid core wood, then in addition to using wood screws (of a maximum length possible for the thickness of the door), you might screw in the screw about two-thirds of its distance. Remove it and squeeze in a very small amount of wood glue, then reinsert the screw and tighten it down. The use of wood glue, or any other type that provides a good bonding power, will ensure a better and more permanent bonding that will better hold the screw to the wood. Whenever feasible and possible, the strike plate or receiving receptacle for the bolt mechanism should be secured with 2" screws.

Many of these type locks can also be used with or without an exterior pin tumbler. If you desire to use the lock for more than a night latch and decide to install the pin tumbler, then you will need to drill a hole in the door. Follow the basic instructions provided earlier for the installation of a regular door lock.

Auxiliary locks also include the door guard, in the chain and chainless varieties (Fig. 4-51). These allow you to keep the door held only partially open (3-6" maximum) and to look out and accept small deliveries or to check on an unknown visitor without totally opening the door, which may compromise your own safety. Various types are available, including those chain locks that have a localized alarm attached (Fig. 4-52).

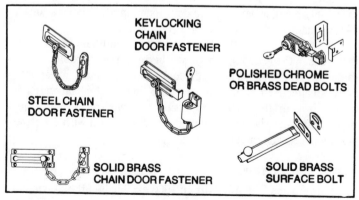

Fig. 4-50. Latch and bolt locks for doors (courtesy of Belwith International, Ltd.)

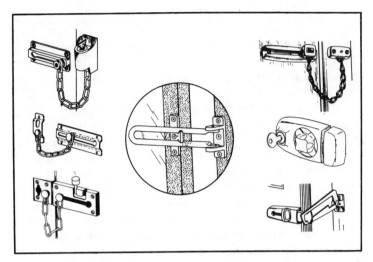

Fig. 4-51. The door guard in chain and chainless varieties (courtesy of Blaine Window Hardware Inc. and Ideal Security Hardware).

SLIDING AND OPEN SWINGING DOOR LOCKS

Houses and apartments frequently have the narrow-stile sliding glass entrance or side doors installed. Dual purposes were the reasoning behind this. First, there is more access to the outside, to include the visual appeal of a large viewing area; second, the architectural trend is toward the use of more and more glass.

Unfortunately, these considerations, while they may be aesthetically appealing and popular, have greatly increased the problems of home security integrity. This is particularly true of the extremely popular narrow stile door found in many homes today, which usually leads out to the patio or backyard.

As the aluminum thickness shrunk in width and in material thickness in these doors, it naturally became more flexible. At the same time, the space to house the locking unit became correspondingly smaller. To retract the locking bolt in the conventional manner is naturally impossible; there is simply no place for it to go. Something had to be done that made the door useful with the same amount of security integrity as before.

Adams Rite MS System

The Adams Rite Mfg. Co. in 1956 established the Maximum Security (MS) system to rate its own hardware and also to study the problem regarding the security and vulnerabilities of sliding doors. To be rated MS, it was determined that a product *must* exceed, in resistance to forced entry, all other components of its surroundings—a very difficult test for many products on the market. While this may seem simple to the reader, product testing to meet such standards has been extremely exhaustive.

The conventional lockbolt (Fig. 4-53) installed in the aluminum frame of glass doors has only a ½" to ⅝" throw with an effective penetration of the strike to as little as ¼". The door is easily sprung open with only a couple of screwdrivers. Burglars are thus presented with a very highly attractive situation: a *very* flexible door that can be easily pried away from its jamb and also a short lock bolt that is supposed to bar the door to forced entry, but doesn't.

Various other techniques have been used over the years to defeat many sliding and double-doors that were not MS designed and rated. The hammer and bar (Fig. 4-54) were used to knock the pivot bolts either upward or downward. The MS system eliminated this by including a massive 3" MS bolt operating on the over-center principle. Pounding down on the bolt would only lock it tighter. Pounding upward would not accomplish anything either.

Adams Rite MS systems will not be defeated by a hacksaw either (Fig. 4-55). The massive MS bolt is of laminated steel—five plies of highly impact-resisting steel. Within the center ply of this

Fig. 4-52. Chain lock alarm (courtesy of Matuska Enterprises).

Fig. 4-53. The door is sprung open with a couple of screwdrivers (courtesy of Adams Rite Manufacturing Co.).

bolt is an alumina-ceramic core. The so-called super hacksaws which supposedly can cut just about anything are easily defeated.

Even burglars learn that they can be defeated by locks. So they turn to circumventing the locks through a new technique called *jamb peeling* (Fig. 4-56). This means, simply, the tearing away of the outswinging door's frame so that no material is left surrounding the lock. Adams Rite's answer to this was the development of the *Armor Strike* (Fig. 4-57), a steel reinforced strike plate that is installed in the hollow jamb (or opposite door of a pair).

Burglars then started another technique, *cylinder pulling* (Fig. 4-58). Because the standard cylinders are of brass, their threads can be stripped quite easily. Also, since the standard cylinder offers a convenient shoulder to pry on, this technique was just about as quick and easy as springing the narrow style. Adams Rite then developed the unique beveled steel guard (Fig. 4-59). The

108

outer portion being beveled, it is also case-hardened and free to swivel. There is no way for gripping tools to hold onto the guard. If the would-be burglar decides to bash in the stile to get behind the outer ring, he would still have to pull the entire inner flange through a round hole. Such leverage is not possible with portable tools.

Let's consider the Adams Rite MS system versus a conventional lock (Fig. 4-60). The Adams Rite MS lock is designed specifically for narrow stile glass doors. Its long pivoted bolt can provide a great measure of protection that cannot be duplicated by any other lock in this type of door. The MS bolt is housed vertically when retracted. Unlike the conventional lock bolt, its length is not restricted by the narrow width of the stile of the door. The MS bolt swings upward into a horizontal locked position with one clean sweep of laminated steel. As much of the 3″ bolt is retained in the locking stile as is projected into the opposite door or jamb.

The conventional bolt, a horizontally projected bolt which is installed in aluminum frame of a glass door has only a ½″ to ⅝″

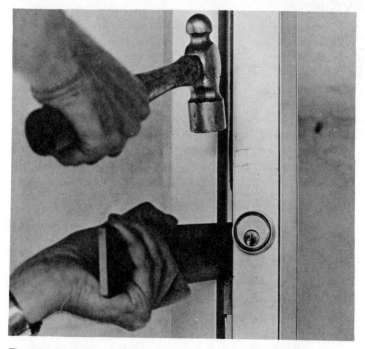

Fig. 4-54. The hammer and bar are used here to knock the pivot holes either upward or downward (courtesy of Adams Rite Manufacturing Co.).

109

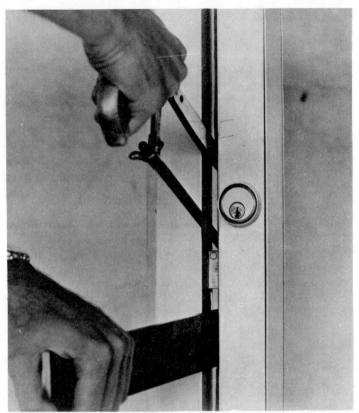

Fig. 4-55. The Adams Rite MS system will *not* be defeated by a hacksaw (courtesy of Adams Rite Manufacturing Co.).

throw with an effective penetration of ¼". The door is easily sprung open. The flexible bar that is supposed to bar the door doesn't, since it is easily pried away.

Understand that security must involve all the component parts of the entire door unit. Figure 4-61 illustrates and identifies the parts of the standard sliding door. A well designed and constructed door will have the pressure (strength) to resist forced entry through the unit.

Most homes will have the narrow stile sliding door, but many with home businesses attached may have the narrow stile swinging door (Fig. 4-62). No matter which is selected, it is extremely important that the selection of the lock be consistent with the features of the Adams Rite MS system. This is a must to ensure maximum security of the door unit.

The sliding door lock by Adams Rite has a stainless steel deadbolt that, in my opinion, is probably the finest the homeowner will ever find for the sliding glass door in homes and apartments (Fig. 4-63). This deadbolt incorporates features not usually found in other sliding door hardware:

☐ It is adjustable. A full 3/16" lengthening or shortening of the bolt projection is possible by turning a screw on the lockface. This can and will compensate for any misalignment between the door and jamb that is prevalent in the newer homes where the sliding door is just thrown into place without any real consideration for the proper alignment of all the features.

☐ The locking bolt is self-protecting. If the door is closed with the bolt in the locked position, the bolt will immediately retract on contact with the jamb, preventing damage or accidental lockout.

☐ The key cylinder is standard so that the glass slider can be keyed in with other types of doors on the premises. The cylinder is

Fig. 4-56. A demonstration of jamb peeling (courtesy of Adams Rite Manufacturing Co.).

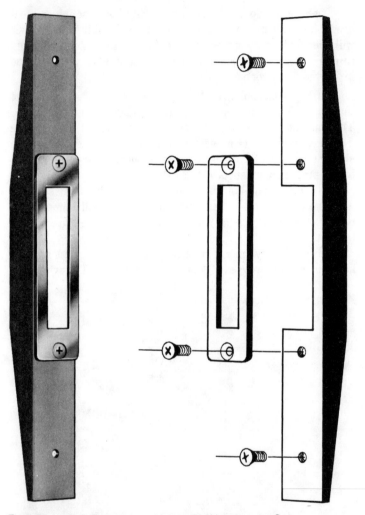

Fig. 4-57. Armor Strike (courtesy of Adams Rite Manufacturing Co.).

a five-pin tumbler insert. The thumb turn mounts directly to the inside of the door.

Patio Door Locks

The Kwikset extra security sliding *patio door lock* provides one of the easiest methods to deter the would-be burglar. Two varieties are currently available: the non-keyed and the keyed patio locks (Fig. 4-64). Notice that the lock is securely fastened to the center rail by two heavy duty metal screws. The locks feature rugged all-metal construction and easy do-it-yourself installation, fitting most sliding aluminum doors.

These locks have the additional advantage of allowing the patio door to be kept partially open (for ventilation) and still maintain security integrity to a great degree. Why? The locking pin goes into a small hole which you have drilled into the base of the sliding door. Actually, you have two holes—one for locking the door when it is closed all the way, and a second hole about 3-5″ away for ventilation. The lock cannot be reached by hand by an individual attempting to get in through the slightly open doorway.

Fig. 4-58. Cylinder pulling (courtesy of Adams Rite Manufacturing Co.).

Fig. 4-59. Beveled steel guard (courtesy of Adams Rite Manufacturing Co.).

The *Deerfield patio lock* (Fig. 4-65) is the recent invention of a master locksmith (within the locksmithing profession it requires 20 years experience before "master" can be added to the title) who was overly concerned that there was no easy method for the average homeowner to secure the patio door. His continued research and design considerations came up with this beautiful, totally extruded metal lock that can be installed in five minutes. Figure 4-66 shows the specific procedures for installing this security lock.

The Deerfield patio lock will lock both panels of a patio door, preventing jimmying or removal of the stationary panel. It will fit any metal door with a 1¼" or wider bottom rail, and the trim style does not interfere with inside sliding screens. The patented principle about which the lock is designed is, essentially, a proven

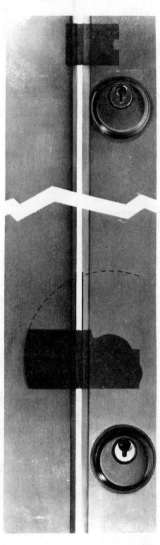

Fig. 4-60. The MS system versus a conventional lock (courtesy of Adams Rite Manufacturing Co.).

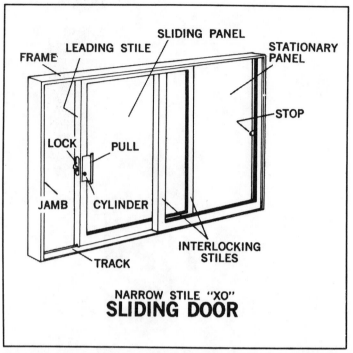

Fig. 4-61. Parts of the standard sliding door (courtesy of Adams Rite Manufacturing Co.).

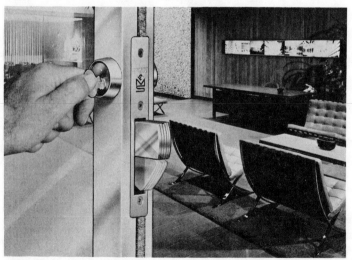

Fig. 4-62. The narrow stile swinging door (courtesy of Adams Rite Manufacturing Co.).

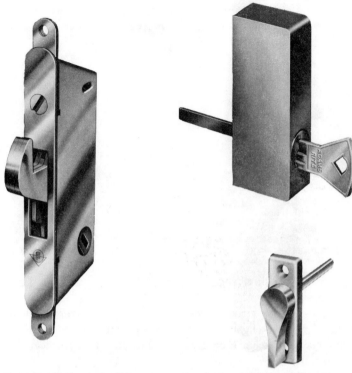

Fig. 4-63. The sliding door lock features a stainless steel deadbolt (courtesy of Adams Rite Manufacturing Co.).

item. It is considered by many to be the safest patio lock available on the market.

ELECTRIC EYE CONTROL UNIT

If you must leave the patio door completely open, or open far enough so that a standard patio lock is of no value in the open position, then Rodann Electronics' *electric eye* should be incorporated into your home security system. The electric eye control unit (the amplifier) is built into the photocell receiver and is powered by a UL approved "plug-in" type transformer. This ensures that all wiring is safe and low voltage type, like a bell, thermostat or burglar alarm wire. It has a solid state relay, and the PR-12 light bulb in the unit is operated at approximately 60% of the rated voltage to ensure a longer bulb life than normal. The amplifier is also a solid state unit utilizing diodes and a phototransistor. The

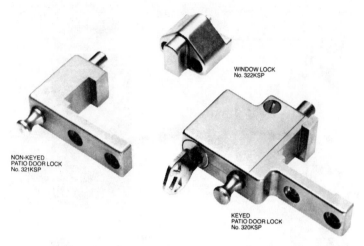

Fig. 4-64. Sliding patio door and window locks (courtesy of Kwikset, Division of Emhart Industries, Inc.).

special optical filter reduces, if not eliminates, ambient light interference.

The system, complete with the photocell receiver and light source, projects a light beam across an opening. Any interference with this beam (when properly focused on the photocell receiver) triggers the alarm.

The fully automatic unit requires no controls to adjust once it has been mounted in place. Universal mounting brackets are provided for easy installation and alignment. Because of the system simplicity, easy focus is obtained by just centering the light on target with the receiver.

Rodann developed an exclusive four second dropout for the unit. Power to the alarm is cut off if the light source is blocked or interfered with, thereby reducing chime burnout. The unit also automatically recycles itself. The receiving alarm unit can be installed just about anywhere so that you can hear it.

WINDOWS

Windows may be the easiest actual entry point into the home, but are the second most common area that the homeowner forgets about, after the door. Like the door, one usually assumes that if the glass is intact, the window is closed, and the simple closing device is in the closed position, burglars will not be able to enter. This is a fallacy.

Fig. 4-65. Patio lock (courtesy of Deerfield Lock Co., Inc.).

Burglars look at the windows after the door. Besides, a window is easier to enter; it's only a sheet of thin glass and a cheap sash lock that can be manipulated with a dinner knife, if need be.

Improvement of home security in regard to the windows takes many forms. This section will deal with improving existing security for various types of windows.

Windows fall into several categories: *double-hung, casement, fanlight* and *skylights* (roof domes). Most other types of windows are variations of these. Note that the standard solid, permanently installed, non-removable window is not covered. This is usually the front window, in the living room wall. Since this window is seen easily, is very large, and of a single sheet of permanently installed glass, it does not require any locking device.

The double-hung (or sash window) has several points that can be considered for home security improvement. Figure 4-67 shows the window in the closed position and partially open position. Security can be achieved to some extent with the window in the partially open position, much less the closed position.

In the closed position, several lock types can be used for improvement: the locking sash lock (Fig. 4-68), the corner lock (Fig. 4-69) or a side mounted locking device (Fig. 4-70). Of the three, the first can only be used in just the closed position, whereas the others can also be used in the partially open position. Low in cost in terms of security provided, they give excellent window security since a key is required in order to unlock the window so it can be moved either up or down.

119

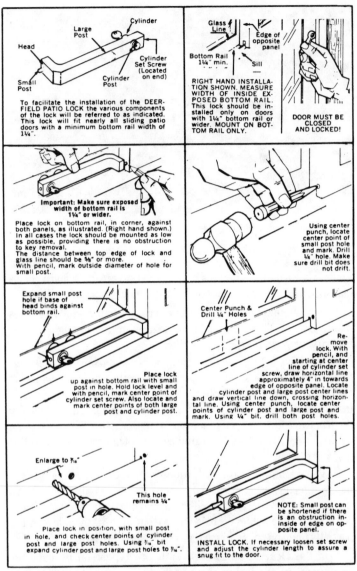

Fig. 4-66. Procedure for installing the patio lock (courtesy of Deerfield Lock Co., Inc.).

The heavy-duty cam lock from Ideal is located at the center point of the window. With this lock, the window will be secure only in the closed position, unless another locking device is used when the window is in the open or partially opened position. These locks are easy to install, each taking less than five minutes.

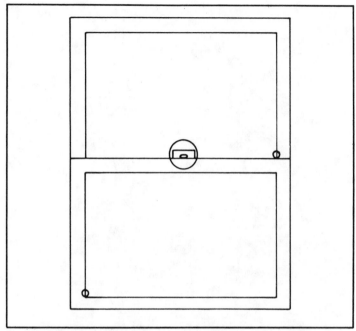

Fig. 4-67. The sash window in the closed and partially opened positions.

Casement Windows

Casement windows come in several variation designs or configurations (Fig. 4-71). The casement window is opened by means of a turning handle located at the base of the windows. Locking is accomplished by a window handle usually located halfway up the window. Unfortunately, 90% of those currently installed can be opened by force, without breaking the glass (although some noise may result), and within 10-15 minutes even the amateur burglar is inside your home.

Increasing the security of the casement window means replacing the current window handle catch feature with the casement window key lock. This involves merely removing the two screws holding the original latch in place and replacing it with the locking latch. The screw holes are the same. Time involved for each window is between three to five minutes. In some instances, homeowners have also brazed or spot-welded the edges of the lock to the metal window frame, and filed the screws down to prevent removal. Unless absolutely necessary, don't file the screws down; check with your local hardware store for special screws that cannot

Fig. 4-68. Locking sash lock (courtesy of Ideal Security Hardware).

be removed with the standard screwdriver. The locking latch is available for either left or right handed installation and can be obtained at your local locksmith or hardware store.

Fanlight Windows

The fanlight window is not as popular as would be expected, but increased installation can be expected in the near future. Fanlight windows are easy to circumvent and get through. Because they open outward from the top, this means a couple of hinges at the bottom, and usually a simple latch device at the top, to secure the windows in the closed position. The windows are held open by a small thin chain or wire cable.

When increasing security for the fanlight window, first look at the hinges. Usually they are small, having two or three screws, with each having a depth factor of about ¾" or 1". The hinges can be removed and heavier hinges should be installed. The screws used, whenever possible, should be at least 2" long and of the flat head type. Improvement to the entire width of the fanlight window is

122

Fig. 4-69. Corner lock (courtesy of Ideal Security Hardware).

accomplished by installing a piano hinge. This type of hinge runs the entire distance of the window, from edge to edge. Numerous screws can be added, increasing the sturdiness of the hinge and warding off possible prying devices that are normally used against the smaller hinges. The simple latch device at the top of the window should be removed and replaced with a locking latch.

Skylight (Dome Windows)

Skylights represent over 75 years of ceiling lighting. In the earlier period, from the turn of the century onward, the skylight provided for the entry of light and ventilation within the home. In older homes even today you may find them without any form of locking device. Sometimes, only a simple hook and eye keep a skylight closed. The dome window is the recent variation of the skylight, but it does not provide for ventilation.

Improving the security of the skylight means ensuring, first of all, that it is made of sturdy wood and possibly has a metal covering over the critical interior area. On the interior side, the use of hinges and locks or the mounting of a window lock or two will keep it basically secure.

A skylight is usually constructed of heavy wood about the edges and thin wood strips into which the glass is placed. Unfortunately, when a piece of glass breaks, it is often covered with a piece of wood which is then nailed into place. It is just too easy to remove.

Thus, it becomes imperative for the homeowner to have a heavy piece of plywood that will cover the entire skylight (on the interior side) and can be firmly attached when the skylight is not actually being used. This is usually when nobody is home, in the

123

Fig. 4-70. Side mounted locking device (courtesy of Deerfield Lock Co., Inc.).

winter months, and during cold or rainy periods.

Also, the use of sheet metal should be considered. The sheet metal can be placed on the inside of the skylight frame. With this in place, the window is closed and locked. The sheet metal portion is then locked in place. Breaking the window makes noise, but imagine the noise as a person attempts to break through heavy-gauge metal to gain entry. One could expect that people several houses away would hear the attempted entry taking place.

For securing the skylight window in the best possible method, and also for a permanent construction, the use of a heavy steel "screen" of bars can be used. The screen may seem unsightly from the inside, but it will provide the best security possible.

The bar grill is made using heavy duty steel as a frame. Drill holes into the frame and insert the bars through so they will fit edge to edge without any give. The frame is bolted into the interior frame. Even in this way, welding is highly recommended.

For domes, security is a slightly different problem. The domes are of a one-piece construction, usually acrylic plastic, and firmly placed and mounted. As such, they are considered permanently attached to the home. The problem here is that the dome can

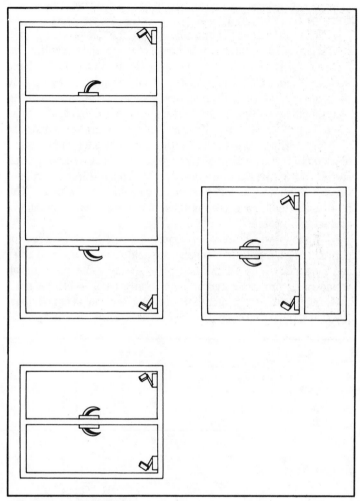

Fig. 4-71. Casement windows.

be broken very easily. Extremely heavy duty cutting knives and even a portable blowtorch (available at any corner store) can be used to open up the dome. The torch flame quickly heats up the plastic and it drops away and pulls aside, so that no rough edges are in the burglar's way. The cutting knife takes several more minutes, but it has no noise or light source (as does the torch) to give away what is going on at night. The best method for protection against dome entry is the use of metal grill work installed just below the dome, as was the case of the skylight window.

Securing Windows

Nails can be inserted into holes drilled into the window frame, so that the window can be closed or partially open for ventilation. Figure 4-72 shows where they can be located in a double-hung window. Figure 4-73 shows how to really secure the window by using a series of nails. Each nail used should be of steel, and the hole should be at least 1/16″ deeper than the nail and drilled at an angle (Fig. 4-74). Removal of the nails is done with a small magnet.

Not all windows in the home, though, require the same degree of protection. As an example, consider an older home with three stories. Naturally, the top floors, over 25′ from the ground, will not require window locks and the use of nails on every window. The first floor should have both of these for the maximum amount of protection possible.

Windows which are never opened should be considered for permanent nailing. If the windows are seldom used, use nail holes and magnets. Keep all the nail holes at the same place on all windows of the same type. Then lightly paint over the hole, covering it with a very light film of paint so the hole is not obvious. If you really need to open the window, use another nail to "punch"

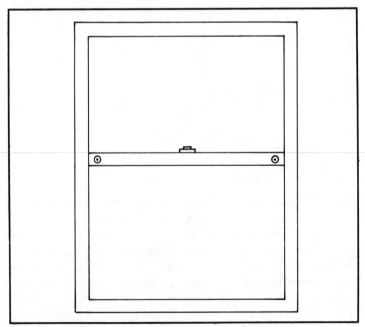

Fig. 4-72. The location of nails in a double-hung window.

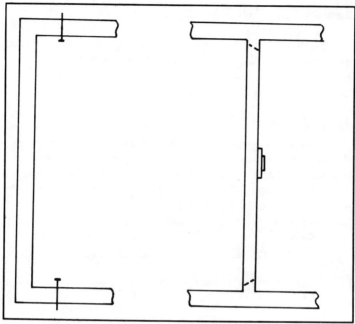

Fig. 4-73. Use a series of nails to secure the window.

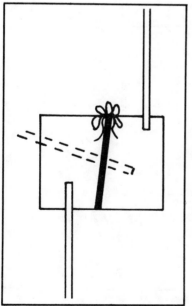

Fig. 4-74. The hole should be at least 1/16″ deeper than the nail and drilled at an angle.

through the paint film. Then take the magnet and open the window by removing the nail.

Strap iron can be used effectively to keep a window closed and safe from a burglar. Short pieces 1″ wide and 3′ 5″ long are sufficient. They are attached to the framework and the window, using long screws (1¼″ minimum).

Basement Windows

Ventilation, hopefully, is not a problem in the basement where the windows must be constantly kept open. Perhaps the windows are hidden by shrubs on the outside, and you don't want to remove them. Since light is the main consideration, you can replace the windows with glass blocks (Fig. 4-75). This will allow for sufficient light to enter the basement and also ensures the maximum security possible.

Fig. 4-75. Replace the basement windows with glass blocks.

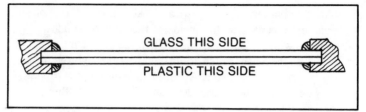

Fig. 4-76. Install the plastic against the glass.

As a final solution, you can literally board up the window from the inside and brick it up from the outside. Cover it so that the brick will match the exterior.

Window shutters have been around for many years. While used more for decoration, they are also a means of security, both for larger basement and also regular home windows.

Window Air Conditioners

A most common mistake in today's home is the *window air conditioner*. Since it is often *installed for the summer only*, the assumption is that it blocks entry through the window. Far from it! Unless proper precautions are taken, this window is less secure than any other window in the home. The use of grill work (discussed later) is only one method that can be used. Easier methods, at lower costs, can increase window security. Scrap iron, corner wedges, steel strips bolted to the frame of the window and the air conditioner, or the addition of padlock type devices and hasp units keep the air conditioner from becoming a point of easy entry for the burglar. It also means the air conditioner is less likely to get stolen by the burglar.

Using Plastic

Plastic is becoming a sought after item. Many security experts are looking at and recommending plastic for windows. While not as clear as glass, the protection afforded is as much as 100 times or more in strength than glass.

The cost of laminated glass can be three to six times the cost of regular glass. If the lamination process is considered, standard installation as for any piece of glass is the procedure.

The use of plastic can be done on the weekend or in an evening by the homeowner. The procedure consists of making the entire glass area thicker by installing the plastic against the glass (Fig. 4-76).

Another variation is to use a thicker piece of the plastic material and mount it on the inside of the door or window (Fig. 4-77). If the window/door glass is broken, the plastic must still be broken through. Screw holes are drilled first through the plastic, then long screws are inserted. At optimum points across windows, you may use shorter screws so the plastic is affixed at other points besides just the edges.

Always allow, in this technique, for an overhang of 1-1¼". Also, always keep the plastic mounted on the inside of the glass. If installed on the outside, an attempt to break through will shower glass across the floor and carpet. If the plastic is on the inside, it will contain the glass. The glass will fall to the outside.

Another method that can be used on back and basement doors/windows in remote areas is the use of *wire glass*. Wire glass comes in sizes from ⅛" to ¼". You've probably seen this type used in a shower door and tub enclosures. Wire glass provides for resistance to the impact of large objects such as a thrown rock or baseball bat being used to break through the glass. Aesthetically, the glass is not always appealing, but it does have its security features which are to be appreciated.

Grillwork

Grills can be simple, fancy, standard purchased ones, or homemade and self-installed. In essence, the grill, while hopefully enhancing to some extent the aesthetic qualities of the home, provides a fantastic amount of physical and psychological security for the homeowner. It also provides a great deterrent to the would-be burglar who, upon seeing the grills over the windows, realizes that this is not a home that will be easy to enter.

Windows and doors can require additional security features such as the installation of grills. Remember, grills are not just for windows alone; they are also prepared for use with or on doors (Fig. 4-78). Other grills, called window guards, can be fixed or adjustable (Fig. 4-79).

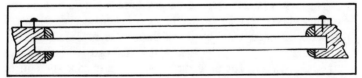

Fig. 4-77. Use a thicker piece of the plastic and mount it on the inside of the door or window.

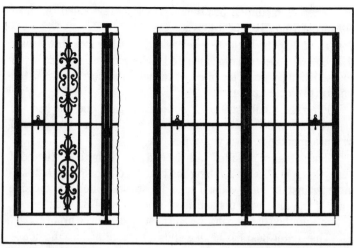

Fig. 4-78. Grills can be used with or on doors as well as windows (courtesy of Superior Security Mfg. Inc.).

Gates

Patio door gates can be obtained that are adjustable in total width from 70 to 80″ with a standard 6′ high gate, and up to 100″ wide for gates with an 8′ height. The proper patio gate has both sides opening by hinging from a center post. The center post offers

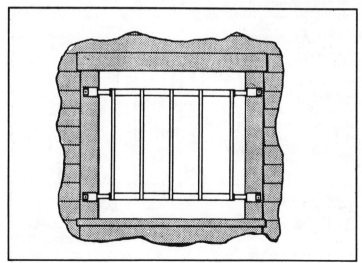

Fig. 4-79. Window guards can be fixed or adjustable (courtesy of Superior Security Mfg. Inc.).

two different mounting positions and can be extended (in most instances) from 78 to 95" in height.

The true patio security gate has a built-in key lock that locks a slide bolt into the steel tube mounted to the wall on each side of the doors. When properly installed, it cannot be removed or adjusted when in the locked position.

Figure 4-80 illustrates a patio door gate and its specific features. Patio door gates can be obtained in various designs and with ornamentation of varying types.

The gates are installed with the end posts being constructed of heavy duty 1½" square tubing for better positioning and attachment against the side walls. The end posts are bolted into the side wall. If the side wall portion is of wood, Fig. 4-81 illustrates a possible method of ensuring the end posts are secured properly.

The center post has angled ends for mounting into the house structure. If the ground portion is cement, then a hole will be drilled and an expanding bolt used for attachment

It must be noted that the installation should be performed by a qualified specialist in the field, but it can be done by the

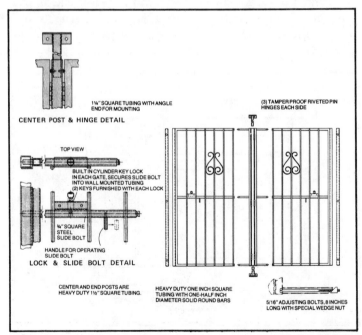

Fig. 4-80. Patio door gate and its features (courtesy of Superior Security Mfg. Inc.).

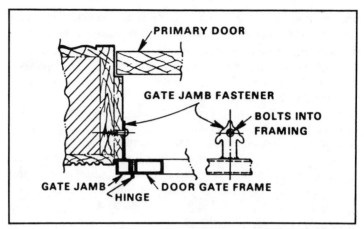

Fig. 4-81. A way to secure the end posts (courtesy of Superior Security Mfg. Inc.).

homeowner. The time required will be at least a half day for the person who does it well, and upwards of a full day for the uninitiated installer.

Superior Security Mfg. has spent many years specializing in gates and gate security for all types of homes and businesses. For the Superior door *Adjust-A-Gate*, there is a gate lock (Fig. 4-82) which is a spring-assisted slide bolt (13/16″ square) that can be

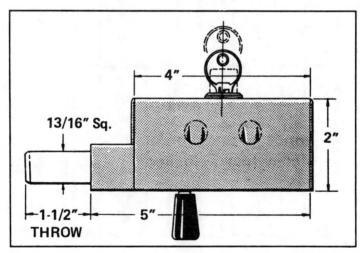

Fig. 4-82. A gate lock for the Adjust-A-Gate (courtesy of Superior Security Mfg. Inc.).

used to latch or create a locked-in positioning, if extended or in the retracted position. The plunger lock can be easily changed to fit different key combinations.

Various single gates are also available (Fig. 4-83). The hinges are tamper-proof.

The Adjust-A-Gate has an adjustable width from 28 to 38″ and is a full 72″ high. The gate is designed to be installed into the existing jamb between the existing door and the storm door, although it can be mounted without the storm door being present.

Because of its adjustable flexibility (not found in many other types of security gates), it will even fit in an out-of-square door jamb and can be hinged on the right or left side of the door frame. The gate can also be installed to open inward or outward, as the homeowner desires.

Fig. 4-83. Single gates (courtesy of Superior Security Mfg. Inc.).

Fig. 4-84. Storm doors (courtesy of Tefco Security Systems).

You may desire a Tefco-designed security storm door (Fig. 4-84). Like the security gate, the door is easily installed in less than an afternoon.

Window Guards

Adjustable window guards are also available to the homeowner. The window guard is fabricated from heavy 1″ square tubing and ½″ round bars on 5″ centers. This main part of the window guard must be of the correct height and no smaller than 10″ in width of the desired window opening in which it is to be used to ensure maximum security protection. Figure 4-85 illustrates a window guard.

A good window guard may or may not have adjustable ends. Standard window guards are also available. They have adjustable ends that can be used to obtain the proper width for the window being protected. Specifically built window guards are also excellent, but because they are contracted for and designed to meet the needs of a specific window, the out-of-pocket cost will be slightly higher than the standard window guard that you may require.

Mounting brackets for these window guards should be of steel. Steel stampings are normally used to attach the guard to the window frame. The mounting can be either a surface or an inside mount.

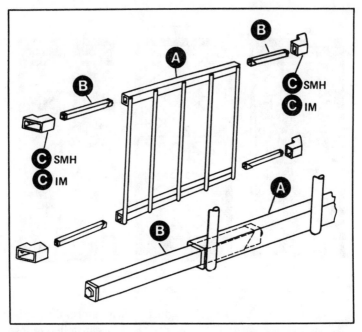

Fig. 4-85. A window guard. (A) Center section. (B) Adjustable ends. (C) Mounting brackets (courtesy of Superior Security Mfg. Inc.).

Do you have two windows, side by side, that need a window guard? Figure 4-86 shows a double window guard that is mounted. This is actually two standard window guards with an intra-window

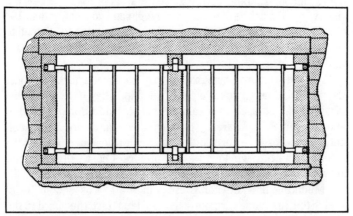

Fig. 4-86. A double window guard that is mounted (courtesy of Superior Security Mfg. Inc.).

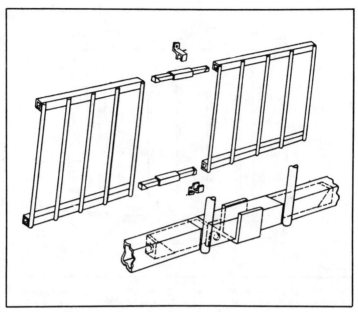

Fig. 4-87. Note the parts layout (courtesy of Superior Security Mfg. Inc.).

set of couplers added. Figure 4-87 shows the installation layout of the various parts.

Window guards also come available in a hinged configuration (Fig. 4-88). These units allow for emergency exit in case of fire,

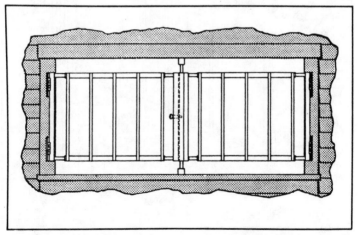

Fig. 4-88. Window guards also come in a hinged configuration (courtesy of Superior Security Mfg. Inc.).

137

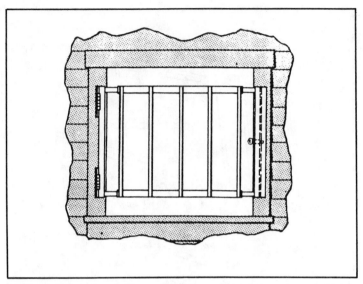

Fig. 4-89. Extra-wide windows need a window guard that can be unlocked in case of emergency (courtesy of Superior Security Mfg. Inc.).

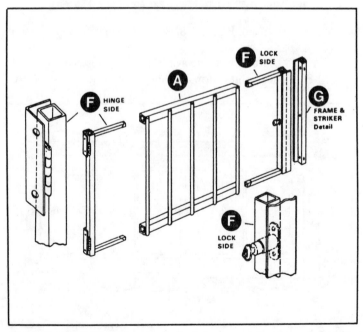

Fig. 4-90. Adaptation of the standard window guard (courtesy of Superior Security Mfg. Inc.).

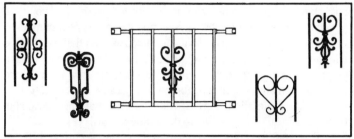

Fig. 4-91. Ornamentation can be attached to the window guards (courtesy of Superior Security Mfg. Inc.).

SECURITY GRILL

FOR HORIZONTAL SLIDING AND CASEMENT WINDOWS

Easily Installed On The Inside

Installs Easily and can be Removed without Damage to Window Frame. Ideal for Apartments Because **You Can Take It With You** When You Move. Can be Transferred to Other Windows. All White Metal Frame Surrounds a White Vinyl Coating on a Carbon Steel Grill Providing Maintenance-Free Protection for Apartment and Home Owners.

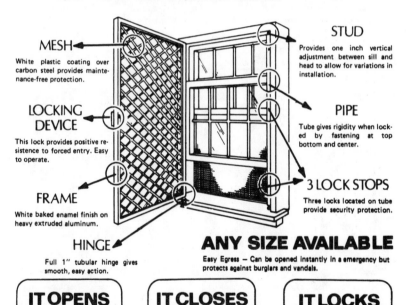

MESH
White plastic coating over carbon steel provides maintenance-free protection.

LOCKING DEVICE
This lock provides positive resistence to forced entry. Easy to operate.

FRAME
White baked enamel finish on heavy extruded aluminum.

HINGE
Full 1" tubular hinge gives smooth, easy action.

STUD
Provides one inch vertical adjustment between sill and head to allow for variations in installation.

PIPE
Tube gives rigidity when locked by fastening at top bottom and center.

3 LOCK STOPS
Three locks located on tube provide security protection.

ANY SIZE AVAILABLE

Easy Egress — Can be opened instantly in a emergency but protects against burglars and vandals.

IT OPENS
No tools or keys required to get instant access to window for cleaning, opening & closing, or emergency exit

IT CLOSES
Providing a major deterrent to would-be intruders by presenting a carbon steel grill.

IT LOCKS
With the simple turn of the knob your Security Grill locks in three places. Easy removal of lock knob & bracket won't open the guard.

Fig. 4-92. A security grill for horizontal sliding and casement windows (courtesy of Blaine Window Hardware Inc.).

139

but also protect against the unauthorized entry of would-be burglars. These units can be surface mounted or inside mounted.

The Superior Security Mfg. Co. also realized that extra-wide windows would want a window guard that could be unlocked in case of emergency (Fig. 4-89). Using the standard window guard configuration and adapting it, the company came up with a terrific unit which is detailed in Fig. 4-90. Ornamentation is available which can be quickly attached to the window guards (Fig. 4-91).

The last item to be considered is the security grill for horizontal sliding and casement windows. Figure 4-92 illustrates this grill and its various features.

Interior Home Security

Feel confident now? You've considered and hopefully selected the proper devices and installed them to make sure your doors and windows will give you the best protection possible. If so, then it's time to move on to the interior of the home.

Security within the home can take many forms, including wired and non-wired alarm systems, ultrasonics, bells and horns, even dogs. I will review various alarm systems, both wired and non-wired, that are highly acceptable for all homes and apartments. Also, I will look at *point protection*, that is, the protection of a given object as it is confined to a very small area. This could be a side room that you use as the home office, and the safe that you want protected above and beyond the general security system that is installed. Point protection can also include doors and windows. Since we finished discussing the physical attributes of doors and windows in the last chapter, a logical extension would be to consider some individual point protection that can apply to them.

MINI-ALARMS

Installed with no tools or wiring, the *Caddi Door Call* mini-alarm announces the attempted entry of any person into the home (Fig. 5-1). Other applications for the unit include the home windows, sliding doors and windows, desk drawers that may contain prescription medicine, the rifle cabinet, etc.

The mini-alarm features a self adhesive tape which makes it so very easy and simple to install anyplace. It is battery operated and

141

self-contained so there are no wires to run. The solid-state construction will ensure a long life with the battery in place. In fact, the average 9 volt transistor battery will operate from one to three years, depending upon the actual use to which the sensor and alarm are put. A key switch arming with a three-position mode (IN, AWAY, and PANIC) ensures the alarm will be ready no matter what the situation. The 85 decibel alarm will be heard throughout the home.

The alarm comes in two basic models, one with a short (8″) wire connecting the alarm to a magnetic detection sensor, and the other with just a magnet outside the unit. The other portion of the sensor is built into the unit.

Since the alarm is so portable, it can also be mounted in a car, such as at the base of the door on the interior side. The unit is out of the way and can easily be activated when leaving the car.

Life-Gard Alarm System

To provide a great amount of security for apartments and homes, the Continental Instruments Corp. developed the *Life-Gard* (model 3400) alarm system. A compact alarm which can be powered by either low voltage ac or by a battery, this solid-state electronic alarm (Fig. 5-2) measures 12″ × 1¾″ × 2½″ and is housed in ultra-streamlined anodized aluminum casing. The designs permit quick installation on any existing door by surface mounting.

The Life-Gard system is activated by its own key and has three different control settings. A 15 second delay also allows time to turn off the alarm when re-entering the home. A second setting will allow someone to open the door and operate the alarm manually with a uniquely designed foolproof "panic" switch. The third setting is used when all persons are at home; anyone attempting entry would be an intruder. In this setting, the alarm will instantly activate when the door is opened.

The unit is designed to send a signal to a remote location when a violation of security is detected. Additional doors and windows can also be monitored with the Life-Gard unit.

You can see in Fig. 5-2 that in addition to the basic unit mounted on the door, a magnetic contact is quickly affixed to the framing opposite the alarm unit. This provides a continuous open circuit when in operation. When the door is opened, the movement closes the alarm circuit, activating the alarm. An auxiliary loop capability can be used to protect additional doors or windows by

Fig. 5-1. Caddi Door Call mini-alarm (courtesy of Convertible Alarm Detection Devices, Inc.).

simply installing contact switches and wiring the normally open loop back to the Life-Gard unit.

The remote signaling capability is remarkable in that it can be used to activate a monitor panel readout, telephone dialer, etc. AA penlight batteries supply auxiliary power to the unit if you don't wish to wire standard ac.

Installation details are shown in Fig. 5-3. The alarm unit can be reverse applied to the frame face on in-swing doors and frames that are flush. Figure 5-4 depicts a sectional view of the Life-Gard alarm unit.

The Life-Gard control panel (model 4400) (Fig. 5-5) is another compact flush-mounted alarm using either low voltage ac or batteries. Like the model 3400, the unit has three settings. Figure 5-6 illustrates the dimensions of the back box for the unit, installation details and typical connections that can be configured with the alarm unit.

Both models 3400 and 4400 require a step-down transformer, available with the alarm unit, if standard ac is to be used in place of batteries. With the 4400 unit, a door plunger contact is installed in

Fig. 5-2. Life-Gard (model 3400) alarm system (courtesy of Continental Instruments Corp.).

the door framing and keeps the alarm from activating until the door is opened.

Matuska Chain-Lock Door Alarm

The *Matuska Chain-Lock door alarm* is one of the growing number of imported home security alarms that are ideal for the small homeowner or apartment dweller. See Fig. 4-52. Small and lightweight, it can be taken from home to home, since installation and/or removal takes only a couple of minutes.

A solid-state electronic alarm for any door, it uses a chain activation system to set off the alarm. Once mounted to the door and frame, it acts as a standard door chain lock. Any attempted unauthorized entry by forcing the door open creates a pressure on the chain. Since the chain will only lengthen for a very short

144

distance, more pressure on the chain trips the alarm which can activate a loud piercing sound.

Matuska has also developed a "secret catch" that should be used when you are home or away. This prevents it from being slipped off the slide. If the chain is moved, it automatically jams and trips the alarm.

Like other standard door chains, the Matuska alarm unit can be opened from the outside only with the proper key. During the night, it is most effective as a spot perimeter alarm. The unit operates with AA batteries which should last the homeowner up to a year.

Matuska Pocket Alarm and Flashlight

A very portable device for personal security in the home (or on the streets) is the Matuska *pocket alarm* and *flashlight*. It provides for both security and safety (Fig. 5-7). Three AA batteries allow for this hand-held unit to be used in the dark for seeing with the flashlight portion. By flipping a switch, it becomes an instant alarm, which can ward off a potential attacker. Easily concealed in a pocket, purse, the hand or in your home work clothes, this is an essential device for women, senior citizens, mass transit riders, joggers, bicyclists and young teenagers in warning them against attacks.

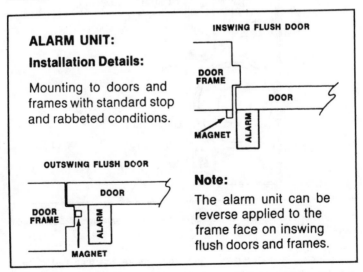

Fig. 5-3. Life-Gard installation details (courtesy of Continental Instruments Corp.).

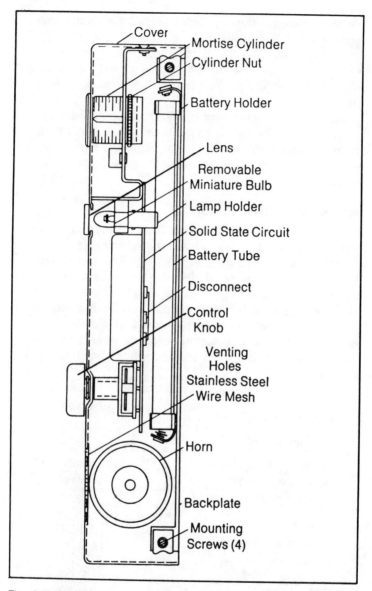

Cover
Mortise Cylinder
Cylinder Nut
Battery Holder
Lens
Removable Miniature Bulb
Lamp Holder
Solid State Circuit
Battery Tube
Disconnect
Control Knob
Venting Holes
Stainless Steel Wire Mesh
Horn
Backplate
Mounting Screws (4)

Fig. 5-4. Sectional view of the Life-Gard unit (courtesy of Continental Instruments Corp.).

During a home fire, when the smoke has created a hazy situation, turning on the flashlight can show you a safe way out. The alarm also can alert the fire department to your exact location within the home. The loud and abrasive sound certainly will be heard over the crackle of flames. This alarm unit can also be used in outbuildings, such as an outdoor tool shed.

LOCATION FOR AN ALARM SYSTEM

If you've decided upon a particular home alarm system to give you partial or around-the-clock protection, are you ready to install it? Also, if you haven't, as yet, selected an alarm system, then this chapter is definitely for you. On the following pages are detailed procedures and alarm units that are available for the home security system. You should be considering where you might be locating the various components.

Most units have a central core to the system. As such, your first consideration is where to put the main unit. It should be centrally located, but not out in plain sight. It is best to consider a closet location or, perhaps, a bookcase or other out-of-the-way place where it won't attract undue attention. Attention is the last thing you want with the system (except for the fact that when a burglar knows you have a professional burglar alarm system installed, he is more likely than not to go somewhere else that is much easier and safer).

Fig. 5-5. Life-Gard control panel (model 4400) (courtesy of Continental Instruments Corp.).

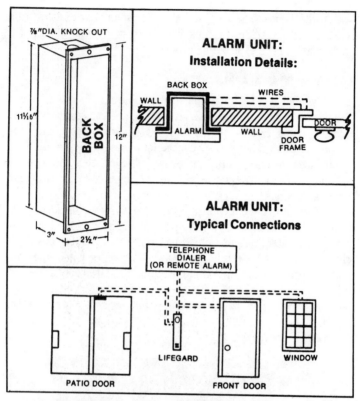

Fig. 5-6. Installation details and typical connections for the Life-Gard control panel (model 4400) (courtesy of Continental Instruments Corp.).

Having determined the placement of the main unit, you will have to move to the various sensors of the system, such as the doors and windows, the indoor alarm, the outdoor single or dual alarm, and the smoke and fire detectors. Figure 5-8 illustrates and identifies various components and their locations within the home.

Figure 5-9 illustrates perimeter, area and point protection. Each type serves a particular function. Figure 5-10 illustrates area protection with two different versions of an alarm. You must determine which of the three types, or combination of the types, that you need and desire within your home to provide optimum protection.

Home security systems take many different forms. Simple, complex, wired and wireless systems are available and will be discussed. The type to select and use is a big decision. The choice is made more difficult because of the many brands that are avail-

Fig. 5-7. Pocket alarm and flashlight (courtesy of Matuska Enterprises).

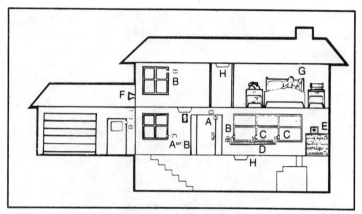

Fig. 5-8. Various alarm system components. (A) Intrusion transmitter/ sensor with on-off and battery test switch. (B) Intrusion transmitter/sensor. (C) Two piece magnetic sensor. (D) Bell wire. (E) Indoor dual alarm. (F) Outdoor dual alarm. (G) Remote emergency transmitter. (H) Remote signaling smoke and fire alarm (courtesy of Chamberlain Manufacturing Corp.).

able. Normally the choice is based on a recommendation from a friend or neighbor; sometimes, regrettably, the choice is based on your pocketbook. Price alone does not mean that you have the best (or worst) system.

The following alarm products cover a variety of price ranges. Each system has been selected because of certain accessories that the homeowner may wish to incorporate for a better system, or because the system or unit is unique and will meet the current and/or growing needs of the individual. Each item/system has been carefully considered. There is, naturally, overlap between systems. Each system is included because of, sometimes, a single feature that you should know about. Each system is considered excellent, feasible and of fine value and use for the home or apartment.

NUTONE S2252 SYSTEM

NuTone, a name that has met quality and reliability in home products for many years, has an excellent selection of security systems and accessories that will fit all homeowner needs. Like many other companies, their security systems are varied, each designed to meet certain types of needs. Some of their systems are more complex than others.

I appreciate the detailed information made available without restriction by the NuTone Housing Division of Scovill Inc. that is presented on the following pages.

Affordable flexibility that includes reliability for home security systems has increased tenfold in the past few years. NuTone has kept pace with this expanding market with the introduction of the superb S-2252 system (Fig. 5-11). Designed primarily for easy installation in the existing home, it is naturally simple to install, too, in new construction. As with other NuTone products that are described in this book, you will see they are not the cheapest on the market—nor the most expensive. Years ago, NuTone realized that pride in a system, and a quality product, is important. The S-2252 system has excellent materials, and no shortcuts in its design or manufacture have been taken. From a massive national survey, NuTone learned what type of electronic system homeowners most needed and wanted. With the in-depth information gained from this survey, the S-2252 was designed and developed.

This is a maximum protection system—not a stripped down model that provides only the bare essentials of security. It can be adapted to virtually every kind of home situation. With the features you need built in, rather than offered as optionally purchased items (as is the case in some other systems), there is a cost savings, along with an installation savings in time.

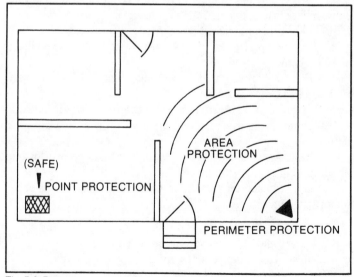

Fig. 5-9. Perimeter, area and point protection.

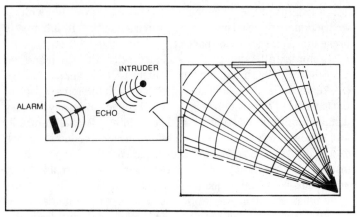

Fig. 5-10. Area protection with two different alarm versions.

Features of this system include:

—Engineered control unit that surface-mounts quickly and easily.

—Power transfer included that plugs into any 120 volt ac outlet.

—A 5 amp/hour rechargeable battery included.

—Automatic alarm shutoff and reset is built in.

—Five protection circuits for ultimate flexibility.

—Switchable interior circuit provides control for homeowner convenience in maintaining 24-hour protection.

—Plug-in printed circuitry board for easy servicing.

—Remote control capability with no additional specialized circuitry being required.

—Fail-safe arming of the system: status LEDs on every remote panel that is installed.

—Optional fire protection circuit with an easy plug-in module.

—Different alarm signals for burglary and fire so you know the difference.

—Test switches and fuse protection ensures no overloading or burning out of the system.

—Dry contact terminals for optional telephone dialer or digital communications.

The system includes the following:

☐ The basic security system control unit.
☐ Optional master remote panel.
☐ Indoor remote panel.
☐ Outdoor remote panel.

152

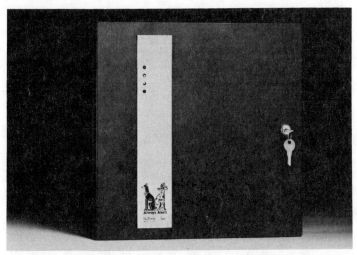

Fig. 5-11. The S-2252 system (courtesy of NuTone Division, Scovill Inc.).

☐ Fire module remote panel.

☐ Remote panel key switch.

☐ A variety of detector sensors: intruder, perimeter, interior, alarms, radio controls, etc.

The S-2252 has all the features you might ever need already built into the system. It consists of the control unit, one to five remote panels for the operation of the system, and the various detection devices and alarms. No matter what variation you need for your particular needs, most likely the S-2252 will meet these needs and still give you ample room later on if you add on another room or move to a larger home that may require an expanded system.

Protection Circuits

For maximum flexibility, as stated earlier, the S-2252 has five protection circuits. Many currently marketed systems have one, perhaps two, circuits. While others are limited to either exterior or interior protection, the S-2252 does both and more. The two perimeter protection circuits can be either open or closed circuit detection devices.

The normal response perimeter circuit is designed to prevent the troublesome false alarms sometimes caused by sensitive detectors making unintentional contact. Any of the closed or open intruder detectors can be connected to the loop circuit. The fast response perimeter circuitry is designed primarily for use with the "glass-break detector" (Fig. 5-12).

The exit-entry time delay circuits accept both open and closed detectors providing an extra measure of protection because the perimeter circuits remain armed at all times, even when you are leaving and returning home. Delays for exiting and entering are separately adjustable from 0-45 seconds. Other similar systems have a fixed time that cannot always be changed. Detectors which guard doors, plus detectors such as ultrasonic and floor mats which serve areas enroute to the doors, can be connected to this loop.

The interior circuit is a switchable circuit for normally open detectors. The fact that it can be switched on and off is important for the homeowner who wants to maintain 24-hour family protection. During the day when the family is moving about the house, the interior detector circuit can be turned off but the perimeter circuit can still be armed. When you are away or after the family retires for the evening, you can turn on the interior circuit for that second line of defense. A switch on the optional master remote panel or an inexpensive shunt switch connected to the control unit turns the interior circuit on and off.

Fig. 5-12. The fast response perimeter circuitry is designed primarily for use with the "glass-break" detector (courtesy of NuTone Division, Scovill Inc.).

The emergency circuit is a 24-hour *always armed* circuit. It trips an alarm instantaneously at just the press of a button. In addition to the "panic" buttons that can be located anywhere within the home, the glass-break detectors used on fixed (non-opening type) windows can be connected to this loop circuit, also. Tamper switches on the outdoor remotes and the optional tamper switch on the control unit are also connected to the emergency circuit.

All of these protective circuits, with the exception of the always armed emergency circuit, are armed and disarmed *with a key* at any of the remote panels. The remotes can be located inside or outside (Fig. 5-13).

The 5 amp/hour rechargeable battery has its own recharging circuit. If there is a power outage, wires cut or even if the transformer is disconnected, the master control unit automatically switches over to dc power so the alarm capability is never interrupted. With a basic system of control and two remote panels, this 5 amp battery (which is larger than most) will provide up to 100 hours of standby operation. Even with the other options such as ultrasonic, infrared, etc. (up to the maximum limit of 200 mA current consumption), this battery will provide at least 20 hours of standby operation and still sound the four minute alarm in case of an emergency situation.

Alarm Shutoff and Automatic Reset

The alarm shutoff and automatic reset feature are built into the control unit. The shutdown time is adjustable from 3-12 minutes. Shutoff of just one protective loop doesn't affect any of the other loops. They will still be capable of sounding an alarm if violated. Also, if the original cause of an alarm is cleared, the circuit that was violated is automatically reset to sound a new alarm in the event of another intrusion.

There is an important difference with the S-2252 system shutoff. Suppose an intruder circuit trips an alarm. Just as it is to be timed out (end of time the alarm sounds), one of the smoke detectors (on another circuit) triggers another alarm. The new violation will initiate a new full-time alarm. Some other systems will only sound the alarm for the time remaining on the first circuit violation, which could be only a matter of seconds, and nobody would realize, until too late, that a fire was in progress.

Test Switch

A test switch on the control unit tests the battery power, the emergency circuit and the alarm circuit. Holding down a spring-

Fig. 5-13. The S-2252 control unit open (courtesy of NuTone Division, Scovill Inc.).

loaded switch to test the system portions shortens the alarm time to 3-12 seconds, (depending upon how long you have set your adjustable shutoff timer (3-12 minutes). Not only is this a quick test of your alarm time adjustment, but holding the switch to test position will quickly silence any unwanted alarm while the cause is found and corrected. The optional telephone dialer or communicator will not activate while you are holding the switch in a test position.

Terminal Board

The terminal board in the control unit provides a 12 volt dc 200 milliamperes (mA) output circuit for continuous power to various ultrasonic, audio and infrared detectors. It also includes the normally open dry contacts for activation of the telephone dialer or a digital dialer or communicator (which can be purchased separately, since NuTone does not have this available).

Circuit Board

The printed circuit board within the control unit plugs in. It is easily removed for servicing, if need be. No wire wrapping at terminals is required, which will speed up the installation time and also eliminate the possibility of cutting the wires. The sophisticated electronic circuitry is protected by three inexpensive, replaceable fuses: one for the battery, one for the auxiliary battery and one for the outdoor alarm circuit.

LEDs

The S-2252 control unit is of all-steel construction, measuring 13 13/16″ high, 14 15/16″ wide and only 3 ⅛″ deep. Access to the interior is by key only, but an optional tamper switch is available. It is unnecessary for the homeowner to ever open the door except to test the system. All the information required is displayed on the front of the control unit, through the display panels' four LEDs: ac power ON is reflected on a green LED, perimeter circuit (red LED), exit-entry time delay circuit (red LED) and the interior circuit (red LED).

The green LED will go out when the system switches to battery power. Using the test switch, you know the system has switched to battery power when this light is extinguished.

The three red LEDs will light up if you attempt to arm the system and it will not arm. This is part of the fail-safe arming that has been built into the system. Whenever an LED goes on, the particular circuit is then known. You know that there is a "fault" within that line. For example, a door might be slightly ajar or a window open, etc.

Multi-Remote Capability

The S-2252 has a multi-remote capability. This capability is specifically built into the S-2252 circuitry for remote panels which will supply important information and perform various functions. Please note that all of the protection circuits of the security system are armed and disarmed by the momentary operation of the key switch on remote panels. Also, all alarms (including the optional fire circuit) and the alarm shutoff feature are reset by the momentary operation of the same key switch. Also, the emergency circuit alarms are always reset at the indoor remotes only.

All remote panels have a green LED which tells you the system is armed. If the LED *flashes* instead of staying on, this would indicate that one of the protection circuits is not ready for arming; that is, a closed circuit detector is open or an open circuit detector is closed. By checking the LEDs on the circuit panel front, you can identify where the fault is and correct it immediately. The special "arming lockout" feature prevents needless false alarms.

Up to five indoor and/or remote panels can be used in the system. All remotes have a precut hole for the installation of a key switch.

Because the homeowner has the option of using a switch to turn on or off the interior circuit, there is a second LED (colored yellow) on the indoor remote panels. This reminds you that the interior circuit is turned off, and it must be turned on before the system can be armed.

The indoor remote panels also feature a buzzer which will sound during the period (from 0-45 seconds) for which entry time delay has been set. The key switch must be used to reset the system so that it will not go into an alarm condition.

The optional master remote panel (Fig. 5-14) is a convenience for the homeowner. It features an alarm horn, emergency button, interior circuit on/off switch, plus the informational LEDs: ac power-on, arming and a mounting hole for a key switch.

Fire Protection Module

A fire protection module capability adds to the multi-faceted security system. By simply plugging this module into the master control unit, complete always armed fire protection capability is added to the system.

The circuitry can accommodate up to 10 smoke detectors and an unlimited number of heat detectors. Power output for the smoke detectors is fuse-protected.

The fire module also includes a remote panel for installation at the end of the fire detection line. It provides complete supervision of the fire circuits.

If there is a power loss to the smoke detectors, or a break of any kind in the fire circuit, a trouble buzzer sounds in the remote panel. A switch on the remote panel lets you know to shut off the buzzer, at which time a red LED activates as a reminder until the trouble is cleared. This same switch will also allow for testing of the buzzers' operation.

Wiring Diagram

There is one problem (not really a problem in terms of security and safety) associated with the NuTone S-2252 system. The system is so flexible and versatile that it is difficult to outline here all the possible ways it can be used in the home. A representative wiring diagram (Fig. 5-15) shows only one configuration. This diagram illustrates the type of wiring needed for a comprehensive NuTone home security system. Note that it is not intended for the actual installation; nor does it include all the devices that might be selected and used by the homeowner. Refer

Fig. 5-14. The Master remote panel (courtesy of NuTone Division, Scovill Inc.).

to this basic diagram as you consider the following parts of the system that make it so flexible and so reliable in the home.

In addition to the control unit which contains all the advanced electronic technological circuitry, you will have to choose the intruder detectors, fire detectors and other alarm devices. The decision as to which of the five protection circuits your intruder detectors will be connected is up to you. Because of the simplicity of S-2252, although it may not seem so simple, the decision may be not to use the exit-entry delay circuit. By using your key at the indoor remote panel located near the door, you can disarm the system while exiting. This would, of course, require an outdoor remote so that when you return, you can use the key again to disarm the system while you enter the house. Since the system is operated by using a key at the remote panels, you will want to decide how many remotes you will need and also where they will be located in the home.

Now that the system has been detailed, and you can see the versatility that is included, let's assume you have selected this total home security system for installation. You live in a home that has a basement and three levels. Included are a master bedroom, several children's bedrooms, two guest rooms, a den, play area (recreation room in the basement) and a walk-in linen closet. You have purchased the system and taken it home. With all the previous information, you can assume that this type of a system is really going to be very complex to install. Not so! The following installation instructions have been included to show that such a system, with many possibilities and with many accessories, is not difficult to install at all. Since most accessories have separate installation instructions, they are detailed separately from the basic system.

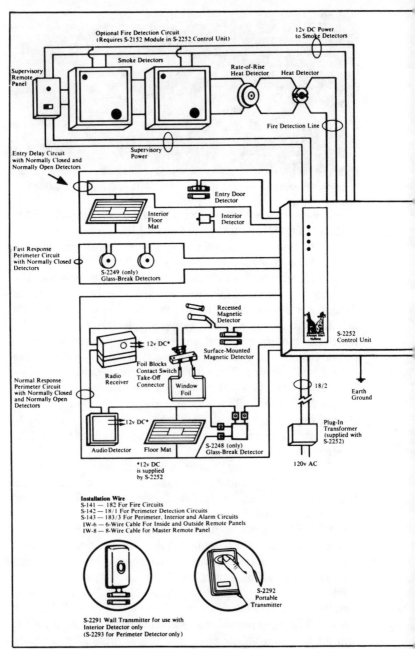

Fig. 5-15. Wiring diagram for the NuTone S-2252 system (courtesy of NuTone Division, Scovill Inc.).

160

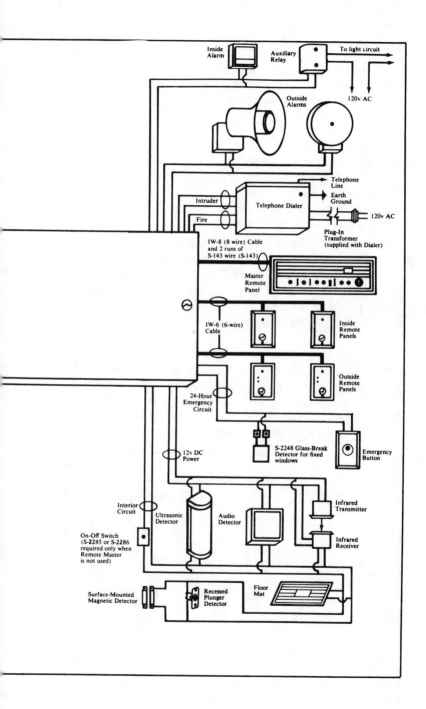

Mounting the Master Control Unit

Remove the printed circuit board from the control unit to facilitate the wiring of the system (also to protect the board from accidental damage). Do not store it in or on plastic. Remove the two screws and carefully work the board down from the terminal strip (Fig. 5-16).

Locate the control unit in an area that is convenient for occasional observation and *weekly testing* but not readily visible to strangers, such as a closet, utility room or even the basement. The control unit should be placed so as to be kept out of the reach of children. Surface mount the unit through the precut keyhole slots, using the screws that are supplied (Fig. 5-17).

Power is supplied to the control unit by a 20 VA transformer. The transformer plugs into a standard grounded 120 volt outlet. The outlet is not to be connected to a switched circuit, but on a branch that is not turned off during absences or vacations. The outlet should be as near as practical to the control unit: 50 maximum when using 18/2 cable; 125 when using 120 volt ac class 1 wire (14/2).

Do not apply power to the control unit until *all* component connections have been made and checked. Observe the local electrical codes and be sure the housing is properly grounded. The internal transformer fuse is not replaceable. If the screw terminals are short-circuited for three-or four minutes, the transformer fuse will blow and the transformer will have to be replaced. Run the

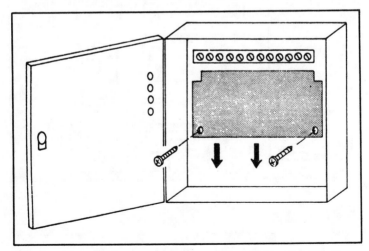

Fig. 5-16. Remove the two screws (courtesy of NuTone Division, Scovill Inc.).

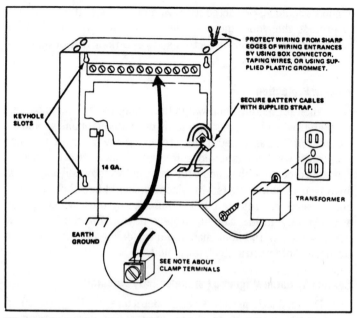

Fig. 5-17. Surface mount the unit through the precut keyhole slots (courtesy of NuTone Division, Scovill Inc.).

wiring between the control unit and all component locations. Label all wires for future reference.

It is important, where practical, to keep the alarm wiring at least 12″ away from the detection circuit. Run the lines to terminals 17-24 through the wiring entrances at the right of the control unit housing.

Here's a note about clamp terminals. Do not wrap wires under the terminal screws. Strip the wires about ⅝″ and seat them under the clamp to the rear of the terminal board. To prevent intermittent contact, do not mix 18 and 22 gauge wires under the same side of the terminal clamp, unless the 22 gauge wires are twisted in pairs. Keep the wires balanced on each side of the screw.

Installing Intruder Detectors for Doors

Here are a few hints on installing the intruder detectors for doors. If using a magnetic switch, mount it on the door frame so that the least practical movement of the door will separate the magnet section from the switch section. If using a plunger-type detector, install it in the door frame on the hinge side only. If the door has a window through which an intruder could enter, the window should be protected with window foil tape. If it is difficult to protect the door, the area directly inside the door can be protected with interior detectors such as a floor mat or an ultrasonic motion detector.

Window Protection

When protecting windows in the home, the surface mounted magnetic switch is the most versatile entry detector and should be considered first as a method for protecting any movable window. Stationary windows (non-movable) as well as movable windows can be protected with window foil tape and window foil accessory switches. Double-hung (sash) windows should have both top and bottom sections protected. If it is difficult to protect windows, the area directly inside can be protected with interior detection devices such as the floor mat, the ultrasonic motion detector or even the photoelectric electric eye unit.

Surface Mounted Magnetic Perimeter Entry Detectors

The magnetic perimeter entry detectors can be mounted on wood, metal or even glass when necessary. They can be mounted with screws, double-sided tape or epoxy type glues. The tape and epoxy are useful on glass, aluminum and metal surfaces where screws cannot be used. If using tape or epoxy, be sure the surface is clean, dry, smooth and at least 65°F when applying.

Position the switch and magnet sections of the detector between 1/16" and 3/16" apart, *in exact alignment*. The two sections can be mounted in any position as long as both sections are right next to each other.

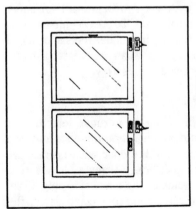

Fig. 5-18. The lower portion of a double-hung window has two magnets mounted on it (courtesy of NuTone Division, Scovill Inc.).

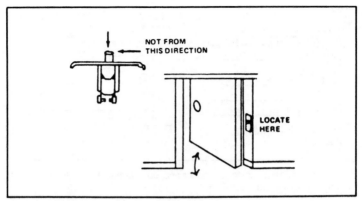

Fig. 5-19. Locate the plunger entry detector as shown.

On metal surfaces or uneven surfaces, use the plastic spacers. On metal surfaces the spacers act as a barrier between the magnet and metal, and on uneven surfaces the spacers align the two separate sections of the entry detector.

Not only can a closed window be protected with an entry detector, but a partially open window can be protected as well. The lower portion of a double-hung window has two magnets mounted on it (Fig. 5-18). The upper magnet protects the window when it is closed. The lower magnet protects the window when it is partially opened, by alignment of the lower magnet to the switch. Allowing the window to be opened for more than 3-5″ is not recommended.

Recess-Mounted Plunger-Type Entry Detector

The plunger entry detector is mounted so the door will contact the plunger at the tip and push the plunger straight in (Fig. 5-19). For protecting doors, there is only one way to install the detector— in the door frame on the hinge side of the door.

Accessory Switches

A variety of accessory convenience switches are available to fit the NuTone S-2252 system for the home.

Outdoor Panel Key Switch And Indoor Panel Key Switch. These are used to arm and disarm the system from inside or outside the home. They are located near the entry door, and are mounted 2½″ deep in a single-gang metal utility box. Figure 5-20 shows the wiring diagram for these two units.

On/Off Switches. These are used for the on/off control of an entry detector. They can be used for the perimeter circuit or the

165

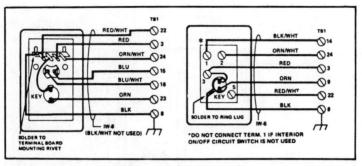

Fig. 5-20. Wiring diagram for the indoor and outdoor panel key switches (courtesy of NuTone Division, Scovill Inc.).

interior circuit and are normally located near the entry detector, but in a place not readily visible to strangers. Closets are the typical locations. They can be surface mounted or recessed.

The Inside Timer Bypass Switch. This has a 60-second timer and is used to bypass the entry detector. The location should be such that it is not visible to strangers. It is a recessed mounted unit.

Emergency Alarm Push Button. It manually activates the alarm in an emergency situation. Typical locations include near entry doors and in bedrooms. These push buttons are wired across terminals 15 and 16 of the control unit (Fig. 5-21).

Outside Key-Operated Timer Switch. Located near the entry door outside the home, it is wired in the perimeter circuit to bypass the entry detector on the door (Fig. 5-22).

Auxiliary-Powered Detectors, Accessories and Remote Alarms

All the auxiliary-powered detectors and accessories have a maximum limitation. Each consumes current; therefore, the number and type of devices must be limited to insure proper system operation, including battery backup power. The maximum number of detectors and accessories is limited by the *total* current load for all devices being used. The total current load must not exceed 0.235 amperes. The battery (fully charged) will operate the system as follows: 0.235 amp-20 hours, 0.150 amp-24 hours, 0.050 amp-50 hours, 0 amp-80 hours. Refer to Table 5-1 for the current load of each device. Table 5-2 illustrates an example of how to compute the current load in the system.

There is also a maximum limitation for alarm devices. The number and type of alarms must be limited to insure proper system

Fig. 5-21. Emergency push button (courtesy of NuTone Division, Scovill Inc.).

operation, including battery backup power. There are two limitation factors to keep in mind when installing this, or any other, system: the alarm current consumed by alarm devices and the current consumed by auxiliary-powered detectors and accessories.

The total alarm current load including alarms, detectors and accessories must *never* exceed 2 amps. Note that more than 1 amp is permitted on the fused alarm circuit. Refer to Table 5-3 for the

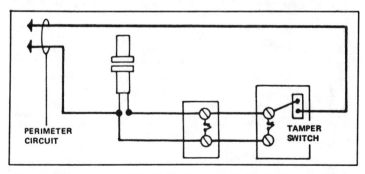

Fig. 5-22. Wiring diagram for the outside key-operated timer switch (courtesy of NuTone Division, Scovill Inc.).

Table 5-1. Current Loads for Auxiliary-Powered Detectors and Accessories (courtesy of NuTone Division, Scovill Inc.).

MODEL — DESCRIPTION	CURRENT LOAD
S-2226 Outdoor Control	0.018 Amp
S-2227 Indoor Control (w/interior circuit)	0.031 Amp
S-2227 Indoor Control (wo/interior circuit)	0.018 Amp
S-2228 Remote Control Panel (w/interior circuit)	0.031 Amp
S-2228 Remote Control Panel (wo/interior circuit)	0.018 Amp
S-2241 Photoelectric Detector	0.040 Amp
S-2244 Audio Detector	0.016 Amp
SA-2245 Ultrasonic Detector	0.045 Amp
S-2290 Radio Control	0.009 Amp

current load of each alarm device and to Table 5-4 for the current load for each auxiliary-powered detector and accessory.

It is most important for the homeowner-installer to know the maximum cable lengths for the various auxiliary-powered detectors and accessories and also for the alarm devices that he is installing. For auxiliary powered detectors and accessories 18/2 cable should be used: 400' maximum for a 0.2 amp load (6 ohms), 800' for 0.1 amp load (12 ohms). If a longer cable run is needed, use the following equation to compute the maximum length:

Table 5-2. Computing the Current Load (courtesy of NuTone Division, Scovill Inc.).

ALARM DEVICE	ALARM LOAD	QTY.	UNIT TOTAL ALARM LOAD
S-2332 Siren	0.300 Amp	1	0.300 Amp
SA-2335 Horn	0.060 Amp	4	0.240 Amp
S-2345 Outdoor Bell	0.450 Amp	1	0.450 Amp
S-2379 Relay	0.175 Amp	2	0.350 Amp

```
  1.340  ◄─────────────────────────────►  1.340 Amp
+ 0.190
  ─────
  1.530 Amp        Total Alarm Load (Max. 2.0 Amp)
```

Table 5-3. Current Loads for Alarm Devices (courtesy of NuTone Division, Scovill Inc.).

DESCRIPTION	LOAD
S-2332 Siren	0.300 Amp
SA-2335 Horn	0.060 Amp
S-2340 Bell	0.180 Amp
S-2345 Outdoor Bell	0.450 Amp
S-2379 Relay	0.180 Amp

$$\text{MAX LENGTH} = \frac{90}{\text{Amp load of all devices on the circuit}}$$

For alarm devices, use 18/2 cable: a maximum 200' for 0.5 amp load (3 ohms), 100' for 1.0 amp load (1.5 ohms). If a longer cable run is needed, use this equation:

$$\text{MAX LENGTH} = \frac{150}{\text{Amp load of all alarms on the circuit}}$$

Always use outdoor alarms in a fused loop. If no outdoor alarms are to be used, connect the indoor alarms to a fused loop (up to a 1 amp load). Figure 5-23 illustrates alarm wiring.

After all wiring is completed and before the transformer (120 volt ac) or battery power is supplied to the control unit, perform continuity testing with an ohmmeter. If the wiring is correct, the

Table 5-4. Current Loads for Auxiliary-Powered Detectors and Accessories (courtesy of NuTone Division, Scovill Inc.).

AUXILIARY — POWERED DETECTOR OR ACCESSORY	CURRENT LOAD	QTY.	UNIT TOTAL CURRENT LOAD
S-2226 Outdoor Control	0.018 Amp	2	0.036 Amp
S-2227 Indoor Control (with interior circuit)	0.031 Amp	2	0.062 Amp
S-2228 Remote Control Panel (with interior circuit)	0.031 Amp	1	0.031 Amp
S-2244 Audio Detector	0.016 Amp	1	0.016 Amp
SA-2245 Ultrasonic	0.045 Amp	1	0.045 Amp

Maximum Total must not exceed 0.235 Amp.   TOTAL: 0.190 Amp

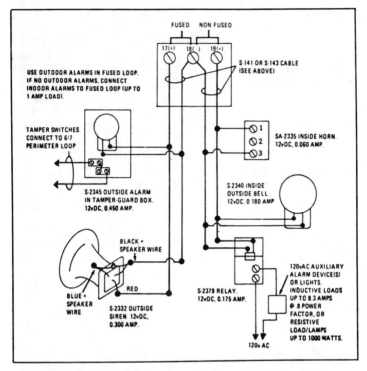

Fig. 5-23. Alarm wiring diagram (courtesy of NuTone Division, Scovill Inc.).

reading on the ohmmeter should match the reading in Table 5-5. Be sure to disconnect the printed circuit board from the terminal strip. Refer to the label that will be found behind the board for specific details.

The discussion has been a few pages long with lots of information, pictures and illustrations, but I believe you get the idea of what a comprehensive home security system is, how it is installed and how it works. On the continuing pages, we will consider other home security systems, some similar to NuTone and others completely different in their approach. We will come back to NuTone, though, as a prime example when we move into other areas of discussion on home security.

INSTALLATION OF ACCESSORIES

As noted previously, there are numerous accessories that can be used with the NuTone S-2252 system. The following information provides more specifics on installation of these accessories.

170

Key-Operated Entry Timer Switch

This is used to bypass the perimeter entry detector from outside the home. It is often used in conjunction with an inside exiting timer switch. Installation would be as follows.

Locate it near the entry door at a convenient operating height outside the home. Cut a hole into the exterior wall that will allow the box to be placed.

Mount the 3" single-gang box at the desired location. Figure 5-24 is an exploded view of the box as it will be mounted and affixed into position.

Make the appropriate wire connections to the timer terminals and wire the connection to the tamper switch. Figure 5-25 shows the wiring for an entry timer switch only. Figure 5-26 shows the switch being used in conjunction with an exit timer switch as part of the installation. Before placing the two plates into position, be sure that the protective coating has been removed.

Table 5-5. Ohm Readings (courtesy of NuTone Division, Scovill Inc.).

TERMINALS ohm meter (+)	ohm meter (−)	OHM READING
1	2	1.5 to 3.5 ohms with transformer output wires connected. But not plugged in.
3	4	infinity if no auxiliary-powered detectors are used. Over 60 ohms if auxiliary-powered detectors are used.
5	6	0 if not used (jumper across 5 and 6 not removed). 100 ohms maximum, typically 5 ohms (5/6 jumper removed).
5	4	infinity.
6	7	0 if not used (6/7 jumper not removed). 100 ohms maximum, typically 5 ohms (6/7 jumper removed). If window foil used in circuit may have up to 500 ohms.
4	7	infinity.
4	9	infinity.
3	9	infinity.
10	11	0 if not used (10/11 jumper not removed). 100 ohms maximum, typically 5 ohms (10/11 jumper removed).
12	11	infinity.
12	4	0 if not used (12/4 jumper not removed). 50 ohms maximum, typically 5 ohms (12/4 jumper removed).
13	14	infinity.
15	14	0 if not used (jumper a-a on P.C. board below terminals in tact). 50 ohms maximum, typically 3 ohms when remote switch is on (jumper a-a on P.C. board cut).
15	16	infinity.
17	18	infinity if not used. Less than 100 ohms if used.
17	19	infinity if not used. Less than 100 ohms if used.
20	21	infinity if not used; x-number of ohms if used.
3	22	over 10,000 ohms.
3	23	infinity.
3	24	over 10,000 ohms.

NOTE: For additional testing, activate each of the detectors or switches in the above circuits to obtain a change in resistance.

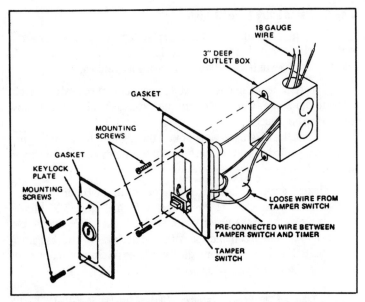

Fig. 5-24. Exploded view of the single-gang box (courtesy of NuTone Division, Scovill Inc.).

Secure the timer switch to the outlet box, using the supplied screws. It may be necessary to remove the knockouts from the outlet box to insert the timer. Be certain the gasket is in place behind the timer switch plate. Caulk around the timer place to seal out moisture when the timer is installed in a rough surface wall.

Secure the keylock plate to the timer switch plate. Be certain the gasket is seated between the keylock plate and the timer plate.

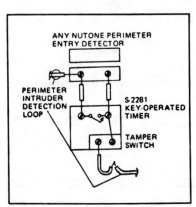

Fig. 5-25. The wiring for an entry timer switch (courtesy of NuTone Division, Scovill Inc.).

172

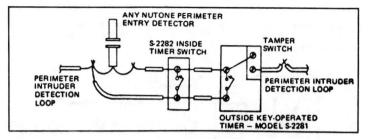

Fig. 5-26. The entry timer switch used in conjunction with an exit timer switch (courtesy of NuTone Division, Scovill Inc.).

Outdoor Remote Panel

The switch should be located near an entry door. It mounts into a 2½″ deep precut hole in the siding of the house in a single-gang utility box. IW-8 (NuTone wiring number) should be used as it is tamper protection wiring. Note that the key switch is not supplied with the panel unit. Figure 5-27 illustrates the placement of the individual parts of the panel unit. Two wiring methods are possible. Figure 5-28 illustrates the preferred wiring method of hookup. Figure 5-29 shows an alternate method.

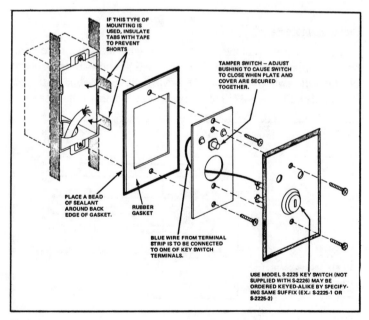

Fig. 5-27. Placement of the panel unit parts (courtesy of NuTone Division, Scovill Inc.).

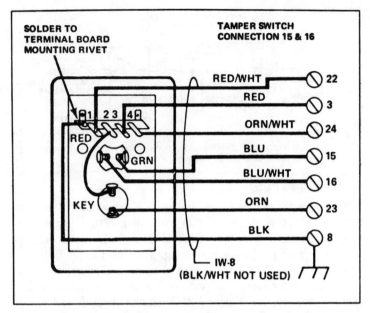

Fig. 5-28. Here is the preferred method of wiring (courtesy of NuTone Division, Scovill Inc.).

Indoor Remote Panel

It is located near the entry door. Figure 5-30 illustrates the basic installation of the utility box. Figure 5-31 shows the mounting of the key switch (not supplied with the panel but obtained separately). Figure 5-32 illustrates the wiring of the remote panel.

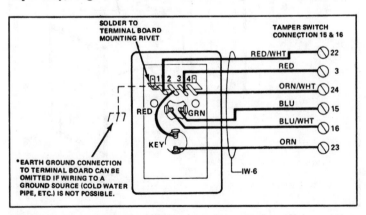

Fig. 5-29. An alternate wiring method (courtesy of NuTone Division, Scovill Inc.).

174

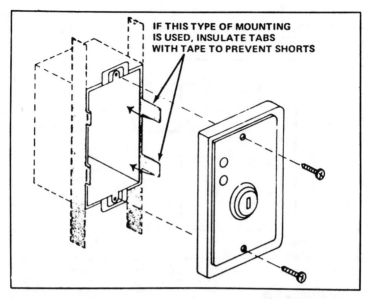

Fig. 5-30. Installation of the utility box (courtesy of NuTone Division, Scovill Inc.).

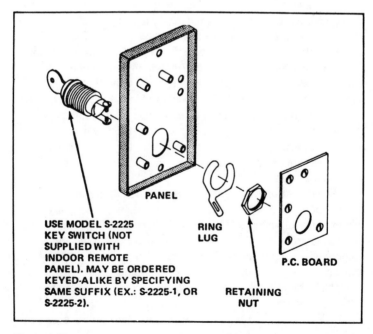

Fig. 5-31. Mounting of the key switch (courtesy of NuTone Division, Scovill Inc.).

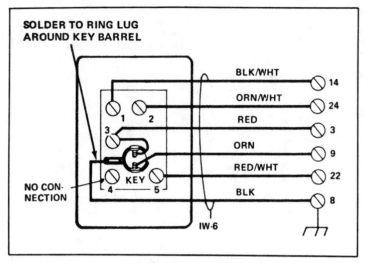

Fig. 5-32. Wiring of the remote panel (courtesy of NuTone Division, Scovill Inc.).

Entry Detection Switch

The switch is used in a closed loop intruder detection circuit. When the switch is depressed, the circuit is closed; when it is *not* depressed, the circuit is open and an alarm condition results. The switch can be mounted to doors and/or windows (Fig. 5-33).

Install the switch in the door frame on the hinge side only. There are two methods of arming/disarming the detector switch: with the on/off switch used inside the home only (this is primarily used at windows and secondary doors) and for situations requiring both inside and outside control (the key-operated entrance switch located outside the house and the timer exit switch which is located inside the house). Specific wiring details for these are found in the control unit installation instructions that come with the S-2252 security alarm unit.

The detection switch should be installed on the top sash, or sill, but not in such a position as to destroy the weather seal on the window. Double-hung windows should have both upper and lower protection provided. The installation area must be large enough to accommodate a mounting flange. Installation of the unit is as follows.

Drill a ¾" diameter hole for mounting completely through the frame. An internal 2 × 4 provides maximum wire clearance (Fig. 5-34). Connect the wires to the switch and insulate with electrical tape.

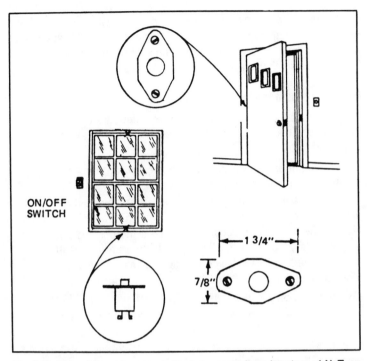

Fig. 5-33. The switch can be mounted to doors or windows (courtesy of NuTone Division, Scovill Inc.).

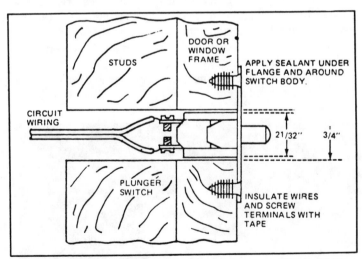

Fig. 5-34. Detection switch installation details (courtesy of NuTone Division, Scovill Inc.).

When installed in a window sill, apply a sealant (GE RTV-108 or its equivalent). The sealant goes under the switch flange and around the body to prevent water from seeping under the switch. Secure the switch in place with the mounting screws.

Recessed-Mounted Magnetic Entry Detectors

The installation of the magnetic entry detector (Fig. 5-35) has several cautions which the homeowner should be aware of and follow.

—Do not damage or destroy any weatherproofing seal on the window or door when installing the switch.

—If installing the magnet in an insulating type window (double pane glass, etc.), be careful when drilling the hole not to hit the glass in the sash. Note that some types of windows may permit the magnet to be glued to the sash without drilling any hole at all.

—Mount the switch and magnet so that the least practical movement of the door or window will separate the magnet from the switch. For example, do not install it on the hinge side of the door.

The entry detectors consist of two components, the switch and the magnet, each with different dimensions (Fig. 5-36). The switch is mounted into the frame and the magnet into the moving portion of the door or window.

Installation is accomplished as follows. Drill the hole where required for the switch and the magnet (if necessary). Use a silicone rubber adhesive to mount the unit pieces. After the adhesive is firmly gripping the unit pieces, go ahead and connect the switch to the perimeter circuit (a closed loop) and perform a final test to ensure that it works properly.

The detector switch and magnet can be mounted in a variety of modes, as illustrated in Fig. 5-37. For a door installation, see Fig.

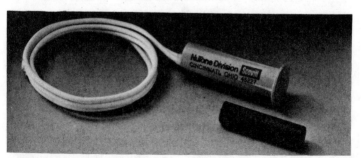

Fig. 5-35. Magnetic entry detector (courtesy of NuTone Division, Scovill Inc.).

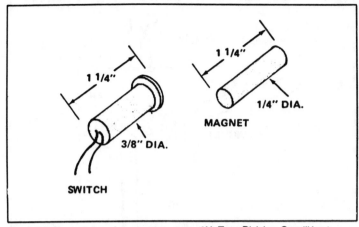

Fig. 5-36. The switch and magnet (courtesy of NuTone Division, Scovill Inc.).

5-38. The Anderson casement window installation is slightly different, as shown in Fig. 5-39. The double hung sash window should have two switches mounted, as seen in Fig. 5-40. For the sliding glass door, Fig. 5-41 illustrates the mounting technique.

The *master remote panel* unit is used to arm, disarm or reset the security system. It also includes an on/off switch control for the interior intruder circuit and a push button for activating an emergency alarm. It serves as a remote monitoring station as well, including LEDs for the intruder circuits. Within the S-2252 security system, only one master remote panel is permitted. The panel uses a four-gang utility box that is 2½" deep (Fig. 5-42). After insertion of the box into a hole cut into the wall, the key

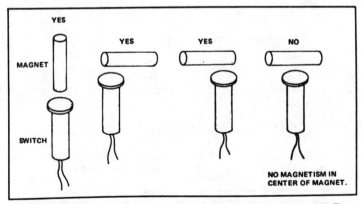

Fig. 5-37. Mounting for the detector switch and magnet (courtesy of NuTone Division, Scovill Inc.).

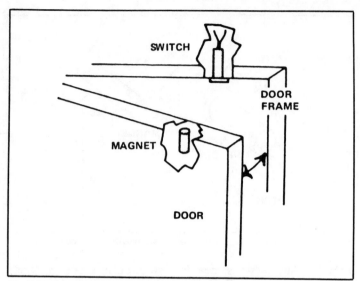

Fig. 5-38. Door installation (courtesy of NuTone Division, Scovill Inc.).

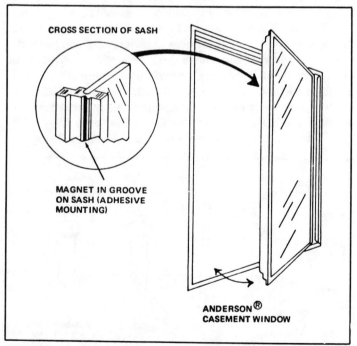

Fig. 5-39. Anderson casement window installation (courtesy of NuTone Division, Scovill Inc.).

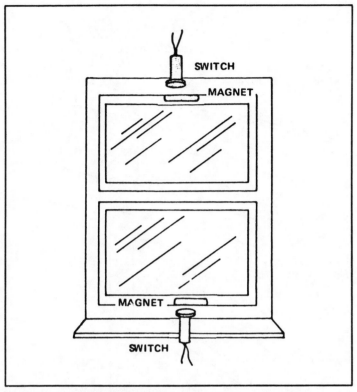

Fig. 5-40. The double hung sash window should have two switches mounted (courtesy of NuTone Division, Scovill Inc.).

switch (not supplied with the panel unit) should be affixed (Fig. 5-43) prior to putting on the cover plate.

Two methods of wiring the panel are available. One run of IW-6 wire and one run of IW-8 wire should be used. The preferred hookup uses 14 wires (Fig. 5-44). An alternate method has 12 wires to the control unit (Fig. 5-45).

The terminal strip/wiring harness assembly supplied with the unit is to be installed in the system control unit housing. The wires are secured to the printed circuit board and affixed with the cable strap. Affix the terminal block to the housing using double-faced tape (Fig. 5-46).

Indoor Key Switch

This switch is used to arm, disarm or reset the system from inside the home (Fig. 5-47)). It mounts into a 2″ single-gang utility

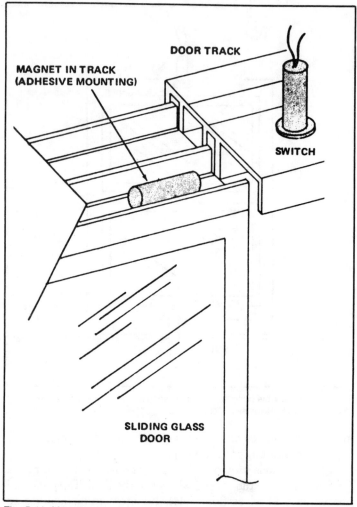

Fig. 5-41. Mounting technique for a sliding glass door (courtesy of NuTone Division, Scovill Inc.).

box. Wiring the switch unit is shown in Fig. 5-48. The mounting cover is attached to the utility box as shown in Fig. 5-49.

INTRUSION PLUS DUAL ALARM SYSTEM

The Chamberlain company recently developed the DS-4011 dual alarm home security system, called the *Intrusion Plus* (Fig. 5-50). It was designed to safeguard a home over the period of many years.

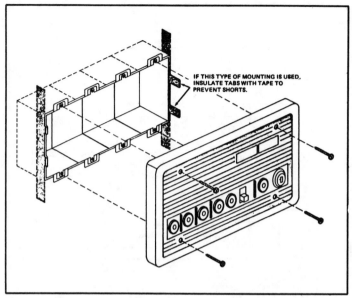

Fig. 5-42. The master remote panel uses a four-gang utility box (courtesy of NuTone Division, Scovill Inc.).

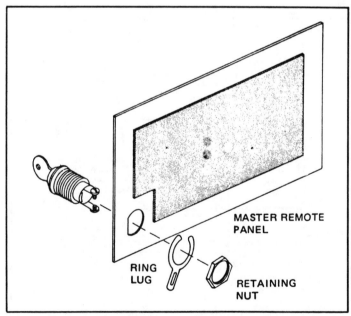

Fig. 5-43. The key switch is affixed prior to putting on the cover plate (courtesy of NuTone Division, Scovill Inc.).

183

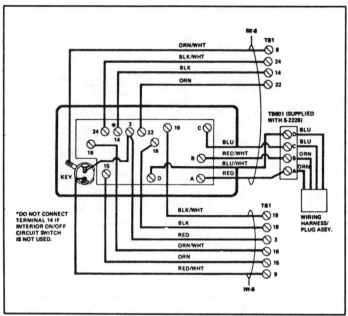

Fig. 5-44. One method of wiring the panel (courtesy of NuTone Division, Scovill Inc.).

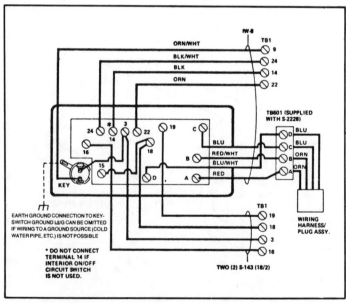

Fig. 5-45. Another method of wiring the panel (courtesy of NuTone Division, Scovill Inc.).

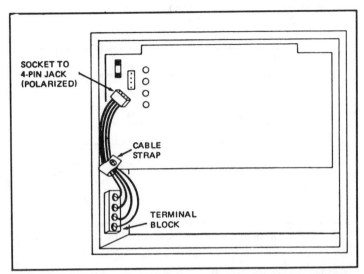

SOCKET TO
4-PIN JACK
(POLARIZED)

CABLE
STRAP

TERMINAL
BLOCK

Fig. 5-46. Affix the terminal block to the housing (courtesy of NuTone Division, Scovill Inc.).

The basic components include the master control receiver, an intrusion transmitter, intrusion sensor, backup battery and the necessary hookup wire. Additional sensors, transmitters and

Fig. 5-47. The indoor remote panel (courtesy of NuTone Division, Scovill Inc.).

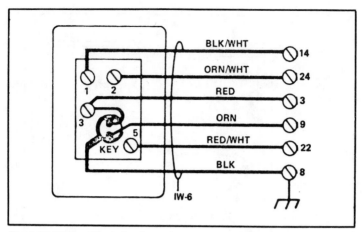

Fig. 5-48. Wiring of the indoor key switch (courtesy of NuTone Division, Scovill Inc.).

external alarms are available so that you can tailor the system to meet your own unique home security requirements.

The Intrusion Plus system does not require new and very costly home wiring. The system is wireless in that the warning of

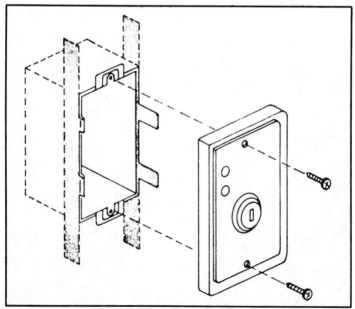

Fig. 5-49. Attachment of the mounting cover to the utility box (courtesy of NuTone Division, Scovill Inc.).

Fig. 5-50. Intrusion Plus dual alarm system (courtesy of Chamberlain Manufacturing Corp.).

intrusions are transmitted from small radio transmitters installed throughout the home.

The system greatly simplifies the problem of living with an alarm system by including several special features such as control settings to let you adjust the system to different situations, such as normal household activity, being away from home or sleeping hours.

The master control receiver is the heart of the system and is used for all sensors and alarm devices. It provides for a constant monitoring of the assigned radio frequency for alert signals transmitted by the various intrusion, emergency or smoke detector transmitters. Any number of units can be monitored. When the alert signal is received, the built-in alarm sounds after a delay or instantly (as directed by your setting of the unit).

The intrusion sensors (Fig. 5-51) are installed on doors and windows where you desire alarm protection. These intrusion sensor transmitters can serve a single or several magnetic sensors. It is easily concealed in close proximity to each sensor, and the transmitter is powered by its own 9 volt battery.

Various external alarm warning devices are available as options to the system, including a loud indoor or outdoor alarm/horn and an automatic telephone dialer. The emergency transmitter unit is optional. It is handheld and can be easily carried with you within the home. By simply pushing its button, you trigger the emergency (also fire) alarm.

Particular features of note on the master control receiver include the following:

☐ Key reset switch. By the insertion of the key and a turn to the right, the system is reset. This is done whenever an alarm has been sounded or the intrusion light goes on.

☐ The internal/external alarm selector. Use in the UP position for only the internal horn, and in the DOWN position for the internal horn plus any optional external alarms, like a siren and/or a telephone dialer (this is switch #1).

☐ Fire/emergency channel. A signal from an optional remote signaling smoke detector will override *all* other signals. Regardless of the control settings, the fire-channel alarm will activate the internal alarm (a beeping sound that is different from the standard intrusion detection alarm), the telephone dialer, and also an external alarm if the controls have been set for external. With the switch OFF (the intrusion system in an inactive mode), a fire/emergency signal will still be given.

☐ Home/away switch (receiver switch #2). The UP-HOME position is used to set the alarm for instant intrusion response. When in the DOWN-AWAY position, the system allows you to depart and return through a protected door without setting off the alarm. You have 60 seconds for exiting, and 30 seconds for entry and turning off the switch before the alarm sounds.

☐ Intrusion ON-OFF (switch #3). This activates or shuts down the system only in the intrusion portion—not the entire system. The fire/emergency channel is always active to receive signals from optional smoke detectors and other emergency transmitters.

☐ Intrusion light (light over switch #2). This red LED indicates that an intrusion has occured and the alarm will sound if it is not reset. If you enter the home with the alarm in the AWAY (delay mode), insert your key into the reset switch and turn it to the right for about two seconds, preventing the alarm horn from sounding. It also rearms the system and turns off the red LED.

☐ Over switch #3 is a yellow LED that glows when the system is in an active (armed) mode.

The emergency switch is located at the top right corner of the control receiver. It will instantly set off the internal horn (and external horn, if any) and also activate a telephone dialer. The switch has ridges located to either side to allow for each location in a darkened room at night. The ridges also protect against the accidental triggering of the alarm unit.

The receiver back panel has the horn/telephone dialer terminals, the ac transformer plug and the battery test switch button. There are five terminals as follows:

☐ Terminals 1 and 2: external alarm connections.

Fig. 5-51. Intrusion sensors can be installed on doors and windows (courtesy of Chamberlain Manufacturing Corp.).

☐ Terminal 2: common ground (negatives) for the alarm and dialer.

☐ Terminals 2, 3, 4 and 5: telephone dialer connections.

☐ Terminal 3: 12 volt dc output.

☐ Terminal 4: intrusion system.

☐ Terminal 5: fire or medical emergency.

Note also that terminals 2 and 3 may be used for more than one device.

Let's assume that you have selected this type of home security system and want to install it. You just don't slap it in quickly, put the various sensors in place, plug in the master unit and say, "Well, that's that; now I'm safe." If you did, then you definitely have defeated the system yourself, by not carefully preparing the system and putting it in properly. The Chamberlain system, while basically simple to install, has certain installation requirements that must be carefully followed in order to ensure that your new system will functionally operate in the correct manner. In order to ensure this correct operation, which makes the system reliable and gives you that extra added security that you desire, certain preinstallation and installation requirements should be followed. They are explained in the following paragraphs.

Preinstallation Receiver Setup

Before installing the Chamberlain dual alarm home security system, it will be necessary to proceed with a few simple steps to prepare the system for proper operation.

Remove the master control receiver cover. The ac power should be disconnected. Carefully turn the receiver upside down and locate the retaining screw in the center of the unit. Remove the screw using a flat blade screwdriver. Then turn the unit right side up and remove the cover.

The battery pack will be held in place by two hook and loop fasteners. Note that there will be two mating pairs of strips. Remove the protective backing from the two identical (non-mating) strips. Press them in place on the battery pack as shown in Fig. 5-52. In a like manner, remove the protective backing from the two remaining strips and press them into positions indicated inside the receiver case. Now position the battery pack in the receiver case so it is firmly held by the mating strips.

Connect the battery to the receiver by snapping the battery connector into a mating connector in the receiver. Note that the

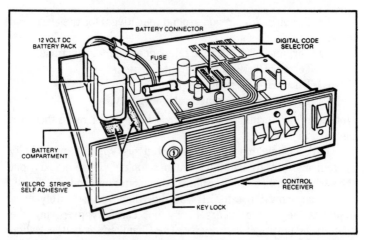

Fig. 5-52. Press the strips into the indicated positions (courtesy of Chamberlain Manufacturing Corp.).

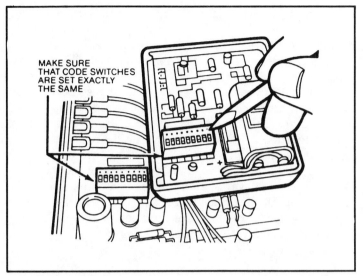

MAKE SURE
THAT CODE SWITCHES
ARE SET EXACTLY
THE SAME

Fig. 5-53. Use a screwdriver or ball point pen to move the switches (courtesy of Chamberlain Manufacturing Corp.).

battery connectors are polarized and will fit together only one way. Do not force the connectors, as damage to the receiver may result.

To set the master control receiver digital code locate the digital code selector switch (Fig. 5-52). Note that the digital switches on the code selector are numbered from 1-9, each with an ON and OFF position. This is the control for *your own personal* digital radio code. By setting your own digital code, your master control receiver will respond only to intrusion transmitters set to the same code. Each switch can be gently switched ON or OFF with the tip of a small screwdriver or ball point pen as shown in Fig. 5-53. By depressing a random combination of ON and OFF switches, such as 1-3-5-6-8 to ON, a specific private code is created. Since any combination of ON or OFF switches can be selected, there are literally hundreds of possible digital radio codes to choose from.

Here's a special note. Switch seven is for the fire channel and must be left in the OFF position. The fire channel code has been preset at the factory to match the smoke detector. After the selection of the digital code for channel 1 (burglary channel), the receiver is set aside and you would move on to the next step.

To set the transmitter digital codes remove the intrusion transmitter and set the control switch to OFF. Place the transmitter face down on a table and remove the retaining screw from its center position. Then remove the cover and snap in a new 9 volt battery.

Place the transmitter and receiver next to each other so that the digital code selector in the transmitter is facing the same direction as the digital code selector of the receiver. Set the switches in the transmitter to exactly match the setting that was selected for the receiver. Every intrusion transmitter to be used with the system *must* be set with this exact code. For that reason, make note of the ON/OFF pattern on a small piece of paper or in the instruction manual.

Carefully replace the cover on the transmitter and secure the retaining screw. Move the switch on the transmitter front to the test position. The LED should light up; if it doesn't, then replace the battery with a *new* one. Reassemble the receiver unit by replacing the receiver cover and securing it in place with the retaining screw.

Installation

You can see now that if you had just slapped the system in quickly, it would likely not be operating. Now you have the basic transmitter(s) set to the proper digital code that matches the master control receiver. You are ready to install the alarm system properly.

Locate the receiver in a central position where an ac outlet is available and not controlled by a wall switch. Favored locations include the first floor bedroom, den, closet or other convenient place. It should be kept in mind that the location should be convenient to your home entrance as well. The entry-delay feature allows you only 30 seconds to enter the home and reset the alarm without activating it. You should time yourself walking from the doors you choose to protect to the location for the receiver. Make sure that you can easily enter the door, put down any packages you might be carrying, close the door, and reach the receiver and use the KEY RESET within the required 30 seconds.

Once you have selected the proper location, plug in the system into the ac outlet (but not an outlet with a wall switch control) and secure the plug in position with the outlet retaining screw. Now set the front panel controls as follows:

—INTERNAL/EXTERNAL ALARM selection UP to IN-TERNAL.

—HOME/AWAY switch UP to HOME.

—INTRUSION switch DOWN to ON.

An intrusion sensor will be required at each window and/or door that you feel requires protection. However, a fewer number of transmitters may be required. One transmitter may be used with a number of nearby sensors, as illustrated in Fig. 5-54.

For a complete and thorough protection, though, all outside windows and doors should be protected with intrusion sensors. With this information in mind, determine the exact number of sensors and transmitters required to completely protect the home.

Each magnetic sensor, as discussed earlier, has two halves, the *switch* half (containing the wire terminals) and the *plain* or *magnetic* half. The magnetic half is mounted at the edge of a door or window and the switch half is *always mounted parallel* on the frame. When the door or window is closed, the distance between the halves should be about ⅛". If only one sensor is to be wired to the transmitter, the switch sensor half is wired directly to the transmitter (see the door in Fig. 5-54). If more than one sensor is used, then the sensors are wired in *series* to the transmitter as illustrated in Fig. 5-55. The sensor transmitter can be wall-mounted close to the window or door and, maybe, hidden behind a curtain or other home furnishing.

Note that the normal condition for the alarm circuit is closed. Thus, if the wire from the sensor to the transmitter is cut or works loose, the alarm will sound immediately.

For sensor and transmitter installation, first split the 22-gauge wire at one end. Separate about 1" and remove ½" of insulation on each wire. Then connect the wire between the sensor and the transmitter. (One end has lug terminals already connected; thus, only the other end will require splitting the wires.) Select the

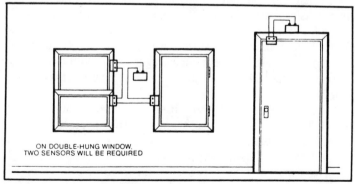

ON DOUBLE-HUNG WINDOW, TWO SENSORS WILL BE REQUIRED

Fig. 5-54. One transmitter may be used with a number of nearby sensors (courtesy of Chamberlain Manufacturing Corp.).

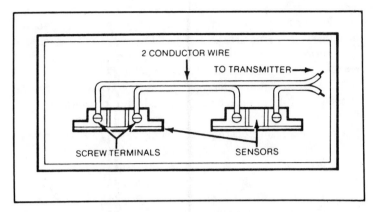

Fig. 5-55. The sensors are wired in series to the transmitter (courtesy of Chamberlain Manufacturing Corp.).

first door or window you plan to protect and locate the position in which the sensor will be mounted.

Always test the transmitter position *before* drilling any holes for attachment, or before affixing with double-faced tape, as the operation of the transmitter may be affected by metal ductwork, pipes or other metal in the walls. Hold the sensor halves together and switch the transmitter control switch ON. Position the transmitter where you expect to mount it, then separate the halves to simulate an intrusion. If the alarm does not sound, try changing the position of the transmitter slightly to avoid possible signal interference/obstructions or else move the receiver. If the alarm still does not sound, recheck the receiver and transmitter digital code settings.

When the transmitter operates satisfactorily, secure the switch halves with screws. Use only wood screws with wood frames and metal screws for metal frames. To mount the transmitter, remove the transmitter cover and battery and place the screws through the open mounting holes. Return the battery and cover to their original position, then cut the wire to the desired length.

As required, repeat transmitter and sensor location. Refer back to Fig. 5-55 for multi-sensors attached to a single transmitter for wiring information.

Figure 5-56 illustrates typical installations for various parts of the dual alarm home security system. Instructions come with the dual alarm system which detail the various testing procedures for the system.

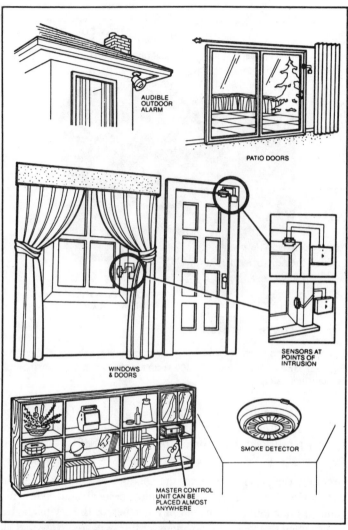

Fig. 5-56. Installations for various parts of the dual alarm security system (courtesy of Chamberlain Manufacturing Corp.).

CHAMBERLAIN DS-3000 SECURITY UNIT

The *Chamberlain DS-3000 security unit* is very acceptable for the home or apartment. The transmitter is a solid-state battery-operated unit, and quick installation/removal is a feature of this system. Figure 5-57 illustrates the unit and identifies the major parts.

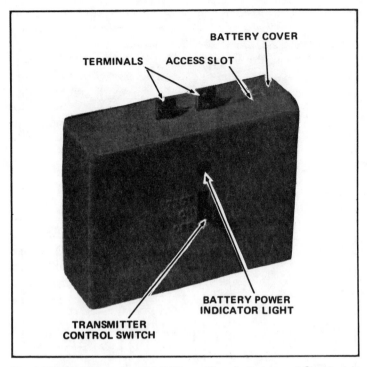

BATTERY COVER

TERMINALS   ACCESS SLOT

BATTERY POWER
INDICATOR LIGHT

TRANSMITTER
CONTROL SWITCH

Fig. 5-57. The Chamberlain DS-3000 security unit (courtesy of Chamberlain Manufacturing Corp.).

The transmitter control has three positions (ON, OFF and TEST). A battery indicator light lights up when there is adequate battery power and the switch is held in the TEST position. If it doesn't light up, then replacement of the battery is necessary.

Like the previous system, the DS-3000 also uses the digital radio code. The technique for selecting a personal radio code is the same, i.e., moving at random any number of the switches 1-9 by changing the ON-OFF positions of the switches. Note that all switches in the OFF position will constitute a code. Switch 7 must be OFF as it is used only in fire codes. There are access slots on each side of the cover (Fig. 5-58). Insert a coin and twist to open. The fastening holes are at the back of the battery compartment.

Before the transmitter has been fastened to the wall, remove the battery cover. Remove the screw from the transmitter back. Carefully turn the unit over and remove the top of the case, being careful not to move the circuit board parts (Fig. 5-59).

Place the transmitter and open receiver cases next to each other. Set the digital channel selectors so the code is exactly the same for both.

The transmitters should be installed close to the magnetic switches. This minimizes the use of wire. Always test the location of the transmitter as wall ductwork, pipes, etc. can reduce the transmitter signal.

Use metal screws to fasten the magnetic switches and transmitter to metal frames. The switches may have to be insulated from the metal with a non-magnetic material.

Use only wood screws to fasten the magnetic switches and transmitters to wooden frames and sashes. Whenever possible, use anchors when fastening a transmitter to a wall.

Remember, the maximum gap should be no greater than ⅛″ between the magnet and terminal sections of the switch. If necessary, use washers or shims under them to keep them even with each other (i.e., on an even plane). Again, transmitters can service one or several switches. Windows that contain a large glass

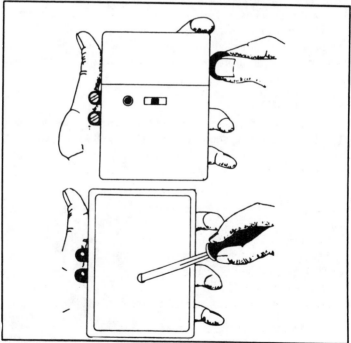

Fig. 5-58. There are access slots on each side of the cover (courtesy of Chamberlain Corp.).

area should be protected with a vibration type detector (i.e., window bug) which can be wired into the DS-3000 transmitter.

CONTROLLOR SYSTEMS CORPORATION PRODUCTS

Controllor Systems Corporation (CSC) has made available to the homeowner a wide selection of various devices that can be integral to the home security concept. Audio discrimination systems allow for the normal sounds to pass. The abnormal sounds such as breaking and entering, breaking glass, etc., can activate the alarm. This is important. FBI Uniform Crime Reports indicate that at least 84% of all business burglaries involve noise. Noise is also a major factor in the detection of a home burglary.

It must be recognized from the start that the sound range of an audio discrimination unit is variable due to the general environment and the acoustics of the building in which it is used. The sensitivity of audio units is adjustable. The audio units have characteristics that are similar to those of ultrasonic systems.

A good audio discrimination unit has many options, including additional pickups, radio transmitters, magnetic contacts for localized trap zones, etc. Audio discrimination will not be just a passing fad within the home security area; it is a fact of security planning. As such, the following material details several Controllor Systems Corporation products with which the home dweller should become familiar.

Model 510 System

The *model 510 system* is one of the better systems available (Fig. 5-60). Naturally, you will look and think, "It's a small system,

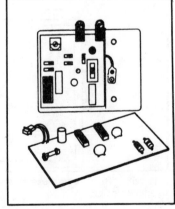

Fig. 5-59. Remove the top of the case carefully (courtesy of Chamberlain Manufacturing Corp.).

but if it can do the job, then I want to know more about it." The advantages and features of the system are extremely important to the potential purchaser. Advantages of this system include:

—Extremely easy to install.

—Being a wireless system, easy placement of the main unit and various remote devices.

—You can limit the number of remote devices; not all are necessary to have a well-defined operating unit in the home.

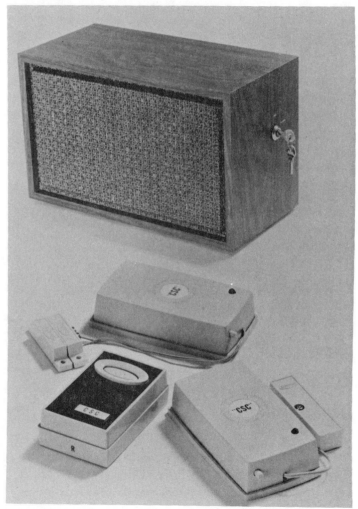

Fig. 5-60. Model 510 system (courtesy of Controllor Systems Corporation).

—Easy to remove when you move to another home.

—Should a part ever break down, it will not affect the entire system.

The model 510 system features entry and exit delays that are adjustable, an electronic *siren* (not just a horn type alarm), gel-cell standby power, 12 volt dc output terminals, the ability to activate a telephone dialer, an external speaker (can also be used for normal paging throughout the home as an intercom type unit), initial arming delay, a digital radio receiver and a key switch feature.

A vibrator transmitter (Fig. 5-61) sensor activates the electronic siren upon the breakage of glass. A test/panic button with an active LED allows you to monitor the battery within the transmitter.

The door/window transmitter (Fig. 5-62) will activate the electronic siren when either the door or window to which it is attached is opened. Since most homes have window frames, the transmitter installation is easily concealed.

An emergency signaling unit (Fig. 5-63) can be carried by the homeowner. It will activate the siren if the button is pushed.

The main control unit has various functions within it. First, the unit must be opened with the key to get at the various external control connection points.

A lamp outlet control switch is provided to automatically switch on a light for entry lighting. The alarm delay control switch allows entry without sounding the electronic siren for 30 seconds.

Fig. 5-61. The vibrator transmitter (courtesy of Controllor Systems Corporation).

Fig. 5-62. The door/window transmitter (courtesy of Controller Systems Corporation).

An automatic battery charger LED lets you know that the gel cell is accepting a trickle charge to keep it fully charged and ready for use in the event of a power failure.

Other auxiliary equipment connections include output terminals that will activate any security device known (normally closed circuits, normally open circuits, etc.), such as an automatic telephone dialer. The external speaker terminals will allow for a connection to reproduce the electronic siren outdoors with any paging speaker (30 watts at 8 ohms). Two additional terminals have been included to supply 12 volts dc power to any device requiring this power like a bell, beacon or other siren.

Fig. 5-63. Handheld radio transmitter (courtesy of Controllor Systems Corporation).

Following on the heels of this system is the CSC model 610, another high frequency security system. I like the simple installation. Just plug in the control cabinet, set the sensitivity dial and the system is in operation. Like the model 510, the various features and system advantages are a tremendous boon to the homeowner.

Model 630 System

Another system is the model 630 which looks just like the previous two systems in the main control unit. It also has various options and unique features that make it ideal for use as a home security unit (Fig. 5-64).

As we look at the various features and discuss some of the specifics of installation and other considerations, remember that these systems are also used by small businessmen. Also, these systems have the advantages of a wired system but are wireless, saving you the cost of installation and the time required to do it yourself (Fig. 5-65).

Model 610 Discriminator

The model 610 is another excellent quality and highly superior sound discriminator from Controllor Systems (Fig. 5-66). This is an easy to install wireless burglary security system that takes a "break-in" sound to activate the siren and turn on home floodlights. The system detects a break-in attempt while ignoring normal household sounds.

The system allows for two outlets of 500 watts for outside floodlights to rapidly bathe the intruder in brilliant light. His only recourse is to immediately flee the scene of his attempted crime.

Model 611 Discriminator

Portable sound discriminators such as the model 611 (Fig. 5-67) are available for hooking into a normally open or closed

Fig. 5-64. The model 630 (courtesy of Controllor Systems Corporation).

Fig. 5-65. The model 630 is ideal as a home security unit. The lady is holding the model 631 (courtesy of Controllor Systems Corporation).

circuit. The model 611 has selective audio processing and full sensitivity adjustment. The unit responds only to the intense frequency sounds of breaking glass, splintering wood, pounding, sawing and metal to metal contact. (For the cost-conscious homeowner, it also sells for about half the cost to which you would probably be accustomed.)

Model 612 Discriminator

The Model 612 discriminator is another CSC development and very new to the industry and homeowner. It performs like no

Fig. 5-66. The model 610 (courtesy of Controllor Systems Corporation).

other sensing device, virtually eliminating false alarms. Installation is very simple. Just mount to the wall or ceiling with one screw in a keyhole slot in the back. Make the sensitivity adjustment in the pot through the bottom recessed hole. Check to be sure the 9 volt battery is hooked up properly. The 612 has a digital code transmitter with a combination of 256 codes, enabling adjustment to match the receiver's frequency. Further, it is adaptable to any wireless or hard wired system.

Model 631 Discriminator

The 631 model sound discriminator has a line carrier transmitter in it (Fig. 5-68). Its principle is just as simple as its operation. Just plug the 631 into any home ac standard outlet, adjust the sensitivity, and the unit is operational. It will activate any of the following companion receivers using the existing ac wiring of the home, or from one building to another: the model 630 control cabinet, the model 632 line carrier receiver, or the model 633 line carrier horn/receiver.

Models 632, 633 and 510

Figure 5-69 illustrates the 632/633 (they look the same). The 632 plugs into any standard ac outlet and contains a relay which closes when it receives a signal from the 631. It can be used with any control panel.

The 633 is a line carrier receiver unit with a built-in horn (which gives 85 decibels at 10') that shouts out the sound when a signal is received from the 631. The 633 can be used in cases where a "buddy system" is desirable, such as a neighboring building.

The model 510 intrusion protection system is detailed in Chapter 7 which will also provide you with an excellent overview of the system's description, operation and details of the main control unit, sensor transmitter and accessory equipment.

FIRST ALERT SELF-CONTAINED BURGLAR INTRUSION ALARM

The *First Alert self-contained burglar intrusion alarm* operates by itself or can also be interconnected with the complete family protection system by First Alert. A wireless perimeter alarm, it is an ultrasonic unit that can be positioned anywhere to provide protection to owners and renters of homes and apartments. It is also used as backup protection for people in a larger home who may already possess the family protection system and want some additional security protection in a specific, defined area.

Powered by the standard house ac, it has a battery backup provision. A interesting feature is that the unit is designed for a lamp, radio or other home appliance to be plugged into the unit,

Fig. 5-67. The model 611 (courtesy of Controllor Systems Corporation).

205

Fig. 5-68. The model 631 (courtesy of Controllor Systems Corporation).

operating in tandem with the alarm. When movement is detected, the light (if that was attached to the unit) would turn on *before* the alarm sounded.

Under such circumstances, a burglar surely would feel caught in the act as the light goes on. As this is immediately followed by the 85 decibel alarm piercing the night, he would be frightened and beat a hasty retreat out of the home.

The alarm also uses a user-programmable three-digit code which will either arm or disarm the system. It can be quickly changed by the owner. This ensures that nobody except the authorized person can easily control the alarm unit.

PLUG-IN SECURITY SYSTEM

Waldom Electronics, realizing that the greatest expense in most alarm systems is incurred in the installation process for complete home security systems, i.e., the installation of the wiring between the control box, detectors and the alarm, developed the "plug in" security system. The system avoids all this expense and hassle by utilizing the exisiting electrical home wiring to transmit a violation signal to the central control center which, in turn, would transmit a signal activating all signal alarms in the system. See Fig.

Fig. 5-69. Front view of the model 632/633 (courtesy of Controllor Systems Corporation).

5-70. The installation is extremely easy for many years of product use. It can be expanded to meet the additional needs of another home, the addition of more rooms, or the conversion of a room to a business office. The plug-in security system provides for a choice of alarm signals that will send the intruder fleeing before he gets a chance to remove valuables.

The alarm can have a flashing light hooked up to the basic unit (Fig. 5-71), or it can be used as a bedroom/neighbor signal horn alarm by itself. In such a case, the tone is moderate and sounds a warning in your bedroom to awaken you, or in your neighbor's home to alert him of the attempted penetration of your home security. He can contact the local police without the intruder being aware of what is happening.

The unit also has the standard indoor signal alarm horn which sounds a loud pulsating 85 decibel alarm. Finally, a 103 decibel outdoor signal alarm horn device is available for exterior installation.

Fig. 5-70. Plug-in security system. (A) Magnetic switch set. (B) Sensor transmitter. (C) Control center. (D) Signal alarms (courtesy of Waldom Electronics, Inc.).

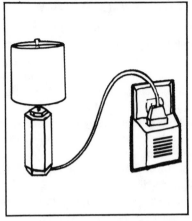

Fig. 5-71. Flashing light signal alarm (courtesy of Waldom Electronics, Inc.).

Looking back at Fig. 5-70, we see the three major functional features of the unit and how easily they can be installed with a minimum of time and trouble.

The magnetic switch set is installed with a couple of screws to the door. A set of wires running to the sensor transmitter which has been plugged into an ac outlet is all that is required for each set of switches and transmitter. Opening the door will cause the switch halves to separate, which will then complete the electrical circuit, activating the sensor transmitter. Likewise, opening a window does the same.

Upon activation, the transmitter sends a special coded signal to the control center through the household wiring system. At the control center, the unit locks onto the signal, waits between 10-15 seconds and then transmits a signal to *all* signal alarms. This happens even if the door or window has been closed again. The purpose of the delay is to provide time for the homeowner to reach and disarm the control center before the alarm sounds. The control center also has a switch that will delete the delay. This means that all the signal alarms will sound immediately upon the opening of a secured door or window.

The control unit provides for a violation light to come on whenever a protected opening is not used. It warns against arming the system before the entire home is secured.

This plug-in system comes also with a smoke/fire detector that will also provide night and day protection. The bedroom/neighbor alert signal alarm can be placed in your friendly neighbor's home which will alert him to a violation in your home, even when you are away on a two-week vacation.

ULTRASON-II ALARM SYSTEM

The *Ultrason-II alarm system* from *Master Lock* is FM coded. The FM signal acts as a "coded key" which guards against satellite false alarms due to such things as power line disturbances.

A powerful, affordable and dependable system, the Ultrason-II is professional quality protection at a lower cost than that of commercial installations throughout the home. The alarm signal that is automatically set to each room's characteristics and remote wireless satellite units relays a loud piercing warning throughout the premises.

The basic master unit is a precision built 26 kHz crystal control device that permits any number of satellite units to operate adjacent to each other without interference. When a signal is received, the unit will analyze the movement to determine whether there is truly intrusion or simply random disturbances due to air currents, passing trucks or whatever.

Within each room or rooms, you attach one or more of the satellite alarms. As they are wireless, you must plug them into a wall outlet (Fig. 5-72). By pressing the "power on" switch, you instantly alarm the Ultrason-II.

TELETALE SYSTEMS

Even though the more traditional perimeter hard-wire security systems are popular, competition and technology requires that newer systems constantly be developed and brought forth to serve the needs and desires of the general public. MRC Alarm Systems & Devices Company recognized this early in the security "game" and started developing their *Teletale* system. Teletale is a patented low frequency intrusion detection system that is currently available to all.

The ASD-2100 portable system is a self-contained detector that is not necessarily permanently wired (Fig. 5-73). No matter what the home protection needs, the ASD-2100 will probably fit them. The basic unit can cover over 1600 and up to 3600 square feet, which is more than ample. It has a further capacity for up to three auxiliary sensors, which will dramatically increase to a total protected area of over 7500 square feet.

The Teletale system provides a low frequency sensing signal of a wavelength that provides for a continuous audible tone creating an effective sound barrier which can be heard just outside the protected area. This signal will not only detect the intruder's presence as he attempts to enter a protected area, but it also

Fig. 5-72. Plug the alarm into a wall outlet (courtesy of Master Lock Co.).

provides a formidable deterrent in that the intruder can hear the tone and realize that a protective sensor system is in current operation. Remember that other systems using ultrasonic or microwave utilize an inaudible sensing frequency above the hearing range of humans.

Phase angle discrimination is another unique feature that has been coupled with the *Doppler shift* principle to provide two-way detection which results in the optimum space protection. The Doppler shift discerns the change in frequency or pitch between the sensor and an object that enters the sound wave pattern. While most types of units recognize motion either toward or away from the detection device, some do not cover the entire area to be protected because of their inherent restricted patterns. The phase angle discrimination adds an extra dimension to the protected area so that motion can be detected in any direction. Phase angle discrimination is accomplished by the sensor's recognition of the normal sound wave pattern of the protected area. This normal or stable condition is compared at the rate of approximately 80 times per second. If a comparison should indicate a changed condition from the normal, an alarm is immediately and automatically triggered.

It should be noted that low frequency sensing wavelengths in the Teletale system will reject the signals caused by thunder or

Fig. 5-73. The ASD-2100 Teletale intrusion detection system (courtesy of MRC Alarm Systems & Devices).

sonic booms, radio station interference, transient signals and the like. These are some of the major causes of false alarms in many other systems. The typical low frequency wavelength is approximately 16" long, as compared to the very small ½" of an ultrasonic alarm. Such things as cats, dogs, etc., can cause false activations in other types of systems, but would immediately be rejected by the Teletale alarm system.

The Teletale II ASD-3100 alarm system has a built-in capacity for up to eight sensing zones, utilizing a maximum of 32 sensors. A solid-state fail-safe circuitry system housed in a tamperproof enclosure, the system can operate for more than four hours from a self-contained power supply in the event of ac power failure. When power is restored, there is no need to replace the batteries; they automatically recharge themselves.

Besides the fast installation and greater flexibility, other Teletale features include: a built-in high power warbler amplifier, automatic reset, entrance/exit delay, standby power and remote key switch operation.

CRIMEFIGHTER ALARM

One of the fastest and most easy do-it-yourself installation alarm systems is the *Crimefighter Alarm* (Fig. 5-74) by the Master Lock Company. A low cost crime-fighting system, it provides a big

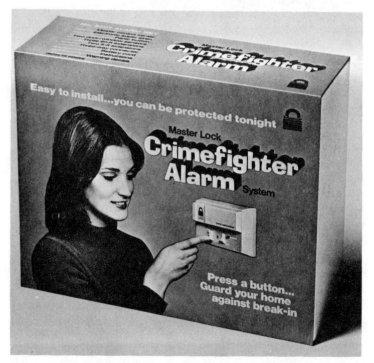

Fig. 5-74. The Crimefighter Alarm (courtesy of Master Lock Co.).

edge for the home handyman. A super device that is just right for the small homeowner or apartment dweller, the system comes with every component prewired and fitted with connectors that will simply plug together. There are no wires that will need cutting or stripping, nor will they require soldering or splicing. The nice thing about this system is that, for the person with absolutely no knowledge of electricity or electronics, the system works by itself. Because of the simplicity of the system and the built-in electrical safety considerations, it's really a safe security system that even a teenager can install with complete safety. The alarm uses a safe low-voltage battery power that makes it totally free of any local wiring code restrictions.

The system offers a unique solid-state built master control panel that can be installed in any room at any point. Other features are the door magnetic contact switches that are quickly attached to a window or door, an emergency button ready to instantly activate the alarm, and the electronic siren which provides a loud, pulsating shriek that can scare off any intruders and also alert neighbors.

Because of the simplicity and low cost of the system, this is probably one of the most effective starter systems for the do-it-yourselfer. In addition, extra detector sensors are obtainable through local hardware stores and home centers so the system can be rapidly enlarged to cover additional doors and windows.

MINUTEMAN II AND MINUTEMAN SENTINEL

The *Minuteman II* from Delta Products, Inc. is considered one of the few complete home security systems on the market. Strategically placed, it will effectively protect the home. If you feel the need for more security, it's expandable. The Minuteman II system is a multi-functional device that is not only a complete detection and alarm system, but can also act as a master control for other units you may wish to add.

The Minuteman II and Minuteman *Sentinel* (Fig. 5-75) are space protectors which use harmless, high frequency ultrasonic sound beams. It can come with or without batteries; the choice is yours. Further, the Minuteman II is a portable system. The system, considered by many as "the key to home security," is the product of 11 intensive years of research to develop the best deterrence method possible.

The basic system consists of the *control detector, power transformer, power isolator, all-weather speakers*, the *Minuteman*

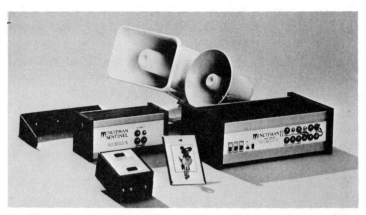

Fig. 5-75. The Minuteman II and Minuteman Sentinel (courtesy of Delta Products, Inc.).

Sentinel, switch assembly and the wall mounting bracket. System features include:

—Total system flexibility.

—Expandability.

—Standby rechargeable batteries to insure continuous operation.

—Time/entry/exit delay.

—Local or remote switching capability.

—Closed loop input for door and window switches but allows for the addition of door and window alarms, if desired.

—Self-testing circuits so you can continually check the system.

The ultrasonic principle of a harmless high frequency sound beam will quickly and quietly blanket an area of approximately 300 square feet. Any movement within this area breaks the beam pattern. The detector senses this motion and activates the alarm signal.

Since the Minuteman II system operates on a closed loop circuit, it activates the alarm only when the circuit is broken. This is exactly opposite of the household lights which utilize an open circuit, where the circuit must be closed before they will turn on.

The Minuteman II control detector and all components work on a single, continuous closed circuit so that any break or disruption which opens the circuit will relay the impulse to the control and activate the alarm system.

Provisions for perimeter, supervised, closed circuit security are included in the system. You can expand your protection to include additional security items such as magnetic door contacts, window foil or other closed circuit detection devices.

The Minuteman Sentinel (Fig. 5-76) is designed to be used as a remote motion detector connected to the Delta Products Minuteman II system. It may also be used with other control systems that require either a contact closure or contact opening for operation. *Any number* of Sentinels may be used in an installation, subject to the limitations of frequency separation, physical isolation and power supply limits.

The Sentinel has three basic circuits, an input voltage regulator, a motion detection circuit, and an output switching relay and "walk light." The Sentinel has no ON/OFF control, EXIT/ENTRY delays or audible alarm. When connected to the Minuteman II, these functions are provided by the Minuteman II. When using the Sentinel with other control systems, these functions must be provided by the control system.

Figure 5-77 illustrates the minimum, medium and maximum range that the Minuteman Sentinel will provide. Figure 5-78 shows two examples of the right and wrong methods of positioning the unit. As with any unit of this type, no matter what the brand name, such positioning considerations are very important in order that you have proper protection and that false alarms will not result. Each manufacturer includes basic information on this area along with the unit.

Fig. 5-76. The Minuteman Sentinel is a remote motion detector (courtesy of Delta Products, Inc.).

216

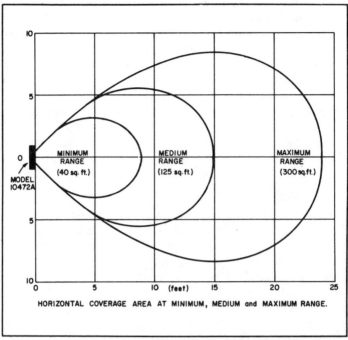

Fig. 5-77. Horizontal coverage area at minimum, medium and maximum range for the Minuteman Sentinel (courtesy of Delta Products, Inc.).

The Minuteman II system with a Minuteman Sentinel should be considered as the basic, fully operating functional system that should be the base for any home security system that uses ultrasonics. Remember that with the Minuteman II alarm system, incorporated are a motion detection device, the delay circuitry, alarm generation (both audible *and* silent), and alarm detection by the opening of the normally closed security loop. The audible horn will produce an ear-shattering 116 decibels at 10'.

Assume that you have just the basic Minuteman II without the Minuteman Sentinel. What will the wiring hookup be for the home, assuming a panic button in the bedroom, door and window switches and a 15 watt speaker? Figure 5-79 illustrates how this design configuration could be wired in the home.

Another system is called, appropriately, the *Delta System Two* (Fig. 5-80) and comes with the ultrasonic alert (12 volt dc), horn system, speaker and power convertor. Addition of a 12 volt battery automatically switches the unit to battery power if the power source is disrupted *or* cut from the outside by an intruder.

217

Non-powered contacts give complete flexibility for working with another alarm system or increasing the number of ultrasonic units.

By use of a Delta relay power isolator (Fig. 5-81), you have instant contact activation from standard household ac. Another model provides for a 20-second delayed activation of contact from ac power; and a third model will give the same 20-second delay activation of contact from a 12 volt dc input. When activated by either the ac or dc input, Delta's series of relays provides dry (non-powered) contacts for both open or closed circuit operation. These relays are commonly referred to as power isolators, and the relays are activated by a powered source and result in a non-powered open or closed circuit activation (contact open or closed).

DIAL & CODER

The final Delta product I wish to discuss briefly is the *Dial & Coder*, a most reliable solid-state universal pulse dialer designed to provide remote dialing of any telephone number up to eight digits (Fig. 5-82). The Dial & Coder initiates its dialing sequence upon a contact (switch) closure and provides an audible *Tone code* for positive identification.

Audio surveillance may be transmitted over the telephone line by using a microphone connected to the microphone input jack of the Dial & Coder. The basic functions of the Dial & Coder are:

—Automatic pulse dialing of any telephone number up to eight digits.

—Automatic hangup and redial in case of a busy signal.

—Generation of up to 110 different tone codes for identification of the Dial & Coder.

—Automatically resetting feature after each completed call.

Since the dialing sequence is initiated upon a contact closure, the unit is readily adaptable to most available sensing devices, such as intrusion alarms, thermostatic switches, pressure switches and other devices providing a single contact closure.

Typical applications of the Dial & Coder include:

—Reporting unauthorized intrusions.

—Reporting of malfunctioning equipment.

—Single button dialing for children, invalids or handicapped persons.

A typical application within the home is shown in Fig. 5-83.

NUTONE RADIO RECEIVER AND TRANSMITTERS

Earlier in this chapter you read about the NuTone home security system. The NuTone company puts out many products

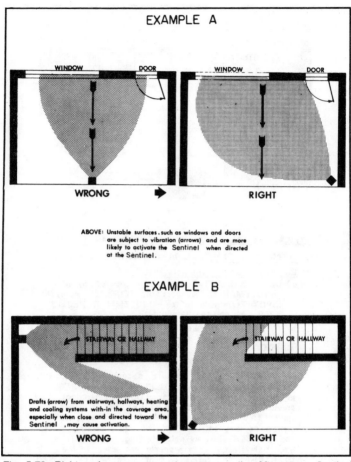

Fig. 5-78. Right and wrong ways of positioning the Minuteman Sentinel (courtesy of Delta Products, Inc.).

that are specifically designed to aid you in combating the potential threat to your home security. The model S-2290 *NuTone radio receiver* is a unique unit in that it can be connected to any circuit, be it a perimeter, interior or emergency (Fig. 5-84). The receiver comes with one of four different frequencies, so additional receivers can be connected to other circuits to work with the master control unit. If desired, each can use a different frequency.

The radio transmitter can be connected to an entry detector. When the entry detector is activated (by opening the door, for example), the transmitter will send a radio signal to the receiver. The receiver is connected to the alarm system control unit. Upon

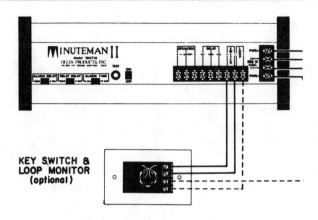

KEY SWITCH &
LOOP MONITOR
(optional)

TYPICAL INSTALLATION WITH MINUTEMAN II

1. **Locate each SENTINEL** at the desired locations.

2. **Connect POWER Terminals.**
   - a) Up to 5 SENTINELS may be powered by the MINUTEMAN II. Connect all SENTINEL POWER INPUT Terminals to the MINUTEMAN II REG. 15 V.D.C. (+) and (−) Terminals.
   - b. If desired, the SENTINELS may be connected to power supplies delivering 10−18 VAC or 12−28 VDC.

3. **Connecting the "LOOP".** The "LOOP" terminals of the MINUTEMAN II require a continuous circuit to be maintained between the LOOP (−) or the REG. 15 VDC (−) terminal and the LOOP (+) terminal to prevent an alarm. Each SENTINEL has a relay contact (N.C.) that makes contact to the relay (COM) contact as long as the SENTINEL is receiving power and the SENTINEL is not detecting motion. Thus, each SENTINEL, when properly connected to the MINUTEMAN II, forms part of a NORMALLY CLOSED, SERIES LOOP. An Alarm will result if the "LOOP" is open for any reason. Any number of switches may be inserted in series with the "LOOP".

   - a) Note the dashed line in the illustration. The dashed line represents the "LOOP." To simplify the installation, the (N.C) relay contact on Unit I is connected to the POWER INPUT terminal that is in turn, connected to the REG. 15 VDC (−) terminal of the MINUTEMAN. [This terminal is internally connected to the LOOP (−) terminal.] *

   - b) If you are installing only one SENTINEL, disregard UNITS 2 and 3. Connect UNIT I relay (COM) to MINUTEMAN II LOOP (+) via any additional switches and KEYSWITCH & LOOP MONITOR, if used.

Fig. 5-79. Wiring for the Minuteman II (courtesy of Delta Products, Inc.).

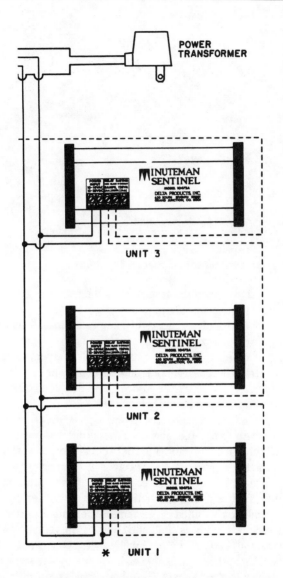

POWER TRANSFORMER

UNIT 3

UNIT 2

✳ UNIT 1

✳ NOTE: IF THE SENTINEL FARTHEST FROM THE MINUTEMAN II (UNIT 1) IS POWERED BY A POWER SOURCE OTHER THAN THE MINUTEMAN II REG. 15 VDC, THE (N.C.) TERMINAL OF UNIT 1 MUST BE CONNECTED TO THE MINUTEMAN LOOP (–) OR REG. 15 VDC (–) TERMINAL.

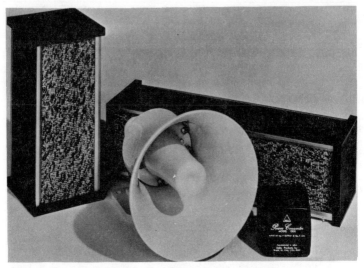

Fig. 5-80. The Delta System Two (courtesy of Delta Products, Inc.).

receiving the signal from the transmitter, the receiver activates the control unit to sound the alarm.

This unit is most advantageous in homes with an addition, and with the door or window(s) not hooked into the general perimeter circuit. In such cases, the radio transmitter and receiver are used. No new circuitry is necessary, nor is another control unit, since the additional monitor works off the already installed control unit, a savings in time and money for the homeowner.

The receiver can be connected to one of three different alarm activating circuits from the alarm control unit: the perimeter intruder circuit, the interior intruder circuit or the manual emergency alarm circuit. If the receiver is connected to the perimeter intruder circuit, it will be controlled by the alarm control panel control knob and also the optional "perimeter" exit/entry switch that has been installed in the home. When connected to the interior intruder circuit, it is controlled only by the interior on/off switch on the alarm control panel. Finally, when connected to the emergency alarm circuit, it will not be controlled by any switch on the main alarm control panel. The emergency alarm circuit is always armed and ready.

Working in tandem with the receiver are the NuTone portable transmitter (Fig. 5-85) and the wall-mounted transmitter (Fig. 5-86). Since these units are very closely related, details of their installation procedures are covered here.

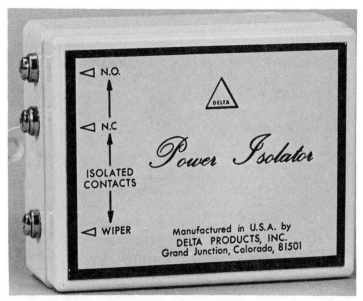

Fig. 5-81. Delta relay power isolator (courtesy of Delta Products, Inc.).

First, though, here are some important facts about installation planning of the radio receiver and associated transmitter units. The installation of the components must be carefully planned. The radio receiver has a maximum range which must not be exceeded. The maximum range will differ slightly with each house. In most cases,

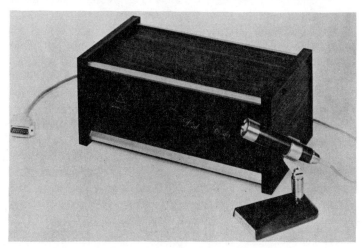

Fig. 5-82. Dial & Coder (courtesy of Delta Products, Inc.).

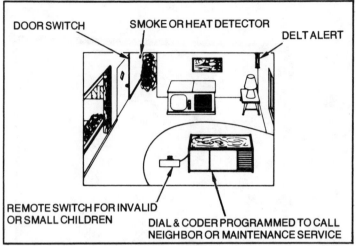

DOOR SWITCH   SMOKE OR HEAT DETECTOR   DELT ALERT

REMOTE SWITCH FOR INVALID OR SMALL CHILDREN   DIAL & CODER PROGRAMMED TO CALL NEIGHBOR OR MAINTENANCE SERVICE

Fig. 5-83. Typical application of the Dial & Coder (courtesy of Delta Products, Inc.).

20' is a good distance between the receiver and transmitter. Never exceed 100' between a receiver and transmitter.

Avoid metal ductwork, dividers and other metallic surfaces that may create a shielding, which will impair the signal from the transmitter to the receiver. If the receiver/transmitter range is low due to radio interference, a receiver/transmitter system with a different frequency may have a greater range. For example, it might be that a F2 frequency system will be greater in a particular location than an F1, Fr or F4 frequency system.

The useful temperature range for the radio-controlled system (except for the 9 volt battery in the transmitters) is −20°F to +140°F. The battery may not work in extremely cold temperatures, which would prevent the transmitter from operating.

There are four methods to test the component locations for their operating range. The homeowner should test each one and select the one that provides the best range and most efficient use of the system to meet the needs within the home.

Using the Finished Control Panel

Turn the signal knob on the master panel to the OFF position. Slide the trouble *signal switch* into the SILENT position.

Construct a temporary installation. Place the transmitters where needed. Locate the receiver in a central position between the transmitters and the control unit.

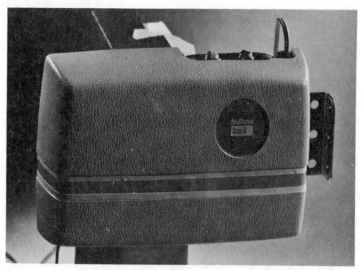

Fig. 5-84. The S-2290 radio receiver (courtesy of NuTone Division, Scovill Inc.).

Temporarily connect the receiver to the control unit terminal strip, as shown in Fig. 5-87. Insert the plug from the control unit terminal strip into the control panel as shown.

Supply power to the control unit in one of the following ways. Supply household ac to the control unit transformer and plug the transformer into the control unit. Using the NuTone rechargeable battery with the battery charger board, plug in the battery charger board and connect the cables to the battery. Use two 6 volt dry cells (Burgess TW-1, Eveready 731 or equivalent) with the dry cell

Fig. 5-85. The portable transmitter (courtesy of NuTone Division, Scovill Inc.).

Fig. 5-86. A wall-mounted transmitter (courtesy of NuTone Division, Scovill Inc.).

battery board. Plug in the board and connect the cables to the battery.

Position the receiver and transmitter(s) in the most convenient locations for the installation and press the transmitter test button. If the location of the transmitter and receiver is within range, the alarm will sound. If there is no alarm, reposition the transmitter. Sometimes only 1 to 3' are necessary.

Using a Voltmeter

Connect a voltmeter to the receiver test points. The tests points are located on the side of the receiver. Refer to the label on the back of the receiver for the test point numbers. Connect the positive lead from the voltmeter to test point #2. Connect the negative lead to the receiver chassis.

Position the receiver and transmitters in the most convenient locations for the installations. If the location is within range, the volt meter will read +.5 volts or higher.

Using dc Power and a Test Lamp

Connect 10 to 28 volts dc power to the receiver wires as indicated in the installation/testing instructions. Connect a continuity test lamp to the receiver terminal "NC" and "COM." Do not use any test lamp over 28 volts.

Position the transmitter(s) and receiver in the best location. Press the transmitter test button. If the location is proper, the test lamp will go out.

Let's jump quickly to the receiver, which has two wire runs: one pair of wires for power and the second for the alarm activation.

The receiver is connected to the power wiring as shown in Fig. 5-88. The NuTone 2300 system for smoke detectors is discussed in a following chapter. But, as shown in the illustration, the receiver could be hooked up to a smoke detection device, also.

It is most important that the receiver be only connected to *one* alarm activation circuit. Never attempt to connect it to more than one circuit.

The receiver could also be connected to the perimeter intruder circuit, as shown in Fig. 5-89, or to the interior intruder

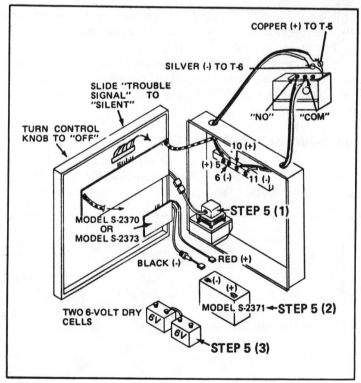

Fig. 5-87. Connect the receiver to the control unit terminal strip (courtesy of NuTone Division, Scovill Inc.).

227

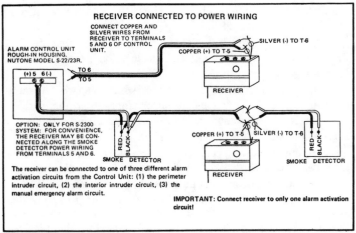

Fig. 5-88. The receiver is connected to power wiring (courtesy of NuTone Division, Scovill Inc.).

circuit as in Fig. 5-90. Finally the receiver can also be connected to the emergency alarm circuit, which is constantly armed and ready for instant activation of the alarm (Fig. 5-91).

The transmitter is a self-contained unit which runs off a 9 volt battery. This, too, can be installed and wired in a variety of ways, as illustrated in Fig. 5-92. Figure 5-93 shows two installation methods for the unit.

NUTONE ULTRASONIC MOTION DETECTOR

The homeowner who likes security that covers all areas should be vitally concerned about the *NuTone Ultrasonic Motion Detector* (Fig. 5-94). The space detectors are used in glass-walled

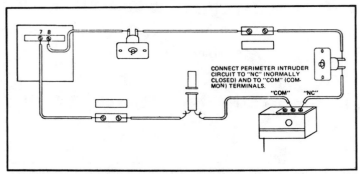

Fig. 5-89. The receiver connected to the perimeter intruder circuit ,courtesy of NuTone Division, Scovill Inc.).

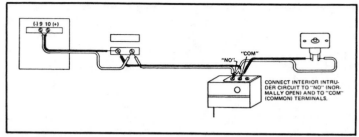

Fig. 5-90. Receiver connected to the interior intruder circuit (courtesy of NuTone Division, Scovill Inc.).

rooms that might otherwise be difficult to protect in order to monitor a room that contains valuable artwork or statuary. Virtually any area an intruder would have to pass through in moving about the home can be used to locate a space detector. Mounted in a strategic location, even on a high wall or ceiling, it will emit inaudible high frequency sound waves in an elliptical pattern ranging from 12-35′ by 3-20′.

How the Unit Works

The detector sends out inaudible sound waves that have a crystal-controlled frequency of 25 kilohertz. If an unauthorized person moves through the protected area, he will cause a change in the frequency of the reflected sound waves (Fig. 5-95). The detector notes this change and signals the security system control unit to sound the alarm.

Remember that the detector receives its power from the NuTone security system control unit. That control unit should have a battery backup; otherwise, the detector would trigger an alarm if the power is interrupted. The alarm will be triggered when the interrupted ac house power is restored to normal.

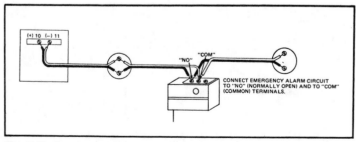

Fig. 5-91. Receiver connected to the emergency alarm circuit (courtesy of NuTone Division, Scovill Inc.).

229

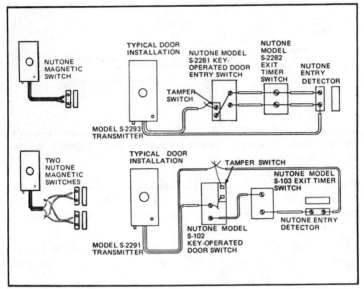

Fig. 5-92. Transmitter installations and wiring (courtesy of NuTone Division, Scovill Inc.).

The detector senses motion by the use of the inaudible high frequency sound waves. When installing the unit, remember that movement as well as high frequency sounds can trigger the detector.

Area Selection

Two things must be kept in mind when selecting the area considered for protection. The detection pattern can be aimed at a specific area; it can be rotated 180 degrees.

The range of the detector is adjustable. Minimum range setting will protect a space 4' high by 5' wide by 12' long. Maximum

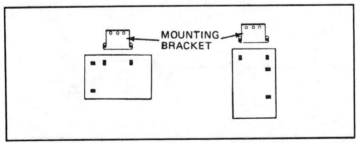

Fig. 5-93. Two installation methods for the transmitter (courtesy of NuTone Division, Scovill Inc.).

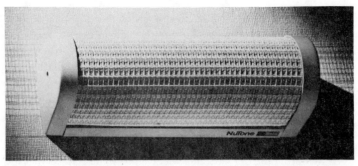

Fig. 5-94. Ultrasonic Motion Detector (courtesy of NuTone Division, Scovill Inc.).

range setting will provide a protection area 15′ high by 15′ wide by 35′ long.

This detector is for indoor use only, in temperatures from 32°F to 122°F. You should use the detector as a second line of defense against intruders to back up your perimeter protection on the doors and windows. The detector can also be used to protect areas immediately inside the perimeter points that do not have intruder detectors.

Use the detector when point source protection (such as a magnetic or plunger switch) is not possible or desirable. However, the detector is designed to protect an interior space rather than just a specific point.

The area chosen should be a normal walking path through the house free of large obstructions, such as partitions. Finally, the area should not be one in which household pets have free access during the period the unit is operational.

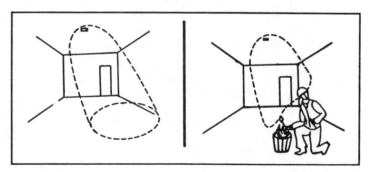

Fig. 5-95. If a person moves through the protected area, there will be a change in the frequency of the reflected sound waves (courtesy of NuTone Division, Scovill Inc.).

Mounting the Detector

Let's look at the installation of the unit in the home. When mounting the basic unit, make sure that you leave at least 25″ of wiring at the detector location to help make the installation and testing of the system easier. If the wiring will be run to the detector on the outside of the wall, there are two plastic knockouts in the detector that will have to be removed. Remember that this intruder detection circuit will be connected to the interior circuit or the perimeter circuit of the NuTone security system.

Mounting the detector in a vertical position requires that the mounting plate be positioned so that the lock-in lip is at the lower left (Fig. 5-96). Place the mounting plate onto the mounting surface. Mark the location of the four mounting holes and the cutout for the wiring entrance. The cutout by the lock-in lip should be used because the detector terminal strip is at that end.

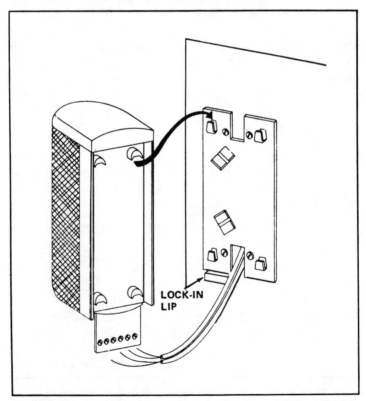

Fig. 5-96. Note the position of the lock-in lip (courtesy of NuTone Division, Scovill Inc.).

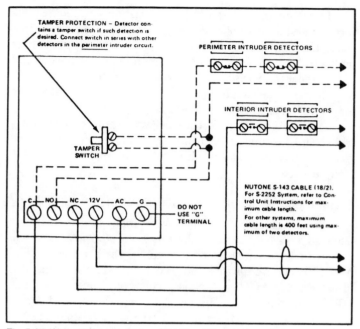

Fig. 5-97. Wiring diagram (courtesy of NuTone Division, Scovill Inc.).

Secure the mounting plate to the surface. Pull the wires through the cutout and mounting plate. Remove the bottom cap from the detector (the top cap is not removable).

Before attaching the detector unit to the mounting plate, aim the unit toward the area requiring protection. Attach the detector to the mounting plate by lining up the four slotted mounting posts on the detector back with the taps on the plate. Apply a slight pressure to the detector to force it onto the mounting plate. To remove the detector, pry up at the lower right corner with a screwdriver.

Wire connections are illustrated in Fig. 5-97. Insert the wires fully into the terminals. No wrapping is required except to the optional tamper switch. Then tighten down the screws.

Range Adjustment and Background Interference

Once positioned and wired, the unit is ready for *range adjustment*. The detector will have to be measured from the farthest point needing protection. Use the range control setting to adjust your unit range. Specific details are in the installation handbook.

If you test the detector, 12 volts must be supplied from the security system control unit to the detector. There are three connections that must be made to the system to supply power from the control unit: connect "12V" and "ac" terminals in the detector to the proper terminals in the control unit (Fig. 5-98), connect the transformer to the control panel, and connect the terminal strip to the control panel printed circuit board.

The background interference and walk testing of the unit will take about 10 minutes to accomplish. Once the detector adjusts and you have the range control setting adjusted properly, the unit is ready for use.

RACON 15000 MICROGUARD MICROWAVE INTRUSION DETECTOR

A new dimension in microwave motion detection was heralded with the advent of the *Racon 15000 Microguard* wall mounted microwave intrusion detector for the homeowner (Fig. 5-99). The detector provides protection against false alarms. It is ideal for multiple unit applications, individual rooms or even long hallways in the home. The standard unit provides adjustable coverage up to a 50' maximum. Common radio frequency interference problems have been eliminated by enclosing the entire sensor in a metal casing which provides shielding, and also by providing a second circuit board to filter all connected lines.

The range control provides for zone adjustment up to 20' wide (maximum) and 50' long. Uniquely, the Racon 15000 is not affected

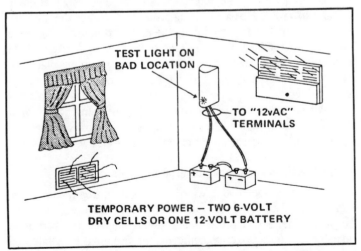

TEST LIGHT ON
BAD LOCATION

TO "12vAC"
TERMINALS

TEMPORARY POWER — TWO 6-VOLT
DRY CELLS OR ONE 12-VOLT BATTERY

Fig. 5-98. Terminal connections (courtesy of NuTone Division, Scovill Inc.).

Fig. 5-99. The Racon 15000 (courtesy of Racon Inc.).

by the normal fluorescent lighting with which so many other units have problems.

The typical installation requires an optional power supply which is designed to operate up to four Racon microwave sensors simultaneously. The power supply comes complete with a standby battery and Class 2 transformer. If using another manufacturer's unit which has 12 volts dc, up to five sensors can still be directly attached to the panel.

Installation is simple. Position the unit so that the area coverage microwave beam covers the desired location, and then mount the unit to the wall or ceiling with the mounting bracket. Of course, the Class 2 power transformer will have to be connected to the home ac outlet.

The alarm duration is a five second opening or closing of the circuit, with an automatic reset feature incorporated into the unit. If you use NO/NC contacts in a panel having two separate circuits, one circuit can be used for a telephone dialer option, a horn driven siren for a local alarm, etc. If this is done, ensure that the attached devices do not exceed 2 milliamps.

RACON 20000 MICROMAX INTRUSION DETECTION SYSTEM

The *Racon 20000 Micromax* intrusion detection system is a completely self-contained unit that operates either from ac or from the built-in battery which is supplied with the unit. Like the model 15000, it has a variety of applications.

Figure 5-100 illustrates the Racon 20000 Micromax maximum coverage patterns of the system. Figure 5-101 is a view of the unit as seen from the rear, in an open position, with identification of the various component parts. The Racon 20000 and 15000 are highly compatible systems which will work very well with high performance and a minimum of disruption, distraction or failure within the home or apartment dwelling.

The ac application has a Class II transformer which puts out 16.5 volts. This low voltage means that no wiring will have to be run inside metal conduit. Low voltage wire (called "zip cord" in the trade) can be safely used.

Two different configurations of the Racon 20000 are currently available for use: the 20000-01, which has a 50' range; and the 20000-02, which has a 75' range.

Where systems are installed in a home that might have powerful air conditioners, air flow and drape movement, it is suggested that the Racon 15000 be used instead of the 20000 system. The 15000 has a 1-2-4-8 step selector on the unit. This is a built-in counter. If the unit does not count 2-4-8 steps (movements), the alarm will not sound. A falling object or the blowing of drapes will not activate the alarm, whereas it would with the Racon 20000. This is because the 20000 unit has a self-detection built-in Doppler shift that will activate the alarm on the first movement.

Here's a quick note on the Racon 15000 power supply. I mentioned using another manufacturer's power panel. If it is 12.6

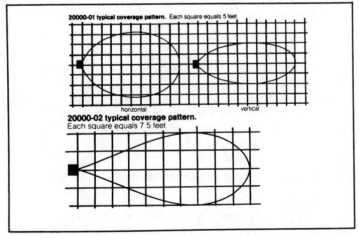

Fig. 5-100. The Racon 20000 Micromax coverage pattern (courtesy of Racon Inc.).

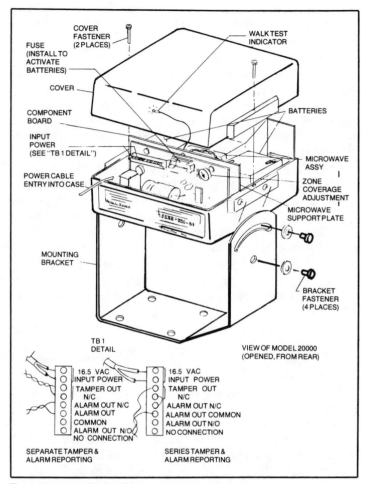

Fig. 5-101. Rear view of the Racon 20000 (courtesy of Racon Inc.).

volts dc, with only 180 mA drive off the 15000 unit, you can hook up the unit directly to the system as long as you don't exceed 2 amps. Finally, in microwave, there is the higher probability of detection and the lowest nuisance (false) alarm ratio when these systems are correctly installed than in others that use a volumetric control, such as infrared.

PIR-78 INFRARED INTRUSION DETECTOR

The following information is based upon detailed material supplied by *Colorado Electro-Optics* (CEO). Several systems are

237

produced by CEO for use by the homeowner, and each should be considered an optimum device if you are looking for an infrared system for your home security.

The CEO passive infrared intrusion detector, *PIR-78*, is a reliable and broad coverage detector (Fig. 5-102). Smaller than most infrared detectors of comparable capability, it operates from either ac or dc power. The plug-in design makes it possible to mount the back plate and connect the internal wiring before the sensor is installed. This procedure reduces the possibility of damaging the sensor during installation and also simplifies wiring the unit. The sealed construction used for this unit minimizes problems that are caused by rapid pressure changes, visible light, moisture, air turbulence or radio interference. Also, the sensor unit has a hard germanium lens, which makes it less susceptible to vandalism. A 24-hour tamper loop circuit inside the unit is broken if the cover is ever removed.

The PIR-78 will effectively cover a room as large as 40 × 40'. Its output is a relay and can be used to trigger both wired and wireless alarms. Standby power is supplied by a rechargeable four-cell battery which will operate for 20 hours in the event of a power failure. The sensor can be obtained with or without the standby battery feature.

Since we have looked at the detailed installation features of other home security units, let's now proceed with the CEO PIR-78 instructions. In general, the PIR-78 represents the latest in the passive infrared technology and design available for the home security system. The unit detects rapid changes in temperature or infrared energy levels within its sensitive region. When one of the six segments of the approximately 40 × 40' sensitive region senses a temperature change, a relay is deactivated to signal an alarm. Many interesting and excellent features are built into the PIR-78 to make it a unique system in the passive infrared field.

☐ A rugged, low profile, easily mounted package system.
☐ Vandal resistant germanium lens.
☐ Coated lens to filter out visible light interference.
☐ ac or dc powered.
☐ Optional 24-hour battery pack.
☐ Dual relay contacts.
☐ Remote walk test capability function.
☐ Latching circuit for field sensor troubleshooting.

The PIR-78 is easily located by simply aiming it at the area to be protected while taking into account the shape of the detector's

238

Fig. 5-102. The PIR-78 passive infrared intrusion detector (courtesy of Colorado Electro-Optics, Inc.).

sensitive region of area coverage. The detector zones are in a teardrop pattern. In addition, there are four *downward-looking* zones for close-in protection.

Don't be worried about the unit not being able to fit into a small corner or any other unusually configured wall space. The unit is 4¼″ wide × 7″ high and has a 2″ diameter.

Mounting and wiring the PIR-78 is accomplished very easily because of the plug-in module board design. When the module board is lifted up and away from the base, it leaves the terminal board readily accessible.

Optimum location of the sensor is achieved by properly relating the PIR-78 sensitive region to the area to be protected. The PIR-78 sensitive region is composed of six sensitive zones extending outward from the lens over an angle of about 80°. When mounted in a vertical position, the bottom edge of the senstitive zone is included to the vertical at 45° down to the floor. The unit is placed approximately 8′ above the floor to provide the optimum use. Note that the PIR-78 is most sensitive to motion across the field of view and less sensitive to distant movement toward or away from it. Therefore, it should be localized where it is most likely that an intruder would cross its field of view.

Since the PIR-78 senses changes in temperature, variable temperature objects should not be included within its field of view. Avoid pointing the detector at any heat source or other object that is likely to change temperature during short intervals of time. A partial listing of things to avoid in the protection pattern include:

☐ Refrigerator motors.
☐ Space/water heaters.
☐ Steam radiators.
☐ Open flames (i.e., fireplaces).
☐ Hot/cold air vents.
☐ Outside facing windows.
☐ Incandescent bulbs within 10′.

Also, do not allow drafts of hot or cold air to come into contact with the casing or sunlight and strike the unit's face. Small household pets should be denied access to the protected area when it is activated. If you keep a dog or cat in the home, its presence should be restricted to rooms or areas other than where the PIR-78 is in operation.

Mounting the Detector

The PIR-78 has four Phillips head screws, 16 plastic washers, a nylon cap nut and a plastic insert to cover the walk test light in the unit. A male/female set of pin connectors is also included for the remote walk test light function, along with a piece of insulated tubing. To gain access to the mounting holes in the base and sides of the case, remove the plug-in module board.

Check to see that the nylon cap nut is removed from the top of the unit. Then insert a screwdriver blade into the slot in the front bottom of the unit. With a slight twist, the plug-in module will move upward and away from the base.

Note the upward travel distance of approximately 1″ when mounting the unit near the ceiling. Leave a minimum of 1″ clearance from the ceiling to the top of the PIR base, so that the module can be plugged in and out.

To avoid ground loops when mounting the unit on a conducting surface, use the insulating washers supplied with the unit to isolate the metal case from the surface. Place the washers with the insert in the hole. The flat washers are used on the opposite side. This procedure should preclude the possibility of establishing ground loops.

Note the hexagonal shape of the case. This allows the unit to be mounted flat, at an angle on a wall or directly into a room corner. The unit should be mounted at a suitable height, usually 6′ to 8′ from the floor.

Electrical Connections

Gain access to the terminal board strip by removing the plug-in module board as previously described. The terminal board pins are numbered 1-12 from the top of the unit. Figure 5-103 is a wiring diagram of the terminal board.

Both ac and dc power connections are made to pins 11 and 12. If dc power is used, connection of the positive wire to pin 12 and the ground to pin 11 are made. Do not apply power supply voltage to terminal 9, which is the battery positive. Terminal is for the battery pack only. If the unit you have selected to mount has the battery option, connect the negative wire to pin 11.

Either of the two sets of normally open/closed relay contacts can be used for the alarm circuit. Since these contacts are isolated

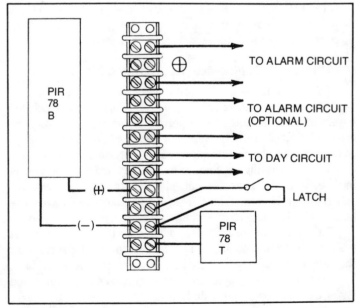

Fig. 5-103. Wiring diagram of the terminal board (courtesy of Colorado Electro-Optics, Inc.).

241

from each other, two separate circuits can be operated simultaneously, if desired.

For a supervised mode operation, connect one lead of the alarm circuit to pin 1 (normally closed) and the other lead to pin 3, the common ground. If the second circuit is to be used, connect between pin 6 (normally closed) and pin 4 (common) for supervised protection.

The tamper circuit will signal an alarm if the equipment case is opened. This circuit can be connected to the alarm day circuit by connecting the day circuit loop to pins 7 and 8 of the terminal board.

Control of the walk test light can be maintained from a remote position. Unplug the walk test light circuit on the back of the circuit board. Wire in pin and sleeve connectors as well as a SPST switch. Size 24 wire will fit this pin connector. Cover the floating connection with a 3/16″ tubing. Do not apply voltage to the walk test light circuit.

The PIR-78 latching function can be activated by shorting together pins 10 and 11. It could be useful to bring this function out of the box with capped wires or to use a SPST switch. Then the latching function can be used for troubleshooting problems without disturbing the case.

The PIR-78 is now wired and ready to operate. Always allow a minimum of five minutes warmup time after power is turned on. Then walk test the unit to check the pattern coverage.

LONG RANGE PULSED INFRARED PHOTOELECTRIC SENSOR

The long range pulsed infrared photoelectric sensor has a 500′ range for reliable outdoor protection (Fig. 5-104). This is included here, instead of with the general perimeter security, as it would be attached to a master control unit that is located inside the home. It would also work the general perimeter and interior alarms.

In an operating system, a momentary alarm condition is initiated whenever the direct optical path between the transmitter and receiver is interrupted. The alarm state deenergizes the output relay which can trigger the alarm system into use.

Because of the broad beam radiated by the transmitter, the IA-502 unit can be installed without special optical alignment tools that would normally be required for other narrow beam devices. The broad beam also facilitates multiple receiver installations and has an excellent operating stability.

For an outdoor installation where an east-west alignment is required, the IA-502 system design includes an automatic sunlight

Fig. 5-104. The IA-502 long range photoelectric sensor (courtesy of Colorado-Electro-Optics, Inc.).

saturation cutoff circuit. It holds the system in an non-alarm state for that short period of time when the rising or setting sun strikes the receiver at the precise angle which would cause the system to signal a false alarm.

Both the receiver and transmitter lens assemblies are heated to prevent internal condensation. An internal switch provides an optical operating mode that cuts off the alarm condition if visibility is reduced slowly, as would occur when fog moves in. This highly reliable detection system includes a built-in rechargeable standby battery and transformer. System specifications are shown in Table 5-6.

Once the locations for the transmitter and receiver have been determined, install the rectangular mounting plates to the mounting surface *with the inserts toward the mounting surface*. Attach the "L" shaped bracket to the plate and the unit to the end of the bracket.

Connect the incoming 12 volt ac to the two exposed terminals in the transmitter. Connect the battery wire (orange) to the positive terminal of the battery. Aim the transmitter at the receiver and carefully align the V notches on top of the transmitter. Tighten down the mounting bolts and replace the cover.

Make the appropriate connections to the five-terminal strip in the receiver beginning from the red painted end as per the following:

☐ 12 volt ac (red mark).
☐ 12 volt ac.
☐ Relay normally open.
☐ Relay common.
☐ Relay normally closed.

Connect the orange battery wire to the positive battery terminal.

Table 5-6. IA-502 System Specifications (courtesy of Colorado Electro-Optics, Inc.).

Range	500 feet
Transmitter Beam Width (typically) *	10 feet at 100 foot range, 20 feet at 300 foot range
Relay Output	S.P.D.T., deenergizes on beam break
Relay Contact Rating	2 amps, 125 volts
Voltage Requirements	12 VAC (transformers supplied)
Standby Capacity	8 hours typically
Sunlight Saturation Cutout	This switch-selectable function locks the receiver in a non-alarm state during operation under rising or setting sun conditions
Lens Heat	The receiver lens assembly is heated to prevent internal condensation
Size	Receiver: 3.0" x 4.5" x 8.0" Transmitter: 3.0" x 4.5" x 8.0"

* The detection pattern is only the direct path between transmitter receiver.

Connect a dc voltmeter to the terminal strip at the bottom of the receiver housing. Set the meter to its low range (readings may range from zero to 3.5 volts dc),. A miniature programming switch is located on the receiver board (red in color). Set both switches to the open position. Align the receiver with the transmitter to obtain a maximum reading on the voltmeter. The red LED on the rear of the receiver will illuminate when the beam is broken.

Should you select this particular unit, Table 5-7 is presented for the selection of the proper wire size per installation. Distances are given in feet from the transformer to the unit and are maximum lengths. Each unit will require a separate transformer.

IP-25 AND IP-50 INFRARED INTRUSION SENSORS

Two other wall mounted CEO passive infrared intrusion sensors include the IP-25 and IP-50. The only difference noticeable in these units are the areas of protection; otherwise, they are identical. Both units are designed for a wide variety of home security applications (Fig. 5-105).

Table 5-7. Wire Guide.

AWG No.	4	6	8	10	12	14	16	18	20	22
Transformer Voltage:										
12 V AC	10000	6250	3850	2500	1550	950	600	350	250	150
16 V AC	30000	18750	11500	7300	4600	2900	1800	1150	700	450
18 V AC	40000	25000	15400	9750	6150	3900	2450	950	950	600

Fig. 5-105. IP-25 and IP-50 passive IR intrusion sensor (courtesy of Colorado Electro-Optics, Inc.).

Like previously discussed CEO units, the IP-25 and IP-50 have heavy metal case plates, strong durable covers and tough germanium lenses to protect the IR detector cell from abuse and vandalism. The many design features which are common to both units include low power consumption, a very low profile, quiet operation, superior RF rejection and conservative ratings for dependable operation. The units are extremely simple and easy to install.

In operation, the infrared sensors detect the rapid changes in infrared radiation that occur within the coverage area. These changes will occur when a person or object, having a temperature which differs from the ambient level, enters the protected area. Since the detectors do not transmit energy or radiation, they cannot interfere with each other. For the same reason, they are totally harmless to both pets and humans.

Both units are designed to be powered from a dc source within the range of 6 to 18 volts. As an alternative source, the CEO PS-1R rechargeable power supply can also be used to operate either unit. The PS-1R is described later.

The IP-25 and IP-50 sensors establish a normal ambient temperature condition and respond when a rapid change is made in the protected area. Because the detectors are entirely passive, they are the most stable and reliable space protective devices available. With no transmitted energy, there is not energy radiation which could be harmful to life. Both these systems are designed to suppress RF interference and will not respond to normal RF signals.

The protective pattern of the IP-25 is shown in Fig. 5-106. The pattern has 10 individual zones covering a total area of 35′ × 25′. The vertical pattern spreads to approximately 4′ at the 35′ range. The IP-50 has four individual zones covering a total area of 20′ × 50′. The vertical pattern spreads to approximately 6′. The IP-50 pattern is shown in Fig. 5-107.

The unit should be mounted in a vertical plane as a higher mounting is possible, but with a corresponding loss of detection directly in front of or below the sensor unit. Avoid mounting locations where sunlight, car headlights, hot/cold heat, open flames, etc., can strike the unit directly or interfere with the infrared detector in operation. Always try to locate the unit sensor at a point where it is most likely to view motion across the pattern.

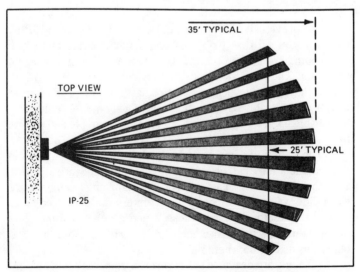

Fig. 5-106. Protective pattern of the IP-25 (courtesy of Colorado Electro-Optics, Inc.).

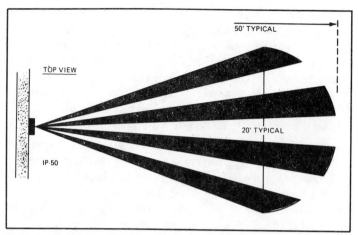

Fig. 5-107. The IP-50 pattern (courtesy of Colorado Electro-Optics, Inc.).

Figure 5-108 illustrates the mounting of the sensor in a vertical position. The cable is routed through the sensor base as follows.

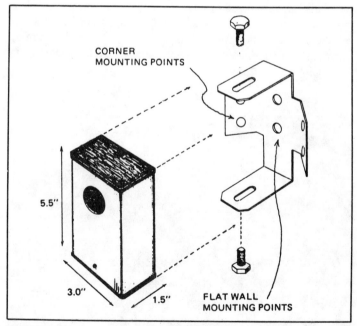

Fig. 5-108. Mounting of the sensor in a vertical sensor (courtesy of Colorado Electro-Optics, Inc.).

Connect the 6-18 volt dc power to the positive and negative terminal strip. Make your loop connections to the appropriate terminals, i.e, the normally open or normally closed circuit.

In testing the system, an LED provides a visual indication of an alarm condition. The light will come on as the unit senses a rapid temperature change in any of the zones of the detection pattern. After completion of the test, the front cover should be placed on the unit and the retaining screws tightened down.

Some panels to which the IP-25 or IP-50 might be connected use a relatively high loop current. Because this may be an inductive load, a high voltage spike is generated which can damage the sensor's relay contacts. A diode is included with the unit to minimize the effect of this spike. The polarity of the loop is measured and the diode is connected across the relay contacts.

In selecting power supplies, certain caution is recommended. Some power supplies use relay transfer from the primary power to the secondary power. In the event of a brownout situation or a slow fadeout of power, a low dc voltage condition may result, causing an alarm from the sensor.

This can be avoided by adding a diode switchover network to the power supply. The minimum supply voltage during transfer will be limited by the battery. This should only be used with relay transfer supplies. Float-charged gel standby systems generally do not employ a relay transfer.

Fig. 5-109. The IA-153 system (courtesy of Colorado Electro-Optics, Inc.).

248

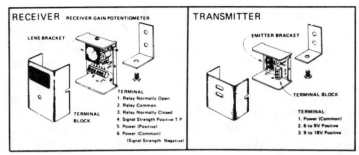

Fig. 5-110. IA-153 receiver and transmitter (courtesy of Colorado Electro-Optics, Inc.).

IA-153 SYSTEM

You might require a broader divergence, and also a greater distance (say over 100') and a full 180° of operation. The IA-153 system from CEO will be just what you need (Fig. 5-109). In addition, both the transmitter's and receiver's optics can be horizontally adjusted up to 20 additional degrees over other type infrared units (Fig. 5-110). This secondary adjustment capability is ideal when an "off-angle" installation is required.

High sensitivity makes possible the use of the photoelectric sensor in many applications such as the penetration of sheet curtains for concealed installations. The wide-beam transmission/reception capability makes it possible for multiple receiver installations in conjunction with one transmitter to provide additional horizontal and/or vertical coverage. Specifications for the IA-153 are shown in Table 5-8.

Table 5-8. IA-153 Specifications (courtesy of Colorado Electro-Optics, Inc.).

Range	150 Feet (nominal)
Transmitter Beam Width (typically)*	30 feet at 25 foot range 25 feet at 50 foot range 20 feet at 100 foot range
Relay Output	S.P.D.T. - Normally Energized. (alarm on broken beam or loss of power)
Relay Contact Rating	100 Ma, 20 volts, resistive.
Size	Receiver: 2.5" x 3.7" x 1.5" Transmitter: 2.5" x 2.3" x 1.3"
Mounting	"L" brackets for general purpose wall mounting supplied. (180° azimuth adj.)
Power Requirements (Recommended power sources include PS-1R or PS-2R rechargeable power supplies or compatible control panel.)	6 to 18 volts DC (Observe Polarity). Current Drain: 6V 12V Receiver: 20 Ma 45 Ma Transmitter: 50 Ma 75 Ma
Alignment Indication	Red LED (on in alarm) and a signal strength output terminal for peaking.

* The detection pattern is only the direct path between the transmitter and the receiver.

249

IA-76 INFRARED PHOTOELECTRIC SENSOR UNIT

CEO has also made available a wall-recessed and mounted pulsed passive infrared photoelectric sensor unit, the IA-76 (Fig. 5-111). Like others of its type, it has a broad beam transmitter and is excellent for use in areas and situations where other bulky, externally mounted sensing units are not acceptable.

In operation, an invisible pulse-modulated infrared beam can be transmitted up to a distance of 150', well over that required in any home. Any interruption of the beam deactivates the SPDT output relay that activates the alarm relay in the master security control unit.

IP-37 SENSOR

The CEO IP-37 is another of the wall-mounted and recessed sensors (Fig. 5-112). The sensing coverage pattern is illustrated in Fig. 5-113. This is as seen from above. Four active zones in the familiar teardrop pattern monitor the area.

Like other units, the relay is supervised (energized in the non-alarm state). The power consumption is typically about 10 milliamperes at 6 volts dc. This level would drain a battery powered system very rapidly, but lower power operation can be achieved in the IP-37 by clipping the wire loop which sits next to the terminal strip. This reverses the function of the relay (energized only in alarm) and limits the alarm pulse to about .5 second. In this mode, you can safely rely upon a year or more of battery life with the IP-37.

Fig. 5-111. The IA-76 (courtesy of Colorado Electro-Optics, Inc.).

HA-99 RESIDENTIAL INTRUSION DETECTOR

The purchase by the homeowner of the *CEO HA-99 Residential Intrusion Detector* (Fig. 5-114) is an important investment and a very positive step toward home safety and security. Because of very moderate pricing, the homeowner may now have the same protection long used by industry.

The Residential Intrusion Detector (RID) is attractively designed to look like a stereo speaker cabinet, but it is an electronic unit which represents a major advance in residential protection. Requiring no wiring, the RID gives the advantage of immediate protection after installation. Simply set the RID in the desired location, turn it on, and it will protect home and property

Fig. 5-112. The IP-37 passive infrared intrusion sensor (courtesy of Colorado Electro-Optics, Inc.).

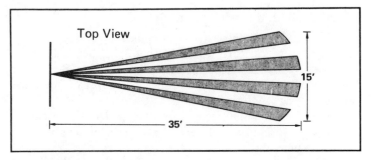

Fig. 5-113. The sensing coverage pattern (courtesy of Colorado Electro-Optics, Inc.).

by sounding a loud alarm when it senses the presence of an intruder.

Most burglars are opportunists. They enter the home quickly during the daytime or nighttime and wish to exit *quickly and quietly*. Since over 80% of burglaries are committed by the inexperienced juvenile offender, the loud and piercing sound of the RID alarm horn will quickly drive them out of the home. The RID may also be connected to most types of perimeter systems for additional protection.

The HA-99 unit utilizes the passive infrared technology, which is the most reliable and sensitive intrusion protection available. Passive means it will emit no energy of any type. The sensor is designed to specifically detect the warm body radiation of an intruder. The following features make the RID HA-99 the safe and reliable home security protection you want and need:

—Battery power for easy installation and maintenance.
—Unique vertical aiming device.
—Visual walk and battery test lights.
—Accessory relay contacts.
—Entry/exit delay.
—Automatic reset.

This unit is ideal for use in all residential settings including the single family dwelling, apartments, mobile homes and condominiums. Figure 5-115 shows the front, back and bottom view of the HA-99 unit and the various parts.

The RID is intended for local alarm use. The area of coverage is relatively large. One unit will protect a room or area approximately 20′ × 25′.

Horizontal coverage has six adjacent zones, three to each side of the detector center line. The field of view is 60°.

252

Fig. 5-114. The HA-99 infrared intrusion detector (courtesy of Colorado Electro-Optics, Inc.).

Vertical coverage is affected by the focusing mirror within the cabinet which is adjustable. The view is 8°. At a distance of 10′ from the unit, the field is approximately 16¼′; at 25′ from the unit, the field of view becomes 42′.

The vertical aiming level gives the homeowner additional control of the protected area. It allows for the adjustment of the mirror, leaving the floor area clear for freedom of movement of small pets through the protected area, while still giving protection and sensing the presence of an intruder. With other intrusion detection devices, any movement within the area, including pets, blowing curtains, etc., will cause an unwanted alarm. The lever is located at the bottom of the detector and can be tilted up or down 15° from the horizontal.

Normal adjustment of the vertical would be +5° or +10°. If the unit were located in a high place, the lever would probably be adjusted downward 5-10° for compensation. Like other units, the location of the RID is important to ensure the maximum optimum coverage.

POWER SUPPLIES

Various units previously described require an uninterruptible dc power supply while employing maintenance free 1.2 amp-hour batteries for standby power. The PS-1R and 2R are rechargeable power supplies for 6 and 12 volt operation with standby power (Fig. 5-116). Primary power is provided by the plug-in transformer

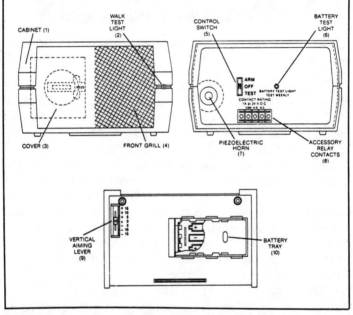

Residential Intrusion Detector...
Parts Identification

1. Cabinet—easy care, plastic woodgrain finish

2. Walk Test Light

3. Polyethylene cover which admits thermal energy to focusing mirror and sensor

4. Front Grill

5. Control Switch

6. Battery Test Light

7. Piezoelectric Horn

8. Accessory Relay Contacts

9. Vertical Aiming Lever

10. Battery Tray

Fig. 5-115. Front, back and bottom views of the HA-99 unit (courtesy of Colorado Electro-Optics, Inc.).

which is part of the basic power supply package for these units. A constant voltage charging technique is used to maximize battery life while allowing for wide variations in the external load. Both high current and current limited outputs are provided for alarm applications with these two units. Specifications for the PS-1R and 2R are provided in Table 5-9.

The PS-1R uninterruptible power source uses a maintenance free rechargeable lead-acid battery to provide 1.2 ampere-hours of

Fig. 5-116. The PS-1R and 2R (courtesy of Colorado Electro-Optics, Inc.).

standby capacity at 6 volts. A constant voltage charging circuit is employed to assure maximum life from the battery while also providing continuous current to an external load. The PS-2R provides the same ampere-hour at a standby capacity of 12 volts.

Depending upon the security system or individual unit you have selected for home protection, you should definitely consider the worthwhile investment of the proper battery for the system. In some systems, the battery is the main source of power; in others, it supplies current to the system when the regular ac is off.

Various types of batteries are available. Most of them will fit one or more of the many systems on the market. Check the system instruction book for the specific battery requirements. Select only a battery that is in the instruction booklet; don't rely upon a possibly inferior product that will not perform when you need it most.

Table 5-9. PS-1R and 2R Specifications (courtesy of Colorado Electro-Optics, Inc.).

	PS-1R	PS-2R
Nominal Voltage	6VDC	12VDC
Standby Capacity	1.2 AH	1.2AH
Maximum Continuous Load	300Ma.	300Ma.
Maximum Intermittent Load	3 A	3 A
Protective Circuit	6V, 30 Ma.	12V, 30 Ma.
Size (inches)	4.3 x 2.5 x 2.0	4.3 x 2.5 x 3.0

Fig. 5-117. Auxiliary power supply (courtesy of NuTone Division, Scovill Inc.).

The auxiliary power supply (Fig. 5-117) is used to turn on your house lights, both interior and/or exterior, when the detection circuits trigger an alarm. The lights will flash for an intrusion or stay on for fire, facilitating the exit of all persons in the house. The unit can also be used to activate an auxiliary high-intensity alarm or motor-driven siren. The auxiliary relay is a surface mounted device using 12 volts dc power when activated. The relay contact rating is 1000 watts or 120 volts ac, 8.3 amps, at 80% power factor.

PLUNGER DETECTORS AND SWITCHES

You may want to use recessed plunger detectors for various applications on perimeter doors and windows (Fig. 5-118), or a two-part detector which uses an invisible pulsed beam. Interruption of this beam will activate the system alarm unit. This is ideal for the protection of various entrances, hallways, seldom-used rooms or larger indoor areas (Fig. 5-119).

Fig. 5-118. Recessed plunger detector (courtesy of NuTone Division, Scovill Inc.).

Fig. 5-119. Infrared detector (courtesy of NuTone Division, Scovill Inc.).

You may also wish to add to your system a key switch (Fig. 5-120) to allow for activation or deactivation of a particular circuit at times when you cannot reach the master control unit.

An outdoor remote switch includes both red and green LEDs. Green indicates the system is armed. Red indicates that there has been an alarm timeout, i.e., the possibility that the intruder may still be within the home.

Depending upon which manufacturer you select, you will find a variety of devices that can be added to the system to give it more flexibility and also provide you with increased security. In many cases, certain devices will adapt from one manufacturer to another.

Fig. 5-120. Key switch (courtesy of NuTone Division, Scovill Inc.).

TELEPHONE DIALER

Earlier we discussed at length the NuTone 2300 system. Suppose you have selected this system and installed it. You think, "Well, suppose I am in the other portion of the house and manage to set off the alarm, but none of the neighbors are home. I'm quite a distance away from the main road, so nobody traveling by will hear the alarm. Maybe I should get an automatic telephone dialer."

Maybe this doesn't quite fit your exact line of thinking, or the situation is not quite right, but it could happen. So you decide to get the telephone dialer (Fig. 5-121) — that is, if you can install it, and if it will fit into the system you have just finished installing. One main thing to remember is that a telephone dialer should not be installed on a party line service. If the party line is being used, the dialer will not be able to dial out. The dialer presented here is from NuTone and matches the comprehensive home security system described earlier.

Dialer Location

The telephone dialer should be located inside a closet that is near the security system master control unit. This location is convenient for testing purposes and for concealment.

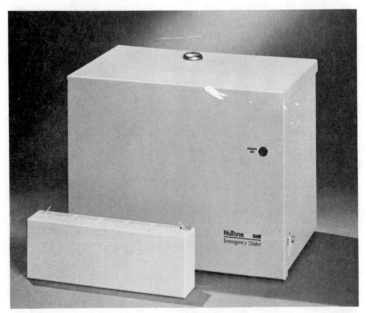

Fig. 5-121. Telephone dialer (courtesy of NuTone Division, Scovill Inc.).

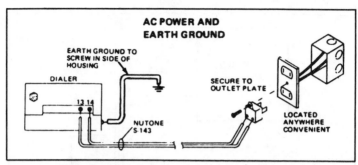

Fig. 5-122. Ground dialer housing (courtesy of NuTone Division, Scovill Inc.).

Wiring the Dialer

Four sets of wires will have to be run for this unit. Depending upon the specific model you select, you will be using standard 18 gauge, flat or twisted wire.

Run One. 18/2 gauge wire from the plug-in transformer to terminals 13 and 14 of the dialer. Locate the plug-in transformer in any convenient ac outlet.

Run Two. Ground dialer housing. Run 14 gauge wire from the screw in the side of the dialer housing to an earth ground source (Fig. 122).

Run Three. Run 18/2 cable from the master control unit to the dialer (Fig. 5-123).

Run Four. Make the appropriate connections to the telephone lines. The NuTone dialer, like others, is registered with the FCC. Under FCC regulations, a proper connection must be made between the dialer and the telephone lines.

Connecting the Dialer to Telephone Lines

There are two methods to connect the dialer to the telephone lines. A telephone coupler is *not* required by FCC regulations. Check the telephone company (Interconnect Department) for their specific requirements for connecting the dialer. The company may permit direct connection into the main entry connector block or may require that the telephone jack be used. The RJ31X telephone jack (supplied and installed by the telephone company), when properly connected, provides for "line seizure" for the dialer. The jack must be connected between the main entry connector block and the household telephone. Wiring is in Fig. 5-124.

Another method is to connect the dialer to the main entry connector block. For direct wiring to the telephone lines, wire the

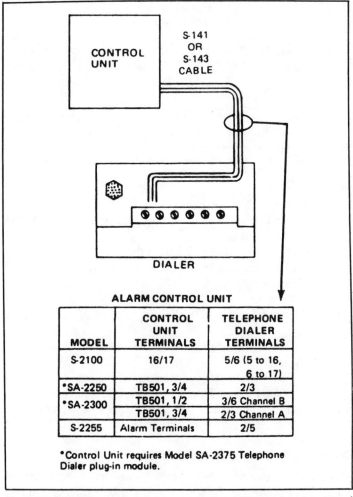

MODEL	CONTROL UNIT TERMINALS	TELEPHONE DIALER TERMINALS
S-2100	16/17	5/6 (5 to 16, 6 to 17)
*SA-2250	TB501, 3/4	2/3
*SA-2300	TB501, 1/2	3/6 Channel B
	TB501, 3/4	2/3 Channel A
S-2255	Alarm Terminals	2/5

*Control Unit requires Model SA-2375 Telephone Dialer plug-in module.

Fig. 5-123. Run 18/2 cable from the master control unit to the dialer (courtesy of NuTone Division, Scovill Inc.).

main entry block. Otherwise, there will be no direct line seizure for the dialer. Figure 5-125 outlines the procedure. In locating the correct line, use a dc voltmeter set at the 0-50 VDC scale. Locate the pair of wires in the connector block that gives a reading of approximately 48 volts. When the telephone is picked up, voltage on these wires drops to 7 volts. Use a telephone headset and locate the wire pair that gives the dial tone. If you have a multi-line system, locate the marked terminal box and find the terminals marked "T" and "R." These wires may be red and green, as some of the previous wires may be.

Disconnect the *red* incoming telephone line from the block and connect to terminal 8 on the dialer. Connect a wire from terminal 7 of the dialer to the block terminal where the red wire from the telephone was connected. Connect a wire from terminal 9 on the dialer to the block where the green wires are connected.

If battery backup is desired for the dialer, use the proper rechargeable battery. With the NuTone system dialer, the proper battery is illustrated in Fig. 5-126. Never use a dry cell battery; the dial battery charger (built-in) will damage the dry cell and also the telephone dialer. Connect the battery to the positive dialer terminal (11) and the negative one (12).

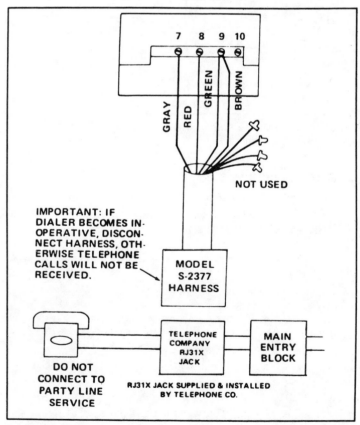

Fig. 5-124. Connecting the dialer to telephone lines (courtesy of NuTone Division, Scovill Inc.).

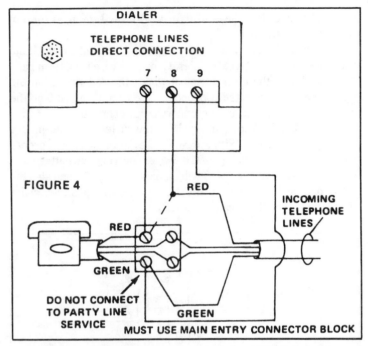

Fig. 5-125. Connecting the dialer to the main entry connector block (courtesy of NuTone Division, Scovill Inc.).

ALARM BELLS AND HORNS

Bells and *horns* are extremely important to the home security system. What good does it do if you have no internal or external alarm device to loudly signal that an intrusion is being attempted?

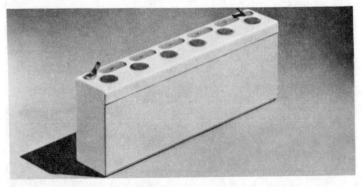

Fig. 5-126. Battery for the dialer (courtesy of NuTone Division, Scovill Inc.).

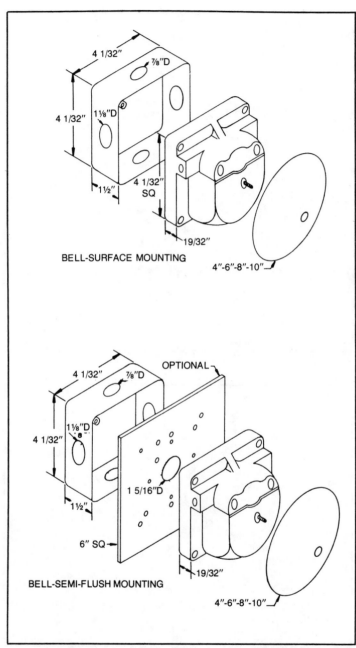

4 1/32"
7/8"D
4 1/32"
1 1/8"D
1 1/2"
4 1/32"
SQ
19/32"

BELL-SURFACE MOUNTING

4"-6"-8"-10"

4 1/32"
7/8"D
OPTIONAL
4 1/32"
1 1/8"D
1 1/2"
1 5/16"D
6" SQ
19/32"

BELL-SEMI-FLUSH MOUNTING

4"-6"-8"-10"

Fig. 5-127. Surface mounting and semi-flush mounting for a bell (courtesy of Fire-Lite Alarms Inc.).

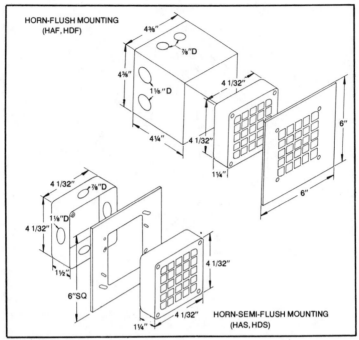

Fig. 5-128. Flush and semi-flush mounting for a horn (courtesy of Fire-Lite Alarms Inc.).

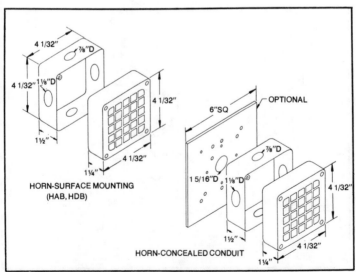

Fig. 5-129. A horn can be surface mounted or mounted with a concealed electrical conduit (courtesy of Fire-Lite Alarms Inc.).

Burglar alarm bells and horns are available with a purchased unit or can be obtained separately. You have either surface mounting or semi-flush mounting bells. Both have the basic electrical mounting box to which the actual alarm unit is attached. In the case of the semi-flush mounting bell, the electrical box can be mounted into the wall. Then an optional panel is attached to which the bell is then affixed. In the surface unit, the electrical box is attached to the wall. Figure 5-127 illustrates these two units and the mounting layout.

Burglar horns can also be flush, semi-flush, surface or mounted with a concealed electrical conduit. These are illustrated in Figs. 5-128 and 5-129.

Smoke and Fire Detection Systems and Devices

During the past year, approximately 10,000 people died in fires. More than 75% of these people died in residential fires. If the homes had been equipped with an early warning fire detector or complete fire detection system, it can be reasonably assumed that over 60% of the people might have been saved. With the opportunity to save so many lives, it becomes incumbent upon everyone to have a fire detection system or smoke detector in the home. At least 20 million smoke detectors have been installed in American homes. Their effectiveness is repeatedly demonstrated over and over again.

TYPES OF DETECTION DEVICES

Detector sensors can be either *ionization* or *photoelectric* models. In general, though, neither the ionization nor the photoelectric models are superior to one another. Whenever possible, it is recommended that both types be used in order to ensure maximum efficiency and the earliest possible alert of a fire.

All smoke detectors used should be UL tested. A UL label mark appears on each unit that has been approved. This means the product has been objectively tested for safety and workability. Over 60 UL standards apply to the detector construction and electronics involved.

Note that the ionization detector responds slightly better to a flaming fire, while the photoelectric detector responds slightly better to a smoky fire. Neither one is considered superior to the other in general use.

Detectors must be optimumly placed so that early warning of a potential fire alerts the residents. Outside (sometimes inside) bedrooms, main through-home hallways, etc., are considered prime areas for their location. Figure 6-1 illustrates a smoke detector installed in a hallway. Note that it is located over 3' from an air register. Installed closer, the air register might blow smoke away from the detector, precluding an early alarm of imminent danger to the household. Likewise, the detector should not be installed between an air return and the sleeping area. This would only cause the smoke to be recirculated and thus diluted. Again, it would result in an alarm delay which could imperil the entire family.

Statitrol SmokeGard Model 809A

The *Statitrol SmokeGard* contains the *dual alarm comparator* (the DAC) which provides for the earliest possible alarm sounding in case of a smoke buildup in the home (Fig. 6-2). Figure 6-3 illustrates the DAC principle. The DAC design provides for the improved detection of *low* smoke concentrations. This unique feature allows for excellent protection from both fast and smoldering type fires.

Features of the battery-powered unit (the model 809A) include:

—DAC.
—Battery is ready when you get the unit.
—Audible "clock" indicates a weak battery.
—Extremely easy installation—no wiring is necessary.
—No special maintenance required of the unit.
—Battery life is one year *or more*.
—Piezoelectric horn.
—Push to test button—tests the horn, battery and electronic circuitry to assure proper operation of the detector.

Stratitrol SmokeGard Model 907

The Statitrol SmokeGard (model 907) also has the DAC feature. This is a hard-wired unit, connecting into your home wiring. With this unit, make sure the electrical circuit is not controlled by a normal light switch, but only from the main circuit breaker box. It doesn't help to have it installed on a switch circuit

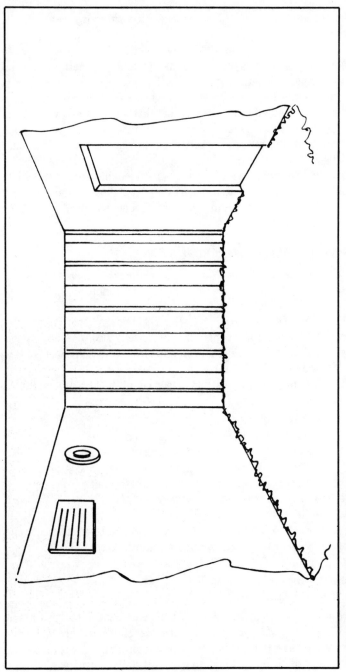

Fig. 6-1. A smoke detector installed in a hallway.

only to learn, too late, that the switch was turned off the night you needed it.

An accessory relay with one set of SPDT contacts is available for use with the SmokeGard. This accessory relay is conveniently designed to be installed remotely from the smoke detector in an electrical panel or other accessible wiring location. It enables the user to have the capability of initiating remote alarm devices such as an external horn, bells, lights, telephone dialers, etc.

Fire-Lite Smoke Detector SD-34

The *Fire-Lite automatic smoke detector*, the *SD-34* is a photoelectric type using a LED source with a rated 40 year service life (Fig. 6-4). Operating on the light scattering principle, the SD-34 has a detection chamber which extends beyond the main housing to provide the best possible smoke entry from any direction. The nominal 1.5% per foot fixed sensitivity calibration of the unit assures early response to slow, smoldering fires. As very rapidly developing fires are possible, an exclusive rate compensation principle senses the abnormal rate of smoke movement, initiating the alarm at a higher sensitivity level, which will insure

Fig. 6-2. The SmokeGard (courtesy of Statitrol Division of Emerson Electric Co.).

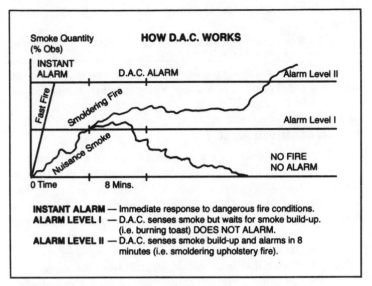

Fig. 6-3. The DAC principle (courtesy of Statitrol Division of Emerson Electric Co.).

that all occupants are alerted at the earliest possible moment. This unit comes in 6 volt, 12 volt, 24 volt or regular household ac electrical power. Typical wiring for a single loop (Class B) panel of double loop (Class A) panel is shown in Fig. 6-5.

Fire-Lite Alarms SD-77 and SD-79

The next two alarms are the residential battery powered smoke detectors by Fire-Lite Alarms, the SD-77 and SD-79 (Figs. 6-6 and 6-7). The Sentry detectors are photoelectric and are highly reliable. Attractive as well as functional, the Sentry combines light weight with rugged durability. Both series are designed for the highest resistance to nuisance alarms. The SD-77 is available with a locking device which deters unauthorized removal of the detector, and the SD-79 is available with or without a 135°F thermal switch. These detectors have a self-contained alarm horn.

Want to test the system to see if it is operational? Just push the button located near the center of the unit front. The LED will come on.

SD-4 Smoke Detector

The SD-4 smoke detector (Fig. 6-8) is a standard outlet plug-in model. The SD-5 is the same except it can be attached directly to a junction box via pigtail leads.

270

Fig. 6-4. The SD-34 smoke detector (courtesy of Fire-Lite Alarms Inc.).

The SD-4 Sentinel detector operates from the household circuit. The detection chamber in the SD-4 is impervious to ambient light. A regulated amount of light is purposely introduced into the darkened chamber and focused to form a sharp beam. Smoke particles entering the chamber cause part of the light beam to be scattered onto the photoelectric cell surface. Exposure of the cell to this reflected light causes its resistance to decrease appreciably which results in an alarm condition. Each Sentinel is equipped with an alarm horn which has a loudness of 85 decibels at 10' away.

Fire-Lite Heat Detector Model Series 40

The *Fire-Lite heat detector* (model series 40) (Fig. 6-9) is a fusible link, fixed temperature detector. It can cover 900 square feet when in operation and is set at 135°F. The fusible link is replaceable and, when popped out, causes a trouble light at the alarm panel to be activated.

The detector doesn't look particularly great by itself, so there is a protective covering. In addition to "dressing" up the detector element, it protects against possible damage and prevents unauthorized removal of the standard heat collector. The cover will fit snugly over the detector body and is secured underneath the

271

TYPICAL WIRING FOR SINGLE LOOP PANEL

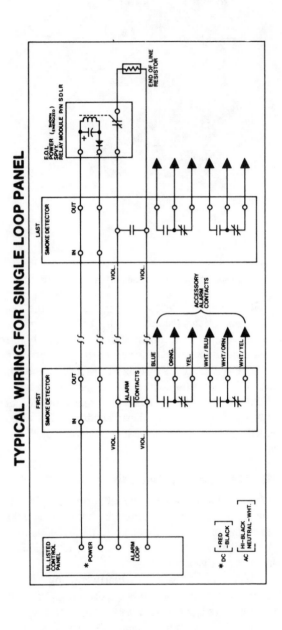

TYPICAL WIRING FOR DOUBLE LOOP PANEL

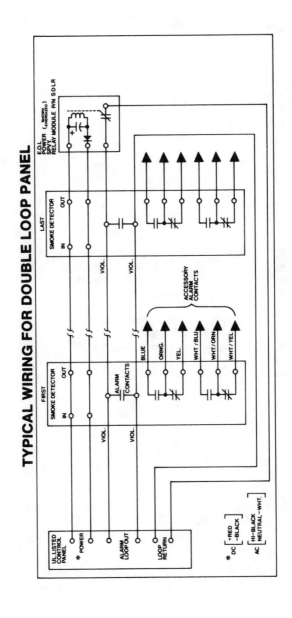

Fig. 6-5. Wiring from single loop and double loop panels (courtesy of Fire-Lite Alarms Inc.).

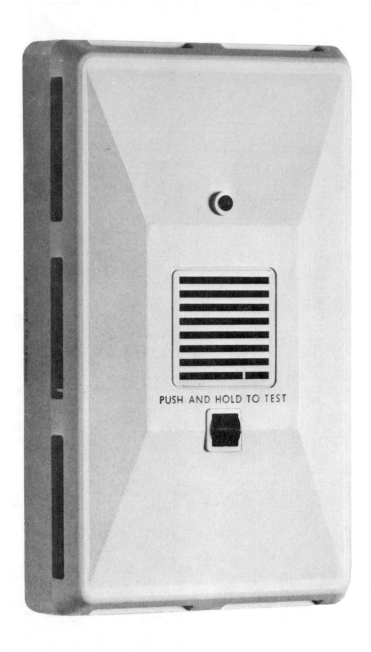

PUSH AND HOLD TO TEST

Fig. 6-6. The SD-77 smoke detector (courtesy of Fire-Lite Alarms Inc.).

Fig. 6-7. The SD-79 smoke detector (courtesy of Fire-Lite Alarms Inc.).

detector mounting screws. Regular operation of the detector is not affected with this cover.

Let's examine a low voltage control panel (Fig. 6-10). This control panel is the basic fire alarm control unit, single zone, designed for use with heat, manual station alarm, smoke and/or ionization detection devices. The control can be used in homes and the solid state circuitry will provide for a long life and excellent system reliability. The unit can be either a single, two or four zone, depending upon the application. It can be expanded to include an optional plug-in relay and contacts, for remote operations when dry contact is required, and has automatic trickle chargers for standby power requirements using a gel type battery.

THE EFFECTIVENESS OF DETECTORS

Over 300,000 people are injured each year by fire in the home. Many home fire injuries are caused by smoke, not flames. You may have used the home safety check that is provided by various fire

Fig. 6-8. SD-4 smoke detector (courtesy of Fire-Lite Alarms Inc.).

departments, but this is only a start. It is only a start for the prevention of fires, not what to do and how to react when a fire starts. A comprehensive fire check is provided at the end of this chapter for your review and use.

Many deaths and injuries occur in fires that happen at night when people are sound asleep. A reliable way to awaken these sleepers before the smoke becomes dense would help more people escape safely, and that's what this chapter is all about. There is a way—the home smoke and fire detection systems that are available at many local outlets.

Should you have a home smoke and/or fire detector or a complete system? If you're not sure, then you share some of the same misconceptions that make many people underestimate the danger from fires. Such misconceptions, such as "The smell of smoke would wake me," and "There's usually plenty of time to get out," or, maybe, "Fires only happen to other people," are the views of people who really don't care, are not interested or, in many instances, are more concerned about saving money than about true safety.

Detectors won't prevent fires. They won't protect property (especially when you aren't at home) and they won't put out the fire for you. What they will do is increase your chances of escaping the fire and alerting the fire department.

IONIZATION DETECTORS

The ionization principle depends on the fact that even a very weak source of radiation will increase the ability of air to conduct electricity. In these detectors, a small and carefully shielded bit of radioactive material ionizes the air in the detector's sensing chamber. As a result, a very weak electrical current flows through that chamber and is sensed by the detector's circuit. When enough particles of smoke have entered the chamber, the current flow is reduced. As it drops below the acceptable threshold, the detector circuit activates the alarm horn or buzzer.

Smoke particles don't have to be very large to reduce the flow of the ionization detector's smoke chamber. Since hot blazing fires

Fig. 6-9. The model 45 heat detector (courtesy of Fire-Lite Alarms Inc.).

Fig. 6-10. Control panel (courtesy of Fire-Lite Alarms Inc.).

tend to produce more smaller smoke particles, and since these flow with the air currents and float further in the hot rising air from the fire, ionization detectors usually have a slight edge in giving an early warning of open, high intensity flames from a fire.

You might wonder about the radiation from the ionization detector. According to the United States Nuclear Regulatory Commission, if you held an ionization detector close to you for eight hours a day throughout an entire year, you would receive only one-tenth as much radiation as you would receive on one round trip airline flight across the United States.

PHOTOELECTRIC DETECTORS

The other most frequently purchased type of home detector uses the photoelectric principle (Fig. 6-11). It detects smoke by seeing it in much the same way as our eyes do—by means of light reflected by particles of smoke.

When particles of smoke are carried into the detector by room air circulating through it, they each reflect or scatter light from a small lamp in the photoelectric detector unit. Some of this reflected light falls on a photocell, causing it to produce a slight

Fig. 6-11. A plug-in photoelectric detector (courtesy of NuTone Division, Scovill Inc.).

electrical current. As more particles enter and scatter more light onto the photocell, more electricity is generated. Finally, when the smoke particles are dense enough to reflect a preset amount of light, the detector circuit actuates the alarm.

Because they sense the light reflected by the smoke particles, photoelectric smoke detectors detect larger particles more readily than they can sense the invisible particles to which ionization detectors can respond. It happens that cooler, smoldering fires produce more of these large particles than do hot, blazing fires. Photoelectric detectors are somewhat more likely to give the alarm while a fire is still smoldering.

Remember, though, that many household fires produce detectable amounts of *both* visible and invisible smoke. Either kind of detector has a high probability of giving you enough warning for a safe escape. To really cover all the possibilities, it is highly recommended that each and every home install at least one of both types of smoke detectors.

HEAT DETECTORS

Some manufacturers offer a heat sensing device either as a standard or an optional part of their smoke detection systems, or as an independent unit that you can use with your current fire detection system. A piece of specially-formed metal is often used which either melts or distorts because of heat in the air around it. Heat detectors built into smoke detectors are usually set off by this occurrence or by a rate-of-rise type thermostat that will set off the main detector's alarm when a certain temperature is exceeded. Separate detection devices sound their own alarm or send an electrical signal to a central alarm.

Heat detectors do add protection. Whether or not you choose to use one is up to you. They are especially useful in environments that could fool or disable some smoke detectors such as a kitchen, where grease particles in the air might cause a smoke detector's sensors to give off a flase alarm. Properly selected heat detectors can also be used in areas that are too hot or cold for smoke detectors to function properly such as attics, furnace rooms and attached garages.

A heat sensor is no substitute for a smoke detector. Remember, it is more often the smoke that causes injury or death than the heat of a home fire. A heat detector is capable of totally ignoring a smoldering fire that is putting out lethal amounts of smoke.

HOUSE CURRENT AND BATTERY-OPERATED DETECTORS

Should you use house current or battery-operated detectors? The answer to this question depends on where you plan to put your detector, how likely you are to test it or the system on a regular basis, and even the likelihood of power failures where you live.

Detectors that operate on batteries tend to take less time and fewer tools to install. Usually most of the effort is devoted to physically attaching the detector itself to the ceiling or wall. This may be done with screws, adhesives or expansion fasteners, depending upon the manufacturer. Once the battery-powered unit is mounted, the owner simply slips in the battery, tests the unit and the job is done. In about a year the detector will begin to emit a "beep" every minute or so, and it will keep this up for as long as a week to tell the owner that the battery should be replaced.

Detectors which operate on household electric current have the power needed to operate as long as there is current to the circuit where they are connected. However, installation is a little more time-consuming with these units if they are not a direct plug-in type. They must be attached directly into the house wiring, which may mean getting the services of an electrician if a person is not "electrically-minded."

A problem can arise, however, when the best location for the detector (in terms of air flow or nearness to the bedrooms) may not have a convenient outlet. In such an instance, it will be necessary to have an electrical outlet installed in the proper location. Avoid having an extension cord put on the detector. It is more likely that if you need a cord "for a minute or so," you may forget to replace it. The cord could be worked loose by kids playing around the cord.

In the event of power failures, detectors which operate on household current will become inoperable, except for those units which contain a standby battery operational mode. In most regions, this may be a somewhat rare event. If power outages are frequent where you live, you might think twice about depending totally on only this type of warning detector.

It is also possible that a fire could actually start in the circuit which supplies power to the detector, and power to the unit might fail before the alarm sounds. However, this is extremely remote and does not appear to be a significant danger.

THE KIND AND NUMBER OF DETECTORS

Because most home fires produce a mixture of smoke types, with a detectable amount of large and small particle smoke early in the fire's growth, either an ionization or a photoelectric detector will meet most needs. Rather than to delay a purchase while you decide between them, just buy one and get it installed immediately. The type you get will provide a greater amount of protection than having no smoke detector at all. At a later date, if you feel the need, another protector of the other type can be purchased and installed.

The number of detectors needed is an important consideration. Tests conducted for the United States Bureau of Standards show that two detectors on different levels of a two story home are twice as likely to provide an adequate amount of time for escape as one detector. The upstairs detector senses smoke wherever it originates, while the downstairs unit will react sooner to a fire which could block escape routes through the first floor.

One detector gives more protection than no detector. Two detectors, if properly installed, provide a more reliable early warning than one. Having two detectors also lets you select an ionization type and a photoelectric model, giving you the best capabilities of both. It also lets you have one battery-powered and one plug-in or direct-wired model, so that neither a battery failure nor a power outage leaves your family defenseless. Finally, two detectors are far less likely to be both "on the blink" when needed than a lone detector might be.

The more detectors you have that are properly situated throughout the home, the greater chance you have of an early detection of a potential disaster. Whenever possible, don't just use the minimum number (2) because somebody you know says so. You know the design of your home, the number of people, the distances to a safe exit, etc. Only you can determine the minimum number required.

This brings up the problem of where to install the detector. Location depends upon the size and layout of the home and on where the family members sleep.

Since the primary function of the detector is to awaken sleeping persons and to warn of early danger, the most critical requirement is to put the detectors as close as possible to the bedrooms in which the family sleeps. If two sleeping areas are separated by any significant distance, each should have its own detector.

Next you should consider the probable path along which smoke would flow from the rest of the home. In a single floor home, this usually means placing the detector in the hallway off of which all bedrooms open. In a home where the bedrooms are upstairs, or in the basement, the detector should be near the top of the stairs to the bedroom area. The simplest rule for locating the basic (or, perhaps the only) detector in the home should be between the bedrooms and the rest of the house, but closer to the bedrooms.

If you're installing multiple detectors, and you've put one near each sleeping area, it is a good idea to make certain there is one on each level of the home. The basement ceiling, near the steps to the rest of the home, is another good location. For extra protection, consider putting a detector in each bedroom, especially if the occupant might be tempted to smoke in bed on occasion. This is especially appropriate if any family members sleep with the bedroom doors shut. Closed bedroom doors actually offer some protection against smoke and fire from outside the room, but they will also make it more difficult to hear a detector alarm situated a short distance from the bedroom. Furthermore, they can keep smoke produced by a fire in a bedroom from reaching a detector in the hall. A detector in the bedroom will serve to awaken the sleeping person before the smoke concentration in the closed room reaches a dangerous level.

THE RIGHT LOCATION FOR A DETECTOR

Check the instructions that may come with the detector. The directions may recommend installing the detector on the ceiling or walls between 6-12″ from the ceiling. This not only takes advantage of the fact that smoke rises, but it also puts the detector safely above accidental bumps and the hands of young children. There is one place *not* to put the detector. Don't put it within 6″ of where a wall and ceiling meet, on either surface. This has proven to be a "dead air" space that gets little air circulation.

Some peculiarities of air flow and ceiling temperatures need to be considered in certain installations. Excessive clean air flow across a detector can keep smoke-filled air from reaching the smoke chamber of the detector. This can happen if the detector is mounted in front of an air supply duct outlet or between the bedroom and furnance cold air return. In either of these instances, relatively clean air may still be "washing" the detector, even when most of the air in the home is unbreathable.

Avoid putting the detector on a ceiling which is substantially warmer or colder than the rest of the house. In either case, an invisible *thermal barrier* near the surface can prevent smoke from reaching the detector. This can be a problem in mobile homes or in older, poorly insulated homes. In such cases, mounting the unit on an inside wall between 12-18″ from the ceiling should provide reliable operation.

NU TONE DETECTORS

NuTone has come out with a variety of home detection units which are highly acceptable for use. The direct-wire photoelectric smoke detectors (Fig. 6-12) provide for a custom designed large-scale integrated circuitry, with an exclusive smoke chamber design incorporating totally unobstructed openings that will permit a faster smoke entry. This means the alarm warning will sound much more earlier than normal. The LEDs in the unit consist of a pulsed infrared light emitting diode and also a photodiode light sensing element which will continuously monitor the air within the smoke chamber. This unique feature is shown in Fig. 6-13.

The in-unit horn can be expanded by the use of an auxiliary power supply (Fig. 6-14) and a relay module (Fig. 6-15). You can

Fig. 6-12. Direct-wire photoelectric smoke detector (courtesy of NuTone Division, Scovill Inc.).

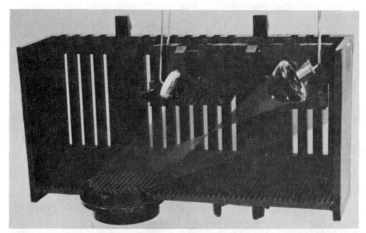

Fig. 6-13. The light sensing photodiode will monitor the air within the smoke chamber (courtesy of NuTone Division, Scovill Inc.).

connect the direct-wire smoke detectors to additional alarms both inside and outside the home, thereby increasing substantially the area over which the emergency signal will be carried. The NuTone telephone dialer can also be connected with the detectors and relay so a message summoning the fire department goes out automatically in an emergency.

The auxiliary power supply is needed to operate the additional inside and/or outside alarms. The number of alarms that can be used varies with the load requirements of your choice of alarms. Always check the instruction sheets that accompany the various alarms to see what the maximum load will be. The relay module activates the auxiliary power supply which is used to sound the remote alarms connected to the detectors.

Fig. 6-14. Auxiliary power supply (courtesy of NuTone Division, Scovill Inc.).

Fig. 6-15. Relay module (courtesy of NuTone Division, Scovill Inc.).

By use of these added units, you have created a smoke alarm system that can be wired in series thorughout the home. If one detects smoke, the alarm will still sound throughout the complete series.

Plug-in smoke detectors are extremely popular in the home. The convenient plug-in model from NuTone is a new product in an engineered line of photoelectric detectors. It has a custom designed integrated circuitry and the unobstructed opening for a faster smoke entry. Like other products, the horn sounds at a loud 85 decibels. The 9′ cord provides for easy connection to nearby wall outlets without the need for an extension cord. Also, a safety-lock feature is provided on the plug so it will not be knocked loose from the ac receptacle.

The battery operated detector (Fig. 6-16) also contains the uniquely designed integrated circuitry and smoke chamber for earlier and faster sensing of smoke. It uses the inexpensive 9 volt alkaline battery. When replacement is needed, the alarm horn will momentarily sound every 30 seconds for a minimum of seven days before the battery goes completely dead. The battery operated detectors can also be used in mobile homes, boats, campers and outbuildings where volatile liquids may be stored.

You may decide to wire a detector to a remote alarm, to remote alarms and/or the auxiliary relay for the lights and telephone dialer, or possibly just to a telephone dialer. Figure 6-17

286

provides the wiring that would be necessary for such additional installations within the home. With such installations, you not only alert yourself with the basic alarm being activated but also the neighbors and fire department.

If you had a comprehensive home security system, as was discussed earlier in another chapter, you could also wire in fire alarm components to the system. Heat and smoke detectors to give early warning can easily be combined with the overall security system. The circuit, in such cases, acts as a detector in case of a malfunction. Trouble lights will alert you to this situation. Figure 6-18 illustrates a home security system that also detects fires.

FIRST ALERT DETECTOR UNITS

The self-contained *First Alert smoke* and *fire detector* with an escape light (Fig. 6-19) illuminates the area surrounding the

Fig. 6-16. Battery operated smoke detector (courtesy of NuTone Division, Scovill Inc.).

detector and lights the way to safety in residential fires. This aids in orienting children and also can illuminate an escape route during a power failure. The light is an extra method of alerting the hard-of-hearing who might not hear the alarm. The detector features a flashlight type bulb covered by a frosted lens which will give a 3.5 candlepower illumination when the horn is activated.

The unit has a dual chamber ionization sensor and the usual solid state circuitry ensuring troublefree service and protection. A test button will check both the sensor and the light, and a warning beep will sound when the batter needs replacing. A flashing LED indicates the unit is on. It requires two 9-volt batteries which separately control the alarm and the light. The multi-functional family protection system alarm units either have a fire protection option or else incorporate it into the basic overall system design.

The homeowner installed unit in Fig. 6-20 has the basic sensors for burglary protection, including the door intrusion transmitter. It monitors fire, gas and personal emergency devices. While smoke and gas detectors and intrusion detectors are very effective on an individual basis, the versatility of a combination system with a centralized monitoring unit can dramatically increase their effectiveness. The single, centrally located receiver unit acts like a 24-hour sentry, watching for a variety of potential home safety hazards. The smoke detectors act on their own 9 volt battery, thus allowing for minimal electrical circuitry. When smoke is detected, the main unit receives a signal and the alarm sounds. Checking the main unit LEDs can tell you exactly what circuit is being activated (there are three different alarms in the unit).

MORE TIPS ON DETECTOR PLACEMENT

Except in unusual circumstances, place detectors between 6-12" from the ceiling. Some detectors, according to the manufacturer, should be placed on the ceiling because they may detect the smoke from a developing fire better than wall-mounted units. Whenever possible, the ceiling detectors should also be mounted near the side walls, within 12". In larger rooms or open areas, such as a full basement, locate detectors 20-25' apart.

Uneven ceilings, or those crossed by beams or open joists, should have a closer installation of detection units, 15-20' apart. In the case of cross beams and joists, they should be mounted on the bottom of the beam/joist, not in the in-between channel.

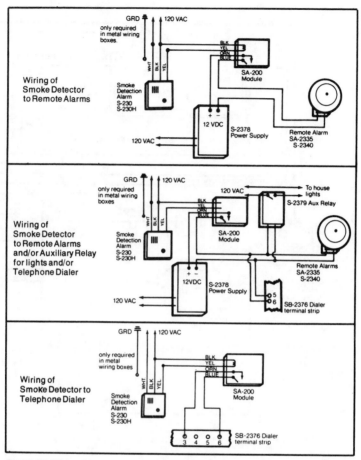

Fig. 6-17. Wiring for various installations (courtesy of NuTone Division, Scovill Inc.).

Cathedral and sloped ceilings can present other detection problems. The air at the top has a higher room temperature. It is maintained as such, creating the so-called thermal barrier which, in effect, blocks the smoke from reaching a detector. Locate the detector at a lower point.

While you should never locate detectors near a hot air duct from the furnace, locating them near the return air duct has certain advantages. Smoke is drawn towards them, allowing for an earlier detection than normal. Never place a detector in dusty or dirty environments, near heating or air conditioning ducts, fans or open windows, near a kitchen stove or metal chimney that slopes

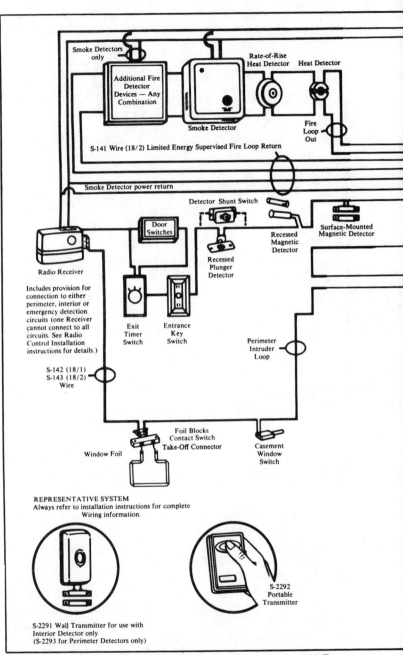

Fig. 6-18. A home security system that detects fires (courtesy of NuTone Division, Scovill Inc.).

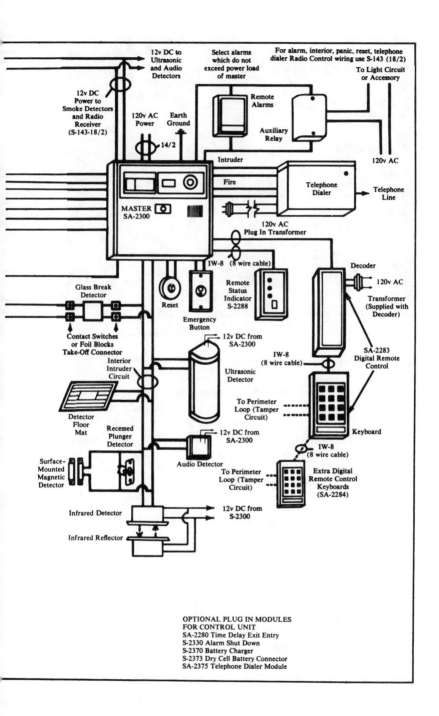

12v DC to Ultrasonic and Audio Detectors

Select alarms which do not exceed power load of master

For alarm, interior, panic, reset, telephone dialer Radio Control wiring use S-143 (18/2)

To Light Circuit or Accessory

12v DC Power to Smoke Detectors and Radio Receiver (S-143-18/2)

120v AC Power

Earth Ground

14/2

Remote Alarms

Auxiliary Relay

120v AC

Intruder

Fire

MASTER SA-2300

Telephone Dialer

Telephone Line

120v AC Plug In Transformer

IW-8 (8 wire cable)

Decoder

120v AC

Remote Status Indicator S-2288

Transformer (Supplied with Decoder)

Reset

Glass Break Detector

Emergency Button

Contact Switches or Foil Blocks Take-Off Connector

12v DC from SA-2300

IW-8 (8 wire cable)

SA-2283 Digital Remote Control

Interior Intruder Circuit

Ultrasonic Detector

Detector Floor Mat

To Perimeter Loop (Tamper Circuit)

Keyboard

Recessed Plunger Detector

12v DC from SA-2300

IW-8 (8 wire cable)

Surface-Mounted Magnetic Detector

Audio Detector

Extra Digital Remote Control Keyboards (SA-2284)

To Perimeter Loop (Tamper Circuit)

Infrared Detector

12v DC from S-2300

Infrared Reflector

OPTIONAL PLUG IN MODULES FOR CONTROL UNIT
SA-2280 Time Delay Exit Entry
S-2330 Alarm Shut Down
S-2370 Battery Charger
S-2373 Dry Cell Battery Connector
SA-2375 Telephone Dialer Module

Fig. 6-19. First Alert smoke and fire detector (courtesy of Pittway Corp.).

upward and to the outside from the stove and in damp or areas of excessive humidity.

The home security system, if properly selected and installed, will also have the circuitry to install a fire protection alarm system without affecting the basic security circuits. Previously discussed comprehensive home protection systems incorporate this feature as part of the basic system. Detailed installation procedures are not included herein.

FIRE LADDER

The emergency fire ladder by Rival (Fig. 6-21) requires no installation. It fits under the bed, in the closet or can be placed by the window.

Made of galvanized steel construction, it won't burn, rot or rust and can hold up to 950 pounds. A secure window sill looping units fits snugly and safely over the window ledge so a quick exit can be made. The ladder comes in two lengths, 15' and 25', for two or three story buildings.

There is nothing to install—no bolts, clamps or screws. When the ladder is pulled from its storage case, a spring-loaded cross bar instantly locks into position. It rigidly braces the 1″ steel side rails, assuring a firm hand hold for safe exit through the window.

The ladder simply loops over the vast majority of sills, and the rungs are dropped out the window. The unit is not cumbersome. Even a child can use it.

Flat rungs offer a non-slip surface for a more secure footing, even without shoes. The reinforced tubular galvanized steel rungs anchor the continuous loop cable.

For extra safety, the Rival ladder is equipped with 4″ heavy-duty standoffs welded to rungs. They brace the ladder away from the wall for a safe descent.

HOME FIRE CHECK

The first step in fire prevention includes a home fire check. This check will let you know where your potential fire hazards are located. There are four basic hazards: *heating and cooking, smoking, storage* and *electrical wiring.* Coupled with the basic hazards are other related ones—household hazards requiring a serviceman to repair and family escape planning in the event of a fire. You should be able to answer the following questions that have been developed by the National Fire Protection Association.

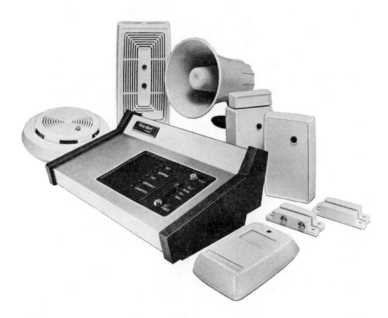

Fig. 6-20. This unit has the basic sensors for burglary protection (courtesy of Pittway Corp.).

Heating and Cooking

—Are fuel-burning space heaters and appliances properly installed and used?

—Has the family been cautioned not to use flammable liquids such as gasoline to start or freshen a fire (or for cleaning purposes)?

—Is the fireplace equipped with a metal fire screen that is always in the closed position when in use?

—Since gas and oil heaters and fireplaces use up oxygen as they burn, do you provide proper ventilation when they are in use?

—Are all space heaters placed *away* from traffic patterns, and are children and older persons also cautioned to keep their clothing away from them?

Smoking

—Do you stop members of the house from smoking in bed?

—Do you check up after others to see that no butts are lodged in upholstered furniture where they can smolder unseen at night?

—Do you dispose of smoking materials carefully (not in wastebaskets or carelessly dumped in an open garbage sack) and do you also keep large, safe ashtrays in the home?

—Are matches and lighters kept away from small children?

Electrical Wiring

—Are all electrical cords in the open—not run under rugs, over hooks or through door openings? Are they routinely checked for wear?

—Is the right size fuse in each socket in the fuse box? Do you replace a fuse with one of the same size?

—If you live in an older or remodeled home, is the wiring adequate to meet *current* electrical code standards?

Storage Areas

—Children get burned climbing on the stove to reach an item overhead. Do you store cookies, cereal or other "bait" away from the stove?

—Do you keep the basement, closets, garage and yard cleared of combustibles like papers, cartons, old furniture and oil-soaked rags?

—Are gasoline and other flammable liquids stored in closed containers (never glass jugs, discarded bleach bottles or other makeshift containers) and away from heat, sparks and children?

Fig. 6-21. Fire ladder (courtesy of Rival Manufacturing Co.).

—Are old paint-laden brushes thrown away? Is paint kept in tightly closed metal containers?

Household Hazards Requiring a Serviceman

—Are the furnace, stove and smokepipes far enough away from combustible walls and ceilings and in good repair?

—Is your heating equipment checked yearly by a serviceman?

—Is the chimney cleaned and checked regularly?

—For safety against chimney and other sparks, is the roof covering fire retardant?

—Are there enough electrical outlets in every room and special circuits for heavy-duty appliances such as space heaters and air conditioners?

—Do you have a qualified electrician to install or extend your wiring?

—Do all of your appliances carry the seal of a nationally known safety testing laboratory, such as Underwriters' Laboratories (UL) or Factory Mutual (FM)?

Other Safety Measures

—Do you have a home fire extinguisher that is acceptable for use on all types of fires? When was the last time it was checked to see if the extinguisher had a "full load"?

—Do you know what to do for a common household fire? Do you know how to fight it?

—Do the younger children and infants have flame retardant sleepwear?

—Do you have quantities of other hazardous materials such as contact cements, hair sprays and oil-based materials kept too close to heat?

—When igniting gas appliances, is the match lighted *before* turning on the gas in order to avoid a flashback from an unsuspected gas buildup?

—Are all gas connections tight fitting?

—Are wastebaskets larger than necessary? Smaller?

—Are rubbish and garbage cans covered?

—Is rubbish, trash, etc., kept away from the stove, water heater, furnace and other ignition sources?

—Do you get rid of old clothes, toys, boxes and rags?

—Are the wall and ceiling materials of safe building materials such as drywall, plasterboard or plaster?

—If the carpeting is fairly old, does it have a limited flammability factor?

—During parties, are the costumes and party dresses fire retardant? If not, are children kept away from lighted candles and flames? Is an adult always supervising the party?

—Are Christmas trees and associated decorations and ornaments fire-safe?

—Do the Christmas tree lights carry a UL label? Are the wires frayed from long use?

—Are the lights turned out before retiring for the night?

Once this home fire check has been completed and reviewed at least once a year (at a bare minimum), you are able to see where the potential fire hazards are. Take appropriate corrective action.

Installation Procedures

Non-wired systems involve the use of ultrasonics and microwaves for the most part. There are also those units and devices which require the installation of various component parts, much less the hard-wiring of the entire system.

In preceding chapters, at least one unit of each type (burglar, fire) was detailed all the way through from the point at which you purchased the system until it was installed, tested and put into an operational mode. This chapter is concerned with these very same systems, but provides specific instructions for the installation of the various devices that go with an entire unit. Beyond this first section of the chapter, we will consider the use of specific products to fit certain previously discussed systems in order to enhance their design performance (and also to better meet the homeowner's needs and desires). Then, the book moves on to the detailed installation instructions for a garage door opener that is radio controlled, and then to the details of various ultrasonic systems that can dramatically enhance home security.

On the next several pages are various uses to which the magnetic sensors can be put to improve home security. Sentrol, Inc., has made these available from their many years of specialized experience. I am deeply indebted to Sentrol for permission to use, at length, the material developed by their security specialists.

GENERAL INFORMATION ON MAGNETIC CONTACTS

Magnetic contacts take various forms and designs, depending upon their application. There are surface mounted magnetic contacts that are self-adhesive, those with screw terminals, concealed contacts, press fit magnetic contacts (SPDT), flanged mounted contacts, steel door application type magnetic contacts (SPDT) and overhead contacts. Several of these types are illustrated in Fig. 7-1.

The various contacts have different minimum and maximum mounting distances (Fig. 7-2 as an example). When selecting a contact set for installation, know what the maximum/minimum distance will be. There are also spacers that can build up the back of the contact set so it will be evenly positioned from the wall to match the other half of the sensor (Fig. 7-3).

These Sentrol security products can be used in almost every typical home application such as the following:

☐ All types of windows, doors and jambs.
☐ Sliding doors and windows.
☐ Art object protection.
☐ Desk drawers.
☐ File cabinets.
☐ Valuables.

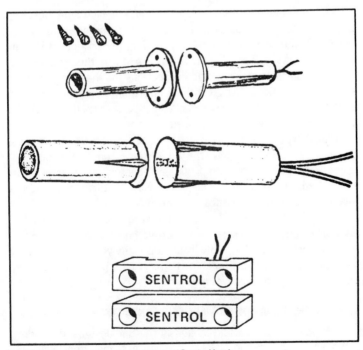

Fig. 7-1. Magnetic contacts (courtesy of Sentrol Inc.).

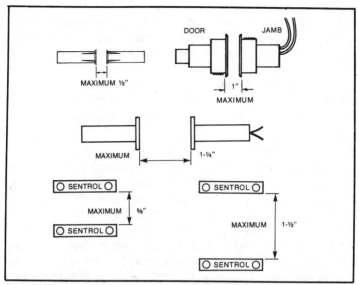

Fig. 7-2. Minimum and maximum mounting distances (courtesy of Sentrol Inc.).

Adjustable Gap

Some contacts are considered "wide gap" in that they do not require very close spacing together. This is a great advantage when false alarms may be caused by a loose fitting door. The wider

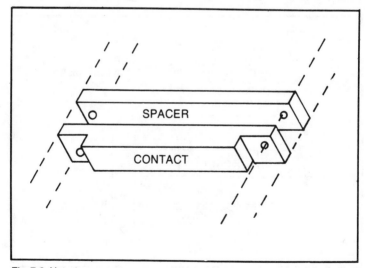

Fig. 7-3. Note the spacer.

gap distance also permits faster installation and accommodates greater misalignment. Figure 7-4 illustrates one typical contact unit, with the minimum and maximum distances shown. Figure 7-5 shows typical gap adjustment curves. These are of great value when you have an adjustable gap magnetic sensor (Fig. 7-6). The adjustment screw on the end is rotated either clockwise or counterclockwise to obtain the gap adjustment desired.

Sensor Gap Wiring

Always refer to the installation instructions that come with a particular magnetic sensor. Some are two-wire; others are three-wire. Depending upon the unit, the wires may be used for specific applications. Table 7-1 illustrates the functions of the wires in several units. Note that depending upon which unit is used, the wire may have a different functional hookup. For some units, the wires will make no difference in the hookup procedure. This is one reason for always rechecking the installation instruction notes.

Sensors are also called magnetic contacts or simply contacts. Either of these names are applicable. Various manufacturers use them separately and in tandem when discussing the units. As a unit, you have a sensor unit; individually, you have a magnet and a sensor. Also, whenever possible and depending upon the manufacturer, the sensor may have a certain alignment for reasons of

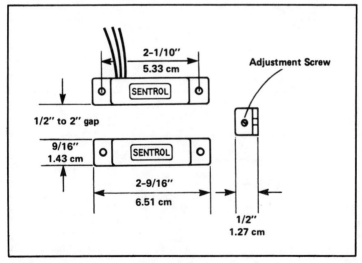

Fig. 7-4. A typical contact unit (courtesy of Sentrol Inc.).

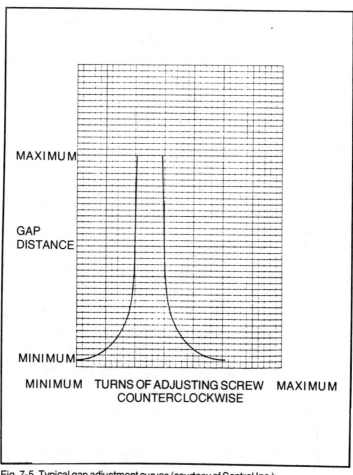

Fig. 7-5. Typical gap adjustment curves (courtesy of Sentrol Inc.).

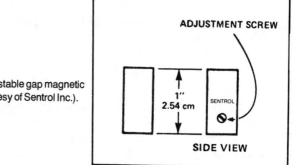

Fig. 7-6. Adjustable gap magnetic sensor (courtesy of Sentrol Inc.).

Table 7-1. Lead Function Charts (courtesy of Sentrol Inc.).

2507, 2507 A, 2507 A-D, 2507 A-H, 2577, 2577 A

Lead Color	Function
Black	Common
White	Closed Loop (N.O.)
Red	Open Loop (N.C.)

2505, 2505A

Lead Color	Function
Black	Closed Loop (N.O.)

2506, 2506A

Lead Color	Function
White	Open Loop (N.C.)

polarity. Be sure that the manufacturer's name is lined up on both the sensor switch and the magnet, when required for correct polarity (Fig. 7-7).

Adjustable Gap Sensor Units

The magnetic contact sensor units having an adjustable gap distance are set by means of the adjustment screw at the end. The *Select-A-Gap* switches from Sentrol are polarity sensitive and *must* be aligned properly.

For a minimum gap, the screw is turned counterclockwise to the near end. With the magnet away from the switch, attach an ohmmeter to the leads; the meter should read INFINITY. Align the Sentrol labels on the magnet and switch so that they both read in the same direction. Bring the magnet up to the switch and watch the meter for an "0" ohm reading. As the screw is turned clockwise, the actuation distance should become greater. When the desired gap is reached, attach the magnet and permanently affix it.

The introduction of ferrous material in the vicinity of the switch will cause a change in the gap distance. For this reason, a non-magnetic screwdriver should be used when adjusting the gap. If a non-magnetic screwdriver is *not* used, it is necessary to remove the screwdriver from the vicinity of the switch before measuring the gap distance.

As the gap is increased, the switch may bias and latch. When latched, the switch will remain closed even when the magnet is removed. Test for a latched condition by removing the magnet; the meter will read INFINITY if the switch opens properly.

VENTILATION OF SLIDING WINDOWS

The following material covers various applications for Sentrol and similar magnetic sensor units in various home security

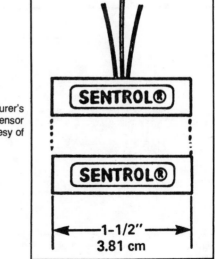

Fig. 7-7. Be sure the manufacturer's name is lined up on both the sensor switch and the magnet (courtesy of Sentrol Inc.).

situations. They include the sliding door, ventilation ideas for sliding windows, steel doors, door chime use, drop-down attic stairs, etc.

Provide ventilation of up to 4″ without disarming the alarm system. This applies to wood or aluminum sliding doors or windows.

Mount wide gap magnets and contact with spacing as shown in Fig. 7-8. Make sure end to end spacing between the switch and magnet is less than ½″.

Wire switch #1 in parallel with switch #2. For surface mounting of the magnet, mount and drill the hole for the switch at the end of the magnet. Install the painted end of the magnet away from the switch.

Mark the window or door at the maximum opening. The window may be opened anywhere between completely closed and the mark without disarming the system. Figure 7-9 illustrates the switches and magnets in place.

MOUNTING THE MAGNETIC CONTACT ON A GARAGE DOOR TRACK

Refer to Fig. 7-10. Make sure the door does not have a guard that extends around the track on the door bottom. Choose the side opposite the rope pull or else move the rope pull to the side opposite the switch.

Mount the bracket on the track with two self-tapping screws. Tighten them evenly against the track.

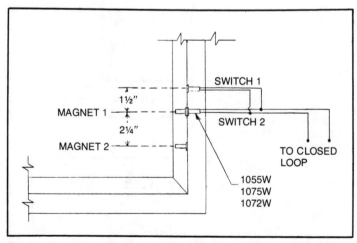

Fig. 7-8. Mount the wide gap magnets and contact with spacing (courtesy of Sentrol Inc.).

304

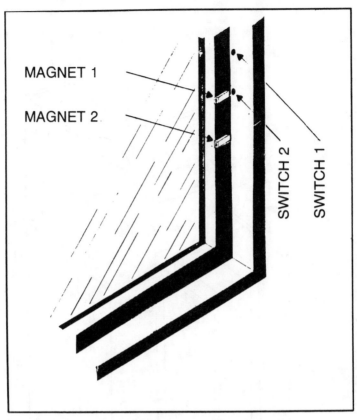

Fig. 7-9. The switches and magnets in place (courtesy of Sentrol Inc.).

Mount the switch to the bracket. Mount the magnet to the bracket. Observe polarity of the switch and magnet. Always line up the switch and magnet labels to read in the same direction. Mount the bracket and magnet to the garage door, allowing about ½″ gap between the switch and magnet.

MAGNETIC CONTACT INSTALLATION IN ROLL-UP DOORS

Refer to Fig. 7-11. Close the gate or door and tape the magnet in place with masking tape.

Mount the magnet with the unpainted end 1/16″ back from the end of the door slat. Space out the magnet as far as possible from the door so it will still have clearance when rolled up. Attach the magnet with clips. Drill a 1″ diameter hole in the channel at the end of the magnet.

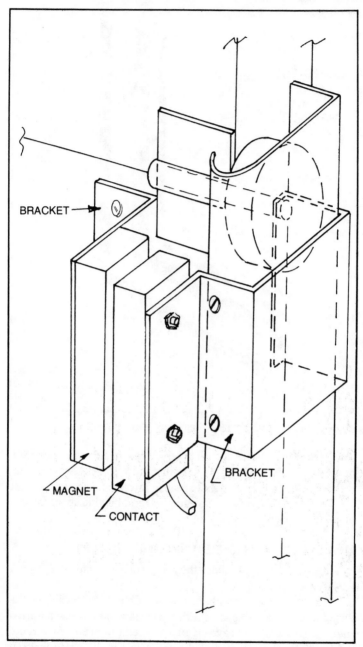

Fig. 7-10. Mounting the magnetic contact on a garage door track (courtesy of Sentrol Inc.).

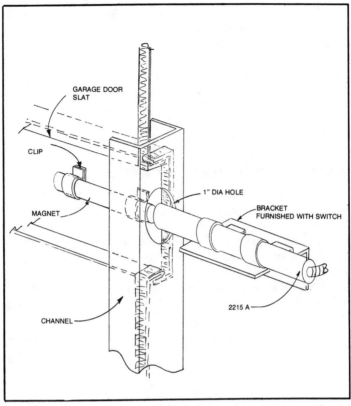

Fig. 7-11. Magnetic contact installation in roll-up doors (courtesy of Sentrol Inc.).

Mount the wall bracket and adjust the switch to the center of the hole. Set it so the end of the switch does not project past the channel inside.

Test for proper operation. Dress the wired leads and hook into the loop. Retest for operation and clearance.

SURFACE MOUNTED MAGNETIC CONTACTS ON STEEL DOORS

Sentrol surface mounted contacts are satisfactory for application in such areas as steel doors, safes, file cabinets, truck doors, roll-up garage doors, etc. Always allow plenty of safety factor in the installation process. It is highly recommended that when installing the contact and magnet, make sure there is no more separation than about 50% of the pull in distance. For instance, depending on which type of contacts are used, the distance will vary. The 1084-T contact switch is .4″ without a spacer and .6″ with a spacer; a maximum separation of .5″ to .6″ will provide a reliable system—not more.

Rules of thumb in this type of application include the following. The gap on the steel is approximately one-half the distance achieved in air. Space the switch and magnet at approximately 25% of the rated gap for air as a safety factor.

Use a spacer whenever it is practical. If only one is used, mount it under the magnet.

MOUNTING SWITCHES ON DESKS AND CABINETS

To protect file cabinets and desk drawers, the self-adhesive switches work extremely well. The wide gap of certain switches provides for a good working distance. Refer to Fig. 7-12.

Choose an area with ¾″ to 1¼″ clearance between the moving and non-moving portions. Clean both surfaces to insure good adhesion of the switch parts.

Install the switch and magnet. Install the magnet with the red-painted end away from the end of the switch. Test with an ohmmeter, and install in the loop.

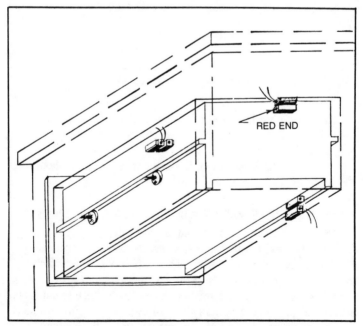
RED END

Fig. 7-12. Mounting a switch on desks and cabinets (courtesy of Sentrol Inc.).

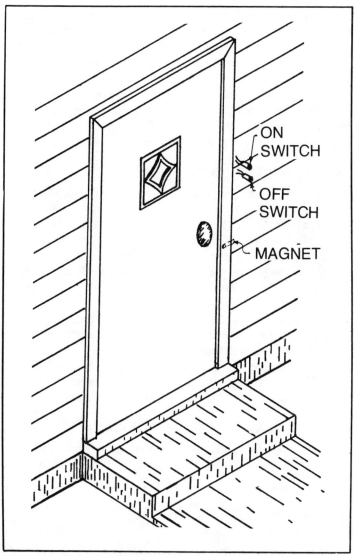

Fig. 7-13. A switch for on-off control (courtesy of Sentrol Inc.).

CONCEALED SWITCHES FOR ON-OFF CONTROL

See Fig. 7-13. Using the closed loop magnetic contacts to arm and disarm certain alarm systems with the magnet can replace a key switch. Some control panels are armed or disarmed using a momentary closure of a single switch (a spring-loaded key switch), and others use two separate switches requiring a momentary closure of one switch to turn on and another switch to turn off. It is possible to use hidden magnetic contacts to accomplish this function in place of a key switch. Hiding the contact near the entry door is a method of eliminating the need for a key. A small steel plate holding the magnet or a hole drilled to hold the magnet will allow entry. This eliminates the need for keys to disarm the system, and you don't have to worry about losing the keys. When used in conjunction with floor mats which must be stepped on to disarm a system, you have an even higher degree of home security.

PROTECTION OF CHAIN LINK FENCE GATES

Since this is an outside application, armored cable should be used. Sentrol also provides specific mounting brackets for gates. See Fig. 7-14.

Determine the switch and magnet position. The cable should be run to a junction box or to the inside of a pipe for splicing.

Mount the brackets on the post and gate with masking tape. Swing the gate to check for clearance. Drill 9/64″ diameter holes to mount the brackets, using self-tapping screws.

Mount the switch and magnet to the brackets, observing polarity. Test the switch for operation with an ohmmeter. Wire the switch into the circuit and test.

If mounting on the hinge side of the gate, be sure you can adjust the gap required to trip the switch when the gate is opened. Use one on each side if a double gate swings from the center.

VENTILATION USING AN OPEN LOOP SWITCH IN A CLOSED LOOP

This allows for ventilation in sliding door or window without disarming the alarm system. The method will allow the alarm user

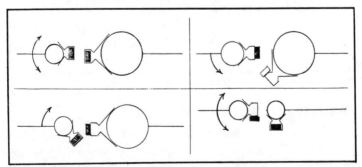

Fig. 7-14. Gates swing in the direction of the arrows (courtesy of Sentrol Inc.).

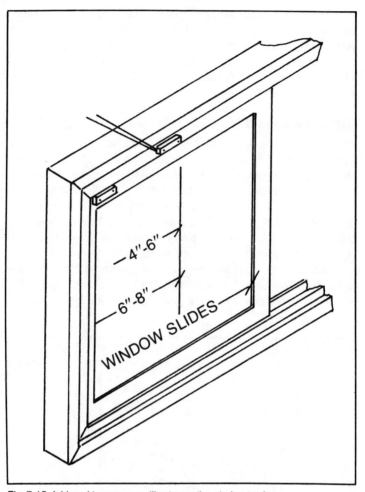

Fig. 7-15. Add markings so you will not open the window too far.

to open or close the window without adding a shunt switch or turning off the alarm system. Using a switch designed for an open loop and offsetting the magnet 4-6″ will provide a closed switch to be wired in series with the closed loop. When the window is moved and the magnet comes in close proximity to the switch, the alarm will be triggered. If the magnet is past the switch when the system is armed, there is no protection. The homeowner will not have an indication on the closed loop circuit light. A stop may be added to prevent this from occurring, or markings may be added so that the person will know not to open the window past the mark (Fig. 7-15).

Mount the switch on the frame 6″ to 8″ in from the window edge in the direction the window slides. Open the window the maximum distance allowed for ventilation (4″ to 6″).

Install the magnet under the switch and test to make sure the switch is opened. Install a stop to keep the window from opening further past this point.

PROTECTING A VAN DOOR

This method provides protection to the rear doors of a van so a minimum opening gap will trigger the alarm (Fig. 7-16). By using an adjustable gap contact, it may be possible to use only one switch to protect both doors, if adjustment can be made to trigger the alarm before the second door is opened. The type of switch depicted, if used to operate a horn, siren or lights, should be buffered with a relay. Use the magnetic contact to drive a relay coil or the relay contacts to drive a high current load.

Select the position for the switch and magnet on the hinge side of the door that opens first (door #1). Drill a 1″ diameter hole with a hole saw in the door and the body of the van. Line up the centers within ⅛″.

Fig. 7-16. Protecting a van door.

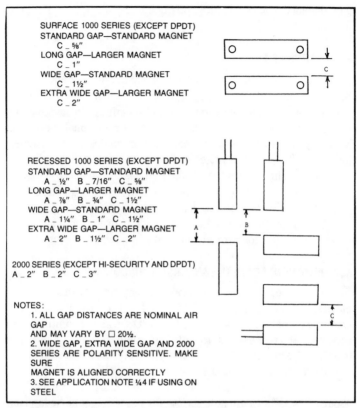

SURFACE 1000 SERIES (EXCEPT DPDT)
STANDARD GAP—STANDARD MAGNET
    C _ ⅝"
LONG GAP—LARGER MAGNET
    C _ 1"
WIDE GAP—STANDARD MAGNET
    C _ 1½"
EXTRA WIDE GAP—LARGER MAGNET
    C _ 2"

RECESSED 1000 SERIES (EXCEPT DPDT)
STANDARD GAP—STANDARD MAGNET
    A _ ½"   B _ 7/16"   C _ ⅝"
LONG GAP—LARGER MAGNET
    A _ ⅞"   B _ ¾"   C _ 1½"
WIDE GAP—STANDARD MAGNET
    A _ 1¼"   B _ 1"   C _ 1½"
EXTRA WIDE GAP—LARGER MAGNET
    A _ 2"   B _ 1½"   C _ 2"

2000 SERIES (EXCEPT HI-SECURITY AND DPDT)
A _ 2"   B _ 2"   C _ 3"

NOTES:
    1. ALL GAP DISTANCES ARE NOMINAL AIR GAP
    AND MAY VARY BY □ 20½.
    2. WIDE GAP, EXTRA WIDE GAP AND 2000 SERIES ARE POLARITY SENSITIVE. MAKE SURE
    MAGNET IS ALIGNED CORRECTLY
    3. SEE APPLICATION NOTE ¼4 IF USING ON STEEL

Fig. 7-17. Gap distances and mounting positions for Sentrol switches (courtesy of Sentrol Inc.).

Insert the switch into the frame. Insert the magnet into the door.

Attach a meter to the switch. Adjust the screw-in end of the switch. Set the gap for a minimum opening to trigger the alarm. Wire the switch to the alarm.

Check to see if door #1 triggers the alarm before door #2 can be opened. If door #2 can be opened without setting off the alarm, add a switch to door #2.

GAP DISTANCES AND MOUNTING POSITIONS FOR SENTROL SWITCHES

See Fig. 7-17. Since Sentrol produces the biggest variety of switches in use, it is very likely that you will use one of their switches in one of your many home applications. Thus, the various

313

gap distances and mounting positions are illustrated for your information.

PROTECTION OF ART

Inspect the frame for an area to place the magnet and switch. See Fig. 7-18. Attach the magnet to the frame using a self-adhesive clip (7-18A). Attach the switch to a wall-mounting clip and install it on the wall behind the magnet (7-18B). An optional method of installing the switch into the wall at right angles to the magnet, forming an "L" with the switch and magnet, is shown in Fig. 7-18D. The attachment at the bottom of the frame is shown in Fig. 7-18C.

Wire into the loop. A 24-hour protective loop is preferable to protect even if a perimeter loop is off.

If the gap is more than ½", use a wider gap sensor. The sensor used should allow for more adjustment without false alarms.

MAGNETIC CONTACT IN THE ANDERSON WINDOW

The Anderson casement window is protected with a recessed magnetic contact. Figures 7-19A and 7-19B are used in the standard model. Figures 7-19C and 7-19D are used if ventilation is required. It is important to note that both models require the magnet to be placed in the sash on the step closest to the inside.

Install the magnet in the sash on the step closest to the inside. Drill a ¼" hole that is 1¼" deep. This step has a cross section of about ½" × ½" and will hold the ¼" diameter magnet by centering the hole in the section.

Drill a hole for the switch opposite the magnet. Angle this hole back toward the inside of the wall about 15°. Install the switch and test.

If you want ventilation, install in the position of Figs. 7-19C and 7-19D. In this method, the switch may have to be recessed more than usual to make sure the window can't open too wide. Cover the ends of the switch and magnet with silicon rubber to protect from the weather.

MAGNETIC CONTACTS FOR PELLA BRAND WINDOWS

Protection of *Pella* brand casement and awning windows with recessed magnetic contacts requires extra care because of the extra pane of glass. The windows may have two separate pieces of glass or may have one thermopane. It is very important when drilling for the magnet that care be exercised to miss the glass.

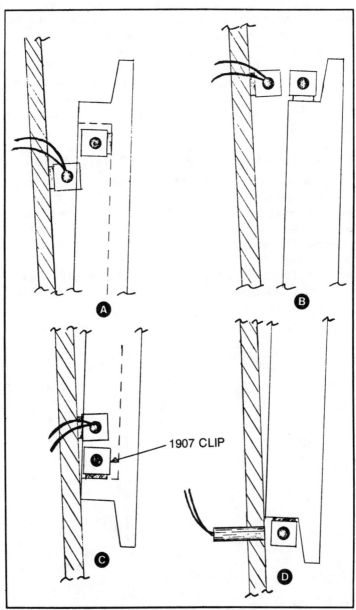

1907 CLIP

Fig. 7-18. Protecting art. (A) Attach the magnet to the frame using a self-adhesive clip. (B) Attach the switch to a wall-mounting clip and install it on the wall behind the magnet. (C) The attachment at the bottom of the frame. (D) Installing the switch into the wall at right angles to the magnet (courtesy of Sentrol Inc.).

Select the position for the switch—in the top of the window if the wires are going to the attic, or in the window bottom if the wires are going to run to the basement. Drill a ¼" diameter hole, 1¼" deep in the window sash. Insert the magnet.

Drill a ¼" hole in the frame. Drill at approximately 15° toward the inside of the wall. Align the switch hole center within ¼" of the magnet's center.

Insert the switch. Test the circuit. Glue the switch and magnet in place.

INSTALLATION OF MAGNETIC CONTACTS ON THIN STEEL FRAMES

Many of the casement and awning windows with the thin frame have been installed during the past 20-30 years. Due to the thin section of the metal and the fact that it is steel, there are problems with drilling and tapping to install normal surface mounted contacts. The method described here requires the use of self-adhesive clips and a wide gap magnetic contact. This will give about ⅝" of gap when placed parallel to the magnet and ⅜" gap end to end with the magnet, when both the switch and magnet are in a clip on a steel surface.

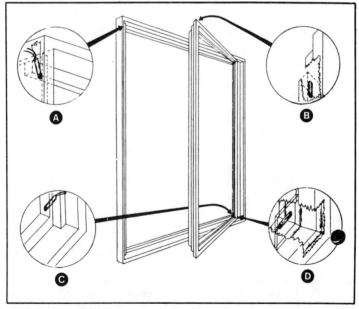

Fig. 7-19. The Anderson casement window is protected with a recessed magnetic contact (courtesy of Sentrol Inc.).

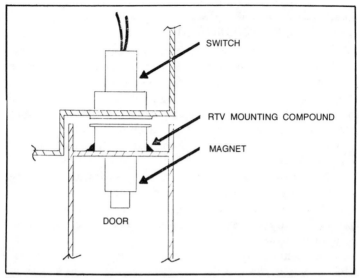

Fig. 7-20. Installing magnetic contacts in a recessed steel door (courtesy of Sentrol Inc.).

Select the position for the switches. Drill a hole for the wires if they are to be hidden.

Clean the frame with alcohol or soap and water to prepare the surface for the sensor unit mounting. Insert the switch and magnet using clips for attachment. Mount on the frame. Test the switch with the ohmmeter, wire the switch into the loop and then retest.

INSTALLING MAGNETIC CONTACTS IN A RECESSED STEEL DOOR

Some steel doors are recessed at the top causing a gap problem in using a concealed magnetic contact. This application, in Fig. 7-20, is useful for many of these doors.

Make sure the recess is at least ½" deep. Carefully align the position for the switch and magnet.

Drill a 1" hole for the switch in the door frame.

Drill a ¾" hole for the magnet in the door top. Wire the switch to the loop and insert it into the frame.

Clean the top of the door and mount the magnet into the ¾" hole. You should use a 1" diameter clip. Hold the clip in place with glue. Close the door and test the circuit. Retest the circuit.

If the recess is more than ¾" deep, use a wide gap set of magnetic contacts *or* build up using washers. If it is over 1" deep, use only the wide gap and build up with washers.

REDUCTION OF THE GAP DISTANCE
ON RECESSED MAGNETIC CONTACTS

In some instances, the homeowner may wish to reduce the gap distance on a recessed magnetic contact to limit the opening of the door. If the magnetic contact, for one reason or another, was mounted on the hinge side of the door, it is sometimes possible to open the door too far before tripping the alarm. The insertion of a steel nail or screw alongside the switch or magnet will reduce the gap, depending on the nail size or the distance from the switch or magnet (Fig. 7-2).

For steel frame and wood doors, drive a #6 nail as close to the magnet as possible. Add an additional nail, if necessary.

For wood doors and frames, drive a #6 nail as close as possible to the switch and test for gap. If still too much gap, add an additional nail by the magnet.

For aluminum or steel doors and frame, insert a #6 × 1¼" steel screw as close to the switch as possible. Add screws as necessary near the switch and magnet to further reduce the gap.

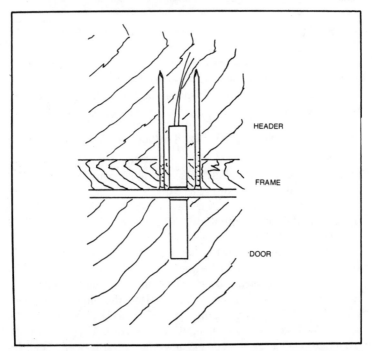

Fig. 7-21. Reducing the gap on a recessed magnetic contact (courtesy of Sentrol Inc.).

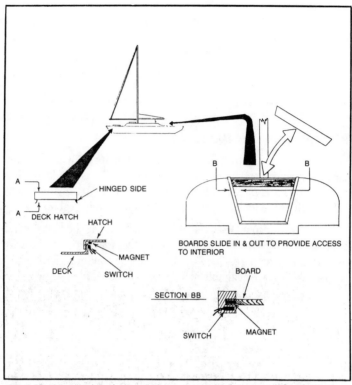

Fig. 7-22. Using the boat battery with no power drain (courtesy of Sentrol Inc.).

INSTALLATION OF MAGNETIC CONTACTS IN BOATS

To install magnetic contacts in boats, Sentrol has developed a fully encapsulated magnetic contact that is ideal for protecting the interior of a boat when used with a simple alarm system. Protecting the hatches and companionway can be easily accomplished by using recessed or small surface mounted units. Using open circuit switches, a relay, a shunt switch and horn, it is possible to use the boat battery with no power drain (Fig. 7-22).

Install the switch in a hatch that can be opened. Use the surface type if it is plastic. Recessed types can be used with a wooden hatch. Install the switch in companionway boards or door.

If using open contacts to drive the horn, install a latching relay to handle the current. Solder and wire connections to prevent corrosion.

Magnets have an effect on compass readings. The compass should be checked after installation of magnetic switches.

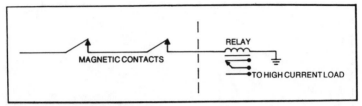

Fig. 7-23. Procedure three.

SWITCHING HIGH CURRENT LOADS

It is occasionally necessary to switch loads with a higher current than the maximum rating on a switch. This would apply to the preceding application for magnetic contacts on boats, among others. Here are four suggestions to help solve this problem.

☐ **Procedure One.** Use a 1 amp switch. Closed loop (switch is closed with the magnet next to the switch) magnetic contacts are available in 1 amp versions in all mounting configurations. Open loop and SPDT are available in most mounting configurations.

☐ **Procedure Two.** Use 3 amp switches. Closed loop magnetic contacts are available in 3 amps for most mounting configurations.

☐ **Procedure Three.** Using the standard magnetic contact to switch the relay, lay out the hookup of the switch to the relay as in Fig. 7-23. Refer to the DPDT switch application, too.

☐ **Procedure Four.** Using a diode to protect the switch from back electromotive force on dc relay coils, the diode addition across the relay coil can protect the switches from a spike created by the electrical field collapsing when the current is removed. See Fig. 7-24.

DOUBLE POLE DOUBLE THROW (DPDT) SWITCHES

Dual switching may be provided with one magnetic contact. DPDT magnetic contacts may be used in place of two contacts or one contact and a floor mat when an annunciator panel is hooked up

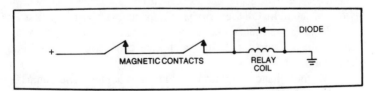

Fig. 7-24. Procedure four.

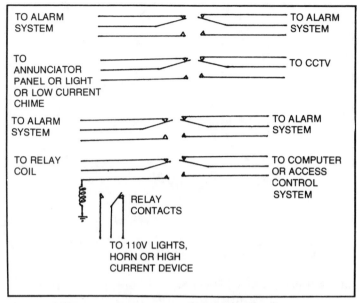

Fig. 7-25. DPDT applications (courtesy of Sentrol Inc.).

to the system. Other applications can include access control systems, lighting control and/or safety systems. (These are not discussed here as they apply more to business concerns that have highly specialized needs.) Each switch is electrically and mechanically isolated from the other and may switch at a slightly different point. See Fig. 7-25.

BURIED SWITCH FOR GARAGE DOORS

It is sometimes necessary to bury a stainless steel contact in concrete due to the door construction. The switch used should be designed for this type of application with the use of stainless steel for corrosion resistance and with an extra wide gap distance. The switch will have a security cable (Sentrol #227A switch specifically designed for this type of application). See Fig. 7-26.

Select the position for mounting that will minimize the amount of concrete to be chipped out. Install the magnet on the door and lay the switch on the floor. Test to make sure at least a 1″ gap exists. If not 1″, adjust the magnet. Chip out the concrete, approximately ½″ deep and ½″ wide.

Lay the switch into the floor and test. Make sure of at least a ½″ extra gap. Fill over the switch and cable with concrete patch.

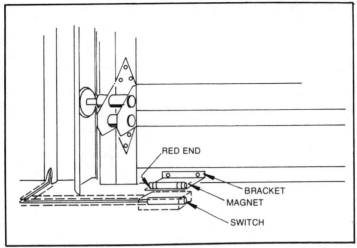

Fig. 7-26. The switch will have a security cable.

REPLACEMENT OF DIAMETER PUSH BUTTON SWITCHES WITH MAGNETIC CONTACTS

In upgrading home security systems, you may wish to remove the ¾" diameter push button switches that were popular at one time, but are not so widely used at the present. By using the Sentrol #1908 bushing, it is possible to replace the mechanical type switches that have problems with dirt, corrosion or binding. In steel doors use the extra gap contacts; in aluminum or wood, use a standard bushing (Fig. 7-27).

Remove the old switch from the frame. If it is a button type, drill a ¾" hole in the door or window frame.

Insert the bushings into the ¾" hole and glue, if necessary. Insert the magnet into the bushing.

Wire the switch to the loop. Put a drop of "superglue" on the switch and press it into the frame bushing. If replacing on the hinge side of the door, don't forget to adjust the gap for the amount of opening.

ARMING OF TRUCK TAILGATES

With many home businesses, the use of various types of trucks, including those with rollup tailgates, has meant increasing the security to include the items left or kept in the truck. This application includes enough durability, gap and vibration resistance to work on the rollup tailgate (Fig. 7-28).

322

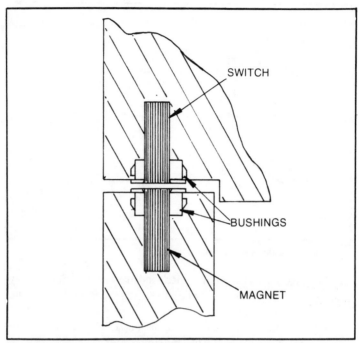

SWITCH

BUSHINGS

MAGNET

Fig. 7-27. In aluminum or wood, use a standard bushing.

Select the location for the switch on wood or aluminum. This will be on the track side, just forward of the track. Usually it is best to mount near the top, at the point where the track starts bending. Install the switch using spacers behind the switch to build it out slightly past the track.

Mount the magnet on the tailgate door with a bracket. Position the magnet and switch as close as possible with the door closed. Mount the end of the magnet about ½″ past the end of the switch. Test and wire in the leads and then dress the wires into place.

Do not hook directly into a high current circuit such as the vehicle horn. Use a relay if switching more than .5 amp. This design can be used to attach a portable alarm that is battery powered.

SURFACE MOUNTED CONTACT
SENSORS ON THE ANDERSON WINDOW

Self-adhesive surface mounted contact sensors are ideally suited for fast and easy installation. With the window closed, the switch and magnet are both concealed. Figure 7-29 applies.

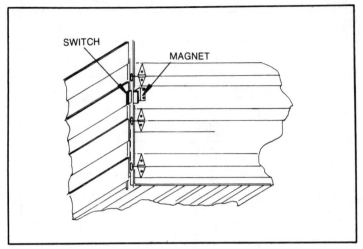

Fig. 7-28. Application for a truck's rollup tailgate.

Locate the position of the switch and magnet. Ventilation may be achieved with the use of a wide gap switch and placed nearer the hinged side of the window.

Drill a hole for the wires. Slant back at 15°-30° to make sure the wires go inside the wall. Drill into the corner as shown.

Clean the surfaces with alcohol to remove dirt, grease and moisture. Mount the switch as shown.

Install the magnet. Insure that the name reading is the same direction on the switch and the magnet for proper polarity. Close the window and test the circuit.

USING A MAGNETIC CONTACT TO OPERATE A DOOR CHIME

This installation replaces the current chime sounding method and offers a more attractive installation. See Fig. 7-30.

Drill a hole for the switch as close to the outer edge of the door frame as possible. Drill a hole for the magnet, offsetting it from the switch hole as far as possible toward the inner edge of the door. Install a closed loop (not an open one) switch and magnet.

Test by putting a meter on the leads and closing the door. The switch should read INFINITY. As the door opens and the magnet passes under the switch, the meter should read 0 ohms. Close the door and the meter should read INFINITY again. If the unit does not switch properly under this test, the magnet may be too strong for the switch. A nail (or steel screw) added as shown will decrease the sensitivity of the switch.

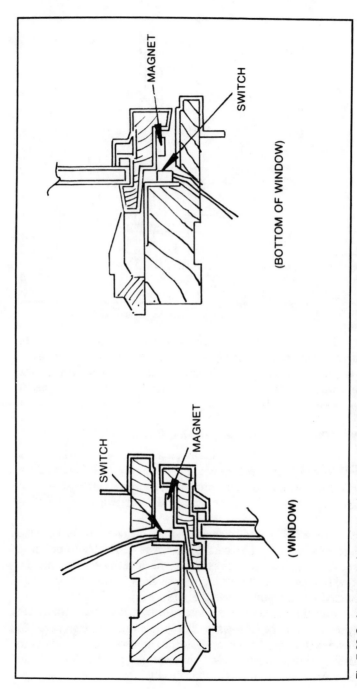

Fig. 7-29. Surface mounted contact sensors for the Anderson window. Note the switch placement.

325

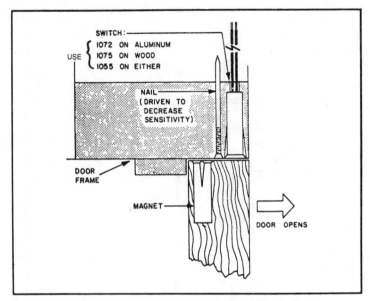

Fig. 7-30. A magnetic contact for a door chime (courtesy of Sentrol Inc.).

The switch is designed for .5 amps. Many bells draw more current than this amount. If this is the case in the application in question, install a relay in the circuit between the switch and the bell. One amp switches are easily obtainable by the homeowner at your local supply store.

MOUNTING A DOOR SWITCH INTO AN EXISTING CONCRETE WALL

The outer wall of the home *may not be of wood but of concrete or brick* (Fig. 7-31). The front door may be a steel one. By using the wide gap flanged contact switch in conjunction with a steel door style magnet, you can have very good security at your main entrance.

Drill a 3/8"-25/16" diameter hole in the door frame. The hole should extend into the concrete as far as necessary to permit a hidden wire to be run, possibly to the level of the ceiling. To provide an exit from the wall, drill an angle approximately 45° from the desired exit point to meet the hole previously drilled.

Run the wires for the switch through the hole. Attach the switch housing with screws or appropriate concrete fasteners. To provide protection for the switch leads and also to make it easier to "fish" the leads through the concrete, it may be desirable to enclose the leads in stainless steel flex tubing.

Drill a 1″ hole in the steel door opposite the switch. Use a press-fit magnet and put it into the hole. A dab of RTV mounting compound will help secure the magnet in the hole. Test for continuity with an ohmmeter; connect to loop.

INSTALLATION OF MAGNETIC CONTACTS ON PATIO DOORS

Sliding aluminum patio doors are especially vulnerable areas in residential structures. This application describes two methods, recessed and surfaced, of protecting these doors.

For recessed installation, remove the door from the frame using the following procedure (Fig. 7-32). Open the door as far as required (some doors have spring "locks" in the upper channel frame, past which the door must be opened before the door can be

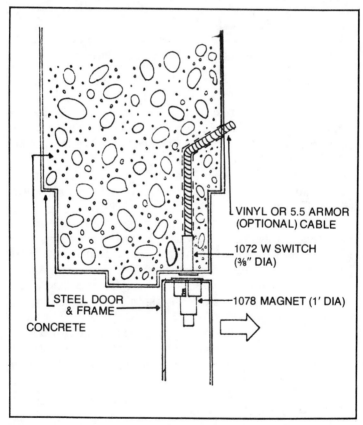

Fig. 7-31. Mounting a door switch into an existing concrete wall (courtesy of Sentrol Inc.).

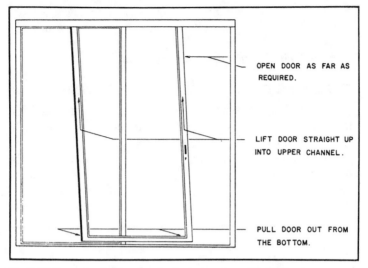

OPEN DOOR AS FAR AS
REQUIRED.

LIFT DOOR STRAIGHT UP
INTO UPPER CHANNEL.

PULL DOOR OUT FROM
THE BOTTOM.

Fig. 7-32. Removing the door from the frame (courtesy of Sentrol Inc.).

removed. Other doors have no such locks. Lift the door straight up into the upper channel. Pull the door out from the bottom.

Locate the desired mounting position for the switch. Note that if the switch will be mounted either parallel to the magnet or perpendicular (with a recessed mounting), a different mounting type switch must be used (Fig. 7-33).

Drill a hole in the door frame and run the wires. Insert the switch into the frame. Whether mounted parallel or perpendicular, use RTV mounting compound to secure the switch.

Mount the magnet on the inside of the upper door channel, toward the top of the channel, with RTV mounting compound. The RTV compound should be sufficiently set in about 15 minutes to permit replacement of the door into the frame.

For surface installation, removal of the door is not necessary, unless the switch leads are to be run into the channel for any reason. Mount the switch on the sash in the desired position. Mount the magnet on the door, directly opposite the switch when the door is closed. RTV mounting compound or a self-adhesive mounting method can be used. Check for continuity when the door is in the closed position.

DROP DOWN STAIR INSTALLATION

Security for the drop-down stairwells in a garage against unauthorized entry is a "must" in situations where the garage door

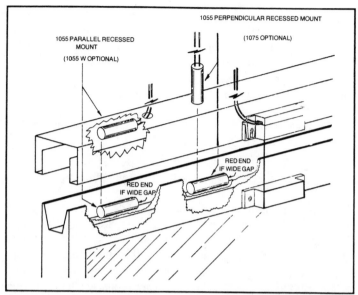

Fig. 7-33. Parallel and perpendicular recessed mounts for switches (courtesy of Sentrol Inc.).

is left unsecured. An intruder could gain access to the garage through the door, enter the attic via the drop-down stairway, cut a hole through the ceiling between the joists and drop into the house, all without triggering an alarm (Fig. 7-34).

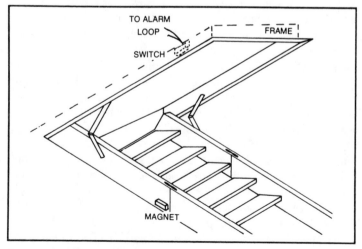

Fig. 7-34. Security for a drop-down stairwell.

Position the switch on the stairway frame and the magnet on the drop-down portion of the stairway. Be certain there is no interference to the stairway mechanism from the switch or magnet.

Permanently attach the switch to the frame, and temporarily attach the magnet to the stairway with masking tape. Connect an ohmmeter to the switch leads, close the stairway and test for continuity.

Permanently attach the magnet to the stairway. Connect the lead from the switch to the alarm loop.

INSTALLING A SWITCH TO AN OVERHEAD GARAGE DOOR

This application is designed to provide protection for an overhead garage door using a high security switch. High security switches (Sentrol #2707A, triple-based high security balanced magnetic contact) are virtually impossible to defeat with an external magnet. They are polarity sensitive and balanced. Be certain that the magnet and the switch are properly aligned in the same direction.

These switches have a nominal operating gap between the magnet and switch of 0.2″ minimum and 0.6″ maximum. Installation instructions take this into account, but it is always best to check for correct operation of the switch before encasing it in concrete.

Select the position of the switch to minimize the amount of concrete to be chipped out. Install the magnet on the door, either directly or with a bracket, as necessary. For installation on the right side (looking at the door from the inside), see Fig. 7-35. Attach the magnet with the Sentrol label upside down and facing away from the door. For installation on the left side of the door, see Fig. 7-36. Attach the magnet with the Sentrol label upside down and facing toward the door.

Close the door. Be certain that the lower edge of the magnet is no further away from the floor than ¼″.

Position the switch so that the label on the switch reads in the same direction as the magnet label, and so that the bottom of the switch is centered on the bottom edge of the magnets. This will assure proper operation of the switch.

Chip away enough concrete (approximately 4½″ long × 1¾″ wide × ⅞″ deep) to permit placement of the switch into the floor cavity. It will be about ⅛″ below the surface of the floor. Also, chip out a channel for the flex cable (approximately ⅜″ × ⅜″).

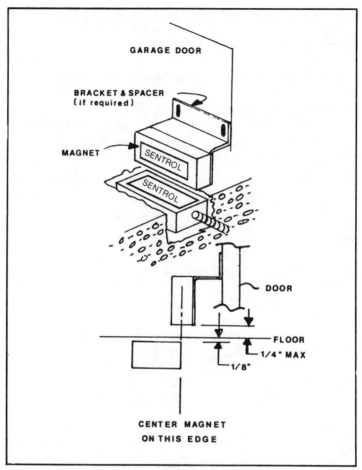

Fig. 7-35. Right side installation (courtesy of Sentrol Inc.).

Lay the switch into the chipped out area, with the cable in the channel. Attach an ohmmeter to the switch, close the door and test for proper operation.

Pour concrete to cover the switch and cable. After the concrete is dry, test the switch again. Connect to the alarm loop. For maximum security, it is best to continue the cable run in conduit after it exits from the floor.

INSTALLATION OF MAGNETIC CONTACTS ON SLIDING WINDOWS

The protection of aluminum sliding windows can be done with either a recessed or surface mounted installation. For the

331

recessed installation, remove the window from the frame as shown in Fig. 7-37. Determine where the switch will be mounted. The switch can be surface mounted (Fig. 7-38).

Depending upon the type of switch used, the size hole in the window frame will always be ⅜" in diameter. RTV compound will be used to hold the switch on (in either a perpendicular or horizontal manner) after the wires have been run.

Mount the magnet on the inside of the upper window channel, toward the top of the channel, with RTV mounting compound. It will take the RTV compound about 15 minutes to set; then replace

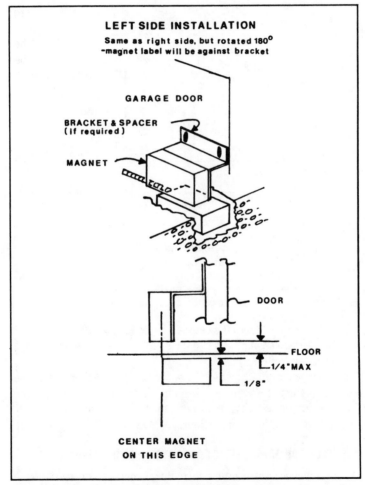

Fig. 7-36. Left side installation (courtesy of Sentrol Inc.).

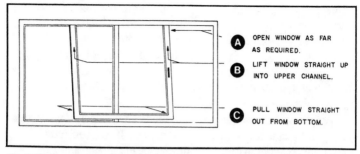

the window. Check continuity when the window is again in a closed position.

For surface installation, removal of the window will not be necessary for this type installation *unless* the switch leads are to be run into the channel. Mount the magnet on the window exactly opposite the switch when the window is closed. Check for continuity when the window is in the closed position.

INSTALLING MAGNETIC CONTACTS ON DOUBLE-HUNG WINDOWS

Here are three methods of mounting switches for this purpose. See Fig. 7-39.

Method one involves recessed installation in the top of the upper window and bottom of the lower window. Use a Sentrol

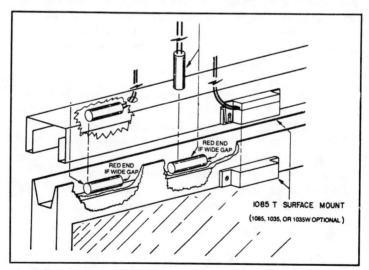

Fig. 7-38. The switch can be surface mounted (courtesy of Sentrol Inc.).

333

series 1055, 1059, 1065 or 1075 magnetic contact. Select the magnet position in the window frame and the position of the switch in the head or sill. Slightly overdrill the holes for the switch and magnet. Coat both the switch and magnet with RTV compound. Insert them in their respective holes. If the switch is a wide-gap one, remember that it is polarity sensitive. If the switch uses a bare magnet, observe correct polarity.

Attach an ohmmeter to the leads and check for proper operation. Connect the switch to the loop. If desired, cover the switch and magnet with wood filler to camouflage and improve appearance of the window.

Method two involves recessed installation in the sides of the window. Drill a vertical hole in the window frame. Coat the magnet with RTV compound and mount it in the hole.

Pick a position for the switch. This is determined by two requirements. First, the magnet must not be centered under the switch. Second, if a wide gap switch is used, observe correct polarity in mounting.

Drill a hole and insert the switch into the hole. Attach an ohmmeter to the leads, close the window and test for correct operation. Connect the switch to the loop.

This type of installation is recommended only when the wall is open and readily accessible for running wires (e.g., during construction or remodeling). A finished wall will make this a very difficult job, requiring extremely awkward "fishing." This application requires the perpendicular mounting of the switch and magnet and may require a wide gap distance between them. It is recommended that a switch from the Sentrol Concealed Contact Series be used for the best installation possible and also to ensure maximum security.

Method three involves surface installation on upper and lower windows. Select the appropriate surface mount switch and mount it on the head, sill or jamb in the desired position.

Mount the magnet on the window, directly opposite the switch when the window is closed. If wide gap or high security switches are used, be certain to align labels for same polarity.

Attach an ohmmeter and test for the proper operation of the switch. Connect the switch into the alarm loop.

PROTECTING A CHINA/SILVER CABINET

Many people like to display their fine silver and works of art in a China cabinet. With the increasing value of silver and various art

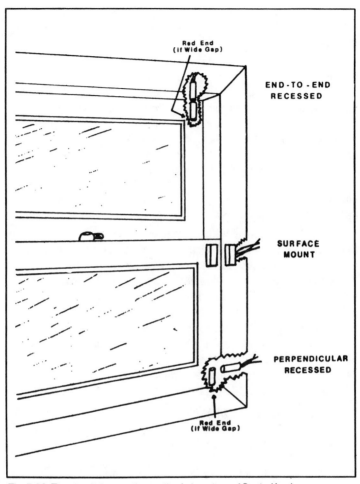

Fig. 7-39. Three switch mounting methods (courtesy of Sentrol Inc.).

pieces, it is highly recommended that these areas receive "spot" protection with an individual alarm switch attached (Fig. 7-40).

Be sure to alarm both doors if protecting a two door cabinet. Wire the switches in series. Contacts should not be placed in the hinged portion of the door, since the door can be opened wide before the switch would trip. For aesthetic reasons, recessed installation is more desirable than a surface mounted switch. If the China cabinet has one or several drawers that should also be secured with a switch, refer to the next possible application of switches.

For recessed installation, select the proper concealed contact to use. Determine the positions for the magnets in the doors and the switches in the cabinet.

Drill a vertical hole in the top of the door(s). Coat the magnet with RTV compound and insert it into the hole.

Drill a vertical hole in the cabinet for the switches. It will also be necessary to drill a hole at an angle from the inside of the cabinet to meet the switch hole, so the wires can be run into the inside of the cabinet. Be extremely careful during this operation to avoid drilling through the front of the cabinet.

Coat the switch with RTV compound and insert it into the hole, fishing the wires through to the cabinet inside. Route the wires in joints of the cabinet, around the top of the cabinet to the back. Drill a hole in the cabinet back and run the wires through.

Test for continuity with an ohmmeter. Connect to the alarm loop (on a 24-hour circuit if desired). Be certain to provide a shunt switch in the circuit, to permit access as needed.

For surface installation, select the place for the surface mount switches and position the magnet(s) on the door(s) and the switch(es) on the cabinet. Mount the switches and magnets, observing proper polarity and gap distances.

Route the wires around the top of the cabinet to the back. Drill a hole in the back and run wires through.

Test for continuity, and then connect to the alarm loop. Install a shunt switch in the 24-hour circuit to permit access as needed.

SECURING A VALUABLES DRAWER

This method can be used to protect a coin or stamp collection or the family silver. It is also an excellent method for securing personal and private papers. See Fig. 7-41.

For surface installation, select an area where the switch and magnet will not interfere with the operation of the drawer. Install the switch in the cabinet and the magnet in the drawer.

Test for continuity with an ohmmeter. Install the wires into the alarm loop (use a 24-hour circuit with shunt switch).

Recessed mounting is not recommended and may not be possible on metal drawers because the metal is usually too thin. If metal drawers are used, use a self-adhering contact, but be sure to allow for a 50% reduction in the gap distance in a steel environment.

Select the appropriate magnet and switch and drill a vertical hole in the side of the drawer. Coat the magnet with RTV compound and insert it into the hole.

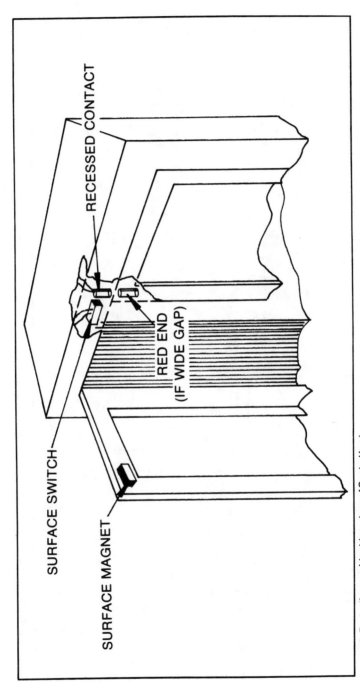

RECESSED CONTACT

RED END
(IF WIDE GAP)

SURFACE SWITCH

SURFACE MAGNET

Fig. 7-40. Protecting a cabinet (courtesy of Sentrol Inc.).

337

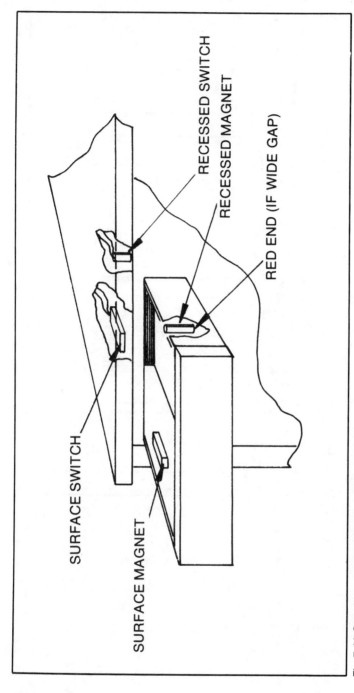

RECESSED SWITCH

RECESSED MAGNET

RED END (IF WIDE GAP)

SURFACE SWITCH

SURFACE MAGNET

Fig. 7-41. Securing a valuables drawer (courtesy of Sentrol Inc.).

Coat the switch with RTV compound and attach it to the cabinet *perpendicular* to the magnet. (Some switches can be mounted in plastic clips or self-adhesive clips.) Be certain the magnet is not centered below the switch, but is near the end of the switch.

Test for continuity. Install the loop.

NU TONE PRODUCTS SYSTEMS
INSTALLATION INSTRUCTIONS AND APPLICATIONS

The NuTone products detailed earlier as examples of specific systems to be installed in the home for both burglar and fire protection have various individual applications. They are described here.

The relay module for a NuTone smoke detector (Fig. 7-42) is used to provide a means for connecting auxiliary alarm devices to the smoke detection system alarms. Most installations require the use of the auxiliary power supply unit which would be wired between the relay and the remote alarm devices. When the relay is activated, it transfers power from the auxiliary power supply to operate the remote alarm device. A possible installation is depicted in Fig. 7-43.

Figure 7-44 is for the connection to various alarm devices including a bell, horn, telephone dialer and auxiliary relay. For a system using the telephone dialer only, Fig. 7-45 applies.

Fig. 7-42. Relay module for a smoke detector (courtesy of NuTone Division, Scovill Inc.).

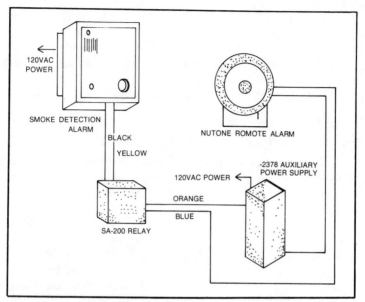

Fig. 7-43. A smoke detector installation.

Multi-family dwellings, an apartment complex building or town house would use the installation procedure in Fig. 7-46.

Mounting the Relay Module

The relay can be installed in a junction box used to mount a smoke detector, or it can be installed separately. It is important to note that the size of the junction box is determined by the number and type of wire connections that will be made in that box.

When installing the module in a separate box, the SA-200 relay module is wired to a single smoke detector or the last detector of a tandem connection. The junction box must have a minimum of 16 cubic inches. Figure 7-47 illustrates installation of the module in single and tandem circuits.

In the first two circuits shown, this is the perferred method when using the NuTone auxiliary power supply with the relay module. The module can be mounted adjacent to the auxiliary power supply to permit maximum distance between the power supply and the remote alarm devices by keeping the wiring between the power supply and the relay to a minimum.

When installing the relay module in a smoke detector box, either to a single detector or in a tandem circuit, the following

340

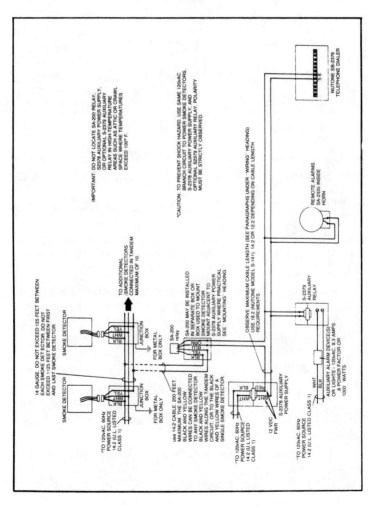

Fig. 7-44. Connecting the smoke detector to various alarms (courtesy of NuTone Division, Scovill Inc.).

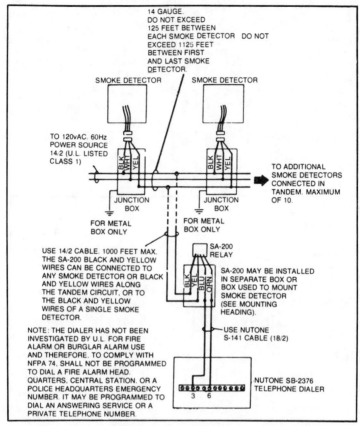

Fig. 7-45. A system using the telephone dialer (courtesy of NuTone Division, Scovill Inc.).

should be observed. A single smoke detector circuit or the last of a tandem connection means at least 20 cubic inches minimum in the box (Fig. 7-48). When wired along the tandem circuit, at least 26 cubic inches is the minimum required at the box (Fig. 7-49).

Wiring the Module

When wiring the module always observe local electrical code requirements. The alarm circuit wiring should also observe the various codes; thus, the following information refers to the maximum cable lengths that may be used.

Maximum cable length for the alarm circuit is determined by the wire gauge and the alarm devices used on that particular wiring circuit. To compute the maximum cable length for any one alarm circuit, add the load factor for each alarm device used on the circuit. Then divide that sum (not to exceed 100) into 4,000 (if using 18/2 cable), 10,000 (if using 14/2 cable) or 18,000 (if using 12/2 cable). Note that the cable length is the length of the wire pair; wire length is double the cable length.

Here are load factors for alarm devices. Load factor is 6 for a NuTone horn. Load factor is 15 for the NuTone auxiliary relay. Load factor is nil for the telephone dialer.

Example: two horns and two auxiliary relays:

$$\frac{4,000 \text{ (for 18/2 cable)}}{42} = 95'$$

If 95' is too short, take one of the alarm devices off that particular circuit and run it on a separate circuit, or use a heavier guage wire (14/2 or 12/2).

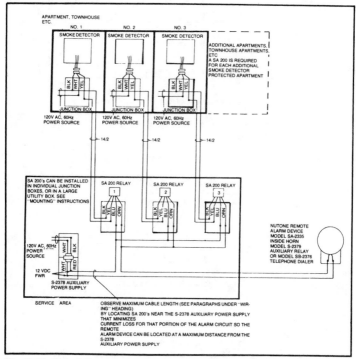

Fig. 7-46. An installation for an apartment or townhouse (courtesy of NuTone Division, Scovill Inc.).

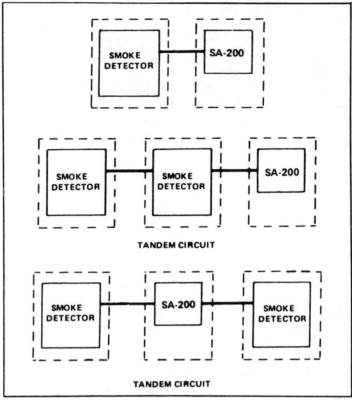

Fig. 7-47. Installation of the relay module in single and tandem circuits (courtesy of NuTone Division, Scovill Inc.).

Example:

$$\frac{4{,}000 \text{ (for 18/2 cable)}}{15 \text{ (one relay)}} = 266'$$

and

$$\frac{4{,}000 \text{ (for 18/2 cable)}}{21 \text{ (one horn and one relay)}} = 190'$$

or

$$\frac{10{,}000 \text{ (for 14/2 cable)}}{42 \text{ (two horns and two relays)}} = 238'$$

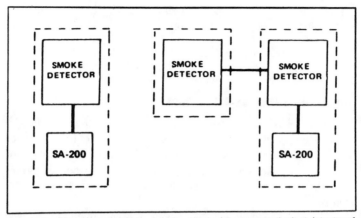

Fig. 7-48. The relay module is wired to a single detector or to the last detector of a tandem connection (courtesy of NuTone Division, Scovill Inc.).

The load factor for the entire system (sum of all alarm load factors) must not exceed 100. For determining cable lengths, cable resistances are as follows: 18 gauge, two-conductor, 13.02 ohms for 1,000'; 16 gauge, two-conductor, 5.16 ohms for 1,000'; and 14 gauge, two-conductor, 3.24 ohms for 1,000'.

Always short one end of your cable. Measure the resistance of the cable loop. Divide your resistance by the resistance of 1,000' of

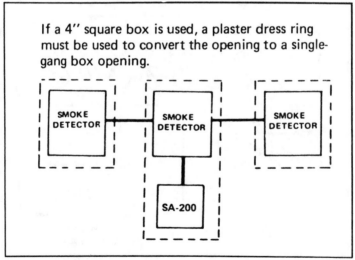

Fig. 7-49. The relay module is wired along a tandem circuit (courtesy of NuTone Division, Scovill Inc.).

345

the specific wire gauge used. Then multiply by 1,000 to calculate the cable length of your installation:

$$\frac{\text{Your Resistance}}{\text{Resistance for 1,000}'} \times 1,000 = \text{Cable length}$$

INSTALLING THE DRIVE-ALERT WARNING SYSTEM

Drive-Alert sensors (more than one sensor can be installed, if done in series) should be buried 6" deep and parallel to the edge of the drive where vehicles will be detected. If there is the danger of damage to the sensor from heavy vehicles, the sensor should be buried deeper. The sensor may be placed up to 5,000' from the control panel.

To avoid possible nuisance tripping, do not install the sensor or cable within 8' of power lines carrying a substantial amount of power. Also, stay as far as possible and feasible from utility lines and transformers and keep a minimum of 30' from high speed traffic.

Maximum sensitivity for the sensor and minimum time for the alert whistle has been factory adjusted. On the inside cover there is a diagram should you need to change this setting.

Extra sensors may be added and, if so, any splices buried or exposed to the weather must be soldered and waterproofed. This may be done by using a waterproof gum seal and/or wrapping with

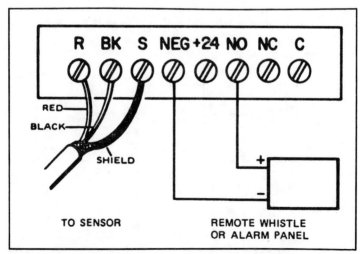

Fig. 7-50. The red, black and shield wires of the sensor cable are attached to the Drive-Alert system as shown (courtesy of B-W Manufacturers, Inc.).

346

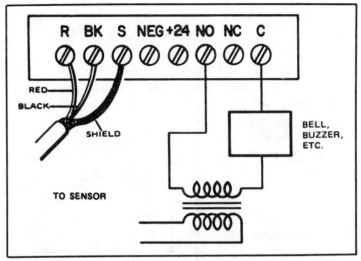

Fig. 7-51. A bell or buzzer is connected to the unit as shown (courtesy of B-W Manufacturers, Inc.).

Scotch brand #33 electrical tape which is available at electrical supply houses and home specialty stores.

The red, black and shield wires of the sensor cable should be attached to the Drive-Alert system as shown in Fig. 7-50. The 24 volt dc remote whistle or alarm panel is attached to the "NEG" and the "NO" points on the control system. The whistle *must* be in the ON position.

A bell, buzzer, etc., should be connected as shown in Fig. 7-51 to the unit using the maximum load of 5 amps at 30 volts ac. The whistle on the unit must be OFF.

To operate remote lamps, bells, etc., connect 24 volt dc 50 mA maximum coil current. The whistle on the unit must now be ON. Use the D_1 diode with inductive loads such as relays. In Fig. 7-52 D_1 is a 1 amp, 100 v diode, number 1N4002 or equivalent.

To connect a 24 volt dc remote whistle, relay or alarm panel with less than 50 mA, 24 volt dc input requirements, the whistle on the unit can be in the ON or OFF position. Use the D_1 diode with inductive loads such as relays (Fig. 7-53). Never connect 120 volt ac to the Drive-Alert terminals.

When used in conjunction with the Drive-Alert, the timer control turns on up to 10 amps of lights, sirens or bells. The unit simply plugs into a 12 volt outlet. The alarms and lights can be adjusted to operate from one to 45 minutes.

347

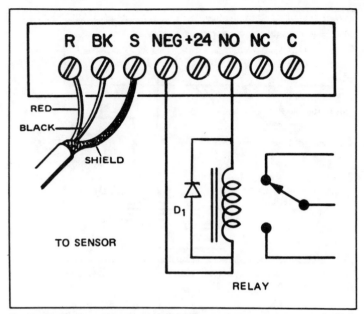

Fig. 7-52. Note the relay (courtesy of B-W Manufacturers, Inc.).

The same electronic whistle contained in the control box can be mounted on a chrome plate for installation in additional areas of the home or surrounding areas. As many as 10 remote whistles can be installed.

RADIO CONTROLLED GARAGE DOOR OPENER

For greater security, especially at night, it is best to enter directly into the garage and have the doors always closed behind the car before stepping out. For excellent security, an electronically controlled garage door unit can be installed (Fig. 7-54).

How the Door Opener Works

To open or close the door, you press the radio transmitter button (Fig. 7-55). When the garage door operator receiver unit gets the signal, it will open or close the door and turn on the light automatically.

To provide for reliable operation, the garage door opener is designed with a sophisticated solid-state circuitry, including an exclusive microcomputer (Fig. 7-56) which operates the motor unit. If the door opener should ever be without electrical power, the microcomputer will lose its memory (become unprogrammed) and may not operate the door properly.

If the electricity is off when you need to open or close the door, the operator's trolley can be disengaged so that manual opening or closing is easily effected. A key operated manual release can be installed to a trigger to open the garage door if this is the only entrance into the garage.

Checking the Garage Door

After purchase of the system, check over the contents very carefully, ensuring that all component parts are there. The first phase of preparation is the checking of the garage door.

Figure 7-57 illustrates two types of garage door counter-balance systems: *stretch* and *torsion springs*. Torsion springs are the most common. Check to see that you have at least 3⅞" clearance above the high arc of the door.

Open and close the door by hand. It must operate smoothly to insure the safe and satisfactory performance of the door system. The counterbalance system must also be properly adjusted.

Remove the garage door lockbar or make it inoperative. The locking device is not necessary because the garage operator's door arm and trolley keep the garage door in the closed position. Remove any ropes or other devices that may be attached to the door.

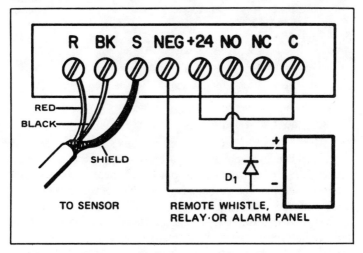

Fig. 7-53. The D_1 diode is used with inductive loads such as relays (courtesy of B-W Manufacturers, Inc.).

Fig. 7-54. The radio controlled garage door opener (courtesy of NuTone Division, Scovill Inc.).

Mounting the Front Wall Bracket

All the forces required to open and close the garage door are applied to the front mounting attachment. It must be adequately secured. If suitable woodwork is not already in place for mounting the front wall bracket, mount a 2″ × 4″ block of wood on the front wall, centered over the garage door, as in Fig. 7-58. If necessary, the front wall bracket may be mounted to a masonry wall by drilling the masonry and using expanding type masonry anchor bolts.

Close the garage door and measure the width of it from the inside. Find the center of the door and mark it with a vertical line on

Fig. 7-55. To open or close the door, press the radio transmitter button (courtesy of NuTone Division, Scovill Inc.).

the front wall, as well as the top edge of the door (see arrow in Fig. 7-59).

Open the garage door to find its highest point of travel. Use a level and mark a line on the front wall of the garage to indicate this point (1 in Fig. 7-60).

Mark another line that is between 2¼″ (minimum) and approximately 20″ (maximum) above the highest point of door travel. For best results, make the line between 3″ and 10″. Use a level to make this second line horizontal, as in 2 of Fig. 7-60.

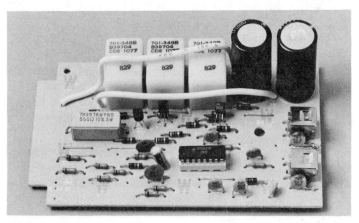

Fig. 7-56. Solid-state circuitry, including a microcomputer (courtesy of NuTone Division, Scovill Inc.).

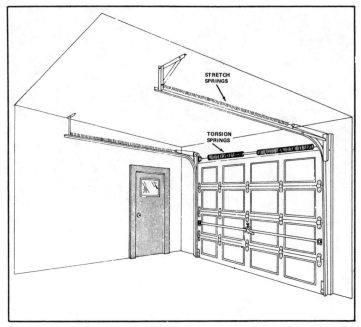

Fig. 7-57. Stretch and torsion springs (courtesy of NuTone Division, Scovill Inc.).

Align the front wall mounting bracket over the center of the garage door, and align it with the horizontal line made previously (1 in Fig. 7-61). Fasten the bracket to the front wall with two 5/16″ × 1½″ lag screws that have been inserted in a previously drilled 3/16″ pilot hole (2 in Fig. 7-61).

Mounting the Unit to the Ceiling

See Fig. 7-62. Position the rail mounting bracket up to the front wall bracket, resting the power unit on the garage door.

Fasten the rail mounting bracket to the front wall bracket using a 3″ drilled pin and hitch pin clip (Fig. 7-63). Prior to fastening, refer to these two notes.

Note 1: Torsion spring counterbalance system offers interference with mounting of the rail mounting bracket. The power unit must be set on a ladder in order to connect the bracket. Never allow the power unit to hang unsupported over the torsion spring or bar.

Note 2: Stretch spring counterbalance system offers no interference to the mounting of the rail mounting unit; therefore, you can leave the power unit resting on the garage floor.

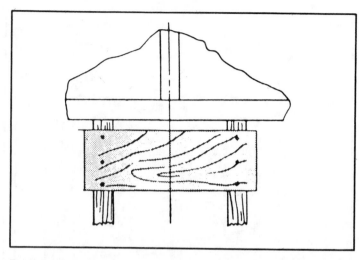

Fig. 7-58. Mount a 2" x 4" on the front wall, centered over the garage door (courtesy of NuTone Division, Scovill Inc.).

Raise the power unit to a point relatively level with the front wall bracket. Open the garage door to its fully opened position. Should the trolley interfere with the opening of the door, pull the trolley release down and slide the trolley back toward the power unit.

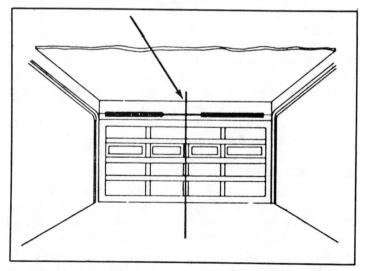

Fig. 7-59. Mark the center of the door with a vertical line (courtesy of NuTone Division, Scovill Inc.).

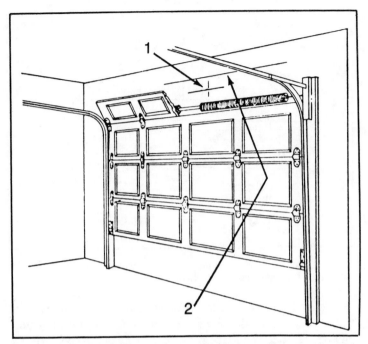

Fig. 7-60. Note the lines (courtesy of NuTone Division, Scovill Inc.).

Center the power unit over the garage door by lining it up with the center line previously made on the top edge of the door (see arrow in Fig. 7-64).

Mount the power unit with the two angle brackets (Fig. 7-65). (These brackets may be cut to meet the requirements of the garage construction.) There are three different mounting methods. See Figs. 7-66 through 7-68. Be sure the power unit hangs level with the front wall bracket.

Securely fasten the angle brackets to the ceiling rafters with the supplied screws. Fasten the power unit to the angle brackets.

Door Arm Attachment

Close the garage door to its *fully* closed position. Relocate the "close" (front) stop/clamp to the front of the garage (1 in Fig. 7-69). Loosen the clamp. Pry the clamp from the track. Slide the stop to the front of the track. Reassemble the clamp to the track. The final location of the "close" stop/clamp is determined later on.

Pull the trolley release lever down and slide the trolley to the front of the garage (2 in Fig. 7-69). Attach the straight door arm between the ears on the trolley, using the drilled pin and hitch pin clip. Note that one end of the straight door arm has a larger hole for this attachment (Fig. 7-70).

Attach the mounting bracket to the curved door arm (or straight arm) using the pin and hitch pin clip (Figs 7-71 and 7-72). For a one piece door with top tracks, do not use the curved arm. Attach the door mounting bracket to the straight arm (Fig. 7-73).

Fastening the Door Mounting Bracket to the Garage Door

If the garage door is a one-piece type with top tracks, disregard steps 1 and 2; go directly to step 3.

1. Move the trolley (with straight door arm attached) to a position which will allow the arm to be joined to the curved arm and provide the best location for the door mounting bracket (1 in Fig. 7-74). The door mounting bracket should be as near to the top of the

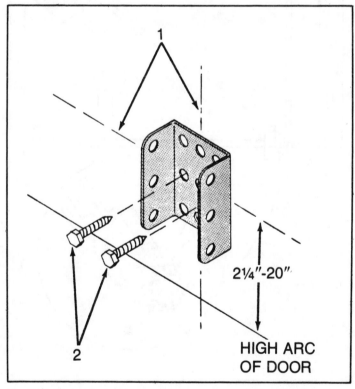

Fig. 7-61. Fasten the bracket as shown (courtesy of NuTone Division, Scovill Inc.).

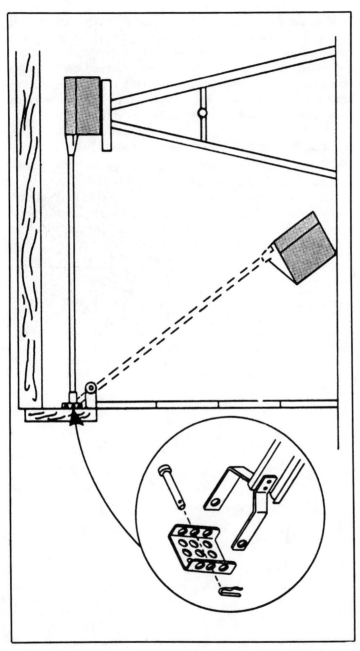

Fig. 7-62. Mounting the unit to the ceiling (courtesy of NuTone Division, Scovill Inc.).

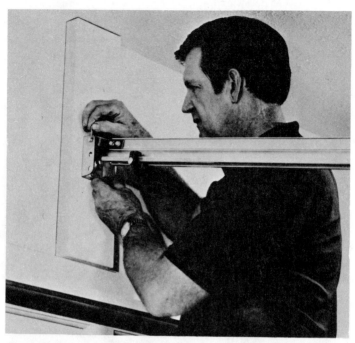

Fig. 7-63. Fasten the rail mounting bracket to the front wall bracket (courtesy of NuTone Division, Scovill Inc.).

garage door as practical. The straight arm should be parallel to the door and perpendicular to the garage floor (2 in Fig. 7-74).

2. Fasten the straight door arm to the curved door arm (3 in Fig. 7-74).

3. Use the door mounting bracket as a template to mark the location of the mounting holes (top of Fig. 7-75).

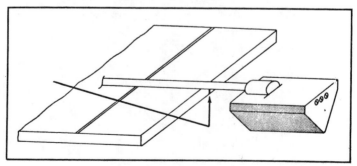

Fig. 7-64. Center the power unit over the garage door (courtesy of NuTone Division, Scovill Inc.).

357

Fig. 7-65. Mount the unit with the two angle brackets (courtesy of NuTone Division, Scovill Inc.).

4. Drill a ¼" diameter hole in the door, approximately ¼" higher than the location marks for the mounting holes. This will assure a tightly closed position for the door (bottom of Fig. 7-75).

5. Secure the door mounting bracket (Fig. 7-76).

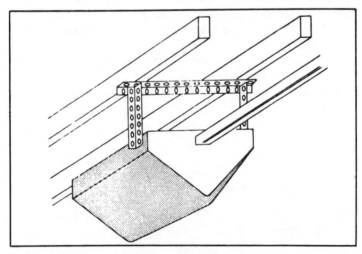

Fig. 7-66. Use this method when the operator rail runs parallel with the ceiling rafters (courtesy of NuTone Division, Scovill Inc.).

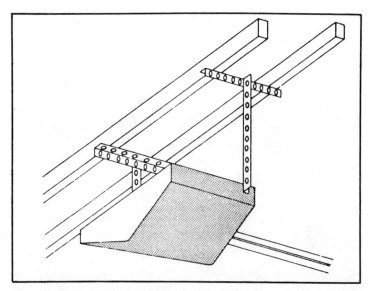

Fig. 7-67. Use this method when the operator rail is perpendicular to the ceiling rafters (courtesy of NuTone Division, Scovill Inc.).

6. Some doors may require reinforcement to prevent damage to the door and to provide a firm mounting point for the door mounting bracket. Use a light gauge or angle bracket for the reinforcement (Fig. 7-77).

Adjusting the Open and Close Stop/Clamps

With the door completely closed and the door arm connected to the door, relocate the stop/clamp against the trolley front rubber

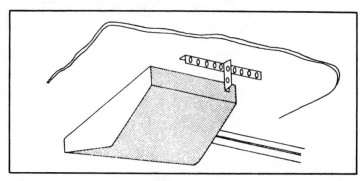

Fig. 7-68. Use this method when the power unit must be mounted directly to the ceiling. Be sure to anchor the screws into ceiling joists (courtesy of NuTone Division, Scovill Inc.).

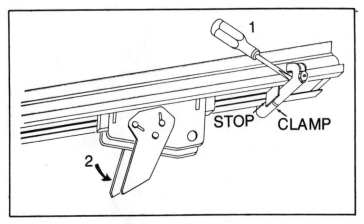

Fig. 7-69. The stop/clamp is relocated to the front of the garage (courtesy of NuTone Division, Scovill Inc.)

bumper (Fig. 7-78, thin arrow). Loosen the clamp nut. Pry the clamp from the track if necessary. Slide the stop against the front rubber bumper. Position the clamp against the stop and secure the clamp to the tack.

    With the trolley release lever disengaged from the screw drive, raise the door to its fully opened position. The bottom of the door should be even with the header in the garage. If the "open"

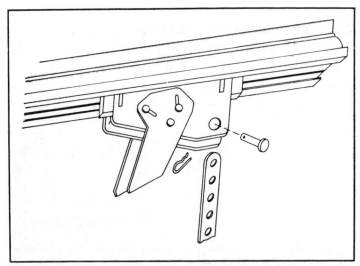

Fig. 7-70. One end of the straight door arm has a larger hole for the attachment (courtesy of NuTone Division, Scovill Inc.).

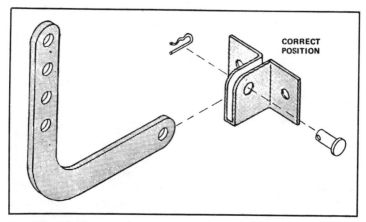

Fig. 7-71. Attach the mounting bracket to the curved door arm (courtesy of NuTone Division, Scovill Inc.).

stop/clamp does not allow the door to be fully opened, loosen the clamp and slide it back toward the power unit (1 in Fig. 7-79).

Hold the door in its fully opened position. Use a prop if necessary. Slide the "open" stop/clamp against the rear edge of the

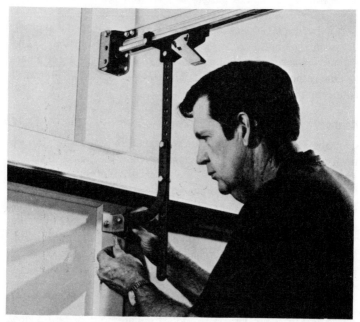

Fig. 7-72. Make the attachment as shown (courtesy of NuTone Division, Scovill Inc.).

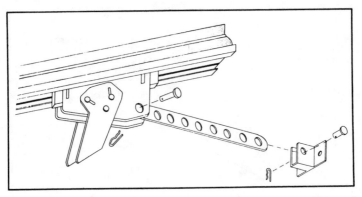

Fig. 7-73. Attach the door mounting bracket to the straight arm (courtesy of NuTone Division, Scovill Inc.).

trolley and securely tighten it in place (2 in Fig. 7-79). The stop/clamps are now adjusted for a closed door and an open door.

Connecting the Radio Receiver to the Power Unit

Figure 7-80 illustrates only one of the various models that come with the automatic garage door opener. We will assume that you have received the model GA585 radio receiver.

If the receiver is supplied with the three Z-terminals, use these to mount the receiver to the operator (Fig. 7-81). The supplied mounting bracket may be used instead of the Z-terminals to mount the receiver to the ceiling or wall. Make the electrical connections using three wires (Fig. 7-82).

Connecting the Wall Push Button Switch

See Fig. 7-83. Mount the wall push button switch where desired (1 in Fig. 7-84). The most common location is near the entry door. Locate it out of the reach of small children.

Run the two-conductor cable between the switch and the operator power unit. Connect the wires on screw terminals 1 and 2 on the power unit (2 in Fig. 7-84). If you use staples to secure the wires, be sure they are insulated to help prevent shorts (3 in Fig. 7-84). Apply the small caution label to a surface near the switch (4 in Fig. 7-84).

Installation of the Emergency Release

See Fig. 7-85. Drill a ⅞" hole through the door stile below where the door mounting bracket is attached (1 in Fig. 7-85).

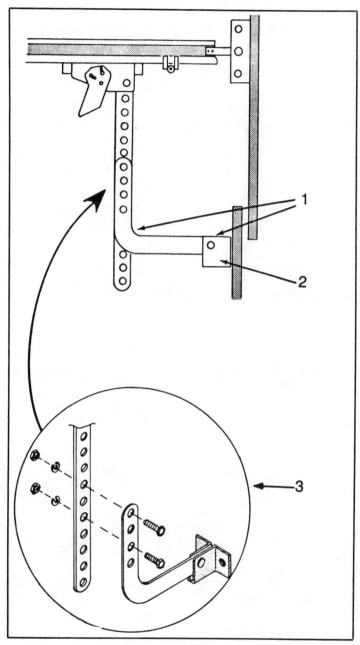

Fig. 7-74. Fasten the straight door arm to the curved door arm (courtesy of NuTone Division, Scovill Inc.).

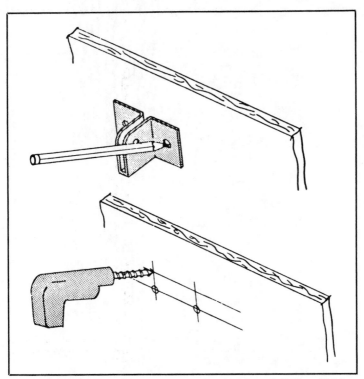

Fig. 7-75. Drill a ¼″ diameter hole in the door (courtesy of NuTone Division, Scovill Inc.).

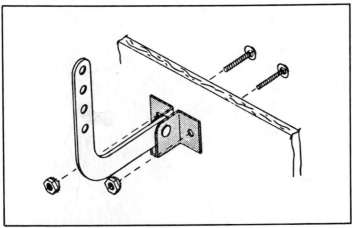

Fig. 7-76. Secure the door mounting bracket (courtesy of NuTone Division, Scovill Inc.).

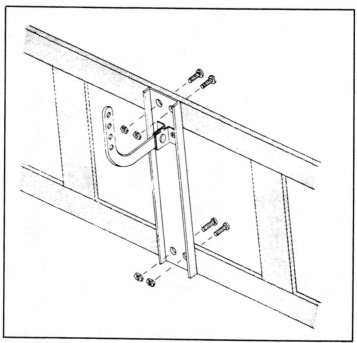

Fig. 7-77. Use a light gauge or angle bracket for the reinforcement (courtesy of NuTone Division, Scovill Inc.).

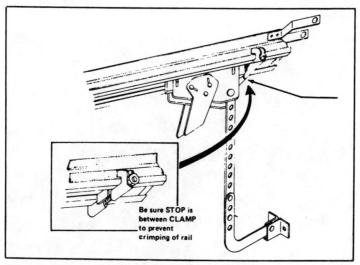

Be sure STOP is
between CLAMP
to prevent
crimping of rail

Fig. 7-78. Relocate the stop/clamp against the trolley front rubber bumper (courtesy of NuTone Division, Scovill Inc.).

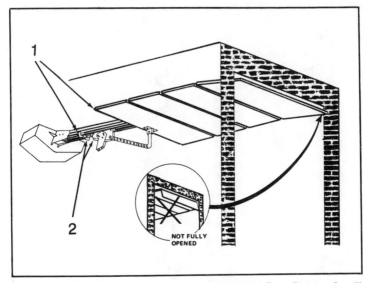

Fig. 7-79. Adjusting the open stop clamp (courtesy of NuTone Division, Scovill Inc.).

Thread cable through the spur washer, door and extension sleeve (2 in Fig. 7-85). With the spur washer around the lock barrel, insert the barrel through the door hole (3 in Fig. 7-85). Thread the extension sleeve onto the lock barrel and hand tighten (4 in Fig. 7-85).

Fig. 7-80. A radio receiver (courtesy of NuTone Division, Scovill Inc.).

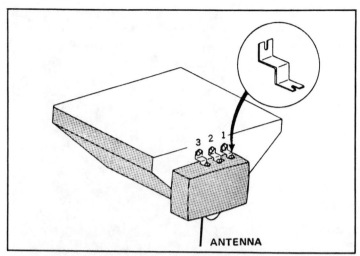

Fig. 7-81. Use the Z-terminals to mount the receiver to the operator (courtesy of NuTone Division, Scovill Inc.).

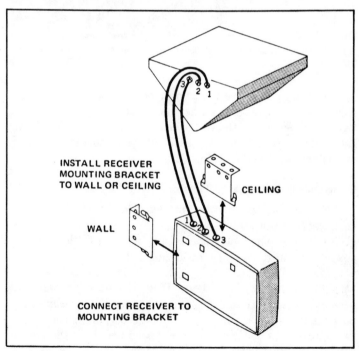

INSTALL RECEIVER
MOUNTING BRACKET
TO WALL OR CEILING

CEILING

WALL

CONNECT RECEIVER TO
MOUNTING BRACKET

Fig. 7-82. Make the connections using three wires (courtesy of NuTone Division, Scovill Inc.).

Fig. 7-83. Connecting the wall push button switch (courtesy of NuTone Division, Scovill Inc.).

Align the key slot vertically with the door, then lightly tap the lock barrel to seat the spur washer into the door face. Next, wrench tighten the extension sleeve to secure the lock (5 in Fig. 7-85). Using the "S" hook, attach the free end of the cable to the trolley manual release (6 in Fig. 7-85).

Connecting the Power to the Operator

Be sure the operator is grounded. Do not wire the circuit controlled by a wall switch.

A three-pronged plug and cord is attached to the operator power unit. Insert the plug into a three-hole receptacle.

The NuTone door opener can be connected to permanent wiring if required by local codes. First, remove the power cord from the electrical receptacle if it is connected. Next, remove the power unit cover. Disconnect the power cord by disconnecting the two wire splices and removing the ground wire from the ground screw. Loosen the strain relief screws and allow the cord to be pulled out. Run permanent wiring to the power unit using proper conduit and fittings as required by local electrical codes. Connect the wires, replace the power unit cover and secure it.

Programming the Operator for Close and Open Limits

Manually close the door and engage the trolley to the drive screw. Press the wall push button and release. The operator will open the door.

Push the wall button and hold in until the operator closes the door completely and the motor shuts off (down limit is now programmed). Press the wall button and release. The operator will open the door (open limit is now programmed).

Radio Control Unit

The NuTone automatic garage door system is designed to provide security and safety for you and your home in that you can

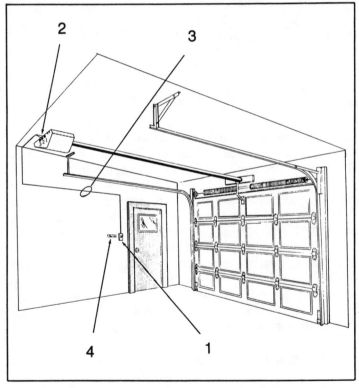

Fig. 7-84. A good location for the wall push button switch is near the entry door (courtesy of NuTone Division, Scovill Inc.).

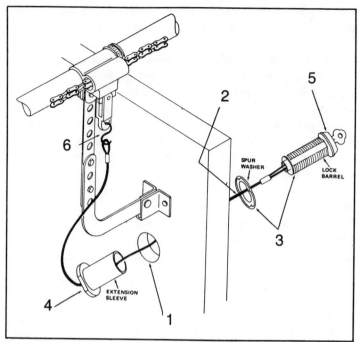

Fig. 7-85. Installing the emergency release (courtesy of NuTone Division, Scovill Inc.).

stay in your car while the operator opens the door and turns on a light. You can keep the door closed and secure when it is not in use. Both of these functions are as easy as pushing a button.

Various radio transmitters are available. No matter which one you use, it is important that the transmitter *not* be stored on an auto dashboard, seat or other location where it will be exposed to direct sunlight. This can damage the battery, transistors, case or other parts. The transmitter can be hand-held, clipped to the sun visor of the car or even mounted under the dashboard (Figs. 7-86 and 7-87).

The transmitter uses the standard 9 volt transistor battery. Replace the battery when the transmitter does not open the garage door. Battery installation is shown in Fig. 7-88.

Reprogramming the Microcomputer

To reprogram the operator, simply run the operator through an open cycle, beginning with the door in the closed position. It is important that if you have disengaged the trolley during a power failure (which would cause the microcomputer to become unprogrammed) in order to manually open/close the door, re-engage the trolley by pushing the release lever up (Fig. 7-89).

Press the wall button and then release it. The operator will open the garage door (or try to do so if the door is currently in the open position). If the door is already fully opened, the operator's light will flash eight times to indicate that the operator is unprogrammed due to a power failure.

Press the wall push button and *hold it in* until the operator completely closes the garage door and stops. Then press the wall push button and release it. The operator will open the garage door and stop. The operator is now properly reprogrammed.

Setting the Radio Transmitter Controls

The NuTone radio controls have a special feature that makes it *extremely* difficult for anyone to open the garage door with another radio transmitter. You set the radio controls to have any one of 256 different codes. Therefore, the chance of someone else in your area having the same code is extremely remote. There are eight tiny switches in the transmitter and a similar set in the receiver

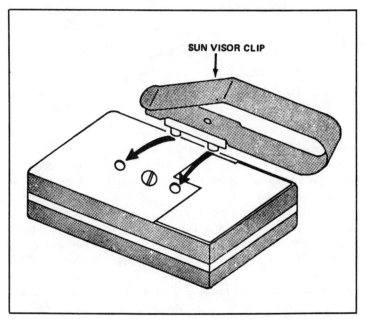

SUN VISOR CLIP

Fig. 7-86. The transmitter can be clipped to the car's sun visor (courtesy of NuTone Division, Scovill Inc.).

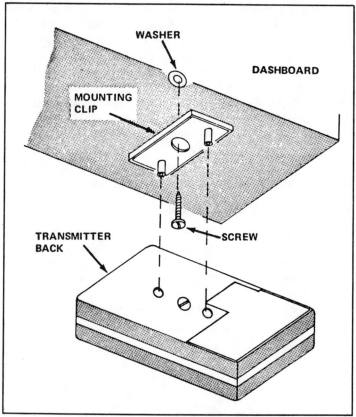

Fig. 7-87. The transmitter can be mounted under the dashboard (courtesy of NuTone Division, Scovill Inc.).

that are used to set the code (Fig. 7-90). Be sure the switches in the transmitter are set the same as the switches in the receiver. Before mounting the receiver in place, you must set the code for the radio controls.

For the receiver, the code switch is set by using a pen, pencil or similar object and changing *two or more* on/off switches to have your own personal code. Do not have all the on/off switches in the ON or OFF position. Such a code could easily be duplicated by someone else.

Put the code away in a safe place such as your personal file drawer in a desk, etc. Never put the code down on the transmitter or receiver where someone else could find, read and memorize it. It could also be hidden in your car.

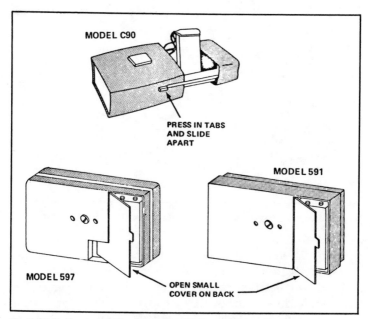

Fig. 7-88. Battery installation (courtesy of NuTone Division, Scovill Inc.).

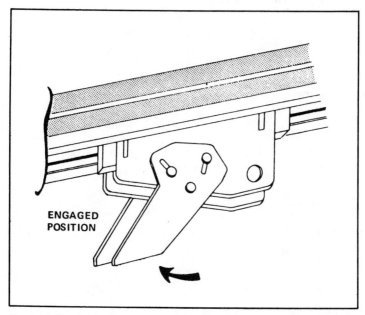

Fig. 7-89. Re-engage the trolley by pushing the release lever up (courtesy of NuTone Division, Scovill Inc.).

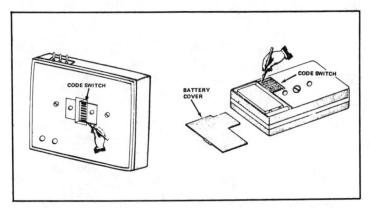

Fig. 7-90. Note the code switches (courtesy of NuTone Division, Scovill Inc.).

For the transmitter, remove the battery cover from the transmitter's back by prying up and lifting it away from the case. Set the code for the transmitter in the same manner as the receiver. Make sure the two are set to exactly the same code. If just one on/off switch is different, the radio control will not work. Replace the battery cover.

Auto Security Systems

The average car is very vulnerable to theft. On today's market, there are unique alarm unit devices that can help to protect the auto and its contents. Be aware, however, that if a thief really has a "need" to get into your car, an alarm unit or other such device will not deter him from attempting such a theft.

MASTER CONNECT SWITCH

One item in your arsenal against the auto thief is the *Master Connect Switch* (Fig. 8-1). It looks like a small lock and key gizmo or perhaps an oversized ignition switch that was misplaced, but in reality it can disconnect and lock up all the electrical circuits required for starting and driving the car. When installed and activated, the switch not only prevents the ignition from being activated in the normal manner but also stops the possibility of the car being started by jumping the wires. The power for operating the auto must pass through the switch or else the auto will not start or run. Power can only pass through when the switch is turned on. It has the advantage of being acceptable to both 6 and 12 volt systems, and also on 24 and 36 volt dc systems. It can be installed just about anywhere on a vehicle (even in the trunk with additional wires running up to the engine points of attachment).

Two other items of note for the Master Disconnect Switch are that the key is part of a coded security lock, so not everyone is going to be able to obtain a key for it. Also, the switch has the

375

Fig. 8-1. Master Connect Switch (courtesy of Bathurst, Inc.).

advantage of forestalling electrical fires and long term battery drain.

AUTO HOOD AND TRUNK LOCK

The *auto hood and trunk lock* (Fig. 8-2) from Ideal Security Hardware effectively secures any hood or trunk to prevent access without the proper key. The unit has a welded link hardened steel chain which also is covered with a plastic sleeve to prevent rattling and marring of the auto's painted surfaces. The lock is attached with *hardened tamperproof screws*. Your car may need two units, one for the hood and the second for the trunk. They can be obtained in a "keyed-alike" mode which means that only one key is required to open both locks.

When installing the lock, the selection of the screw attachment points is important. Naturally, you would not drill starter holes into the exterior auto metal. So you should look at the locking unit structure on both the trunk (or hood) and the body. There are excellent attachment points—you select exactly where you want the lock attached. Only minutes are required to attach the lock. Once in place, you are able to unlock the trunk (or hood) and open it just far enough to insert a second key and unlock the safety chain lock, which allows full entrance and access to the trunk. Very detailed installation instructions are included with the lock.

ANTI-THEFT IGNITION LOCK

Available data reveals that the anti-theft ignition locks required by the *Department of Transportation (DOT) Vehicle Safety Standard #114* do not provide for an adequate defense against theft. The time needed to defeat many of these locks varies from only a few seconds to several minutes. Further, the buzzers required by DOT to be installed in the cars for warning the driver that the ignition key is left in the ignition do not appear to be effective to any great extent. It is clear that additional and more stringent vehicle theft protection must be designed and put into effect to defeat the criminal element.

During a recent six year period, the number of auto theft offenses rose 23%. This loss exceeds over $1 billion annually. With over a million autos stolen annually, it is no wonder that every means possible should be taken to protect your auto from being stolen.

The *Lock Technology Corporation* (New Rochelle, New York) has developed a true, anti-theft device (Fig. 8-3). Installed in a few minutes, the steering column lock features a hardened face guard, special deadlocking retainer, a unique stress displacement ring and the world-famous Medeco high security cylinder and keys. It *cannot* be pulled, is drill resistant, pick resistant, and the cylinder has over 250,000 possible uniquely configured key combinations.

Since your car represents probably the second largest investment after your home, doesn't it seem prudent to provide the appropriate security to protect this large investment? The high security ignition lock is not currently available for all models of cars. When it is available for all models, you will be able to obtain

Fig. 8-2. Auto hood and trunk lock (courtesy of Ideal Security Hardware).

Fig. 8-3. A steering column lock (courtesy of Lock Technology Corp.).

the best protection possible by contacting your local qualified locksmith for such an anti-theft ignition lock. Two models of the lock that fit General Motors and Ford cars can now be obtained.

If your local locksmith/security supply store does not carry the high security anti-theft lock, contact may be made directly with the manufacturer. The address is in Appendix C of this book.

GARD-A-CAR AUTO IMMOBILIZER

The *Gard-A-Car auto immobilizer* (Fig. 8-4) is a low-cost answer to your auto security problem. Using the electrical circuit interruption principle, this small unit (2″ square) immobilizes the car when a thief attempts to start the vehicle.

In less than eight seconds, the timed circuit breaker within the unit will cut off all electricity flowing to the auto's distributor. A situation in which this unit could prevent your auto from being stolen might be as follows. While you are shopping downtown, a thief enters your car and quickly jumps the wires to start the engine. Putting the car in gear, he starts to move away. To his great surprise, the car suddenly stops working. The engine is dead! The thief cannot restart the engine since the auto immobilizer has effectively stopped the flow of current to the distributor. Being caught off guard, he must either flee or be caught red-handed. Your car is left behind. Even if the thief had a second key to the ignition switch, the car would still be immobilized.

The installation for this unit is extremely simple and takes almost no time at all. Unlike some devices, it requires no drilling to mount the unit, and it can be hidden anywhere in the car. Installation would be as follows. While there are no holes to drill, you should have a knife or pliers handy to help. Find a convenient place to locate the unit. The unit can be located at any point so long as the wires will reach the distributor. You can attach more wire to the unit if you feel, for safety's sake, that you want to mount the unit in the trunk or rear of the car.

Using the self-sticking adhesive backing, affix the Gard-A-Car unit. Pass the wires through any convenient hole up and through the firewall to the engine compartment. Cut the thin wires between the coil and distributor with the knife or pliers.

Connect the wires to the Gard-A-Car wires. It is best to use the insulated splice connectors that are supplied with the unit for this purpose. The wires will not be pulled apart. Crimp the splice

Fig. 8-4. Auto immobilizer (courtesy of Gard-A-Car, Inc.).

connectors with the pliers. Figure 8-5 illustrates the basic installation procedures.

Operation of the unit is by the simple flipping of the switch to the ON position. You turn it back to the OFF position when reentering the car. If an attempt is made to operate the car while the unit is in the ON position, pushing the reset button will reactivate the unit. Then you would flip the switch to the OFF position to use the auto.

Given time, these units can be defeated if a very determined auto thief figures out how the system operates. He could, possibly, trace the system wires back to the basic unit and flip the switch, but this would take time—time he cannot afford without being caught. While this unit immobilizes the auto, it does not sound a warning alarm to indicate that the car is being stolen.

AUTO PAGE ALERT SYSTEM

The more sophisticated auto alert system is exemplified by the *Auto Page* models 4000 and 4200 (Fig. 8-6). You are alerted by beeps and a LED flashing on your Auto Page receiver unit (Fig. 8-7).

The Auto Page 4000 is a powerful, low cost four-watt theft warning system which uses a coded radio signal. Having a continuous tone coding, of which there are over 1,000 possible code combinations, the system virtually eliminates false alarms and interference from other units. By use of a CB antenna, the system can transmit an individually coded signal up to eight miles away under ideal conditions, depending upon terrain and local atmospheric conditions.

Almost unlimited applications can be performed with the model 4000 since it is equipped with both positive and negative trigger terminals, which many other comparable systems do not feature. Because of these terminals, security can be included for

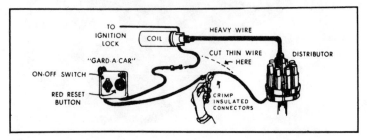

Fig. 8-5. Installation for the auto immobilizer (courtesy of Gard-A-Car, Inc.).

Fig. 8-6. The model 4200 auto alert system (courtesy of Auto Page Inc.).

other items to be protected from theft such as trucks, RV vans, boats and even private airplanes.

Essentially developed, though, for the car, the 4000 system can be also installed in the home, office or a storage facility for increased security. It can operate alongside other security systems which you may choose to install.

The Auto Page 4000 is also equipped with a terminal to defeat transmitting signals while you are driving. Thus, unnecessary transmitting is cut off and the transmitter unit can be protected. The miniature transmitter is mounted within the auto. Its signal is triggered when the sensors detect an attempted theft. The transmitter sends a signal to the small, highly sensitive (and lightweight) personal pocket receiver you carry on your person. The receiver warns you with its continuous beeping tone and the LED flashing only when it receives its own specially coded signal.

The Auto Page kit includes the following:

☐ The transmitter.

☐ The receiver.

☐ Two door-type microsensors.

☐ Two 1.5 AA batteries.

☐ Two mounting screws for the transmitter installation attachment.

☐ A coaxial cable for the car radio antenna.

You will need a drill and a screwdriver, some epoxy glue for the microsensors and a standard radio antenna (if you don't already have one mounted on the vehicle).

Fig. 8-7. 1.1e receiver unit (courtesy of Auto Page Inc.).

The batteries in the receiver should last up to three months in normal use. The battery life can be extended, though, if you will turn off the receiver when it is not in use.

Installing the Transmitter

The best place for mounting the transmitter is usually under the dashboard, on the firewall. This places the transmitter near your car radio and simplifies the connection to the car's radio antenna.

Carefully study how and where you will install the transmitter unit before you start. Don't mount it in the path of the heater or air conditioning air stream.

Mark the location under the dashboard where the two mounting holes will be drilled. Be careful that the area to be drilled is free from other wiring, trim or other possible obstructions. Drill the hole on the location marks and fasten the transmitter. Be sure to tighten down the screws securely.

The Auto Page system is designed to be powered from only a 12 volt dc negative grounded system. Most vehicles use the negative ground systems, but check yours before installing the unit. If connected to a positive ground system, it may damage the unit.

382

Antenna Mounting

Disconnect the car radio antenna and connect it to the antenna jack on the transmitter (Fig. 8-8). Connect the coaxial cable between the radio's antenna jack and the car radio jack on the transmitter. The connection will give your transmitter its maximum transmission range. However, if your antenna is broken off or if it retracts into the auto automatically, your security warning system may become ineffective. In such cases, you might want to add another antenna or connect a 1 to 2' piece of wire to the antenna jack of the transmitter. Then tape this wire near the window. The Auto Page 4000 is also equipped with a M-type CB antenna connector. By use of the CB antenna, transmission range can be extended up to eight miles.

Note that after connecting the transmitter to the antenna, you may want to repeak your AM radio's antenna trimmer for the best AM reception. Also, you should never use the CB antenna together with the car radio antenna.

Door Type Microsensors and/or Optional Plunger Switches

The wires from the door type microsensor must be connected to the positive sensor screws on the transmitter. The plain wire is the ground and should be connected to the negative sensor screws of the transmitter. The microsensors must be securely glued to the car door post or other location (Fig. 8-9). It is highly recommended that you use an epoxy glue for this purpose. To adjust the

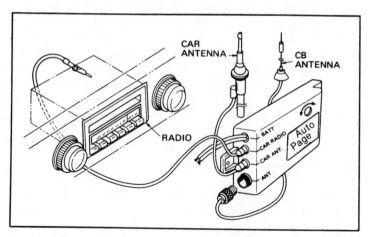

Fig. 8-8. Connect the antenna to the antenna jack on the transmitter (courtesy of Auto Page Inc.).

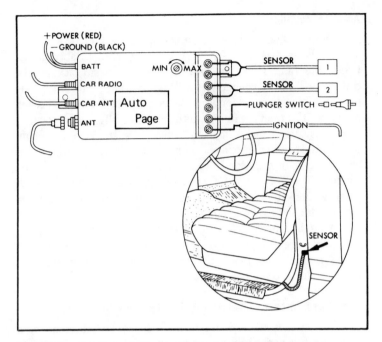

Fig. 8-9. Glue the microsensors properly (courtesy of Auto Page Inc.).

sensitivity, turn on the receiver using the ON-OFF switch and pushing the RESET button. Adjust the MIN-MAX sensitivity control on the transmitter until the opening of the car door activates the transmitter, thus triggering the receiver. Note that excessive sensitivity may cause false triggering of the transmitter unit.

The trigger screw terminals on the transmitter can be used for connecting optional switches (or even vibration type sensors). Positive and negative trigger terminals make many methods of triggering the transmitter possible, i.e., by the dome light switch, dome light and other switches, or plunger and other optional switches for the trunk, hood, passenger door, etc.

If you want the trigger on the transmitter by the dome switch, the lead wire should be connected to the trigger terminals as follows. If the dome light switch is placed on the negative side, the lead wire is connected between the lamp and the switch. It should be connected to the negative trigger terminal. If the dome light switch is placed on the positive side, the leadwire should be connected to the positive trigger terminal. Figure 8-10 illustrates this procedure.

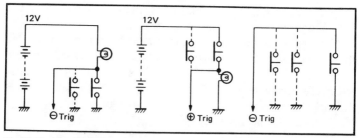

Fig. 8-10. The lead wire should be connected to the positive trigger terminal (courtesy of Auto Page Inc.).

Mount the plunger switches at the point of closure or the door frame jamb (Fig. 8-11). Do not mount them in any plastic or other non-metal surface in the car because the switches must be grounded. You will have to drill a ⅜" hole at each closure point.

Note that the Auto Page system is also used for one-way triggering. This is accomplished by connecting a push button switch to the negative trigger terminal and ground, or by connecting a push button switch to the positive terminal and the positive side of the battery. To "page" the receiver, just press the push button.

Connect a length of 16-22 gauge wire to the connector which will fit over the end of the plunger switch. Crimp the connector. Of course, the wire should be long enough to reach the transmitter. Screw the plunger switch into the hole and attach the connector with wire to the end of the plunger switch.

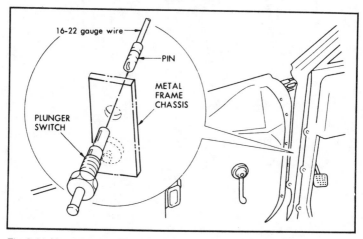

Fig. 8-11. Mount the plunger switches correctly (courtesy of Auto Page Inc.).

The Auto Page system also has a special application. The normally open trigger circuit (this is the internal circuit connected to the positive or negative trigger terminal) can also be triggered by a voltage sensor. A voltage sensor, which senses a voltage drop when the vehicle's dome light goes on as the door is opened, is connected to the negative trigger terminal. When the voltage goes up when the dome light goes on, the voltage sensor should be connected to the positive screw.

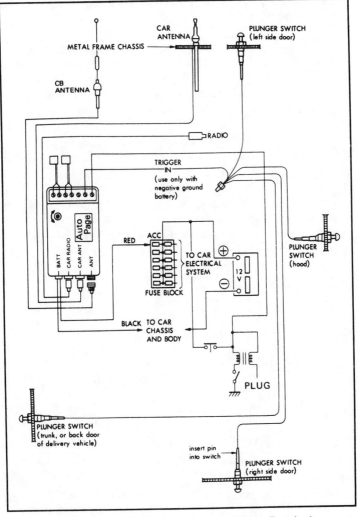

Fig. 8-12. Auto Page system wiring diagram (courtesy of Auto Page Inc.).

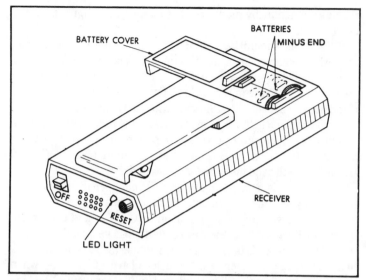

Fig. 8-13. Check to see if the batteries are properly installed (courtesy of Auto Page Inc.).

It must be noted that a good ground connection is important for the efficient operation of the Auto Page unit. Connect the ground wire (BATT on the transmitter) from the transmitter to a point on the frame or firewall of the auto. This must be connected to a metal contact point as shown in Fig. 8-12. For 12 volt dc power, connect the red BATT power wire from the transmitter to a point on the vehicle fuse block that is always hot, i.e, not switched off when the ignition is off.

Ignition Lead

To cut off unnecessary transmitting and protect the transmitter unit, connect this lead to the positive side of the vehicle ignition coil. Thus, the transmitting signals while you are driving can be defeated. If this lead is not used, your transmitter may operate while you are driving your own car.

Operating the Auto Page System

Set the receiver ON-OFF switch to ON. You should hear a beep sound from the receiver. If there is no beep or the LED doesn't flash, you should check to see if the batteries are properly installed (Fig. 8-13). When the receiver is beeping in the ON position, the RESET button should be pressed. This puts the receiver in a standby mode, ready to receive the signal from the unit transmitter.

Switches should be tested to insure that they have been properly connected and are functioning. This is performed by opening and closing each switch or else by rapping sharply with a metal tool next to the microsensors. Each time the receiver beeps, it should be reset and then the next switch or sensor tested.

Unless the RESET button is pressed, the receiver will always continue to beep after it receives a transmitter signal. Once activated, the beep tone is "latched" on until turned off. The transmitter will send the code for six seconds.

A warning is noted with this unit. Do not open the transmitter to make any internal adjustments. Such adjustments should only be made by a person in possession of an FCC 1st or 2nd class radio operator's license. Also, the Auto Page 4000 is designed for use by individuals with a CB license. This is because the system functions in the CB band of frequencies. If you don't have a CB license when you purchase this unit, fill out and mail in FCC form 505 CB which comes with the unit.

Like the 4000, the Auto Page 4200 theft warning system is an excellent system for vehicle theft protection. More complex, it has

Fig. 8-14. Auto Alarm (courtesy of GC Electronics).

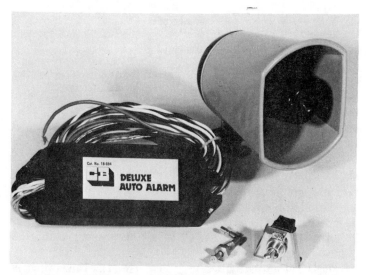

Fig. 8-15. Deluxe Auto Alarm (courtesy of GC Electronics).

a greater number of variables that can be included with the system, including the provision for a siren alert that can be mounted to the vehicle.

GC ELECTRONICS AUTO ALARMS

The *Auto Alarm* (Fig. 8-14) and *Deluxe Auto Alarm* (Fig. 8-15) from GC Electronics (Rockford, Illinois) are 100% solid state units. *Auto Alarm* features include the following: all solid state, weatherproof, operates off the car battery, 96 decibel horn, voltage sensing circuit and engine compartment installation. *Deluxe Auto Alarm* features include the following: all solid state, weatherproof, operates off the car battery, 96 decibel siren (high-low type), voltage sensing circuit and engine compartment installation, automatic reset and automatic delay, no external switch and an automatic siren reset after four minutes.

Additional sensor switches could be added to cover all doors, hood and the car trunk, if desired. Both these units have very desirable features and provide a high state of alarm security for any vehicle.

UNGO BOX

Techne Electronics' Ungo Box is the most advanced electronic security system designed especially to protect vehicles from theft

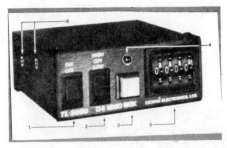

Fig. 8-16. Ungo Box (courtesy of Techné Electronics).

and vandalism. It contains one of the most advanced semiconductor technology systems available on today's market. Using the latest and most advanced digital integrated circuitry, the Ungo Box has been engineered to be a completely foolproof security system. Figure 8-16 illustrates the Ungo Box and the numbers identify the following system features.

ON/OFF Phase Interlock Switch (1). The switch is designed to deactivate the ARM/DISARM push button switch. The ON/OFF switch is to prevent any accidental arming of the UNGO Box and should be in the OFF position when the vehicle is left for servicing or when you are carrying passengers.

Motion Sensitivity Switch (2). This three-position switch is designed to let you set the motion memory of the Ungo Box to HI-OFF or LOW. In the HI position, the full motion detection system is in operation. In the LOW position, the less sensitive part of the motion detection system is in operation. In the OFF position, all motion is turned off. This switch should be in the HIGH position unless you are parked in a windy area or in a multi-story parking garage.

ARM/DISARM (A/D) Switch (3). When pressed, the switch will arm or disarm the Ungo Box.

LED (4). The LED will turn on when you open the car door, letting you know that the Ungo Box has been triggered. You now have 10 seconds to dial in your personal combination and press the A/D switch to disarm it.

Thumbwheel Switch (5). The switch is an in-line digital readout switch which functions in conjunction with the A/D switch. Rotating the number has no effect on the Ungo Box until you press the A/D switch.

Motion Sensitivity Adjustment (6). Always make sure the motion control is set in the HIGH position. This is a factory set point and is adequate for most vehicles. For a particular vehicle sensation, you can fine tune the unit's sensitivity.

Miscellaneous Home Security Applications

The incidence of automobile theft is high. People are turning to bicycles, mopeds and other forms of transportation. The greater availablity of these devices has led to a greater theft of them. One of the major reasons has been that, until recently, there has been no really safe way of securing them.

On the average, bicycles are locked up with just any available chain and lock the owner can obtain—usually as cheaply as possible. What is not always considered is the actual security integrity of either the chain or the locking device.

CITADEL ULTRA-HIGH SECURITY LOCK

For bicycles and mopeds, the best locking device is the *Citadel ultra-high security lock*, as seen in Fig. 9-1. A self-contained unit, it is the result of research performed at the Massachusetts Institute of Technology, which was done to design a lock that would be invulnerable to the tools used by the bicycle thief such as wire cutters, hacksaws, hammers, screwdrivers and the like.

Somewhat unusual in design, the lock has excellent security protection, which is increased by a special alloy material hardening. These alloying elements permit an extreme hardness of metal and also make it extremely tough and impact resistant. It uses a double locking mechanism at each end of the "U" shaped shackle.

The locking mechanism is the seven-pin circular key tumbler which means that just another key is not going to be cut by anyone,

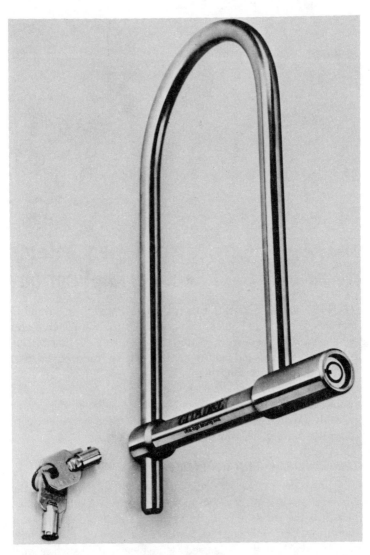

Fig. 9-1. Citadel ultra-high security lock (courtesy of Acro-Fab Industries, Inc., Bike Security Systems Division).

including even the locksmith down the street. The lock is electroplated for rust protection and covered with a tough polyvinyl-chloride plastic to prevent the marring of the bicycle's finish.

In tests of the ability to withstand cutting with the Citadel against other standard chains and cable locks and also coiled cable, (bolt cutters, cable cutters, hacksaws and prybar smashing were

Fig. 9-2. The Citadel is fine for securing bicycles (courtesy of Acro-Fab Industries, Inc., Bike Security Systems Division).

used), only the Citadel passed every test without being cut. Remember this when you purchase such a lock. The Citadel is not cheap ($25-$40 being the going price). The Citadel doesn't have to be used just for the bicycle; it can also be used on mopeds and motorcycles (Figs. 9-2 and 9-3).

Fig. 9-3. The Citadel can be used on mopeds and motorcycles (courtesy of Acro-Fab Industries, Inc., Bike Security Systems Division).

CHAINS AND CABLES

Naturally, not everyone can afford up to $40 to protect a bicycle. Let's look at some other products in other price ranges that are also very effective as deterrents to bike and moped theft.

Anti-theft chain and cable is specially designed in a security chain or cable configuration. Any chain used should be one that is either called "hardened" chain or "anti-theft" chain. These are specially designed security chains resistant to saws. Many contain a boron bearing alloy allowing for extreme hardness,. Also, they are heat treated to the core of each individual chain link.

In conjunction with the chain should be a well-built lock that has a locking mechanism which is difficult to open with another key. Figure 9-4 illustrates such a lock. Note it has the popular *Ace* key; this is one of the most difficult locks to pick, even for the locksmith. Casings for bicycle locks should be rustproof and of

Fig. 9-4. A rustproof lock (courtesy of Campbell Chain Co.).

case-hardened steel. The locking shackle should also be of hardened steel to resist cutting and attacks by saws.

The *snap-back cable* is popular for securing bicycles (Fig. 9-5). It is a flexible, aircraft type galvanized cable that has a self-recoiling feature which makes it easy to store when not in actual use (Fig. 9-6). Normal anti-theft snap-back cables come in 6' lengths, which are adequate to go through both bicycle wheels, around the frame and around a stationary object (Fig. 9-7).

A recent development by the Campbell Chain Co. in motorcycle and moped security is the *moped chain and lock* (Fig. 9-8). The chain lock is a two piece unit, which attaches through the chain links (Fig. 9-9) and then is locked in place (Fig. 9-10). An unusual lock, it looks different because of not having the conventional locking shackle so closely associated with a standard lock. Figure 9-11 shows the locking/unlocking procedure required to use the moped security lock.

BOAT SECURITY

Many homeowners have a boat tucked away at a boat slip—usually quite some distance from their home. While there

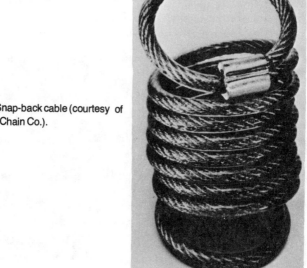

Fig. 9-5. Snap-back cable (courtesy of Campbell Chain Co.).

Fig. 9-6. The cable is easy to store (courtesy of Campbell Chain Co.).

may be just a few boats also present, it is not always possible for each one to be personally observed and checked by the boat dock area security guard team. As such, it becomes imperative that the security-minded boat owner take appropriate steps to provide for the security of the boat—steps that will ensure that either another boat owner or the security team is aware of an intrusion on your boat. The *Racon Boat Watch Marine Security System* does just that.

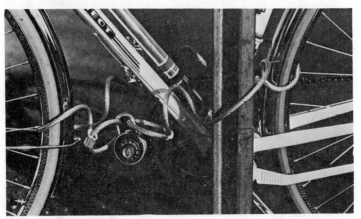

Fig. 9-7. The cable comes in 6' lengths (courtesy of Campbell Chain Co.).

Fig. 9-8. Moped chain and lock (courtesy of Campbell Chain Co.).

A self-contained microwave protection unit, the Boat Watch (Fig. 9-12) provides full protection around the clock. The unit mounts inside the boat cabin and sounds an alarm when an intruder is detected. It operates from the boat's existing 12 volt dc battery system and its wired into the ship's horn. A key switch (ideally located near a logical entry point to the boat) can be used to disable the system by the boat owner upon his return to the craft.

The Boat Watch can be installed in any convenient location, such as a bulkhead or cabin top. The unit comes supplied with its own mounting bracket which allows rotation for the best coverage.

The range of the Boat Watch (the coverage pattern) is adjustable up to a maximum of 30'. The detection sensitivity is also adjustable.

Figure 9-13 illustrates a typical horizontal coverage pattern. The vertical pattern would be slightly smaller. Each square in the illustration represents 3'.

Installation instructions are as follows. The Boat Watch must be mounted on a solid area, like the bulkhead, so the area of protection covers the most valuable items. Connect #18 wire from

Fig. 9-9. The lock is a two piece unit (courtesy of Campbell Chain Co.).

the ship's battery to TB-1, terminals 1 and 2 (refer to Fig. 9-14, typical wiring diagram for all electrical connections). This line should be protected with a .5 amp fuse.

Connect #18 wire from TB-1, terminals 5 and 6, to the ship's horn button (or horn relay) via a STST key switch (an optional device) located near the boat's entryway. This allows the system to be disabled upon owner entry to the boat.

With the key switch turned OFF, turn the power to the Boat Watch to ON. You may have to pull the tamper switch.

Allow the system to settle in for a full five minutes. Then adjust the range to provide coverage over the area of desired protection. The LED will blink when movement occurs and then stay on, indicating an alarm condition. Walk around the outside of the cabin to walk test for excess sensitivity and then readjust the range, if necessary, until detection is observed outside.

Fig. 9-10. The lock is in place (courtesy of Campbell Chain Co.).

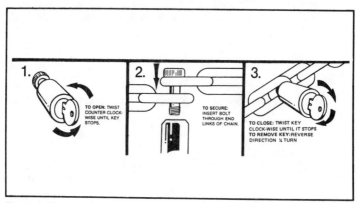

1. TO OPEN: TWIST COUNTER CLOCK-WISE UNTIL KEY STOPS.

2. TO SECURE: INSERT BOLT THROUGH END LINKS OF CHAIN.

3. TO CLOSE: TWIST KEY CLOCK-WISE UNTIL IT STOPS TO REMOVE KEY: REVERSE DIRECTION ¼ TURN

Fig. 9-11. The locking/unlocking procedure for the moped lock (courtesy of Campbell Chain Co.).

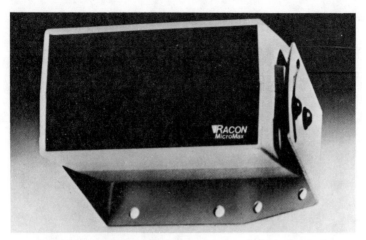

Fig. 9-12. The Boat Watch (courtesy of Racon Inc.).

Test the complete system, as follows. Exit the cabin and turn the key switch ON. Enter the cabin; the boat horn should sound after approximately two steps inside the cabin. Stand still; the horn should go off in approximately five seconds. If a faster or slower detection is desired, the detection sensitivity jumper may be moved to a lower or higher number, respectively.

Hanging lamps and cabin curtains in the protection area zone should be secured. If nuisance alarms occur, detection coverage and sensitivity should be reduced. This is accomplished by turning the potentiometer counterclockwise and making higher settings on the step detection jumper.

Double check all electrical connections and replace the unit cover tightly. The Boat Watch is now ready to detect and warn of intruders on your boat.

ZEISS LOCK

Trailers, mobile homes and campers have the need for solid, well-built door locks. Since the door is the weakest point, it is also

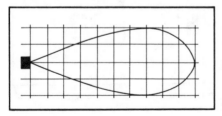

Fig. 9-13. Horizontal coverage pattern (courtesy of Racon Inc.).

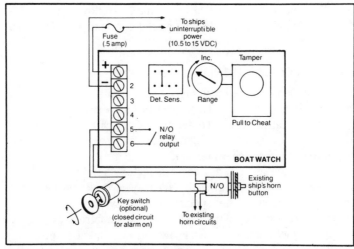

Fig. 9-14. Boat Watch wiring diagram (courtesy of Racon Inc.).

the most vunerable and only realistic method of gaining entry. As such, a secondary door lock is an absolute must.

The Zeiss lock is a well-crafted lock, especially created for this purpose. Figure 9-15 illustrates the lock as it would have to be affixed to the door of a house trailer or small camper. The extra protection provided by this lock includes:

☐ Double-bitted key and double-pinned cylinder.
☐ Six pin true security.
☐ Metal plate to prevent rapid break-in.
☐ Heavy duty bolts through the door for extra protection.
☐ Strike backup pieces for greater strength and added security.

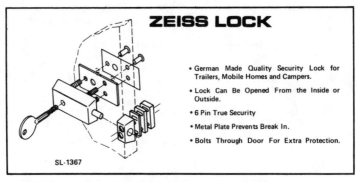

Fig. 9-15. Zeiss lock (courtesy of Blaine Window Hardware Inc.).

The installation of the lock is as simple as following Fig. 9-15. Time for installation should not exceed one hour under normal circumstances.

HOME OFFICE EQUIPMENT PROTECTION

Many people have home offices or at least several pieces of office equipment around. These can include expensive electric typewriters, calculators and other movable machines. Figure 9-16 illustrates the uniquely designed and patented Bolen locking system devices for such equipment.

Each Bolen security device has been tested and approved as a foolproof method of insuring the security of desk and table top business machines. The special locking system dramatically reduces the possibility of theft. The locks are unobtrusive and easy to apply. Once installed, you know the equipment is properly guarded. The equipment becomes unremovable unless your seven-pin tumbler burglar alarm type key (the Ace key again) is used to unlock the tough locking body that is free-spinning and wrench-resistant. The locks are also crushproof and designed to

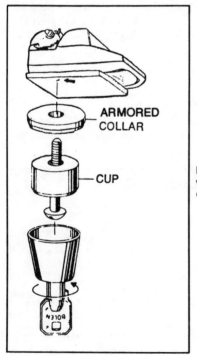

ARMORED COLLAR

CUP

Fig. 9-16. Bolen locking system devices for office equipment (courtesy of Bolen Industries, Inc.).

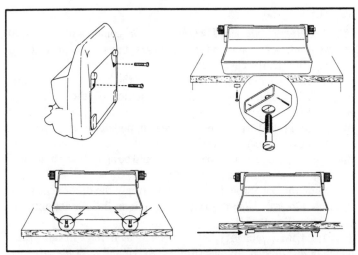

Fig. 9-17. Attaching the Bolen 200 to a typewriter (courtesy of Bolen Industries, Inc.).

withstand attempts to batter them apart. The steel locking bars of the various units have been heat treated and hardened.

The Bolen 200 is the most simplilified of the locking units. Figure 9-17 shows an exploded view of the device and how it would attach to a typewriter. With this particular unit, the lock is used in conjunction with the mounting screws originally provided by the equipment manufacturer. Installation would be as follows.

Mark and drill a hole for the mounting screw. Insert the key into the lock so that the "wing" at the key bottom enters the slot in the brass ring. Push the key in as far as it will go. Then turn it clockwise until the slot is at "0." Shake or pull out the cup inside the lock.

Insert the mounting screw through the hole in the cup. The head of the screw should be inside the cup. If necessary, you may use a washer.

Place the armored collar over the screw. The center groove should seat on top of the cup. Insert the assembly through the drilled hole and tighten the screw to the equipment.

Slip the lock over the cup. Holding the lock in place, push the key in and turn it counterclockwise until the slot is lined up with the "L." Remove the key. If the lock fully covers the cup and rotates freely, the equipment is securely locked in place. Removing the lock means holding firmly while inserting and turning the key clockwise to "0."

Bolen Locking Bars

The *Bolen Universal Locking Bar #95* comes with two ¼-20 screws to fit most common typewriters. If the screws prove to be too long, they can be cut to size.

Insert the mounting bolts in place at the base of the machine (Fig. 9-17A). Place the machine in position on the desk (Fig. 9-17B). Mark the spots where the holes are to be drilled. Remove the typewriter and drill the holes to accommodate the two screws.

Remove the screws from the machine's base. Insert a screw through the bracket. The small hole should be against the bottom of the desk. Tighten the screw down (Fig. 9-17C).

Slide the bar through the bracket. Apply the other screw and the Bolen lock through the remaining hole in the bar and into the typewriter (Fig. 9-17D).

The IBM Selectric typewriter has its own *Bolen Locking Bar*, which is installed as follows (Fig. 9-18). Upend the typewriter so the bottom faces you. Remove the two plastic blocks from the machine base where the bar will be applied.

If the typewriter is a Selectric II model, peel the adhesive backing from the felt pads. Apply the pads to the feet of the typewriter to prevent rattle or excessive vibration. If the machine is a Selectric I model, the pads are not necessary.

The Selectric I will use the short spaces and short holes in the Locking Bar. Install the bar on the base of the machine with the center stud pointing toward you. The spacers must be used in order to prevent warping of the typewriter frame.

Set the machine into position and mark where the stud will go through the desk. A ⅜" hole is drilled for the stud.

Place the typewriter down so the stud enters the hole. Put the Bolen lock in place. The center screw *cannot* be longer than the thickness of the desk; if it is, cut it to the proper length.

Bolen Cable Lock

The *Bolen Cable Lock* is used with other pieces of office equipment and is installed as follows. Most equipment is installed in a two-part case which comes apart easily when you remove the screws which hold it together. Turn the equipment over and remove the screws. Turn the case right side up again and separate the two sections.

Locate a place to the side of the bottom section where there is space enough to accommodate the grooved metal stem of the cable. Be sure the place selected ensures that the stem of the cable will

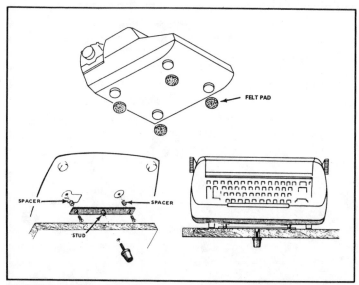

Fig. 9-18. Installation of the Bolen Locking Bar for an IBM Selectric typewriter (courtesy of Bolen Industries, Inc.).

not come into contact with any of the electrical or mechanical parts (Fig. 9-19A). If you cannot find such a space on the bottom section, then find one on the top section. Drill a ¼" hole in the case at that point (Fig. 9-19B).

Space washers are provided with the cable lock so, if necessary, add a sufficient number so the stem extends into the case far enough to accept only one washer and the provided spring clip. The purpose is to create a rigid "sandwich" that will prevent the stem from wobbling or moving in or out of the case (Fig. 9-19C).

The spring clip should be firmly pushed into the groove of the stem. This will hold the cable stem in place. The clip should be on the outside of the case.

To install the locking end of the cable, place the machine with the attached cable on the desk in the approximate position where it will be used. Allow for the length of the cable, finding a convenient and unobtrusive place to mount the shoe (the piece of metal that will have two holes and a hollow stem). It may be mounted on the leg of the desk, under the desk top or even into a wall stud, etc. Install the shoe, using the screws provided (Fig. 9-19D).

Place the loop of cable over the hollow stem (Fig. 9-19E). Place the cover assembly over the shoe, making sure that the sides

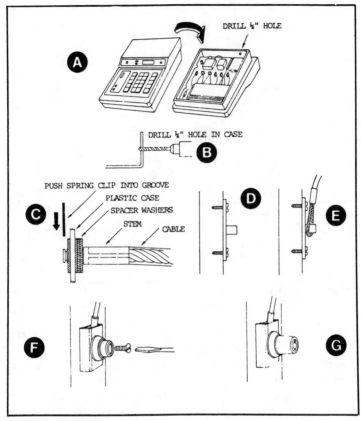

Fig. 9-19. Installing the Bolen Cable Lock (courtesy of Bolen Industries, Inc.).

of the cover straddle the shoe plate to prevent rotating.

Fasten the cover by applying the machine screw through the cup. Insert the lock cylinder over the cup and lock with the key (Figs. 9-19F and 9-19G).

With all the Bolen locking devices, always record the number of the key. If you ever lose the key or require another one, you will have to forward this particular number to Bolen Industries (along with $2.50 for a replacement key). The address may be found in Appendix C.

WEIL PRODUCTS LOCKS

Thinking about keys, let's look at a number of locks that you might just purchase for the home. They may be used to lock up a small child's bicycle that doesn't cost a lot, as an added lock to

Fig. 9-20. Some Weil Service Products locks (courtesy of Weil Service Products Corp.).

Fig. 9-21. The Time-All II (courtesy of Intermatic Inc.).

another bicycle chain, or for the garage, barn or other outbuilding. Also, you may have a tool chest or other items that can be secured with a lock (and/or with a lock and chain). When selecting a padlock, it's important to select the lock that meets your security demands. Appendix B is a discussion of possible considerations when you are selecting a padlock.

Weil Service Products has a number of different locks that can be considered for home use. Included are the *brass case cylinder lock,* the *combination lock* and the *laminated steel hardened shackle lock* (Fig 9-20). In addition, the magnetic super security padlock is an excellent choice in that there is no keyway for picking. It operates off a magnetic keying principle with each key different as with any lock. It is pickproof, weatherproof, contains no combination, resists hacksaws and bolt cutters, and has a super tough strength shackle.

Fig. 9-22. The Master Control (courtesy of Intermatic Inc.).

Fig. 9-23. All-Weather Time-All (courtesy of Intermatic Inc.).

AUTOMATIC TIMING DEVICES

Outside or inside the home, the *automatic timing device* is a great boon to home security. Records of police departments across the nation testify that a home protected with automatic timing devices is less likely to be the target for burglars and vandals. Such timers can control and light a home, giving the home a lived-in appearance. Several Intermatic models are presented here for your consideration.

The *Time-All II* is a compact table top timer (Fig. 9-21). It is fully automatic and controls lights and appliances at preselected times. Temporary and permanent controls are built into the unit.

The *Master Control* (Fig. 9-22) has 24 different tabs that allow for multiple daily programming. Control several lamps, a radio and the TV when you're away from home. The unit also has a manual on/off to permit the use of individual home devices without disturbing the automatic operation of the unit.

The *All-Weather Time-All* (Fig. 9-23) is another multiple timer, except that this one is weatherproof. A 24-hour multiple program dial allows the preselection of up to 12 on/off cycles for indoor or outdoor applications.

Closed Circuit Television (CCTV)

Closed circuit television (CCTV) is basically the same as having your home camera take pictures live and seeing them instantly on television. The most basic system consists of a camera, the TV monitor and a coaxial cable which connects the first two. While these are the basics of the system, it would not do you much good to have one unless you could monitor its use constantly.

CCTV CAMERAS

Several types of lenses can be used with a CCTV camera: a *telephoto, wide-angle* or the *regular lens* unit. CCTV cameras can be manual or automatic. The automatic camera is motor-driven and is constantly moving, surveying a wide area that cannot be viewed by a manually mounted camera that does not see an entire spectrum but rather just a small portion of it. Some cameras can also have a tilt unit built-in addition to the motor function for automatic scanning. These camera systems, with all the functions, are somewhat costly and are usually used in commercial or industrial type applications, wherein there is a constant security guard monitoring the systems.

CCTV has made many advances during the short period of time it has been offered to the general public. The security aspects and possibilities of CCTV are almost endless. While many homeowners will never need to have a CCTV type monitoring unit for their premises, there is a proven need for a system that allows for the safety and security of the individual while at home.

Fig. 10-1. Talk-A-Vision (courtesy of Koyo International Inc. of America).

TALK-A-VISION

Talk-A-Vision (Fig. 10-1) is a very new concept for the homeowner from Koyo International of America. It has proven applications for watching the front door or remote areas of the grounds. It can be used for visitor reception and control and also is excellent for use by invalids who are unable to monitor certain areas of the building and grounds.

The Koyo Talk-A-Vision system is easy to operate and install. Consisting of four units, the CCTV camera, a monitor, interphone and the remote interphone unit, the system is activated when the call button is pressed by a visitor to the home. This sounds a two-tone chime at the intercom handset master. At the same time,

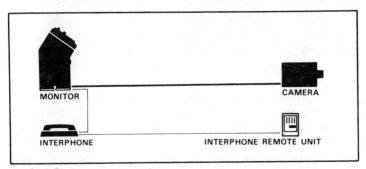

Fig. 10-2. Basic system connections.

412

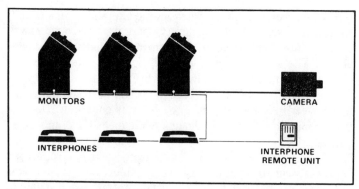

Fig. 10-3. An interconnection design.

the camera and monitor go into operation. The camera and monitor are always in a standby condition. This will allow for an instant live picture on the monitor as soon as the intercom remote door station call button is pushed. The camera and monitor can be adjusted to operate from just 30 seconds to three minutes after starting up. The system can also be held in a continual monitoring mode, so you can always check and see if someone is at the door or not. This procedure is done by setting a standby switch on top of the CCTV monitor to "picture on." The camera and monitor goes instantly to the "on" condition and the picture appears continuously. Figure 10-2 illustrates the basic system connections.

Talk-A-Vision can also be used with multiple monitors and/or interphones. In this interconnection design (Fig. 10-3) you have the power supply set to "on" as well as the power switch of the monitor, which is connected to the power supply of the camera.

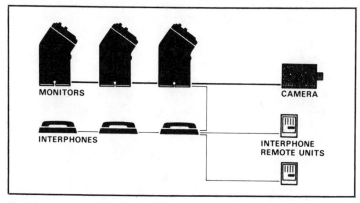

Fig. 10-4. Two interphone remote units are used.

When pressing the call button of the interphone remote unit, the camera and monitor (up to three monitors) are activated as well as the two-tone chime on the intercom master unit and submaster unit(s). The system can use multiple monitors, interphones and interphone remote units, as illustrated in Fig. 10-4.

As a solid-state line-wired unit, it can be installed by the homeowner in one afternoon. The system is quite new. Detailed instructions are provided, though, with the CCTV unit when purchased.

Remember that CCTV is a sophisticated device. If you are not completely sure that you can install the system exactly as indicated in the directions, you might contact a professional installer to perform the task for you.

Do-It-Yourself
(DITY) Security Systems

Do-it-yourself, or DITY, is just that—doing it yourself without having to purchase off-the-shelf type security systems. You can create some form of a defensible perimeter and interior security alerting system without having to spend several hundred dollars or more. Of course, such systems are never as effective and efficient as professionally-designed and built systems, but they do provide a strong deterrent.

Before we get into some specific concepts and ideas for DITY, let me explain what will not be discussed. Fire sensor systems are not covered because a home fire sensor system depends solely upon the specialized systems and components that have already been discussed. For these systems in the home, it is best if you use localized battery-operated sensors that have a self-contained alarm.

While necessity may be the mother of invention, certainly innovation is its father. Innovation, the use of existing products and materials, much less the reconfiguration of certain individual items, can greatly increase home and apartment security. This chapter is a compilation of thoughts, ideas, concepts and designs to further assist the reader in upgrading home physical security.

Naturally, some of the items that are included are off-the-shelf ones, but they are of the type that the average person would normally purchase to enhance the security of the home. This means spending $10 or even $20, not several hundred dollars, as in the

415

case of the more fancy and comprehensive systems that you can purchase.

DITY has become an American way of life. In recent years, inflation has meant that an alternative must be developed by the homeowner. The field of home security is no exception. DITY means creativity, using existing materials and supplies and, sometimes, some of the individual system components to make your own system.

ALARMS

Figure 11-1 illustrates a simple alarm circuit. This could be for just a door in an apartment, a door and a window, or two doors and several windows in a home. It consists of a battery unit, several switches (the sensors) and a bell unit.

Such a system can be used successfully. A localized alarm can be built and installed for an individual window and mounted directly inside the window. Have the wires and sensors run to a specific window (or door) and the battery and alarm at some other point. A variation would be to have a plug-in system, with one of the step-down transformer plug-in devices used, and then running the alarm and sensors off it. Depending upon what is desired, multiple alarms can be installed, each one being very localized or covering a specific "zone" of the home.

Pull trap sensors can be made with a clothes pin, a piece of plastic and some string, as shown in Fig. 11-2. These could be used at a door to the home, the garage or even on the auto, if desired. Commercially available sensors, such as a Sentrol magnetic

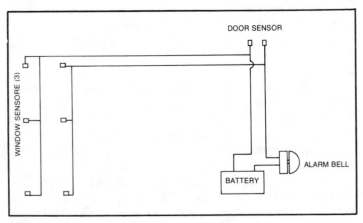

Fig. 11-1. A simple alarm circuit.

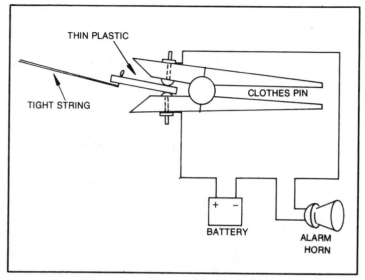

Fig. 11-2. Pull trap sensors can be made with a clothes pin, plastic and string.

sensor, an auto horn and battery, could be used for the doors and trunk of a car (Fig. 11-3). A variation would be to install such a unit in the car.

As long as the circuit is not completely closed, the battery drain is extremely minimal over a period of time. Batteries should be checked on a biweekly basis to ensure that they do not run down.

You can also put in an emergency switch, either a regular ON/OFF or a push button, into any circuit. This gives you the opportunity to sound an alarm immediately, without waiting for the sensors, or else to sound the alarm when the sensor may have been bypassed by the burglar. Such emergency switches can be set up by your bed, at one or more central locations in the home, or outside the home. The main thing to do is not indicate with a big sign, or whatever, that it is an emergency alarm switch. Figure 11-4 illustrates such a switch put into the system.

SECURITY FOR CASEMENT WINDOWS

Casement windows can have their security increased by replacing the current window latch/locking unit with a keyed window lock (Fig. 11-5). This easily replaces the existing non-locking casement window handle. Even if the glass is broken or cut by a burglar, the window cannot be opened. The key lock also has an indicator button to the side which indicates at a glance if the

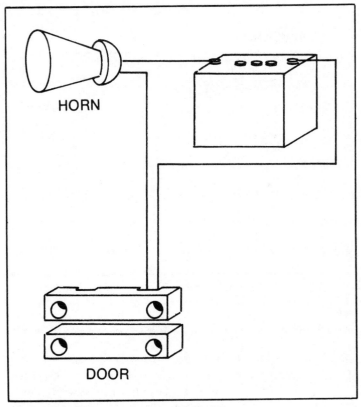

HORN

DOOR

Fig. 11-3. A magnetic sensor, auto horn and battery.

window is locked or unlocked. Installation time is less than five minutes; all that is required is to remove two screws, take out the old non-locking handle unit and replace it with a locking one, and put the two screws back in.

BLAINE WINDOW HARDWARE PRODUCTS

Blaine Window Hardware, a specialist in window hardware and devices for the home, has for many years carried a full and expanded *total* line of home security products that are highly recommended for use. The top or bottom mounted sliding door lock is in Fig. 11-6. A German lock that holds the sliding door to the non-moving portion, rather than to the frame edging, gives a much stronger holding. It uses a double-bitted key for increased security. Cost is very low for such a quality lock, and the installation time is extremely short.

418

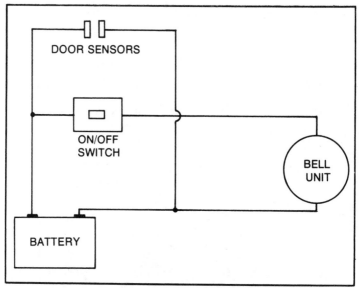

Fig. 11-4. An emergency alarm switch.

You might use the steel pin which drops into a hole in the door frame (Fig. 11-7). The pin is long enough to go through both door frames within a 3/16" hole which is drilled by the homeowner. When in the unlocked position, the pin hangs on its own hook ready for use. The pin hook is attached by a small screw, but it can also be attached by epoxy glue.

When installing the steel pin, drill the hole slightly slanted downward for greater security. This will ensure that by forcibly

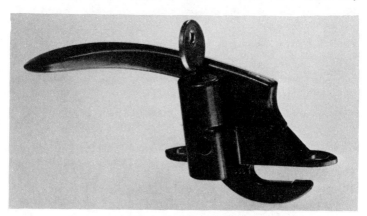

Fig. 11-5. A keyed window lock (courtesy of Ideal Security Hardware).

419

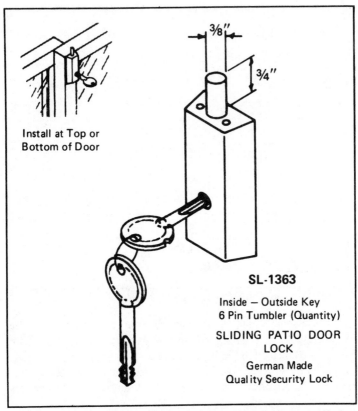

3/8″

3/4″

Install at Top or
Bottom of Door

SL-1363

Inside — Outside Key
6 Pin Tumbler (Quantity)

SLIDING PATIO DOOR
LOCK

German Made
Quality Security Lock

Fig. 11-6. Top or bottom mounted sliding door lock (courtesy of Blaine Window Hardware Inc.).

shaking the door from the outside, the pin will not work loose and fall out.

Charlie-Bar Safety Lock

Consider using the *Charley-Bar safety lock* to prevent the sliding door from being jimmied open (Fig. 11-8). The end bracket is secured into the side stile and the bar is held up with its own holding hook, ready for immediate dropping into place. The Charley-Bar fits any sliding door 36″-48″ wide. Installation time is less than 30 minutes.

Lok-Safe Patio Door

Another easy installation, an off-the-shelf item from Blaine Window Hardware, is the *Lok-Safe patio door lock* (Fig. 11-9) which

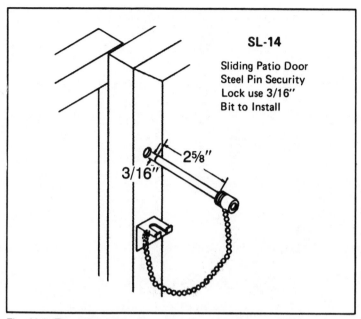

SL-14

Sliding Patio Door
Steel Pin Security
Lock use 3/16"
Bit to Install

2⅝"

3/16"

Fig. 11-7. The sliding patio door steel pin security lock (courtesy of Blaine Window Hardware Inc.).

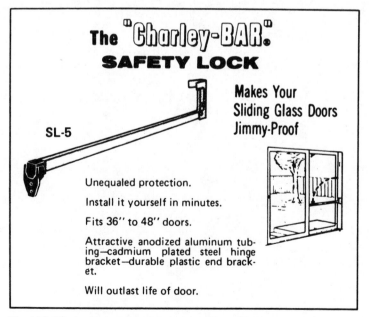

The "Charley-BAR."
SAFETY LOCK

**Makes Your
Sliding Glass Doors
Jimmy-Proof**

SL-5

Unequaled protection.

Install it yourself in minutes.

Fits 36" to 48" doors.

Attractive anodized aluminum tubing—cadmium plated steel hinge bracket—durable plastic end bracket.

Will outlast life of door.

Fig. 11-8. Charley-Bar safety lock (courtesy of Blaine Window Hardware Inc.).

EASY TO INSTALL
patio door lock

SL-1357 w/key
Universal Lock

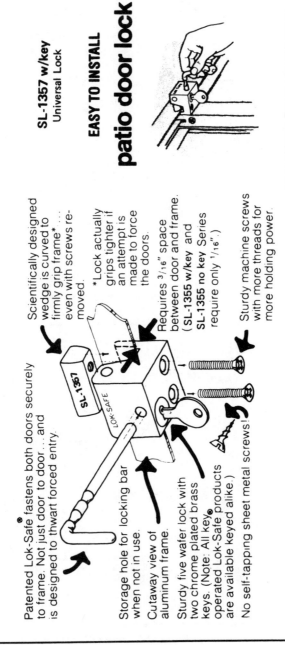

Keyed Model. Forms a bond between door and frame that resists forced entry.

Patented Lok-Safe fastens both doors securely to frame. Not just door to door... and is designed to thwart forced entry.

Scientifically designed wedge is curved to firmly grip frame*... even with screws removed.

*Lock actually grips tighter if an attempt is made to force the doors.

Storage hole for locking bar when not in use.

Requires 3/16" space between door and frame. (**SL-1355 w/key** and **SL-1355 no key** Series require only 1/16".)

Cutaway view of aluminum frame.

Sturdy machine screws with more threads for more holding power.

Sturdy five wafer lock with two chrome plated brass keys. (Note: All key operated Lok-Safe products are available keyed alike.)

No self-tapping sheet metal screws!

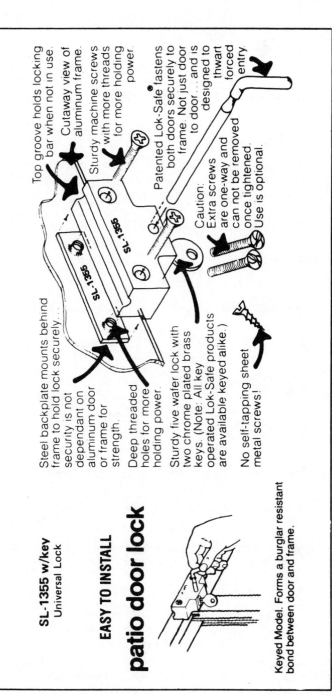

SL-1355 w/key
Universal Lock

EASY TO INSTALL

patio door lock

Top groove holds locking bar when not in use.

Cutaway view of aluminum frame.

Sturdy machine screws with more threads for more holding power.

Patented Lok-Safe® fastens both doors securely to frame. Not just door to door....and is designed to thwart forced entry

Caution: Extra screws are one-way and can not be removed once tightened. Use is optional.

Steel backplate mounts behind frame to hold lock securely.... security is not dependant on aluminum door or frame for strength.

Deep threaded holes for more holding power.

Sturdy five wafer lock with two chrome plated brass keys. (Note: All key operated Lok-Safe products are available keyed alike.)

No self-tapping sheet metal screws!

Keyed Model. Forms a burglar resistant bond between door and frame.

Fig. 11-9. The Lok-Safe patio door lock (courtesy of Blaine Window Hardware Inc.).

423

can form a burglar resistant bond between the door and the frame. Unlike some patio door locks, the Lok-Safe further fastens *both* doors together to the frame. This feature also thwarts further forced entry. Two variations of the lock are currently available to the DITY homeowner. Their features and specifics are shown in Fig. 11-9.

Sash Window Locks

The *sash window screw lock* is a very inexpensive device that holds the windows together through a bonding application. The window can be closed, ventilated or set for an air conditioner. Figure 11-10 shows the screw lock and illustrates its use. Because of its method of installation, it will provide superior protection and cannot be pried away from the framing without destroying the entire window.

Fig. 11-10. Sash window screw lock (courtesy of Blaine Window Hardware Inc.).

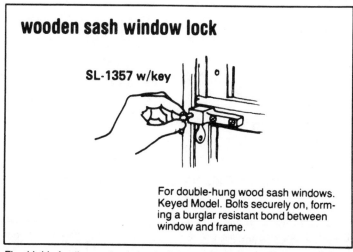

wooden sash window lock

SL-1357 w/key

For double-hung wood sash windows.
Keyed Model. Bolts securely on, forming a burglar resistant bond between
window and frame.

Fig. 11-11. Another sash window lock (courtesy of Blaine Window Hardware Inc.).

Installation is effected by a simple hole drilled through the sash. Screws can be put at various positions on the window to allow for different window opening levels, such as partially opened for minor ventilation (never more than 5″, though) or for the air conditioner to be installed. In this case, once the air conditioner is mounted, the screw lock is positioned and mounted, not being removed until the air conditioner is taken out in the fall.

Another sash window lock is depicted in Fig. 11-11. It uses a key and mounts at the side of the window.

You might want a sash window lock that allows for ventilation, but not a screw lock, so a standard ventilation lock would be desirable (Fig. 11-12). It comes with two strikes for different positions on the window. Whether closed or partially open for ventilation, it is always kept locked so the window cannot be further opened to allow illegal entry into the home.

There is also the Charley-Bar available for a sliding window in the home, as shown in Fig. 11-13. Installation is less than 30 minutes.

SLIDING WINDOW OR DOOR LOCK

Maybe a safety sliding window (or door) lock is what you want (Fig. 11-14). Like some of the previous window locks, it can be put in the closed or ventilation position and kept locked to prevent unauthorized entry.

425

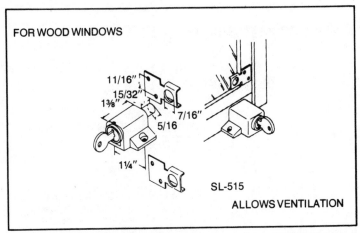

FOR WOOD WINDOWS

11/16"
15/32"
1⅜"
7/16"
5/16
1¼"
SL-515
ALLOWS VENTILATION

Fig. 11-12. A standard ventilation lock (courtesy of Blaine Window Hardware Inc.).

Note that many of the products herein, even though you may consider them very "low cost" type items, have proven their worth. They are above average home security devices that are recommended by various organizations, law enforcement officials, and groups which are concerned with all aspects of home and personal safety and security.

The "Charley-BAR" SAFETY LOCK
JIMMY-PROOF

is easily installed by any DO-IT-YOURSELFER.
And Assures you of Safety against Burglarizing through Sliding Windows. No ordinary key lock can give you this protection.

SL-536

Fig. 11-13. The Charley-Bar is available for a sliding window (courtesy of Blaine Window Hardware Inc.).

426

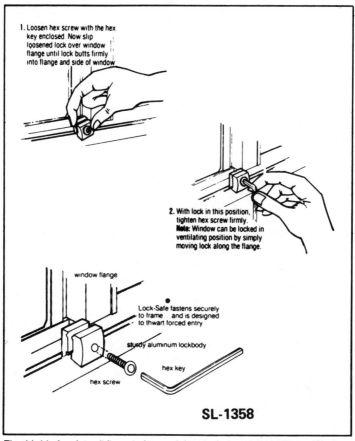

Fig. 11-14. A safety sliding window and door lock (courtesy of Blaine Window Hardware Inc.).

USING MISCELLANEOUS MATERIALS TO IMPROVE SECURITY

The use of miscellaneous materials around the home can be used to improve your security. At the front, side or back door, you can use a piece of 2″ × 4″, a piece of foam rubber, carpeting or other similar material, and a hinge to prevent the door from being opened. The 2 × 4 is cut so that it will reach the distance between the door and the facing wall or corner point. The hinge is affixed to one end of the 2 × 4 and the floor. The other end of the board is covered with material so it will not damage or deface the door. It can easily be lifted up and out of the way for exiting.

You can use a piece of chain and bolt it down to the frame. Use a heavy duty hook to the interior side of the door as an emergency door chain. It's a lot heavier and will withstand more attempted pressure than some of the less expensive door chains on the market.

Improve the window security by installing several nails in the sash frame. You can drill a hole slightly downward through the sashes and insert a nail into the hole. To get the nail out, you use a magnet. The nail sets just below the surface of the sash (about 1/16″). I recommend that you use at least two nails, one on each side, set in 2-4″ from the sash edge. You can also put a third one in the center of the sash rail.

For outbuildings, consider using a cane bolt on double doors such as the garage to retain one of the two doors. On the other door, put a heavy duty latching safety hasp. Make sure you do not lay the hasp totally flat to install the screws. The hinging portion must be positioned underneath the locking portion of the hinge. When the hasp is pushed over the staple, it is automatically latched to prevent movement of the door. The lock then totally secures the hasp.

For screws on various items that could be removed to gain entry, use one-way tamperproof screws. These are specifically designed for easy installation on products which are exposed to prowlers and vandals. Each screw has a one-way head which is easily screwed in but cannot be removed.

On hinges for the door, use a quality steel hinge, with a non-removable hinge pin. Next, when installing the hinge, whenever possible use screws that are at least 2″ long. In at least one of the screw holes put a long (3-4″) nail in instead of a screw.

For the door, be sure to use some type of a door viewer. You might consider putting in one that goes with the door knocker or just a viewer by itself.

You can have a secondary lock for night security that has a vertical locking feature. In this case you install the basic lock, but do not install the cylinder, by drilling a hole in the door. From the

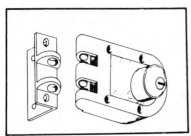

Fig. 11-15. Secondary locks (courtesy of Ideal Security Hardware).

Fig. 11-16. This lock has a hardened steel shackle (courtesy of Security Locks, Inc.).

outside, nobody will know that you have this extra security. The time for this is less than 15 minutes. Figure 11-15 illustrates different locks that could be installed.

You might want to put a hasp and lock on your main door, also. While the hasp unit should be of high quality steel, it should be put in with long screws or, if possible, bolts.

The lock that should be used cannot be of the 59¢ or $1.98 variety. It should have a hardened steel shackle and be as pick-resistant as possible (Fig. 11-16).

WINDOW FOIL

The use of window foil to cover various open glass areas is of great value to the homeowner and the home security process. Foil tape can be used on doors and windows as part of the overall home security perimeter protection plan (Figs. 11-17 and 11-18).

When installing foil, there are certain cautions:

—Foil will not stick to wet, dirty or cold windows.

—Window must fit tight in the frame.

—Severe bending and creasing will break the foil.

—Foil must not touch any metal surface.

—Foil must be completely covered with a foil sealer after installation to protect it from moisture and dirt.

In its basic application, foil is mounted over a glass surface and goes to a connector block where it is wired into the rest of the security system (Fig. 11-19). As was depicted in Fig. 11-18 it can

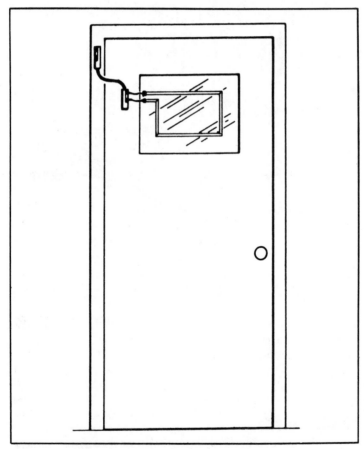

Fig. 11-17. Foil tape on a door (courtesy of NuTone Division, Scovill Inc.).

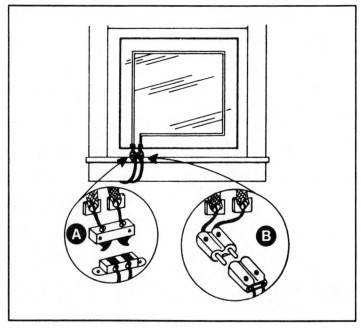

Fig. 11-18. Foil tape on a window (courtesy of NuTone Division, Scovill Inc.).

also be installed on a sliding window by use of a contact switch or a takeoff connector. The basic equipment you will have to purchase for the installation of foil on windows will be the foil and connector blocks (Fig. 11-20) and a can of window foil protective sealer (Fig. 11-21).

Window Preparation

Using a 3″ × 3″ block of wood (plastic, bakelite, etc.) and a grease pencil or tailor's chalk, mark outside the window. This will be the guide for the foil (Fig. 11-22). Note from Fig. 11-23 that the block is held firmly against the window edge to insure a smooth and straight line.

To help make the installation, don't use the foil roll as it is received. Rather, hang the foil reel above the window in a foil holder-dispenser (Fig. 11-24). If you purchase your foil installation kit from NuTone, this will be supplied. A holder dispenser can be made by sandwiching the foil reel between two pieces of cardboard and inserting a nail through the center.

Clean the window with a clean, lint-free cloth and a solvent such as alcohol or benzine. Do not use window cleaner. Store

Fig. 11-19. Foil is mounted over a glass surface and goes to a connector block where it is wired into the rest of the security system (courtesy of NuTone Division, Scovill Inc.).

Fig. 11-20. Foil and connector blocks (courtesy of NuTone Division, Scovill Inc.).

Fig. 11-21. Window foil protective sealer (courtesy of NuTone Division, Scovill Inc.).

cloths carefully and allow the windows to dry completely (Fig. 11-25).

Installation

Before the actual installation is started, there are four very important things to know.

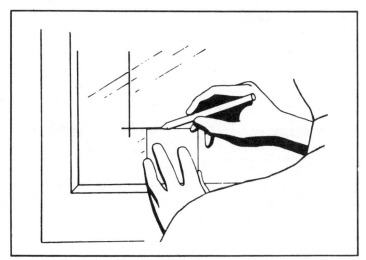

Fig. 11-22. Mark a guide for the foil (courtesy of NuTone Division, Scovill Inc.).

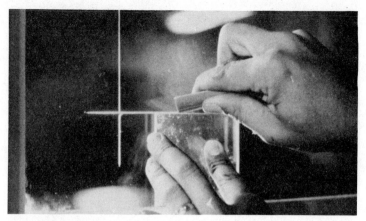

Fig. 11-23. Hold the block firmly against the window edge (courtesy of NuTone Division, Scovill Inc.).

☐ Foil must be stretched to assure that it will break easily if the window is broken.

☐ Foil must be smooth across the window—use a matchbook cover to smooth out the foil.

☐ Foil should be applied in one continuous strip to make the best possible electrical circuit. If foil breaks during the process of installing, there are two recommended remedies. If the area

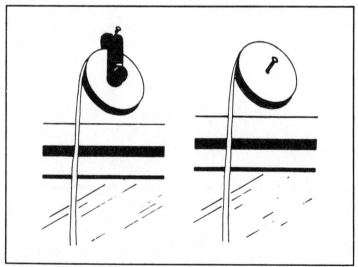

Fig. 11-24. Hang the foil reel above the window (courtesy of NuTone Division, Scovill Inc.).

Fig. 11-25. Clean the window properly (courtesy of NuTone Division, Scovill Inc.).

preceding the break covers a small or medium area, remove all the foil completely from the window and begin a new strip. If the area preceding the break covers a large area or an area with difficult turns or window frame crossings, splice the tape (see the section on repairing foil breaks).

Mark the location where the intruder detection circuit will meet the window. If accessory components such as a contact switch, takeoff connector or a flexible cord will be used, mark the exact location (Fig. 11-26).

Peel off the paper backing from a section of the foil. Begin at the point where the intruder circuit will meet the window. Allow a 2″ piece of foil to extend over the window frame. Press and hold the foil at the edge of the glass. Stretch the foil away from the starting point and stick it to the glass (Fig. 11-27). Foil *must* be stretched in order for it to break if the glass is broken. Make the foil smooth on the glass by rubbing over it with a match book cover (Fig. 11-28). Figure 11-29 shows the stretching of the foil at a corner point; notice that the line is very exact where the foil has been stretched.

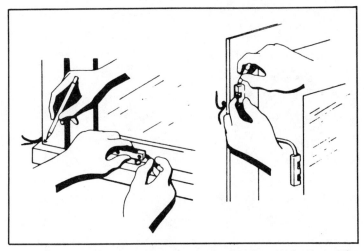

Fig. 11-26. Mark the location where the intruder detection circuit will meet the window (courtesy of NuTone Division, Scovill Inc.).

For right angle turns, stick the foil to the glass up to the edge of the intersecting guide line (Fig. 11-30). Have at least 5″ of the paper backing removed from the foil. Fold the foil back over itself, gently creasing it (*severe creasing and bending may break the foil*) (Fig. 11-30A).

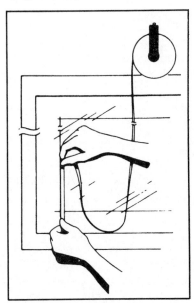

Fig. 11-27. Stick the foil to the glass (courtesy of NuTone Division, Scovill Inc.).

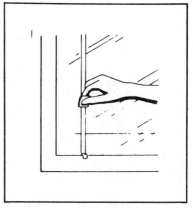

Fig. 11-28. Rub over the foil with a matchbook cover (courtesy of NuTone Division, Scovill Inc.).

Fold the foil at a 45° angle and press the corner down (Fig. 11-30B). Begin running the foil along the new guide, holding it at the corner and stretching it as it is placed on the window. Smooth over the corner with a matchbook (Fig. 11-30C).

Continue to follow the guide lines around the window and work your way back to the starting area. Remember to stretch the foil as you stick it to the glass and smooth the foil with a matchbook cover.

Remove the paper backing from the bottom of the connector block. Pull foil back away from the window frame and stick the connector block to the window, overlapping about ⅛″ of the foil (Fig. 11-31A). Remove screw and clasp from the connector block. Lay the foil over the connector block (Fig. 11-31B). Replace the clamp, screw it to the block and remove excess foil (Fig. 11-31C).

Coat the foil over with foil sealer (Fig. 11-32). Add mineral spirits if the sealer is too thick to spread evenly. The sealer should overlap both edges of the tape.

Fig. 11-29. Stretching the foil at a corner point (courtesy of NuTone Division, Scovill Inc.).

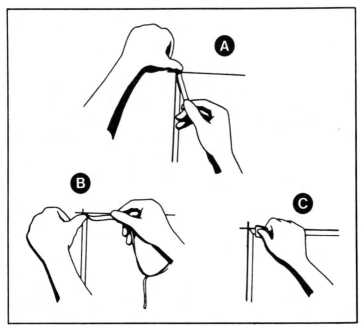

Fig. 11-30. Making a right angle turn with the foil (courtesy of NuTone Division, Scovill Inc.).

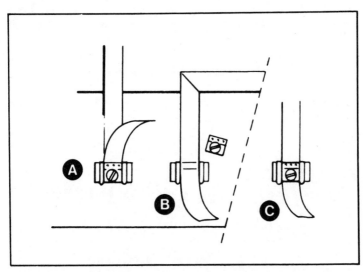

Fig. 11-31. (A) Pull the foil back away from the window frame and stick the connector block to the window. (B) Lay the foil over the connector block. (C) Replace the clamp (courtesy of NuTone Division, Scovill Inc.).

Fig. 11-32. Apply foil sealer (courtesy of NuTone Division, Scovill Inc.).

ADD MINERAL SPIRITS IF SEALER IS TOO THICK TO SPREAD EVENLY

Sliding Windows

Foil can be installed on sliding windows by using a contact switch or a takeoff connector (Figs. 11-33A and 11-33B).

The contact switch is recommended for windows that are used daily or weekly. This switch should never be used on seldom used windows because the contacts on the switch may become oxidized if the switch contacts are not regularly active, which may result in

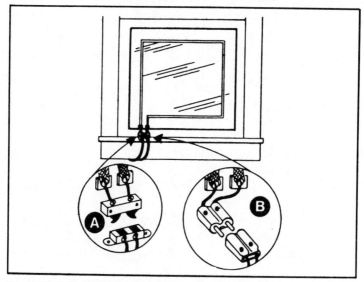

Fig. 11-33. Foil can be installed on sliding windows by using a contact switch (A) or a takeoff connector (B) (courtesy of NuTone Division, Scovill Inc.).

Fig. 11-34. Contact switch (courtesy of NuTone Division, Scovill Inc.).

unwanted alarms. When installing, be sure to line up both sections of the switch so the rocker contacts on the larger section are fully depressed by the contact plates on the smaller section. Figure 11-34 shows a contact switch.

The takeoff connector is recommended for windows that are seldom used. This plug-in socket connector is not recommended for frequently used windows because the contact switch is more convenient to the opening and closing of a window. The plug section should be wired to the foil; the socket section should be wired to the security system wiring. To install wire, back off the screws in the connectors, insert stripped wires and then tighten

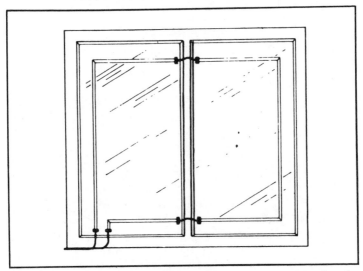

Fig. 11-35. Connect the blocks with 18 gauge insulated approved burglar wire (courtesy of NuTone Division, Scovill Inc.).

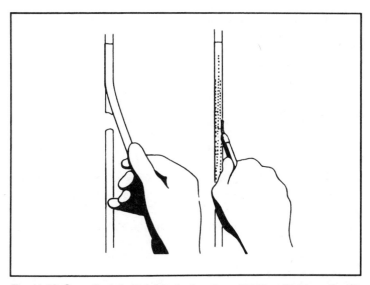

Fig. 11-36. Cover the foil with foil sealer (courtesy of NuTone Division, Scovill Inc.).

screws. Plug and/or socket sections can be fastened down with a No. 6 sheet metal screw if desired. For this purpose, drill a 5/32" hole through the center of the case.

Crossing Metal Frames

It is important that the foil must not touch metal crossbars or frames on windows. These windows may be grounded. A short circuit to ground may cause the alarm to sound. Most alarm

Fig. 11-37. A completed installation (courtesy of NuTone Division, Scovill Inc.).

grounds occur at poorly insulated foil connector blocks and crossbar locations.

To cross over a crossbar, install a connector block on each side of the crossbar. Connect the blocks together with 18 gauge insulated approved burglar wire (Fig. 11-35).

Repairing Foil Breaks

Remove the foil sealer (if it has already been applied) with steel wool. Stick a new foil strip over the existing foil, overlapping the existing foil with new foil about 3″. Use the foil splicing tool (which is supplied with the NuTone foil installation kit) to prick holes over the overlapping foil. Check to be sure the circuit is complete through splicing. Cover the foil with foil sealer (Fig. 11-36). When completed, your installation should look like Fig. 11-37.

12

Other Security
Products for the Homeowner

There are many available products that do not fall strictly into my guidelines for the external, perimeter or interior security and fire threats, much less other threats such as auto vandalism and theft. This isn't to say that they are not as important to home safety and security; they are just as important.

GAS SENSORS

Increasingly, residential homes are using *natural gas* and mobile homes use *propane gas*. Gas sensors are now available to sense the gas before it builds up to an explosive and deadly concentration. The National Fire Protection Association's statistics place the annual number of gas leak related explosions and fires at 9,500.

First Alert Corp. recently introduced their new gas sensor. The heart of the unit is a specially designed long-life sensor device which will activate a solid-state alarm when *methane* is sensed. Methane is the major component of natural gas. So sensitive is the unit that it will detect and react to as little as 300-5000 parts per million (ppm) of methane or 1000-2000 ppm of propane. Once sensed, the alarm is quickly activated.

Manufactured to extremely rigid U.S. standards, the solid-state circuit ensures that the unit itself will not act as an ignition source catalyst should it ever sound in a totally gas-filled room. This is a totally maintenance-free unit, powered by standard ac. It should be located near a furnace, liquid propane storage tank or the like.

The *gas sentry* by GC Electronics (Fig. 12-1) is a mobile carbon monoxide alarm unit. This unit is specifically designed for use in automobiles, trucks, vans, recreational vehicles and campers or any small enclosed area where a dangerous buildup of carbon monoxide might occur.

It will detect carbon monoxide at 425 parts per million, which is just the amount it would take to give a person a frontal headache within one to two hours of breathing carbon monoxide. This detection and warning will come long before the concentration can reach a dangerous level. The unit also detects butane and other hydrocarbons.

You start your car on a cold day and rev up the engine. The level will exceed 425 ppm, but the unit has a built-in delay feature to prevent the buzzer from sounding during the warmup period. Later on, while driving, if the level again builds up to 425 ppm, the alarm will sound. If the level drops below 425 ppm, the unit will

Fig. 12-1. Gas sentry mobile carbon monoxide alarm (courtesy of GC Electronics).

Fig. 12-2. Water Alarm (courtesy of Northern Electric Co., Division of Sunbeam Corp.).

automatically reset itself. This item is a "must" type that should be carried in every vehicle, new or old.

WATER ALARM

The Northern Electric Company (Sunbeam Corp.) developed the *Water Alarm* for every person who dreads costly water damage (Fig. 12-2). This is a dependable and inexpensive way to guard against water damage from sump pump failure, laundry overflow, broken water heaters, air conditioner water runoff into the home or even a leaking roof.

This new water alarm needs just a drop of water beneath the unit to activate the precision electronic water-sensing circuit. This would set off a loud, high-pitched warning signal. To distinguish the unit from other alarms such as a smoke detector signal, the Water Alarm signal is an intermittent one and continues for at least 24 hours, or until the unit is reset.

The Water Alarm features solid state circuitry, a 100% *polypropylene* housing to ensure water will not short out the circuit and make the alarm inactive. It also has a low battery indicator, an adjustable depth gauge setting, reset button and a unit test button. It will operate with any commercially available alkaline 9-volt battery for longer life.

There is no wiring, tools or complicated installation. The Water Alarm even floats while in operation, so it will not be flooded into inactivity. Placement of the alarm after hooking up the battery and the unit is all that is needed.

RADIO INTERCOM SYSTEM AND WALL RECEPTACLE

Perhaps you have a small home office, shut off from the rest of the home so you won't be disturbed, or maybe you are in the middle of making a cake and the doorbell rings. Who is there? Instead of leaving what you are doing or not answering at all, you reach across and push a switch on the *radio intercom system* (Fig. 12-3). After inquiry, you know that you must go to the door. You can open the door in relative safety since you know who is there; the person has been talking into the outside speaker unit (Fig. 12-4).

By using the *wall receptacle* (Fig. 12-5), you can place portable speakers throughout the home. This allows you to monitor the entire house at night in case you believe someone else is in the house. You can safely check this without leaving your bedside. The unit is also very useful in talking with other people in different parts of the house. For invalid people or the elderly, this is more than a time saver; it may help to save lives.

SAFES

The Meilink Safe Company has three particular safe models that should be seriously considered for the home. The first is the stand-alone model 300-S (Fig. 12-6). The body and the rear of the safe are formed of electrically welded double steel walls almost 2″ thick. The cavity between these walls is completely filled with a proven *Thermo-Cel insulation* — a special insulation material which contains latent moisture in crystal form. Heat from a fire vaporizes the moisture crystals and provides an efficient vapor barrier against heat entry.

Fig. 12-3. Radio intercom system (courtesy of NuTone Division, Scovill Inc.).

Fig. 12-4. Outside speaker unit (courtesy of NuTone Division, Scovill Inc.).

The doors are 2½" thick and also Thermo-Cel insulated. Deep, continuous tongue-and-groove joints seal out heat.

In-ground safes are also a Meilink specialty. The MLOC-4 model is designed for in-floor installation (Fig. 12-7). Set in concrete, this model gives outstanding burglary protection. The cover plate is flush with the floor and almost impossible to detect

Fig. 12-5. Wall receptacle (courtesy of NuTone Division, Scovill Inc.).

Fig. 12-6. Model 300-S safe (courtesy of Meilink Safe Co.).

under a rug or furniture. A UL listed changeable combination lock, electrically welded steel body and a relocking device complete the unit. The unit can be put into the floor after construction or during the pouring of the basement.

The square *"C" rated money safe* (Fig. 12-8) also contains the UL listed changeable combination lock, relocking device and a 1" thick body of carbon steel that is electrically welded. Like the previous safe, it can be installed in the floor.

Heavy duty floor safes of excellent quality steel are also available from the Deerfield Lock Company. Figure 12-9 illustrates just one of several models available. Constructed of electrically welded steel walls and sides, and with a rugged steel top that cannot be pried open or hammered in, the safe is easy to install in the floor.

This model includes a keyed lock, but a combination could be used—assuming you can always remember the combination. The lock is an "Ace," meaning that it is one of the most difficult locks to pick, even for a locksmith with many years of experience in the field.

Figure 12-9 illustrates the planning and design that hides the floor safe, which has been mounted between two floor joists. The basement walls can also be used to secure this unit.

The safe has been designed to fit a variety of homeowner needs and come in four different sizes: the *tight-space model* (5" × 5" × 7" deep), a *standard model* (6" wide × 8" × 7" deep); the *deluxe* (6" wide, 12" long × 7" deep) and the *supper deluxe model* (10" wide, 14" long and 8" deep). All safes come with a complete set of mounting hardware and detailed installation instructions.

IDEAL SECURITY TRAVEL LOCK

The *Ideal security travel lock* (Fig. 12-10) was originally intended to add additional security to the conventional doors found

Fig. 12-7. The MLOC-4 is designed for in-floor installation (courtesy of Meilink Safe Co.).

449

Fig. 12-8. The square "C" rated money safe (courtesy of Meilink Safe Co.).

in motel or hotel rooms. The unit was designed and is still used very widely for travelers to increase their room security.

What is nice about the travel lock is that you can use it at home to ensure that, if your home or apartment is broken into, *your* room is securely locked against unauthorized entry. The lock is easy to install and remove. Just place the clip over the jamb and into the strike recess. Close the door. The lock slides onto the ratchet clip and prevents the door from being opened from the outside. The engagement of the lock over the ratchet clip requires the key to unlock it and remove it from the clip in order to open the door.

DOOR VIEWERS

Door viewers have become increasingly important to the homeowner and apartment dweller. In many areas, legislation mandates that these doors now must have an installed viewer. The Kwikset door viewer is of the same type required by many of these local laws (Fig. 12-11).

Though small in size, the door viewer provides a significant additional measure of protection. Many police departments put the

450

Fig. 12-9. A heavy duty floor safe (courtesy of Deerfield Lock Co.).

door viewer high on their list of recommended residential security measures.

The door viewer features a precision-made glass lens that provides a full 160° viewing panorama from inside the door, enabling the resident to see out without callers or unwanted intruders seeing inward. The viewer will fit all doors from 1⅜" to 2" thick.

Fig. 12-10. Security travel lock (courtesy of Ideal Security Hardware).

451

Fig. 12-11. The door viewer (courtesy of Kwikset, Division of Emhart Industries, Inc.).

To install, drill a ½″ hole through the door. Insert the viewer halves through the hole and tighten down. It cannot be removed from the outside.

MARKING PEN

If the police ask you to come down and identify some stolen property they have recovered, can you be sure that the particular property is yours? Perhaps you don't have the serial numbers written down or specific pictures of the objects. What can you do? Nothing! But you should have done something a lot earlier. You could have used the Brink's *security marking pen* by the Sanford Corporation (Fig. 12-12). An invisible non-defacing marker pen, it writes on any surface, be it porous or non-porous. The markings show up later only under ultraviolet light. For greater security, you

Fig. 12-12. Brink's security marking pen (courtesy of Sanford Corp.).

453

should also keep in a safe place a listing of your property, noting where on each item you marked your name, address, telephone number, date of birth or other identifying data.

SHRIEK ALERT

The *Shriek Alert* can become your personal bodyguard (Fig. 12-13). A very inconspicuous object, it looks like a tube of lipstick that fits easily in the palm of the hand, purse or pocket. The Shriek Alert is a must for anyone out at night or walking through lonely areas. Simply depressing the cap down will send out a powerful shriek that scares off attackers and attracts needed attention. The price is low (less than $5 in most stores), and each unit is good for 50-60 uses. Powered by an aerosol, it requires no batteries to operate.

FIRE EXTINGUISHERS

Fire extinguishers can be used in areas like the kitchen, garage, auto trunk, etc. In case of a flash fire from kerosene or flammable paint, an appropriate extinguisher should be available.

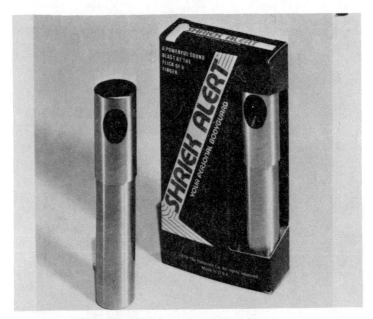

Fig. 12-13. The Shriek Alert (courtesy of The Peterzell Co.).

Fig. 12-14. A home fire extinguisher (courtesy of Pem All Fire Extinguisher Corp.).

The *Pem All Fire Extinguisher Corp.* produces a wide variety of extinguishers for all types of uses. The home extinguisher in Fig. 12-14 is a handheld unit weighing less than five pounds. A mounting bracket is provided. This unit can be used on all types of fires:

☐ Class A fires—paper, wood, fabrics, etc.

☐ Class B fires—burning flammable liquids (gasoline, oils, cooking fats, etc.).

☐ Class C fires—fires in electrical equipment.

For the home workshop, which is usually filled with a variety of easily combustible, the Pem All Halon 1211 ceiling-hanging extinguisher (Fig. 12-15) is very desirable. This is a total flooding unit, which will cover a floor area of 64 square feet, and 512 cubic feet.

The Halon 1211 features quick penetration of an endangered area, leaving no messy residue. It is non-corrosive and non-conductive, penventing flashback or reignition of fires.

The "in place" hanging units require no special plumbing or electrical service for installation, since the unit is completely self-contained and reacts to increasing temperatures. An easy-to-read gauge lets you know when recharging is necessary.

455

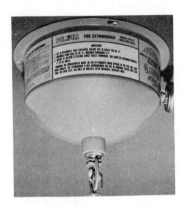

Fig. 12-15. The Halon 1211 extinguisher (courtesy of Pem All Fire Extinguisher Corp.).

AGRI-GARD

Disaster planning can also apply to those buildings not directly associated with the home. It may be an outbuilding where you have

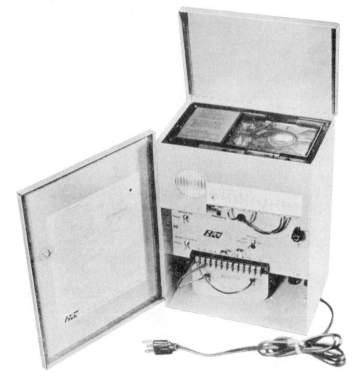

Fig. 12-16. The Agri-Gard (courtesy of B-W Manufacturers, Inc.).

Fig. 12-17. The Security Lite (courtesy of Rival Manufacturing Co.).

items stored, such as a barn on the farm, or other like buildings. These structures are normally referred to as *confinement buildings*. For a storage building or one where you may have a horse or other livestock, the *Agri-Gard* (Fig. 12-16) is a very important investment. Many other alarm types will not stand the harsh environmental conditions of these buildings. Having to withstand

457

Fig. 12-18. An electric engraver (courtesy of Rockwell International).

all types of weather and temperatures, the Agri-Gard continues to operate efficiently. The unit has a built-in telephone dialer and power-off sensor. It can detect intrusion, fire and a rise in temperature.

RIVAL SECURITY LITE

You are in the attic or basement and the lights go out. With no flashlight, you will be stumbling around for several minutes. Rival has the *Security Lite* (Fig. 12-17) that prevents this from happening. It is able to provide instant light during a power failure. The light turns on automatically when the electricity goes off. It can also serve as a rechargeable flashlight and night light. You just keep it plugged into an ac outlet.

The Security Lite has a special "beaming lens" design to give maximum illumination to the front and the sides. A three position switch goes ON for flashlight, AUTO for power failure and night light functions and OFF for charging of the unit only. A 24-hour charge keeps the unit going for up to 90 minutes due to the extra capacity batteries built into the unit.

ELECTRIC ENGRAVER

The *electric engraver* (Fig. 12-18) can be used to engrave metal, glass, plastic and wood. It discourages theft by allowing you to permanently etch an identification number on various items of value. This is something that should be done by everyone. Engravers, such as the one by Rockwell International are available at a wide variety of home repair, hardware and other stores.

Home Lightning Protection

Information for this chapter is provided through the courtesy of the Lightning Protection Institute, Thompson Lightning Protection, Inc., and the Independent Protection Co. I am extremely greatful for their cooperation and assistance.

Did you know that, on the average, lightning will strike from 90 to 135 times a year within a half-mile radius of your front door? More people are injured by lightning than by floods, tornados or hurricanes. Yearly, about 37% of all fires in rural and suburban areas are caused by lightning.

When Benjamin Franklin installed the first lightning protection device on his home in Philadelphia in 1753, it only had two parts: a sharpened copper wire at the top "about the size of a common knitting needle" and an iron rod stuck from 3 to 4' into the ground, projecting about 6' above the house.

MAJOR SYSTEM ELEMENTS

We have advanced a long way in terms of the design and development of lightning protection systems. Today's systems have six major elements:

—Lightning rods (also called air terminals) (Fig. 13-1).
—Main conductor wires (Fig. 13-2).
—Bonds (Fig. 13-3).
—Lightning arresters (Fig. 13-4).
—Tree protection.
—Grounding devices (Fig. 13-5).

459

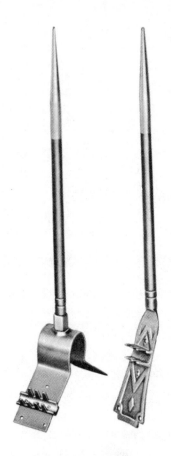

Fig. 13-1. Lightning rods (courtesy of Thompson Lightning Protection, Inc.).

TARGETS OF LIGHTNING

Where does lightning strike? Four major areas of the home are prime targets of lightning. Roof and projections will receive 31.8%, the TV antenna will receive 29.2%, overhead power lines that are very close account for 28.9%, and various adjacent trees will attract 10.1% of all lightning.

Fig. 13-2. Main conductor wires (courtesy of Independent Protection Co., Inc.).

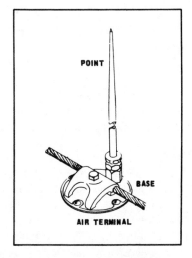

Fig. 13-3. The bonding of conductor wires to the air terminal base ensures continuity of electrical charge (courtesy of Independent Protection Co., Inc.).

Lightning's likeliest targets are structures that standout due to height, ground area, isolation or a combination of these. It's dangerous to assume that a tall object will shield a nearby lower one, for lightning does not select its target until the leader stroke of the bolt nears the ground.

COMPARISON OF LIGHTNING AND A HOME'S ELECTRICAL POWER

Lightning and its effects and potential dangers can be best understood by a comparison with the everyday electrical power in

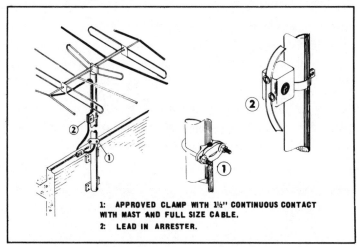

1: APPROVED CLAMP WITH 1½" CONTINUOUS CONTACT WITH MAST AND FULL SIZE CABLE.
2: LEAD IN ARRESTER.

Fig. 13-4. TV antenna protection (courtesy of Lightning Protection Institute).

461

the home. The ordinary house current has from 110 to 240 volts and about 100 amperes. Such current can be lethal. If shorted, it can start a fire.

Powerful as it is, the home current would have to be increased a thousand times for the current to jump 1' through the air. Lightning's 10 million to 100 million volts, on the other hand, are so great that a bolt containing 1,000 to 300,000 or more amperes of current may leap a mile or more through the air.

The lightning bolt has a core of pure electrical energy averaging ½" to ¾" thick, surrounded by a 4" thick channel of heated air. The thunderclap that you hear is caused by heating, ionizing and exploding of air molecules within this channel.

It is quite obvious that a force as powerful as lightning cannot be safely controlled by the materials and methods used for common household electricity. Lightning protection is a special and exacting science.

Since most lightning fires, home damages and casualties are caused by the direct strikes to the roof, chimney, dormer or other high portions of the home, including antennas, with bolts then jumping to plumbing pipes, house wiring or other metal attached outside the home, a proper lightning protection system is a *must*. Such a system, by necessity, must divert any lightning bolt onto itself, leading the powerful bolt of electricity safely deep into the ground without allowing the current to enter the home. A system which does not protect all possible points of the lightning's entry is not adequate for home safety and security.

EVALUATION OF POTENTIAL DANGER

The protection of a home starts with an evaluation of the potential danger. Once the homeowner can admit that the home is not secure from lightning, then the real work begins. While it is best and *strongly recommended* that the actual lightning protection system be installed by a Lightning Protection Institute (LPI) certified installer, there are numerous steps that the homeowner can take ahead of time to prepare for the installation.

First, the evaluation of the home *and surrounding area* is a must. Height, the pitch of the roof, distances between high and low objects, and trees should be indicated on paper. A rough diagram should be prepared of the possible danger points that should be protected. Figure 13-6 illustrates this evaluation.

Next, determine what is necessary to have even a minimal amount of lightning protection. This consideration must be

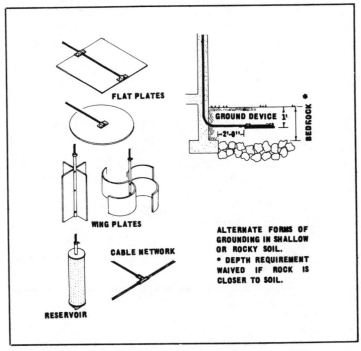

FLAT PLATES

GROUND DEVICE 1'

BEDROCK

2'-0"

WING PLATES

CABLE NETWORK

ALTERNATE FORMS OF
GROUNDING IN SHALLOW
OR ROCKY SOIL.
• DEPTH REQUIREMENT
WAIVED IF ROCK IS
CLOSER TO SOIL.

RESERVOIR

Fig. 13-5. Grounding devices (courtesy of Lightning Protection Institute).

tempered by the knowledge that the materials available are somewhat expensive (when considered in line with an internal/external home security system), and that second-rate materials are a definite "no-no."

LIGHTNING PROTECTION EQUIPMENT

Let's look at the basic pieces of lightning protection equipment that an average home would probably have and understand each piece's function, where it would probably be installed and to what it would connect.

☐ **Air Terminal.** This is the topmost element of the lightning protection system, designed to intercept a direct stroke (Fig. 13-7). The air terminal consists of a solid or tubular rod(s) of specified size and material that is mounted in an approved base and includes an approved (meets or exceeds UL standards) conductor connection.

☐ **Bonding.** This is a connection by a full-size conductor between a conductive metal object and an element of lighting

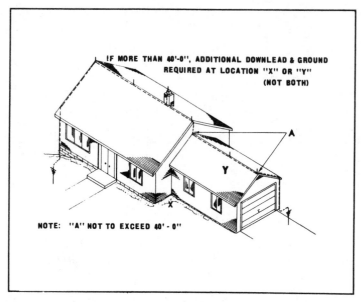

Fig. 13-6. Diagram of places where lightning could strike a home (courtesy of Lightning Protection Institute).

Fig. 13-7. Air terminal (courtesy of Independent Protection Co., Inc.).

protection that accomplishes an electrical continuity between the two, preventing a "side flash" (Fig. 13-8).

☐ **Main Conductor Wires.** These wires are used to interconnect various parts of the lightning protection system. They serve as a downward lead to the ground from the roof system, accomplish various bondings and serve as ground electrodes in some cases.

☐ **Lightning Arresters.** These are small devices mounted at the entrance points of the overhead electrical service wires and on the tv antenna (Fig. 13-9). They are connected to the system's grounding and arrest surges of power.

☐ **Tree Protection.** You should have special systems for any trees that are taller than the house, which are located (usually) within 10-15' of the house. You may have a extremely tall tree (60-75') at the corner of your property. Even though it is 40' away, it should be considered for a tree protection system.

☐ **Grounding Devices.** For all homes on moist clay soil, at least two copper ground rods, ½" diameter or larger, are preferred. They should be located at opposite corners of the house and sunk to a minimum of 10' into moist soil. When the ground soil is too hard to drive a 10' rod into the ground, then an encircling of the foundation should be done.

LIGHTNING RODS

Lightning rods should be placed on every sharp corner on a roof. Pipes and ventilators are hooked into the system. Conductors

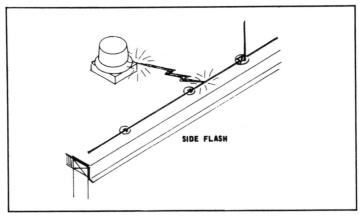

Fig. 13-8. A side flash should be prevented (courtesy of Lightning Protection Institute).

Fig. 13-9. Lightning arresters (courtesy of Thompson Lightning Protection, Inc.).

lead to the grounds on diagonal corners of the system, as shown in Fig. 13-10.

Figure 13-11 illustrates various considerations in measurement and placement that must be determined in laying out the basic

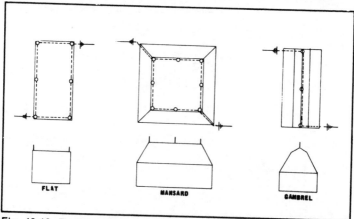

FLAT   MANSARD   GAMBREL

Fig. 13-10. Roof types and protection methods (courtesy of Lightning Protection Institute).

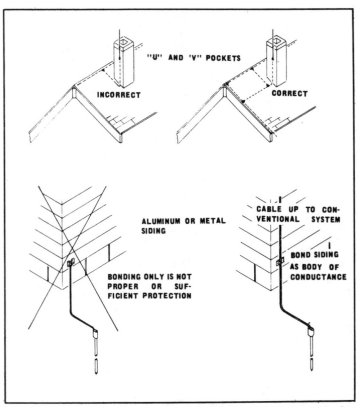

Fig. 13-11. Some things to consider when placing a lightning protection system (courtesy of Lightning Protection Institute).

home lightning protection system. Tables 13-1 and 13-2 show the minimal material requirements for Class I *main conductors* and the minimal material requirements for the Class I *secondary conductors* that will have to be installed on the home.

Main Conductors Table 13-1. Minimal Material Requirements for Class I (courtesy of Lightning Protection Institute).

TYPE OF CONDUCTOR		COPPER		ALUMINUM	
		Standard	Metric	Standard	Metric
CABLE	Min. Size ea. Strand	17 AWG	1.15 mm	14 AWG	1.63 mm
	Wgt. per 1000 Ft.	187½ lbs.	85 Kg.	95 Lbs.	43 Kg.
	Cross Sect. Area	59,500 CM	.30 Sq. Cm	98,500 CM	.499 Sq. Cm
SOLID STRIP	Thickness	14 AWG	1.63 mm	12 AWG	2.05 mm
	Width	1 inch	25.4 mm	1 inch	25.4 mm
SOLID BAR	Wgt. per 1000 Ft.	187½ lbs.	85 Kg.	95 lbs.	43 Kg.
TUBULAR BAR	Wgt. per 1000 Ft.	187½ lbs.	85 Kg.	95 lbs.	43 Kg.
	Min. Wall Thickness	.032 inch	.815 mm	0.0641 in.	1.63 mm

467

TYPE OF CONDUCTOR		COPPER		ALUMINUM	
		Standard	Metric	Standard	Metric
CABLE	Wire Size	17 AWG	1.15 mm	14 AWG	1.63 mm
	Number of Wires	14	14	10	10
SOLID STRIP	Thickness	16 AWG	1.29 mm	16 AWG	1.29 mm
	Width	1/2 inch	12.7 mm	1/2 inch	12.7 mm
SOLID ROD	Wire Size	6 AWG	4.12 mm	4 AWG	5.19 mm

Remember that *each and every* high point must be protected. From the high points, you should look at where the connecting wire cable will run. Distance is important! If there are more than three rods and the overall distance is 40' or more, then a secondary grounding must be done.

All parts of the lightning rod assembly system, right down to the ground rod, must meet fire regulations. For total protection, all equipment should exceed the minimum UL standards. To repeat, when considering installation, look for a professional installer who is a member in good standing of the Lightning Protection Institute or one of its member manufacturers. The homeowner should be very careful to check the credentials of professional installers. For further information on lightning protection, and a list of LPI certified installers in your area, you may contact LPI at the following address: *Lightning Protection Institute, 48 North Ayer Street—P.O. Box 406, Harvard, Illinois 60033.*

14

The Home Security Closet

Why have a *security closet* or room? Even in the days of old England, castles had secret rooms—either to hide valuables or for the protection of the castle owner. It really hasn't changed that much today.

In the late 1950s, Civil Defense efforts prompted many people to put in a bomb shelter. In the 1970s these rooms had been converted to basement-like rooms, additional bedrooms or wine cellars. Such rooms, or any sized room, can be converted quite easily into a security closet. Also, large space areas, like a corner of the basement, or a second floor walk-in linen closet or clothes closet, can be converted into a room for the safety of the household occupants. A basement corner area can also double as a food storage area.

Essentially, the security closet or room is a very temporary space that is used by the occupants as a refuge of safety during a crisis situation that could arise when someone succeeds in breaking into a home. In many homes, the security room can be concealed (i.e., a secret door that looks like part of a wall), but it can be a corner room that has a reinforced door and walls and also contains certain basic emergency needs. It can also be used for the temporary storage of valuables, art objects, coin or stamp collections, and the like (including firearms, if they are kept in the home).

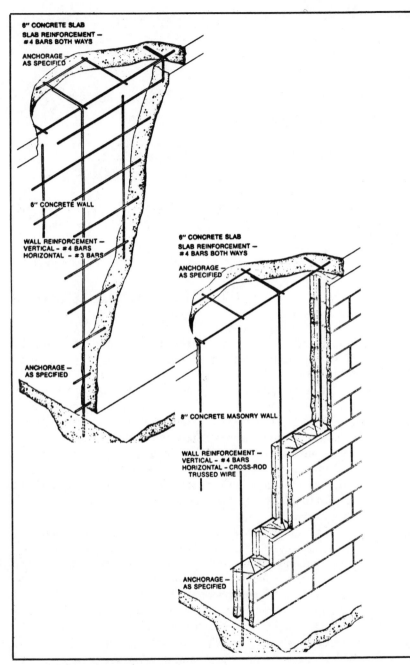

Fig. 14-1. Wall possibilities for a security room.

470

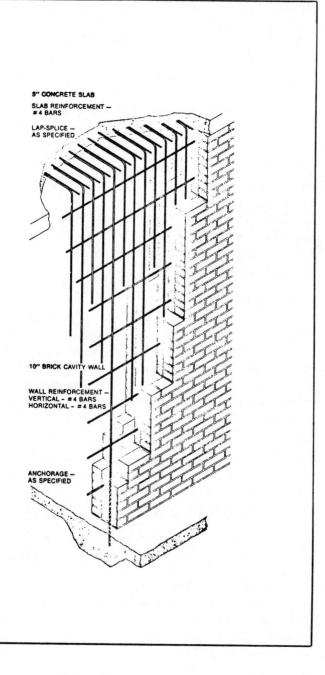

5" CONCRETE SLAB

SLAB REINFORCEMENT —
#4 BARS

LAP-SPLICE —
AS SPECIFIED

10" BRICK CAVITY WALL

WALL REINFORCEMENT —
VERTICAL - #4 BARS
HORIZONTAL - #4 BARS

ANCHORAGE —
AS SPECIFIED

LOCATING THE SECURITY ROOM

In determining the location of the security room, the homeowner must take into consideration the following:

—Ease of accessibility from all points of the residence to the room.

—Size of the room.

—Cost of creating the room from an empty space.

—If the room will serve more than one purpose: mini-office for home use, Civil Defense fallout shelter, valuables storage area, occasional storage of certain items and/or food storage, electrical outlets, lighting and ventilation.

—If the room is to be used for the storage of items, consider the size and number of items to be stored.

Once an area has been selected, do you want it known that its selected purpose is that of a security closet? Do you want it to look like just another small room? Or do you want it totally hidden from view?

ROOM DESIGN AND CONSTRUCTION

Once this has been determined, we must next consider the variable designs that can be developed to make the security closet a place of real security and not just a miniature room. The cost of the room will be based on the design, size, location (as relates to the amount of building or remodeling that will have to be undertaken) and other improvements needed.

In any security room, the walls, doors, and possibly the ceiling or floor may have to be strengthened to create what is known as a 'hardened' area, i.e., one that cannot be easily entered except through the use of excessive force.

The walls must be built up, perhaps with concrete blocks and metal rod inserts. The alternative of a sheet metal lining may also be considered. Figure 14-1 illustrates several wall types that could be used.

The door should be of solid wood, at least 2¼" thick, and preferably having a steel sheet overlaid on one or both sides of the door for additional strength (Fig. 14-2). The door must fit flush into the frame and be properly aligned with the corresponding wall. The frame should be of steel. The door should open out, ideally, but this is impractical due to the hinge pins that would be outside the door. So, the door closing and retaining features, locks and the like will also have to be top quality.

Depending upon the door, assuming a wood one, several hinge types can be used, ensuring that they are of high quality steel (Fig. 14-3). Screws for the hinge should be at least 2" long. Three hinges are required, never just two.

Locks that are used should be controlled from the inside; a double-locking lock is suggested. This requires a key from either side to open (Fig. 14-4).

You should have heavy duty bolts, that slide into the metal door frame, attached to the interior side of the door. You can also have a crossbar put on the door (Fig. 14-5).

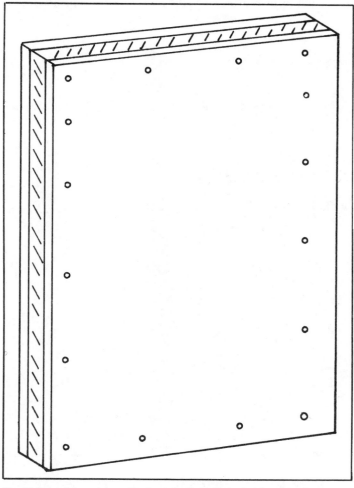

Fig. 14-2. A solid wood door with sheet steel bolted to both sides of the door.

VENTILATION

It seems somewhat ridiculous, but home builders often neglect to consider that the occupants of a security closet or room must have air to breath. Ventilation is a prime consideration in building the room. For additional security, the ventilation should go to the outside or be developed in such a way that the outlet is far from the room (or seems to be).

The use of a standard air vent can be safely used. A vent which runs through the wall to another room can be used. From within the room, it might look like part of the internal air conditioning system or heating system; no one would suspect its real purpose. Figure 14-6 illustrates possible ventilation concepts.

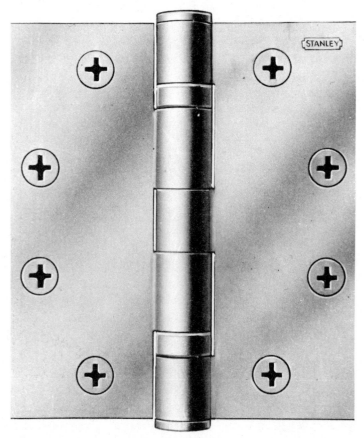

Fig. 14-3. A hinge for the door (courtesy of Stanley Hardware).

Fig. 14-4. A double cylinder dead-lock (courtesy of Kwikset, Division of Emhart Industries, Inc.).

FLOOR AND CEILING

What about floor or the ceiling? If you really want a security closet that can protect your valuables, whether home or away, then the floors and/or ceiling should also be reinforced. If you are away on vacation, and a burglar gets in, he might consider breaking into your security room. He can't get through the door or the walls, so he considers going into the basement security room by going right through your living room floor. It's not his home; he could care less. In such instances, you will want to reinforce the ceiling of the room. This is undertaken during the construction phase or after initial construction of the corner room has been done.

You could do several things:

—Run strips of structural steel in a checkerboard fashion across the top of the security room.

—Use hardwood and sheet steel.

—Use a structural steel frame, sheet steel and concrete or brick.

If you have, as your security room, a large closet on the second floor, you may also have another closet on the first floor that is directly underneath. This provides another opportunity for you. You can put in a small rope ladder on the second area, and then cut away a portion of the floor and make a flush type trap door between the two. See Fig. 14-7.

ELECTRICAL POWER

Some form of electrical power is required for the security room. Power can be drawn off another source, such as an electrical outlet in the room, or a separate line from the main electrical box can be run. If so, then the line should not be identified as the "security room" inside the box. Also, the control switch for the

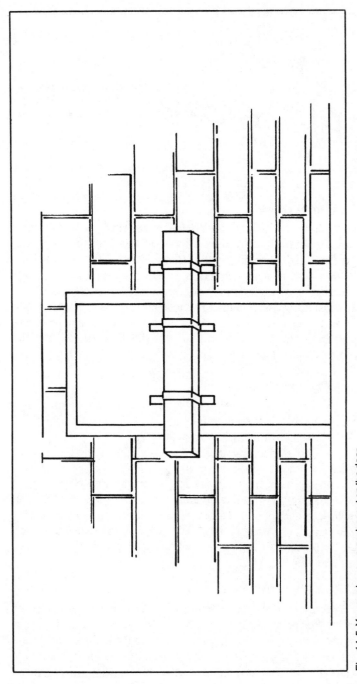

Fig. 14-5. You can have a crossbar put on the door.

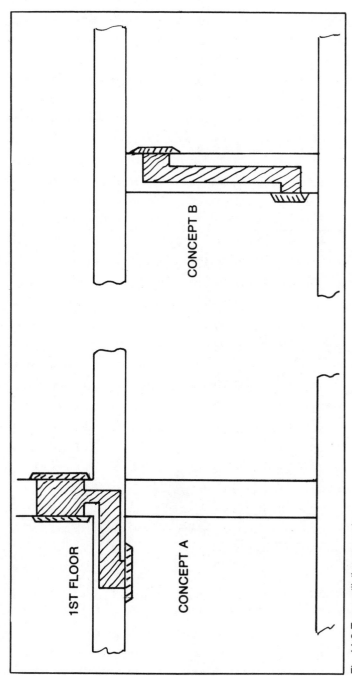

1ST FLOOR

CONCEPT A

CONCEPT B

Fig. 14-6. Two ventilation concepts.

477

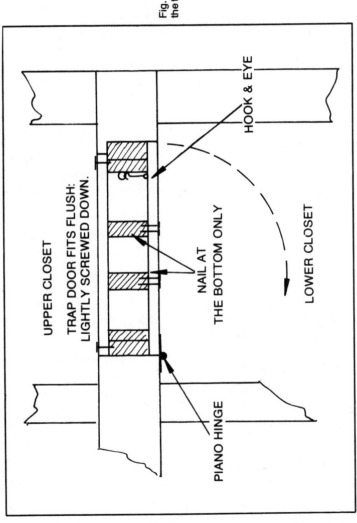

Fig. 14-7. Make a trap door between the two closets.

UPPER CLOSET

TRAP DOOR FITS FLUSH;
LIGHTLY SCREWED DOWN.

HOOK & EYE

NAIL AT
THE BOTTOM ONLY

LOWER CLOSET

PIANO HINGE

478

power (if one is used) should be *inside* the security room, not outside.

SECURITY CLOSET ITEMS

Within the security closet should be at least one flashlight and extra batteries. Keep the batteries outside the flashlight, putting them in only when needed. Check the batteries every several months. Rotate the batteries with others so you ensure that the batteries are always good.

If you happen to be a ham radio operator, you might give consideration to locating your radio set, or an auxiliary one, within the security room. Again, separate power lines are necessary. CB type walkie-talkie units can also be included. Those with multiple frequencies are good in that you might easily be able to contact someone on one of the frequencies, if need be. Since the telephone is not normally kept in the security closet, consider running an extra line to that room.

If you have an interior security alarm that has an outside alarm, put an auxiliary control switch in the security closet so you can activate the alarm. You might also consider installing a separate alarm outside that is controlled by a switch in the security closet. In doing so, consider the placement of the alarm up high where it cannot be easily reached.

A switch that will turn on your outside lights should be installed. You can, by working the switch (or installing a flasher), attract attention by flashing the lights in a particular pattern. This would certainly be noticed by someone passing by who would notify the proper authorities. You may also want to have some monitoring equipment to allow you to monitor the sounds in various rooms of the home.

Appendix A
Home Security Checklist

The home security checklist on the following pages is designed to allow the homeowner to determine the home security areas that need to be improved, upgraded or added to a non-existent security plan; check yearly for additions to, or variations that should be considered, in home security; or to determine the current status of the home security system. The checklist should be reviewed at least yearly.

The list does not purport to be all-inclusive to fit the needs of every possible variation in home living. It is a viable point of departure from which you can select the specifics that relate to your own particular environment.

PERIMETER BARRIERS

☐ Type of barrier, including height and presence or absence of a top guard?

☐ Do buildings or bodies of water form any portion of the perimeter?

☐ If so, what protective measures are being employed?

☐ Are outside windows and doors properly secured?

☐ What is the frequency of any inspections to check maintenance and operation of security devices on doors/windows?

☐ Are clear zones maintained on both sides of the perimeter fence? If not, are they feasible?

☐ Are electric or electronic alarm or intrusion detection devices used on the perimeter?

☐ Are warning signs posted?

☐ Are ground seismic detection alarms installed?

☐ Are there unprotected areas of the perimeter?

☐ What is the present condition of the perimeter fence? Any holes, breaks, posts down, etc.?

☐ Are holes or tunnels under the fence?

☐ Are boxes or refuse piled up or other material stored near the fence?

☐ Are there weak places in the perimeter caused by a stream, body of water or other opening through which an unauthorized person could enter?

☐ What is the frequency of local police patrols past the residence?

☐ Are all of the points where a break-in might occur lighted by street lights, signs or your own "burglar" lights?

☐ Have you protected blind alleys where a burglar might work unobserved?

☐ Are piles of material placed so as not to give burglars hiding places?

☐ If a fence would help your protection, do you have one?

☐ Is your fence high enough or protected with barbed wire?

☐ Is your fence in good repair?

☐ Is your fence fixed so that an intruder cannot crawl under it?

☐ Are boxes, materials, etc., that might help a burglar over the fence placed a safe distance from the fence?

☐ Are the gates solid and in good repair?

☐ Are the gates properly locked?

☐ Are the gate hinges secure?

☐ Have you eliminated unused gates?

☐ Have you eliminated poles or similar things *outside* the fence that would help a burglar over the fence?

☐ Have you protected solid brick or wood fences that a burglar could climb and then be shielded from view?

☐ Do you check regularly to see that your gates are locked?

☐ Do you regularly clean out trash or weeds on the outside of your fence where a burglar might be concealed?

PERIMETER ENTRANCES

☐ Number and type and location of most frequently used gates?

☐ When gates are not in use, are they securely locked?

☐ Type of locking devices on gates, if any?

☐ Is there adequate key control, i.e., who has? Any keys lost recently?

☐ Is the *entire* driveway clearly visible from one or more windows or doors?

OUTSIDE LIGHTING

☐ Are there good power facilities available (i.e., low percentage of power failures, etc.)?

☐ Is there an auxiliary power source for emergency lighting? Or do lighting sources have a battery operation during period of power outages?

☐ Are lights controlled by automatic timer or manually operated?

☐ Are switchboxes secured if they are outside of the residence?

☐ What other emergency lighting is available?

☐ Are perimeter areas adequately lighted during hours of darkness?

☐ Do the light sources aid or hinder a trespasser?

☐ Do light sources cover entranceways, side and back windows, outbuildings, etc., wherein access would be made extremely easy without the lighting?

☐ Are the entrance and gate areas sufficiently lighted?

☐ Are lights at the gate/driveway arranged to light up the vehicles entering the area?

☐ Are buildings/immediate surrounding areas well illuminated?

SHRUBBERY

☐ Are trees located in positions that would allow a person to use them in gaining entrance to the area (i.e., help to get over the fence)?

☐ Can individuals hide in trees, free from general scrutiny?

☐ Are bushes big enough to hide a person so he cannot be seen by a casual observer?

☐ Are bushes located close to buildings?

☐ Are bushes located where they would hide a person attempting access through a window?

☐ Are bushes located by an exterior doorway?

☐ Are bushes provided adequate lighting (even low level) so you can casually check to see if someone is hiding behind them?

☐ Do tree branches capable of holding a person extend close to second/third story windows?

☐ Can trees be easily climbed by a person?

DOORS

☐ Are all doors lockable from the inside?

☐ Is there some type of control (or alarm) so that unauthorized entry will be detected?

☐ If doors must be opened for ventilation, are they properly protected (chain lock, etc.)?

☐ Are doors themselves, locks and hardware in good repair?

☐ Are exterior doors as strong as aesthetically possible?

☐ What kind(s) of hardware are used on exterior doors?

☐ Have serial numbers been removed from any padlocks?

☐ Are padlocks rotated every several months?

☐ Where are keys to padlocks kept?

☐ Would the doors be more secure if faced with sheet metal? Heavy wire mesh or grillwork? Other exposed glass surfaces?

☐ Are door locks of the deadbolt type?

☐ Are auxiliary locks used?

☐ What is the door's thickness?

☐ Is the door hollow core? Solid? Does it have thin panels? Glass areas?

☐ Can door frames be readily pried apart from the door so as to release the locking bolt?

☐ Are door frames of metal or solid wood with a strong backing of wood?

☐ Have you secured all unused doors?

☐ Are door panels strong enough and securely fastened in place?

☐ Is the glass in back doors and similar locations protected by wire or bars?

☐ Are all of your doors designed so that the lock cannot be reached by breaking out glass or a lightweight panel?

☐ Are the hinges so designed or located that the pins cannot be pulled?

☐ Is the lock bolt so designed or protected that it cannot be pushed back with a thin instrument?

☐ Is the lock so designed or the door frame built so that the door cannot be forced by spreading the frame?

☐ Is the bolt protected or constructed so that it cannot be cut?

☐ Is the lock firmly mounted so that it cannot be pried off?

☐ Is the lock a cylinder type?

☐ Are your locks in good working order?

☐ Are the setscrews holding the cylinders firmly in place?

☐ Do you lock your padlocks in place when the door is unlocked?

☐ Are the padlocks' hasps installed so that the screws cannot be removed?

☐ Are the hasps heavy enough?

☐ Are they of a grade of steel that is difficult to cut?

☐ Are they mounted so that they cannot be pried or twisted off?

☐ Have locks been rekeyed within the past two years?

☐ Do you lock all doors in your home every time you go out?

☐ Do you have a chain latch on both your front and back doors?

☐ Do you use the chain latch every time you answer the door?

☐ Are your doors equipped with strong, pin tumbler locks?

☐ Do you have the type of hinges that cannot be forced from the outside?

☐ Do you have a peephole in your front and back doors?

☐ If your doors have a window in them, do you have the type of lock that must be opened from the inside, as well as the outside, by a key?

☐ Are the locks on your most used outside doors of the cylinder type?

☐ Are they of either the "deadlocking" or "jimmyproof" type?

☐ Do you use chain locks or other auxiliary locks in your most frequently used doors?

☐ Do the doors without cylinder locks have a heavy bolt or some similar secure device that can be operated only from the inside? Can all of your doors (basement, porch, French, balcony) be *securely* locked?

☐ Do your basement doors have locks that allow you to isolate that part of your house?

☐ Do you know everyone who has a key to your house? (Or are there some still in possession of previous owners and their friends?)

KEYS

☐ Did you have the lock tumblers changed when you moved into your new home?

☐ Are you careful in giving out duplicate keys?

☐ Do you always separate your home and automobile keys when you leave your car in a parking lot?

☐ Have you removed all identification tags from your key ring so if you lose it, a burglar won't know where to go?

☐ Are you sure that no one in your family tries to "hide" the door key in such places as the mailbox or under the door mat?

☐ If you lost your keys, would you have the lock tumblers changed at once?

WINDOWS

☐ Are windows located at a sufficient height from the ground to afford better than average protection? Is safety glass used in any windows?

☐ Are windows removable so that large objects could be passed through them?

☐ Are windows permanently sealed or covered with grill or bars?

☐ Can windows be opened sufficiently to allow an outsider to open a window lock, other latch or opening device easily?

☐ Are steel bars or heavy wire mesh/grill work *adequately* protecting the windows?

☐ Are windows secured with lag bolts?

☐ Are window bars no more than 5½″ apart and, if more than two of them, are there crossing bars? Are they interlaced together?

☐ Are valuable pieces of artwork, pictures, etc., readily visible and identifiable through windows?

☐ Are easily accessible windows protected by heavy screens, grills or bars?

☐ Are unused windows permanently closed?

☐ Are your bars or screens mounted securely?

☐ In the case of windows not protected by bars or alarms, do you keep the windows locked or shuttered?

☐ Are unused or infrequently used winodws barred, locked or alarmed?

☐ Are the window locks so designed or located that they cannot be opened by just breaking the glass?

☐ Have you protected all of your seldom used windows and small windows?

☐ Have you considered the use of glass brick in place of some windows?

☐ Do you close and lock every window in your home whenever you go out?

☐ Do you have bars or grillwork over "out of the way" windows such as those that lead to your garage or basement?

☐ Do you have pin tumbler locks on your windows?

☐ Are your window locks properly and securely mounted?

☐ Do you keep your windows locked when they are shut?

☐ Do you use locks that allow you to lock a window that is partly open?

☐ In high hazard locations, do you use bars or ornamental grills?

☐ Are you as careful of basement and second floor windows as you are of those on the first floor?

☐ Have you made it more difficult for the burglar by locking up your ladder?

OTHER OPENINGS

☐ Have you eliminated unnecessary skylights?

☐ Are your accessible skylights protected with bars or burglar alarms?

☐ Are your exposed roof hatches properly secured?

☐ Are the doors to the roof or elevator penthouses strong, in good condition and securely locked?

☐ Have you protected any fan openings through which a burglar might come?

☐ If your transoms that open to the outside are large enough to admit even a small burglar, are they properly locked or protected with bars, screens or chains?

ALARM SYSTEMS

☐ Is there a protective burglar alarm system for the premises?

☐ Is it a single unit? Are there multiple units?

☐ Are units self-contained (battery operated) or do they run off an ac circuit?

☐ Will the defensive procedures lessen to a great extent if the ac power goes off?

☐ Is there a safe or other security container in the residence?

☐ Following an alarm, is there a rapid follow-up by police?

☐ Are all alarm units Underwriter Laboratory (UL) certified?

☐ When was the last time batteries were checked on self-contained units?

☐ Are batteries regularly changed on a fixed schedule (whether or not they need replacing)?

☐ When was the unit installed?

☐ If over five years ago, have you given thought to upgrading or replacing with a more modern, up-to-date system?

☐ Does the alarm system cover all exterior openings in the home?

☐ Has the alarm malfunctioned within the past year?

☐ When was maintenance last performed? Adequate? Superior? Poor?

☐ Is the company that manufactured the alarm system still in business?

☐ Is the master alarm unit located in an out-of-the-way place in the home (closet, etc.)?

☐ When was the entire alarm system tested?

☐ When were individual alarm components tested?

☐ If you have self-contained units, when were they last tested?

FIRE PROTECTION

☐ Do you have a home fire alarm system?

☐ Is it connected to the burglar system? Or is it separate?

☐ Do you have self-contained fire sensing units?

☐ Are they battery operated or ac operated?

☐ Do you monitor the units on a weekly or monthly basis?

☐ For battery operated units: Are batteries changed every 8-10 months, or more frequently? Are units tested individually every month? Are sensors cleaned monthly? Do individual units have a LED to indicate the unit is active?

☐ Do you conduct a fire drill within the home on a semi- or annual basis?

☐ Does everyone know what to do in different situations?

☐ Do you have portable home fire extinguishers?

☐ Are there extinguishers for all types of fires?

☐ Are extinguishers located in areas where fires may break out? Or in an adjacent area?

☐ Is an extinguisher in the work room area? In the garage?

☐ Is an extinguisher in the family automobile?

☐ Do you have an emergency fire ladder in rooms on floors above ground level for escape?

☐ Has the ladder been tested recently?

☐ Do you have a lightning protection system?

☐ How old is the system?

☐ Are all component parts UL certified?

☐ Was the system installed by a certified lightning protection specialist?

☐ Since the system was installed, have additional rooms been built onto the house?

☐ Do you have large trees or electrical lines near the home?

GENERAL SECURITY

☐ Do you always require identification from repairmen and utility company representatives?

☐ Is the chain latch in place every time you answer the door?

☐ Do you make a note of the license tag numbers of suspicious vehicles that you notice in your neighborhood?

☐ Do you have a mail slot in your door so that an accumulation of mail will not advertise that you are away from home?

☐ Do you stop delivery of milk and newspapers when you are going away?

☐ Do you have an automatic device that will turn on your lights and radio at dusk when you are away?

☐ Do you make arrangements to have the grass cut or the snow shoveled when you are going out of town?

☐ Do you close the garage door each time you leave?

☐ Do you always close the curtains and draw the shades after dark?

☐ If you are a woman and live alone, do you use your initials rather than your first name on your mailbox, your door and in the telephone book?

☐ Do you let the police know when you are going out of town?

☐ Do you always call police when you see or hear anything suspicious in your neighborhood?

☐ Do you have pin tumbler cylinder locks on all exterior doors? If not, have you installed auxiliary night latches to protect such doors?

☐ Do you make certain that strange callers have no opportunity to tamper with your door lock?

☐ When you leave your home, do you avoid leaving notes which tell where the house key can be found?

☐ Do you wait until after your return to tell the local paper about your vacation?

☐ Before leaving your home, do you make certain that shades are left up and venetian blinds are partially open?

☐ When you leave your home, do you check to make sure that all exterior doors and windows are securely locked and all ladders securely fastened with pin tumbler padlocks?

☐ Do you keep a record of the serial numbers and descriptions of your valuables? Do you rent a safe deposit box for storage of valuables?

☐ Do you arrange to keep the house and lawn looking neat?

☐ Do you plan so that you do not need to "hide" a key under the door mat?

☐ Do you keep as much cash as possible and other valuables in a bank (or bonded storage in the case of large items)?

☐ Do you keep a list of all valuable property?

☐ Do you have a list of the serial numbers of your watches, cameras, typewriters and similar items?

☐ Do you have a description of other valuable property that does not have a number?

☐ Do you avoid unnecessary display or publicity of your valuables?

☐ Have you told your family what to do if they discover a burglar breaking in or already in the house?

☐ Have you told your family to leave the house undisturbed and call the police if they discover a burglary has been committed?

☐ Do you know the phone number of the law enforcement agency that takes care of your home?

☐ If you have a gun, do you know the laws regarding its use?

☐ If you have a gun, is it kept in perfect condition?

☐ If you have a gun, is it kept where it can be found only by persons who can legally and safely use it?

☐ When you move to a new residence, do you hire a reliable locksmith to rekey all locks?

☐ Do you lock garage doors?

☐ Do you have a peephole or interview grill in your door?

☐ Are cabinets, closets and drawers where you keep valuables properly locked?

□ Do you hide your spare key in a place where it cannot easily be found?

□ When arriving home late at night, are your keys ready immediately?

□ Do you conceal your single status on your door and mailbox name plates?

□ Do you have a "Charley Bar" or a secondary lock for sliding glass doors?

□ Do you lock your car when you leave it?

□ Do you take all but ignition keys with you when a garage attendant parks your car?

WALLS

□ Are your walls actually as solid as they look; have you eliminated insecure openings in otherwise solid walls?

□ In checking walls, have you paid particular attention to points where a burglar can work unobserved?

□ Is your roof area near openings either secure or protected by an alarm system?

□ Have you eliminated weak points in your walls where entrance could be gained from an adjoining building?

□ Have walls been built-in near doorways?

HOME SAFES

□ Is your safe designed for burglary protection as well as fire protection?

□ Is your safe approved by the Underwriters Laboratories?

□ Is the safe fastened securely to the floor, the wall or set in concrete?

□ Is your safe located in an inaccessible area?

□ Is the safe concealed (hidden)? Where?

□ If you have a vault, are the walls, as well as the door, secure?

□ Do you keep sizable amounts of money in your safe?

□ Do you keep your cash on hand at a minimum?

□ Do you spin the dial when you lock the safe?

□ Have you changed the combination in the last two years?

□ Do you use care in working the combination so that you cannot be spied on by visitors?

APARTMENT SECURITY

☐ Have you put a strong, short chain on your apartment door?

☐ Do you leave your door unlocked even when you are home?

☐ Do you keep the door chained when a stranger knocks until you are satisfied his purpose is legitimate?

☐ Do you double-lock your door when you leave?

☐ Have you put extra locks on windows facing on fire escapes?

☐ When you have your car serviced, do you remove house keys from the key case? Keys are easily duplicated when cars are in parking lots, being repaired or serviced.

☐ Do you urge your apartment manager to keep hallways, parking lots, laundry rooms and all outside areas well lighted?

☐ Do you see that shrubbery which might provide an easy hiding place is kept trimmed?

☐ Do you check thoroughly the references of service/ maintenance people who are given access to your apartment?

☐ Are you alert for strangers who loiter in hallways, elevators and laundry rooms?

☐ Do you have an apartment entrance lock capable of withstanding great force?

☐ If you have an apartment with windows opening onto a fire escape, patio or balcony, do you lock all windows when you go to bed?

☐ Do you provide secure locks for all doors in your apartment?

☐ Do you have a double cylinder lock on all doors with glass?

☐ Do you have a night chain on your door?

☐ When you leave your home for any period of time, do you lock all windows and doors?

PROTECTING YOUR HOME FROM BURGLARIES

☐ Do you lock outside doors at all times, even when you are on the premises?

☐ Do you open the door to strangers?

☐ Have you installed slide bolts and chains on the inside of all outer doors?

☐ When you move into a new house or apartment, did you have new locks installed or keys changed?

☐ Have you checked door moldings for tight fit?

☐ Are doors hinged so no pins can be removed from outside?

☐ Have you replaced locks with the double cylinder type, particularly doors with glass panels?

☐ Are the garage and tool shed locked when not being used?

☐ Have all obstructions in your yard been removed that could conceal a burglar breaking into your house?

AWAY FROM HOME

☐ Have you purchased a timer to switch lights on and off?

☐ Have you arranged to have mail, milk and newspaper deliveries discontinued or taken care of by a responsible neighbor?

☐ Have you informed neighbors and local police of your traveling plans so that special attention will be paid to your home?

HELPING THE POLICE

☐ Have you written down the license numbers of vehicles used by suspicious persons in your neighborhood?

☐ Do you keep an inventory of valuables so that you will know immediately if anything is missing?

Appendix B
How To Select A Padlock

You may have carefully selected the alarm system, the exterior lighting and even grill work for your windows. There may be outbuildings or bicycles that can use a padlock to keep them secure.

Hopefully, the following discussion on selecting a padlock will be of great interest and value. Developed by the Master Lock Co., this information is very applicable to the many padlocks on today's market.

What is the real key to security when you pick out a padlock? Locks vary tremendously in the amount of protection provided. Important differences may be hard for you to spot. Keep the following in mind when you're shopping.

WROUGHT STEEL PADLOCKS

Wrought steel or "shell" padlocks are the lowest priced locks you can buy. They're intended mainly for nuisance protection—keeping the kids out of your toolbox, restricting access to a mailbox or storeroom, etc. Costing little, they can prevent misadventures or injury from hazardous household items.

WARDED LAMINATED PADLOCKS

Master laminated construction results in a lock far sturdier than "shell" types and much more resistant if anyone tries to hammer open the case. The multi-spring, warded mechanism operates a strong shackle-locking lever. The design permits a wider range of key variations than offered by shell locks and less chance of duplication.

Costing more than shell types, but less than those with pin tumbler mechanisms, warded locks give dependable protection. Use them to secure oil tank caps, well covers, beach lockers, barn doors, etc.

Because of the relatively large clearances between internal moving parts, warded locks are frequently chosen for applications where sand, water, ice and other contaminants are a problem. While the locks look almost the same as Master pin tumbler padlocks at first glance, there's a decided difference in the security provided. The most *visible* difference with the warded lock is seen in the type of key employed.

PIN TUMBLER LAMINATED LOCKS

Since warded locks cost about half the price and pin tumbler and warded locks look so much alike, many unknowing consumers make the wrong buying decision where *high security* is essential. When locked property has substantial value, the pin tumbler lock with its many hidden strengths is infinitely superior, well worth the additional money.

Controlled by precision mechanisms, these Master locks offer premium protection and thousands of key changes. Compared to a warded lock mechanism with only four working parts, similar appearing Master pin tumbler locks use 19 precision parts to assure top security. A patented *double-locking* feature multiplies this protection by independently locking each shackle leg. The result is a lock extremely difficult to open by forcing, shimming or rapping.

For added security, look for the legend "HARDENED" on the shackle. Case hardening gives an extra-hard outer layer to resist cutting or sawing, and a tough, inner core to keep the shackle from becoming brittle.

Key numbers of better Master locks are temporarily *inked* onto the casing. Once the owner records it in a safe place, he can erase the number from the lock so no one can obtain a copy by subterfuge.

BRASS PADLOCKS

Hard-wrought brass versions of Master high security laminated padlocks are designed to withstand severe corrosion problems encountered along seacoasts, aboard boats, and in areas of high humidity and atmospheric pollution. For theft deterrence, the shackle typically will be chrome-plated hardened steel. For extreme conditions, even the shackle can be brass. Expect the price of maximum security brass padlocks to run substantially higher than for steel.

A lower cost medium-security alternative for the average user is the *solid brass* padlock. Again, look for pin tumbler locking and a case-hardened shackle to protect valued property. Priced substantially less than heavy duty laminated brass padlocks, solid brass locks are naturals for many coastal users, boats, outdoor lockers, gates and similar applications. In addition, the sleek styling and golden luster of Master solid brass padlocks make them ideal for indoor use on gun cases, display cabinets and other places where fashion is a key factor.

COMBINATION PADLOCKS

The chief reason for these locks is *keyless convenience*—particularly with children where lost keys may be a problem. Protection features to look for include reinforced double-wall construction—tough stainless steel outer case over a sturdy wrought steel inner case—and a hardened steel shackle for added resistance against cutting and sawing. Combination locks are classed as medium security, with strength equivalent to a quality warded padlock.

HASP LOCK

People should consider more than just the strength of the padlock they choose. The finest lock affords little protection if burglars find it hung from an undersized or unhardened hasp that they can cut with ease. To avoid a weak link in security, get a hasp that matches the quality of the lock. Look for adequate size, a pinless hinge, concealed screws, case-hardened staple (the metal loop the lock passes through) and steel ribbing for added strength.

An evolutionary step beyond the hasp is the *hasp lock*. Instead of using a separate padlock, the lock and hasp are one. It is permanently joined so the lock can't be misplaced or stolen. Hasp locks give built-in convenience akin to the deadbolt door lock while offering much easier installation, which accounts for their popularity with builders, contractors, farmers and do-it-yourselfers. Their uses range from securing garage doors and sheds to boathouses, warehouses and a host of other places.

CHOOSING CHAIN AND CABLE

When it comes to movable property, the use of a strong padlock with a properly matched chain or steel cable is the way to go. Common chain available in hardware stores should be passed over in favor of chain specifically designed for locking applications. Be sure it is case-hardened for high resistance to cutters, saws and files. Individual links should be welded, not just twisted, to resist being pried apart. Multi-stranded security cable is available for equivalent protection, with the added benefit of light weight. In either case, the thicker the chain or cable, the greater the protection. Examine cable closely as some manufacturers add a thick coating of vinyl to make a small steel strand look bigger.

For greatest protection, position the lock and cable (or chain) as high above the ground as possible. This makes it difficult for thieves to gain extra leverage by bracing one leg of a bolt cutter against the ground.

ARMOR LOCK

In the contest of thief against property holder, this advanced padlock introduces a special shackle to frustrate thieves armed with hacksaws and bolt cutters. The *Armor lock* is designed with these cutting tools in mind; its free-spinning shackle sleeve of case-hardened steel turns like a roller bearing so a saw blade will slide over its surface instead of biting in. Thick armor protects the rest of the shackle—simply too big a bite to fit the jaws of most bolt cutters. By outwitting thieves rather than relying on brute strength alone, the *Armor lock* gives extra protection at substantial cost savings. Uses include locking trailers on cars; beefing up protection for bikes, snowmobiles, cabins and recreational vehicles; securely anchoring valuable portable equipment and locking up other prime theft targets.

GUN LOCK

This is a life saver as well as a "theft thwarter." The lock blocks access to the trigger, stopping anyone from firing rifles, shotguns or handguns inadvertently. Unobtrusive, it can be used even for firearms on display.

TRAILER LOCK

The trailer lock guards against towaway theft of trailer and contents. Too many people leave trailers with expensive boats,

snowmobiles, etc., unhitched and unguarded in their driveways—
easy targets for thieves. A Master *trailer lock* completely blocks
access to the coupler cavity and cannot be pried off.

OUTBOARD MOTOR LOCK

The lock secures the motor to the transom of the boat by
making it impossible to unscrew the clamp handles. Too often theft
of an outboard takes little more effort than stealing an unlocked
bicycle. These motors are among the most poorly protected pieces
of property people own. This lock provides the security of
case-hardened steel combined with pin tumbler locking. It defies
cutting by saws or bolt cutters.

SKI LOCK

It insures against theft of skis and poles, a serious growing
threat to sports enthusiasts. The Master combination lock
mechanism with oversize dial can be operated with ease even with
gloves on. The generous cable length secures both skis and poles
to the tree, rack or any other suitable immovable object. The lock
is designed so the owner can carry it effortlessly around the waist
while skiing.

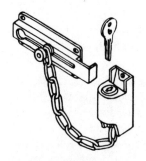

Appendix C
List of Manufacturers

Refer to this list when considering items for home use. Remember what the item will be protecting, the value of the item and the amount you wish to spend. When looking for products in your local area, check first the local telephone or other directory of business. If there is no local retailer store for the product, or a distributor nearby, then contact the manufacturer at the address listed. For those marked with an asterisk (*), you may write directly in order to receive more information about the product or to purchase it directly. Always check with local stores prior to contacting manufacturers directly.

Adams Rite Manufacturing Co.
P. O. Box 1301
4040 South Capital Ave.
City of Industry, CA 91749

Aqualarm, Inc. (*)
544 West 182nd Street
Gardena, CA 90248

Arrow Fastener Company, Inc.
271 Mayhill Street
Saddle Brook, NJ 07662

Auto Page Inc. (*)
3718 South Western Ave.
Los Angeles, CA 90018

Bathurst, Inc. (*)
801 West 15 Street
P. O. Box 27
Tyrone, PA 16686

Belwith International Ltd. (*)
7600 Industry Ave.
P. O. Box 1057
Pico Rivera, CA 90660
Bike Security Systems Division
Acro-Fab Industries, Inc.
177 Tosca Drive
Stoughton, MA 02072
Blaine Window Hardware Inc. (*)
1919 Blaine Drive
Hagerstown, MD 21740
BMR Security Products Corporation
203 Broad Street
Milford, CT 06460
B-W Manufacturers, Inc. (*)
P. O. Box 739
721 North Webster Street
Kokomo, IN 46901

Campbell Chain Company
3990 E. Market St.
York, PA 17402
Chamberlain Manufacturing Corporation
Corporate Headquarters
845 Larch Avenue
Elmhurst, IL 60126
Colorado Electro-Optics, Inc.
2200 Central Avenue
Boulder, CO 80301
Continental Instruments Corporation
70 Hopper Street
Westbury, NY 11590
Controllor Systems Corporation (CSC) (*)
21363 Gratiot Ave.
East Detroit, MI 48021
Convertible Alarm Detection Devices, Inc. (CADDI) (*)
824 E. Methvin Street
Longview, TX 75601

Deerfield Lock Co., Inc. (*)
758 Hoffman Lane
Deerfield, IL 60015

Delta Products, Inc.
630 South 7th Street
P. O. Box 1147
Grand Junction, CO 81501

Don Gilbert Industries, Inc. (*)
P. O. Box 2188
5700 Krueger Drive
Jonesboro, AR 72401

Dremel Creative Power Tools
Division of Emerson Electric Co.
4915 21st Street
Racine, WI 53406

Fire Lite Alarms Incorporated
40 Albert St.
New Haven, CT 06504

Fox Police Lock Co.
46 West 21st Street
New York 10, NY

Gard-A-Car, Inc. (*)
P. O. Box 294
Grosse Ile, MI 48138

GC Electronics
400 South Wyman Street
Rockford, IL 61101

Ideal Security Hardware Corp.
215 East Ninth St.
St. Paul, MN 55101

Imperial Screen Co., Inc. (*)
5336 W. 145th Street
Lawndale, CA 90260

Independent Protection Co., Inc. (*)
1603-09 South Main Street
Goshen, IN 46526

Intermatic Incorporated
Intermatic Plaza
Spring Grove, IL 60081

Koyo International Inc. of America (*)
1855 New Highway
Farmingdale, NY 11735

Kwikset Division
Emhart Hardware Group
516 E. Santa Ana Street
Anaheim, CA 92803

Lightning Protection Institute (*)
48 North Ayer Street
P. O. Box 406
Harvard, IL 60033

Linear Corporation
347 S. Glasgow Ave.
P. O. Box 6019
Inglewood, CA 90301

Lock Technology Corp. (*)
685 Main Street
New Rochelle, NY 10801

Master Lock Company
2600 N. 32nd Street
Milwaukee, WI 53210

Matuska Enterprises (*)
P. O. Box 6084
San Rafael, CA 94903

Medeco Security Locks, Inc.
P. O. Box 1075
Salem, VA 24153

Meilink Safe Company (*)
Division of Meilink Industries, Inc.
6245 Industrial Parkway
Box 2458
Whitehouse, OH 43571

Milbar
530 Washington Street
P. O. Box 400
Chagrin Falls, OH 44022

MRC Alarm Systems & Devices Co.
700 West Virginia Street
Milwaukee, WI 53204

Northern Electric Company
Division of Sunbeam Corp.
5224 North Kedzie Ave.
Chicago, IL 60625

NuTone Division
Scovill Housing Products Group
Madison & Red Bank Roads
Cincinnati, OH 45227

Pem All Fire Extinguisher Corp.
394 Myrtle Street
Cranford, NJ 07016

Peterzell Company (*)
Box 966, M-020
Winter Park, FL 32790

PSG Industries, Inc.
1225 Tunnel Road
Perkasie, PA 18944

Racon Inc.
Boeing Field International
8490 Perimeter Rd. S.
Seattle, WA 98108

Rival Manufacturing Company
36th and Bennington
Kansas City, MO 64129

Rixson-Firemark, Inc.
9100 West Belmont Ave.
Franklin Park, IL 60131

Robboy Electric Mfg. Co. (*)
4565 N.W. 37th Ave.
Miami, FL 33142

Rockwell International
Power Tool Division
400 North Lexington Ave.
Pittsburgh, PA 15208

Rodann Electronics Mfg. Co.
133 South Brea Blvd.
Brea, CA 92621

Rossin Corporation
1411 Norman Firestone Rd.
Goleta, CA 93017

Sanford Coporation
2740 Washington Blvd.
Bellwood, IL 60104

Sargent
Division of Walter Kidde & Co., Inc.
100 Sargent Drive
New Haven, CT 06509

Security Products Division
Scovill Security Products
P.O. Box 25288
Charlotte, NC 28212

Sentrol Inc.
10950 S.W. 5th St., Bldg 250
Beaverton, OR 97005

Simplex Security Systems, Inc.
Front and Main Streets
Collinsville, CT 06022

Soar Electronics (U.S.A.) Corp. (*)
200 13th Avenue
Ronkonkoma, NY 11779

Statitrol
Division of Emerson Electric Co.
140 South Union Boulevard
Lakewood, CO 80228

Steelcraft Manufacturing Company
9017 Blue Ash Road
Cincinnati, OH 45242

Superior Security Mfg. Inc. (*)
6301 St. Louis Avenue
St. Louis, MO 63121

Techne Electronics, Ltd. (*)
961 Commercial
Palo Alto, CA 94303

Tefco Security Systems (*)
2368 Prospect Street
Memphis, TN 38106

Thompson Lightning Protection, Inc. (*)
901 Sibley Highway
St. Paul, MN 55118

United States Gypsum Company
Metal Products Division
101 South Wacker Drive
Chicago, IL 60606

Waldom Electronics, Inc.
Subsidiary of HMW Industries, Inc.
4301 West 69th Street
Chicago, IL 60629
Weil Service Products Corp.
2434 West Fletcher Street
Chicago, IL 60618
Weslock
TRE Corporation
13344 S. Main Street
Los Angeles, CA 90061

Index

The Complete Security Handbook — for home, office, car, boat, RV, anything

by C.A. Roper

Have you ever worried about your home or office being burgularized? Would you have adequate warning if your home caught fire or a gas pipe burst? Is your car, RV, or boat protected against theft or vandalism? Or, could a potentially dangerous prowler invade your property without your even realizing it? Today, more than ever, proper personal and home security can make the difference between worryfree living, and possible disaster. Now, this timely, up-to-the-minute sourcebook provides you with all the answers you need to protect your family *and* your property from almost any kind of threat—fire, theft, gas and water leaks, smoke, lightning, and more.

Here's where you'll find all the how-to's for selecting *and* installing all kinds of security devices and systems to protect any home, building, or vehicle . . . directions so simple to follow that anyone can do it with a minimum of home-handyman experience. There's a full section on home security planning which shows you how to determine your security needs, then develop, design, purchase, and install the system that fits your own special requirements. You'll also find sound advice on exterior security—from fences, walls, and outside lighting to alarms, intruder detectors, and window and door locking devices.

Jam packed with literally hundreds of illustrations, this all-inclusive security manual includes an in-depth discussion of the advantages, disadvantages, characteristics, and placement of different types of fire and smoke detectors—photoelectric and ionization. There's a whole range of ideas for using magnetic sensors, radio controlled devices, and several kinds of ultrasonic systems, plus there's an entire chapter covering every kind of automotive security device imaginable. Loads of security hints and devices for boats, RVs, campers, and other vehicles, too.

If you're looking for practical, proven advice on every type of personal and property security device, with easy instructions on both choosing and installing them . . . then this is definitely *the book* to have!

C.A. Roper is an expert on all types of security systems and devices and is the author of TAB's *The Complete Handbook of Locks and Locksmithing*.